COMMUNICATIONS AND THE FUTURE

PROSPECTS, PROMISES, AND PROBLEMS

Edited by
Howard F. Didsbury, Jr.

World Future Society
Bethesda, MD • U.S.A.

Editor: Howard F. Didsbury, Jr.

Editorial Review Board: Deirdre H. Banks, James J. Crider, Howard F. Didsbury, Jr. (Chairman), Theodore J. Maziarski, Andrew A. Spekke

Staff Editors: Edward Cornish, Lane Jennings, Jerry Richardson

Production Manager: Jefferson Cornish

Editorial Coordinator: Sarah Warner

Editorial Assistants: Ellen Dudley, Ann Gardner, Melinda Katz, Henry Marien, Jean Ruffin, Frances Segraves, David Smith, Cynthia G. Wagner, Beth A. Walters

Cover Art: Diane Smirnow

Typesetting: Unicorn Graphics

Published by:
World Future Society
4916 St. Elmo Avenue
Bethesda, Maryland 20814-5089 • U.S.A.

Library of Congress Catalog Number: 82-50664

International Standard Book Number: 0-930242-16-5

Printed in the United States of America

Contents

iii

PROMISES

PROBLEMS

v

Note

This volume was prepared in conjunction with the Fourth General Assembly of the World Future Society, held in Washington, D. C., July 18-22, 1982. Donald C. Rosene served as General Chairman of the Assembly. The Assembly Program was developed under the chairmanship of Kenneth W. Hunter.

The papers presented here were selected from the very large number submitted to the Editorial Review Committee. The committee regrets that space limitations permitted only a small number of papers to be published in this volume. In addition, many papers had to be cut substantially. Footnotes and other scholarly paraphernalia were minimized, so that as wide a selection of thoughts as possible could be presented.

Introduction

The papers that comprise this volume view the current telecommunications revolution and its likely developments and probable effects from a wide range of perspectives. The numerous authors, each in his own way, attest to the fact that modern telecommunications serve as the "nerve cells" of humanity. Representative of this broad spectrum of perspectives are such subjects as the future of American microelectronics technology, telecommunications alternatives to transportation, and the promise of information technology in the expansion of trade (both national and global). There are also succinct surveys of current developments in, and future prospects for, global satellite communications. Businessmen and educators will be especially interested in assessing the Japanese example of the "information society." The global impact of modern communications technology receives appropriate attention (for example, by examining the effects of such an impact on the peoples of developing nations). International economic and political tensions accompanying telecommunication innovations are explored. An incisive critique of the MacBride Commission Report on global communications is of special interest to the American reader. In an effort to ensure "balanced coverage," the volume does not ignore possible negative effects of anticipated telecommunication innovations. Psychological, social, and political dangers inherent in these innovations are noted. In sum, this volume will serve to alert a large audience to the promise and problems associated with the advent of this new dramatic phase of human development and global civilization.

—Howard F. Didsbury, Jr.

Prospects

The Future of Literature

by

Michael H. Begnal

The future of the arts is one that will be modified and undoubtedly impaired by the technological society in which we live. Certainly technology has the potential to be a great boon to mankind, and perhaps it already is, if for nothing else than for providing labor-saving devices to increase each individual's leisure time. Theoretically, these empty hours should weigh in favor of the arts, since free time can be filled with reading, listening to music, or going to the theater or cinema. But technology is a force that gives with one hand and takes away with the other. While it provides time, it also fills it with mindless entertainment.

In 1595, Sir Philip Sidney wrote that the duty of literature was to teach and to delight, and this dictate could serve as a criterion for art throughout the ages. Sidney went on to say, "The final end is to draw us to as high a perfection as our degenerate souls, made worse by their clayey lodgings, can be capable of." While he may have been a bit harsh on our spiritual conditions, it is interesting to speculate about what he might have thought of the recently published "Generic Novels," titled *Western*, *Science Fiction*, *Romance*, and *Mystery*. Each has its no-frills, supermarket black-and-white cover. For $1.50 a volume, we receive 60 pages of each genre, written by Anonymous. A *New York Times* book reviewer, also anonymous, said that the books "actually satisfy the need for a garbage read." What is significant about these novels, for our purpose, is their complete and total emphasis upon plot. We have no knowledge of the name of the author and find that he or she just wants to tell a story, so that theme, the "teaching" part of Sidney's duality, disappears into the tale. If we pick up a novel by Saul Bellow, for example, we probably have some prior idea of what to expect in terms of a comment upon experience, because it is Bellow, but with *Western* we look for little more than a stereotyped narrative, a "garbage read."

One of the central ways in which technology can be held responsible for this erosion of literature's ability to make serious comment lies in technology's emphasis upon the concrete and the immediate. As well, the products of technology (a prime example is the television set) instill a passivity in the human participant, since one needs to do little more than to sit back and be entertained. And this begins to set a behavioral pattern. In other words, it is

Michael H. Begnal is professor of English and comparative literature at the Pennsylvania State University.

easier to read *Western*, since one really doesn't have to think about it, than it is to contemplate *Crime and Punishment* or *Ulysses*. A comic book version of the complete Old and New Testaments is already on sale, as well as a "translation" of the King James version into simple and more modern English. Television is probably not the awful culprit, but it is instead yet another example of technological culture at its easiest. It offers an alternative to literature.

Television provides instant gratification, since one can flick the dial to another channel whenever a program is not satisfying. With a complicated or a dull novel, all one can do is put it down guiltily and stare out the window or go out to do some yard work. Normally the video program is brief, less than 20 minutes when commercial time is subtracted, and in this short time a trivial problem is posited and resolved. Will the murderer be discovered, or will one roommate get back on friendly terms with another? In most cases, the character of the actors is known from previous shows and remains fixed each week as the problems change. The abstract nature of the concerns of the serious novel make it a completely different animal.

And it is the very essence of serious literature that technology and its parent, science, have called into question. From one point of view, anything that is utilitarian in our society is valuable, while anything else is not. Utilitarian can be interpreted as physical, demonstrable, something that improves everyday existence. The light bulb is obviously of value, while the novel or the painting may be another question. Some of our time is for work, and some of it is for play, and one area is not really supposed to intrude upon another. Work provides for the needs of material existence, while playtime is important for relaxation. Play and playtime, words usually used for childhood, now commonly describe adult behavior.

If my proposed division here is valid, then where do literature and the arts fit in? Obviously, to qualify at all, they must contribute to relaxation and become entertainment. Thus we find that the novels that capture the first 10 spots on best-seller lists are those that concentrate almost entirely upon plot. They are gothic romances, suspense thrillers, sexy confessions, or sentimental accounts of growing up with idiosyncratic relatives or neighbors. In many cases, these contemporary novels are episodic and have no real development of theme and character, so that they can be read in pieces, in the same way that one experiences an evening of television viewing. These novels are not criminal or evil, even to an academic like me; they are simple tales, much like children's bedtime stories, which demand very little exertion on the part of a reader who is looking for passive entertainment.

As a projection, then, it would seem that the importance of literature in the societal scheme of things should continue to shrink appreciably. Another factor supporting this is the economic. It is rare to find an idealistic book publisher, so that, in a kind of vicious circle, the more the public turns away from serious literature the less that literature will be available. Best-seller lists are the novelistic Nielsen ratings, and in fewer and fewer instances will a publisher take a chance on an unknown quantity. It is certainly a safer business proposition to commission the fictional version of an extremely popular movie than it is to invest in the work of a novelist who has not yet published, who has no established track record, no matter how interesting his manuscript might seem. As well, with the tremendous amounts of money to be made from the movie rights to popular novels, there is certainly a psychological pressure on any writer to take the path of least resistance. The artist is unconsciously corrupted by the process in which he lives.

One of the most telling aspects of the progression of civilization in the twentieth century has been the gradual predominance of the image over the word. While I would not go so far as to say that the tube is mightier than the sword, the image is fast becoming the most widely used means of communication in our culture. Already we have wallsize television screens, video games, and video movie cassettes, and more and more people go to the movies than ever before. Not very far into the future, records will be replaced by video discs, so that we can watch pictures of the performers while they sing —and not too much later will come laser holograms, so that it will be possible to have Mick Jagger or Luciano Pavarotti singing and/or dancing in three dimensions in our living rooms. At least initially this will be sensational, but once again the emphasis will be upon what the artist does and how he or she looks, not what he or she says. In music we will look at the sound, not listen to the lyrics. In such an atmosphere, the significance of the word must lessen and lessen, and the audience for poetry, the novel, and paradoxically even the static painting, must shrink along with it. It is debatable, aesthetically, whether or not a picture is worth a thousand words, but undoubtedly this will certainly be true in the marketplace.

What will happen will happen, but I do believe that unfortunately the image, the picture, will not serve to bring us together as human beings as literature has done. The shared cultural knowledge of works such as the Bible, the *Iliad*, the *Odyssey*, and the *Divine Comedy*, which in the past provided a basis for historical and artistic perspective, will be eroded by an immediate technological view that celebrates only what can be known now. While it might seem that the act of reading a novel is a private experience, as in many ways it is, it is actually not so private and solitary a thing as watching television. Reading an important novel was an experience that almost forced one to discuss it with someone else, to ask: did you think it meant this? That is: did it mean the same thing to you that it did to me? (When I was much younger, a friend once challenged me to a fistfight over what I had said about Shakespeare's *Richard II*.) The slapstick resolution in *Laverne and Shirley* and even the somewhat sophisticated irony in *MASH* are not events that we really need to talk about. We all get it, and we know that we do, so that we proceed in isolation to the kitchen for snacks or something to drink before the next program begins. Literature makes us stop and look backward to what we have experienced, while the televised image only pushes us forward to what will entertain us next.

This is not to prophesy that literature will be relegated to cultural monasteries, as Hermann Hesse predicted in *Magister Ludi*, but its appreciators will be greatly reduced in numbers. A literature that teaches and delights demands an active audience that is willing to take it on its own terms and to treat it seriously. As the word itself lessens in value, we lose our ability to appreciate style, and thus to appreciate theme. In recent times, writers and artists have been accused of being ivory towerists, art for art's sake types, and perhaps this may come to be. In the nineteenth century, every parlor

5

table displayed a copy of Longfellow's poems and crowds thronged the docks in New York harbor waiting for the next installment of the current novel by Charles Dickens. In our time, and in our children's time, this sort of thing is not to be, and the world will be the worse for it, though there is little we can do about it. The computer can duplicate words faster than we can think them, but, without the human being, or even the artist, the computer screen must always remain a pretty picture fit for little else than the next programming of a game of *Space Invaders*.

Brazil and the Information Societies of the Twenty-First Century

by

P.J. Castelo Branco

When one thinks of information societies, one usually thinks of Japan, the United States, Germany, France, and perhaps other OECD countries like Canada or the Netherlands. One does not tend to think of developing countries, even industrializing ones like Brazil and Singapore, but this is perhaps the result of looking at the future through a rearview mirror. By the twenty-first century, Brazil, if current development trends continue, will indeed be a full-fledged information society.

Brazil is a large country—indeed, geographically it is the fifth largest country in the world, with an area of 8.5 million square kilometers. Because of the terrain, topography, and vegetation of Brazil, an advanced communications system is a prerequisite to our development. Brazil is also large in population, being the seventh most heavily populated country in the world, with a total population of approximately 125 million. Brazil also has the world's tenth largest economy, with a gross national product currently at the level of $260 billion (U.S.) per annum.

Brazil is already in many ways an industrial economy. Its industrial exports were valued at $23 million in 1960, $109 million in 1965, $424 million in 1971, and over $10 billion in 1981. Brazil has thus sustained a growth rate, in terms of manufactured exports, of over 38% per annum over the last decade.

To sustain its economic growth, Brazil is already engaged in a number of ambitious projects, such as building the world's largest hydroelectric plant (in cooperation with Paraguay) and attempting to have 25% of all automobiles in Brazil powered by alcohol by the mid 1980s. Brazil is also developing important new economic regions, such as the Carajas project in the state of Para. This project is designed to exploit the considerable mineral resources of this region, which have already been valued at close to one-half trillion U.S. dollars.

Brazil has long recognized that there is a critical link between telecom-

P. J. Castelo Branco is chief executive of the Washington, D.C., office of EMBRATEL, the Brazilian Telecommunications Company. He is governor for Brazil on the INTELSAT Board of Governors, and recently completed a one-year term as chairman.

munications, economic development, and national technological growth. Both economic growth and expansion of communications facilities in Brazil for the last 15 years have sustained a real annual expansion rate in excess of 10% per annum. This parallel growth is no accident. In the early 1960s there existed in Brazil more potential subscribers on waiting lists than there were telephones in service. This pent-up demand for telecommunications service was largely the result of a lack of capital for financing the expansion of the telecommunications network. The solution found was a simple and effective one—namely, to use potential subscribers as a source of capital financing. Thus, over the last 17 years, a Brazilian self-capitalization scheme has allowed subscribers to invest in future expansion. Pent-up demand thus became an asset, in terms of obtaining local financing for system expansion.

This program has proved enormously successful in the Brazilian experience. In fact, the results have been remarkably impressive. The number of telephones in the Brazilian system has, over the last 15 years, grown from 500,000 to over 7.5 million. The number of installed telephones per 1,000 population has increased from 20 to over 60 during this period. Less than a handful of countries around the world have achieved a similar rate of growth during the 1960s and 1970s. Indeed, if Brazil is able to sustain its telephone expansion at a similar rate until the twenty-first century, it will have more than 125 million telephones.

A second reason for Brazil's dramatic breakthroughs in telecommunications is a product of the telecommunications institutional structures in Brazil. Brazil's telecommunications are organized as follows: a Ministry of Communications; a national telecommunications holding company known as Telebras; an entity for international and long-distance telecommunications telex and data, within Brazil known as EMBRATEL, that is within the Telebras structure; and, finally, individual telecommunications companies, one in each state, that are subsidiaries of Telebras and handle all local and intra-state telephone traffic.

This structure allows a sharing of technical and financial resources within the Telebras holding company system to meet telecommunications needs as they arise. In particular, a portion of EMBRATEL's revenues along with a portion of revenues from other Telebras companies are paid each year into a national telecommunications development fund. These funds are used to meet the most urgent of Brazil's telecommunications needs—be they local, long distance, or international in nature. In practice, the most important result of this procedure has been that the significant growth of profitable overseas telecommunications services during the 1970s has assisted in Brazil's national telecommunications development. Thus, overseas telecommunications facilities and services for Brazil have not only experienced remarkable growth in the last few years, but also, through the generation of new revenues, have served to bolster national telecommunications expansion as well.

Several other important telecommunications developments have taken place in Brazil in recent years. In partnership with Spain, the United States, and Portugal, Brazil has deployed during the past 10 years two submarine cables (BRACAN I, 160 circuits, and the just installed U.S.-Brazil system, BRUS, 1640 circuits), and will soon be installing a third cable, ATLANTIS, with capacity for 1380 circuits, which will connect Brazil to Africa and Europe. Brazil's use of the INTELSAT global satellite system for international service has grown 150% during the last five years, from 300 voice circuits to 700.

Lastly, Brazil has implemented a national satellite system through the lease of three transponders from INTELSAT for domestic service. Already this system allows reliable service to Brazil's interior, to such locations as Boa Vista, Manaus, Porto Velho, and Rio Branco. This network will continue to grow rapidly in future years.

The future for Brazilian telecommunications is likely to present an even more challenging series of goals than did the 1960s and 1970s. These efforts will, however, also likely produce spectacular results.

In the area of international telecommunications, we project international satellite circuits for telephones to increase from approximately 700 today to 3500 by 1993, and perhaps to 15,000 by the end of the twentieth century. We also anticipate significant new Brazilian investment in advanced submarine systems, including fiber optics systems over the next 20 years, in order to achieve a balance between terrestrial and space telecommunications systems. We anticipate that the technologies represented by the INTELSAT VI and subsequent satellites, as well as fiber optic cable systems, will allow the cost of international service to continue to decline. These cost reductions should serve to stimulate a continually high rate of growth for overseas service; therefore, we expect a parallel growth of this service and Brazil's economic growth.

Domestically, we see a similar pattern of growth in telecommunications that relies on the following major points—expanded use of satellite communications and other advanced wideband systems for national telecommunications services; the growth and implementation of digital communications systems and electronic switching systems; continued rapid implementation of new telephone stations, particularly in the most rapidly industrializing parts of Brazil; and finally, a progressive nationalization of advanced telecommunications and electronics technology.

These domestic objectives will be pursued on several fronts. First of all, Brazil will attempt to sustain the growth of available telephones in the national network.

To interconnect an extensive network of more than 100 million telephones, Brazil will rely heavily on microwave communications (and, increasingly, on satellite communications). Already Brazil provides through INTELSAT transponder leases, service to the interior of the country. This national satellite communications network, which provides telephone, telex, data, and television service, is expected to expand significantly in the next five years. Furthermore, Brazil has filed with the International Frequency Registration Board for frequency assignments for the BRAZILSAT domestic satellite network. Although the exact technical requirements of this satellite system, as well as the implementation date, have not been finally resolved, it is currently anticipated that certainly some time during the 1980s (or, conceivably, early in the 1990s) the domestic long-distance telephone traffic requirements of Brazil will be provided by a Brazilian domestic satellite system.

Finally, it is anticipated that, during the 1980s and 1990s, Brazil will move to implement an increasing amount of digital communications technology and to implement new electronic signaling and switching exchanges. Brazil will also upgrade its intercity networks. Already, five kilometers of high-capacity fiber optic links have been installed in Rio de Janeiro. Just as AT&T is implementing the Advanced Communications System in the United States and similar systems have been planned or are already implemented in France, the United Kingdom, Canada, the Netherlands, etc., Brazil would also anticipate rapid implementation of pocketswitched digital electronic telecommunications equipment.

The most dramatic goal for the 1980s and 1990s for Brazil, however, is to become a developer and manufacturer of advanced telecommunications equipment. We believe that, for the future, Brazil must not think of "technology transfer," but instead think in terms of "progressive incorporation of technology." What is meant by this statement is that new electronic technologies, if they are actually developed and mastered by the developing countries themselves, can become a means for industrializing countries like Brazil to leapfrog forward. In particular, most industrialized countries, like the U.K., U.S., Germany, France, etc., must revise their industrial structures, perhaps dramatically so, to accommodate the new technologies. Countries such as Brazil can shape their industries from the outset to produce products and services competitive on the world market, because they do not yet have an established technology base.

Brazilian technology goals are not simply based upon wishful thinking. There are indeed detailed plans for implementing this long-term strategy. One of the key aspects in this regard is detailed plans to establish the Telebrás Research and Development Center, currently being built in Campinas, in the state of São Paulo. This center is considered crucial to Brazil's plans for the "nationalization of technology." We believe that the new R&D center, which is intended to ultimately house 1,000 people and over 500 engineers, is the start of Brazil's answer to the U.S. Silicon Valley in California and Bell Labs in New Jersey.

The objectives of the Campinas R&D center are both demanding and long-term in scope. Among the programs to be undertaken at this center are the development of digital transmission equipment, the design of optical laser communications systems, development of digital satellite communications technology, and the design and engineering of a wide range of advanced electronic switching systems based upon the so-called TROPICO family of equipment that Brazil has already started to develop. The key to the TROPICO system will be intelligent subsystems connected together by means of distributed processing techniques, thus allowing a gradual buildup of components to achieve higher and higher levels of performance. We feel that the TROPICO system has much greater flexibility to meet the demands of industrializing countries than other systems (such as System X, being developed in the United Kingdom).

Thus, it can be seen that Brazil has placed enormous emphasis on the rapid growth of modern telecommunications over the last 20 years and that its plans for the next 20 years are yet more ambitious still. Brazil intends to achieve by the year 2000 one of the world's most reliable and sophisticated networks for both national and international telecommunications. Perhaps more significantly, we anticipate that Brazil will be a major exporter of advanced telecommunications and electronics equipment by the year 2000 as well. Although achieving these goals will depend on many aspects, such as finance capital, development of a national technology base, and perhaps a little luck, we are, nevertheless, quite serious about our national telecommunications goals. By the twenty-first century, we seriously believe that Brazil will be an advanced technological country in terms of computers, communications, and energy, and as a full-fledged information society we will be sharing our technology and our advanced industrial products with the rest of the world.

The Future of Language: Basic Tool of Communication

by

William Exton, Jr.

If we are to anticipate major linguistic developments on a rational basis, we should state the basic assumptions that we deem essential to such projections. We begin with these:

1. Language may be defined as a body of (verbal) symbols representing a variety of meanings; together with an operational system of usage (via grammar, syntax, code, etc.). Languages originate in oral form; and written forms are subsequently developed.

2. Written language may be preserved, over time, in its original form; but a language "lives" only in its usage and is therefore an ongoing creation of its users. As conditions alter usage, a language undergoes change.

3. Language is an essential tool, not only for its externally directed functioning for interactive, direct, indirect and large-scale communication but also for internal processing (i.e.: pre-communication, post-communication, and self-communication; as in conceptualization, contemplation, formulation, "thought," logic, reaction, evaluation, consideration, analysis, synthesis, calculation, etc.—none of which are necessarily—or can be completely—communicated).

4. All purposeful communication (beyond such visual indices as facial expressions, "body language," and a relatively few conventionally established or special signs, signals, gestures, etc.) depends upon the use of a verbal language.

5. The structure, the symbolic resources, the specificity, and other functional characteristics and associated values of a language must determine not only its applicability to and effectiveness for various communication purposes, but also its suitability for and its inherent operational effects upon those internal processes to which it is applied.

6. The purposes, forms, and media of communication change with cultural and social changes; with developments in technology, economics, and institutional and governmental practices; and with the effects of political, military, international, geographic, and environmental considerations. Con-

---

William Exton, Jr. is president of William Exton, Jr. and Associates, management consultants, New York, New York.

sequently, languages tend to change with the changing requirements for their use in various forms and applications of and developments in communication—and also with the changes in the nature, direction, orientation, and content of "thought processes."

Clearly, if the dynamism implied here is justified, then we may well assume that:

7. Languages, generally, are in a state of flux (as students of linguistics generally contend that all but those of closed and static societies have always been).

And we may also assume further that:

8. Languages current in the more technologically advanced, and the more socially, culturally, intellectually, and politically progressing societies, and in those more ethnically and linguistically diverse, will change more, and more rapidly, than those languages current in other societies.

In order to develop an acceptable projection of such changes, it is in order to review (briefly) at least a few significant and historically demonstrable changes in language that have transpired in response to past developments of various kinds; and then to consider the possible/probable results of those changes in conditions—current or anticipated—that are affecting or may be expected to alter the current state of our linguistic heritage.

Among those factors now—or soon to be—contributing in a major way to changes in language, are these:

1. The need or occasion for the introduction of new terminology, arising from:
    a. Scientific discoveries
    b. Technological developments (other than 4, below)
    c. Cultural changes; changes in life-style and in consumer tastes and habits
    d. Developments in operational characteristics of manufacturing and service industries, office work, bureaucratic functions, etc.
2. The introduction of new linguistic terminology and patterns, through:
    a. International trade
    b. Intercultural exchanges, contacts or experience (travel, tourism, immigration, etc.)
    c. International gatherings of all kinds
    d. Diplomatic and other official relations
    e. International relations generally: alliances, hostilities, interchanges, etc.
    f. Education aimed at inculcation of communication skills
    g. Effects of racially, culturally, socially, economically and educationally differentiated elements within the population
3. The development of new ideas, and new ways of "thinking" about matters of more-or-less general interest:
    a. Political change
    b. Philosophical, spiritual, religious developments
    c. Intellectual, artistic, literary developments
    d. Examples set by role-models, leaders, innovators, etc.
    e. Examples set by the media

    f. Education for advanced understanding of communication processes
4. The development of and use of communication-related technology (other than 1a, above):
    a. Advanced hardware and software for computerized processing of communications of many kinds, including the non-linguistic (i.e.: graphic; dynamic)
    b. Enhanced transmission/distribution capabilities
    c. Widespread availability and use of advanced hardware/software for computer processing and for the transmission of communication of many different kinds—linguistic and other
5. Progress in linguistic sciences, arts, and skills:
    a. Advanced operational languages for computers, robots, automatons, etc.
    b. Advances in communication theory
    c. Progress in linguistics
    d. Better understanding of neuro-verbal-syntactic processes
    e. Development of linguistic discipline (i.e.: General Semantics) for enhanced and more widespread "sanity" of language and behavior
    f. Planned change in language to exploit new knowledge and understanding, to render it a more accurate, precise, and efficient tool both for communication and for internalized processing

For perspective on the constant, inevitable, and often drastic changes and developments in language, we should consider at least such obvious historical matters as these:

• However "pure" the original Indo-European (Aryan) tongue may have been, it evolved over time into such diverse forms as Latin, Greek, Slavic, Gaelic, Hindi, and other rather extreme variants. Latin further diversified into Italian, French, Spanish, Rumanian, Romansch, Portuguese, and a few minor dialects. Greek itself branched into many local versions; and its mainstream transformed from Homeric grandeur (now comprehensible only to scholars) to modern Greek—which is currently in the process of further transformation into a government-sponsored "demotic" mode. The Slavic and Gaelic forms also spun off their derivations; and the earlier forms of Hindi, likewise, have many parallel but differing linguistic offspring in India.

Meanwhile, each identifiable language, so derived, has undergone and is undergoing major transformations. French, for instance, branched from Gallic-flavored Latin into a wide variety of regional (Langue d'Oc; Langue d'Oeil) and local (Norman, Breton, Burgundian, etc.) dialects—some of them verging on the mutually incomprehensible—and its transformation over the years is clearly illustrated by comparing the ninth-century *Chanson de Roland*, the works of Molière and Balzac, and the "patois" of much modern French literature with the everyday idioms of today's Paris, Lyon, Marseilles, Nantes, Strasbourg, etc.

France provides also the unique example of an official (and vain) effort to preserve linguistic purity: the French Academy (the 40 "immortals") controls the national lexicographic authority and refuses to authorize the acceptance of alien words. This has not prevented increasingly popular usage of many imported words and expressions (such as the "Franglais" of *le cock-*

14

tail, *le drugstore*, *le bifteck* and *le whisky*—not to mention *le hot dog*, *le weekend*, *le software*, *le hardware*, etc.).

• The deeply felt loyalty to and the personal importance of language are clearly demonstrated in the militance evoked by linguistic conflicts. Belgium is torn politically, culturally, and economically by the apparently unresolvable competition between the two major ethnic-linguistic groupings within its population: the French-speaking Walloons and the Flemish—whose language is related to Dutch. Canada has been riven—and Montreal has lost many important corporate operations—over the problems raised by French-speaking Quebec. India is home to hundreds of tongues, but has long relied on English (spoken by only about 5% of the population, but that includes the better educated, the political, professional, and managerial elite, etc.) as the official language of the government and courts. When Indira Gandhi attempted to make (modern) Hindi (most generally spoken of the native languages) the official language, she ran into such vehement opposition that the project had to be dropped.

• Contacts with other nations and cultures commonly result in the adoption of words from other languages. For example, we have totally absorbed such words as *algebra* and *admiral* from the Arabic, *Jehovah* and *messiah* from Hebrew, *litre* and *table-d'hôte* from the French, *mafia* and *spaghetti* from the Italian, *wigwam* and *squaw* from the Indians, *vodka* and *sputnik* from the Russians, *guerrilla* and *chili* from the Spanish, etc. In addition, many other alien words have at least limited currency. Examples are *ciao*, *shalom*, *chutzpah*, *mensch*, *mach*, *schnell*, *prosit*, *nyet*, *sayonara*, *toodle-oo*, *papoose*, *bambino*, *blitz*, *discotheque*, *casino*, *vino*, *bonbon*, *couturier*, *derrière*, *corrida*, *gulag*, *schnapps*, etc.

Let us now consider at least the major changes in the development of the language we call English. Many scholars believe that King Alfred (900 A.D.) was the first king in the British Isles to think he was speaking English, which they trace back to Anglo-Saxon, or "old English," as exemplified in the Saga of Beowulf (750 A.D.?)—now virtually unintelligible to all but a few philologists. Development through the Dark Ages is suggested in the barely decipherable monkish Anglo-Saxon Chronicle (891 A.D.?). Further changes in the language can be traced in such landmarks as the Domesday Book (1085 A.D.) and Piers Ploughman (1362 A.D.).

After the Normans invaded England in 1066, they formed a new aristocracy, with Norman French as its tongue. This, of course, introduced much in the way of new vocabulary, pronunciation, and cultural ideas into what had been the English of Edward the Confessor. The most notable result of this is to be found in the works of Chaucer, who died in 1400 A.D. Here is a sample from his "Troilus and Cresyde," written approximately six centuries ago:

> And for ther is so gret diversite
> In English and in writyng of our tonge,
> So prey I God that non myswrite the,
> Ne the mysmetre for defaute of tonge.

We skip a bit to the Elizabethan period (late sixteenth and early seventeenth centuries), which yielded the English of Shakespeare; and on to the Victorian Era (late nineteenth century), with its Dickens and Thackeray—

but also with its Darwin, Spencer, and other innovators and popularizers of science.

In the meantime, of course, English was popularizing many scientific terms adapted from the Greek (*geography*, *megalith*, etc.) and absorbing a great wealth of words from Latin—not only from legal and medical parlance, but also from many other fields of knowledge and activity (*hibernate*, *armament*, *reservoir*, etc.).

In the twentieth century, we can note the speeding progression from Kipling to Hemingway, and on to Mailer and Bellow—with side excursions to the likes of Joyce; and from the lyrics of W.S. Gilbert to those of the Beatles.

English has—and tends to cling to—many obvious defects. Among these, perhaps the most widely recognized is its highly inconsistent and often indefensibly archaic orthography. Our spelling comes down to us, only slightly modified, from feudal times—and continues to baffle school children and foreigners (not to mention our college and graduate students, secretaries, executives, and professionals). For example, why should "ough" be pronounced so differently in *thought*, *though*, *through*, *drought* and *rough*; and why shouldn't they be spelled *thot*, *tho*, *thru*, *drowt* and *ruf*? Why do we use *c* to make the sounds of both *k* and *s*?

Theodore Roosevelt tried to introduce "simplified spelling" early in this century. He ordered the Government Printing Office to publish the Congressional Record in that way. But he had to retreat when senators and representatives saw their words immortalized in such unfamiliar form—and feared the imputation of near-illiteracy by their constituents.

It is high time we ceased to burden outselves with such useless vestiges of the adolescence of our language and gave it a friendly boost toward potent and flourishing maturity.

Many English verbs are highly irregular (*am*, *are*, *is*; *was*, *were*; *go*, *went*) and are the despair of foreigners attempting to learn the language. Surely the resources exist to amend this situation by providing more regular conjugations.

Since language lives only as constantly created by those who use it, we should at least identify the major factors effecting change in the use of language—and those factors that make such changes in usage more, or less, influential. We should also distinguish—among changes—those which are superficial, trivial, temporary, passing, or otherwise unimportant and those which are organic, significantly functional, "built in," and likely to be lasting.

There are changes, and there are changes. Virtually every season brings some new words into circulation; the adoption of new synthetic terminology (*modem*, *sitcom*, *smog*); the popularization of scientific terms (*byte*, *chip*, *transistor*); the creation of labels to fit social phenomena (*jailbait*, *mugger*, *drop-out*); the spread of slang (*uppers* and *downers*, *French leave*, *schnozzle*); the use of proper names to suggest somehow associated subjects (*bikini*, *roscoe*, *John Hancock*); the easing of trade names into the common vocabulary (*victrola*, *frigidaire*, *levis*); metonymy: the naming of a part to suggest the whole (*wheels*, *silver screen*, *turntable*); and other changes in or additions to current usage of the language.

Unpredictable, haphazard changes in or additions to language can flow from such a diversity of origins as phenomenally popular authors, motion pictures, songs, comic strips, or well-known characters (real or fictional). Or they can arise from the impact of a discrete ethnic/linguistic group (*soul*); or from a major media event (as occurred with the early space shots (*astronaut*), the atom bomb (*fallout*), and the wars (*dog-face, doughboy*), etc.).

Some of these changes and additions will be transient; some will remain in use for a long time; and some will undergo their own changes from original meanings and applications, as the conditions that brought them into being also change. (*Scoff-law*, originally created to label those who bought and drank liquor illegally during Prohibition, is currently applied to those who ignore parking tickets.)

Such changes and additions are many, but most of them are relatively minor. Over the years, they provide needed labels for new things, ideas, concepts, experiences, processes, and other matters entering into the consciousness of users of the language; and they enrich the vocabulary. Without such accretions and modifications, the language would become inadequate for daily use. But such bits and pieces of change in its idiom leave the fundamental nature of the language—in its structure and syntax—basically unaltered; and its general usage is largely unaffected by such discrete factors.

If the language we use is to become more useful to us—better adapted to our present and future communication needs—then changes of a much more fundamental and structural nature will be needed. And we may well ask, Will they come? And if so, will they develop slowly, by gradual usage—or deliberately, by plan?

A careful, thorough, and competent review of the deficiencies of the English language could be the first step toward a renovation that would make it as well adapted to common and literary usage in the twenty-first century as it was to Shakespeare's genius, almost 400 years ago. Here are a few suggestions:

Compared to highly inflected languages, English is often rather vague. (This is especially apparent when formulating legislation, precise legal instruments, and in other such exacting applications.) By comparison, German verbs, for instance, end in suffixes that clearly indicate the person (first, second, third), number (singular, plural), and tense. German nouns call for a clear designation (*der, die, das*) of gender; and the enclitic is inflected through all cases (nominative, genitive, dative, and accusative).

Whatever the disadvantages of so elaborate a grammar, it does provide an often needed clarity. Conceivably, a grammar could be devised for at least optional use in English. With a "Two-Style English," the more elaborate form would provide a high degree of specificity when required; but it would be acceptable to dispense with the elaborations and use "folk English" for less exacting or formal purposes.

There are some linguistic needs that appear, and become obvious—but remain unmet. Individuals may initiate their own solutions, and others may follow; but such a need is not satisfied until a satisfactory and workable way of meeting it is generally accepted and used. For example, if languages are to change in order to meet emerging needs, then it is high time our usage of English should provide an acceptable accommodation of the development, during the past decade or two, of the changing status, and the scope of activi-

17

ties, of women. We truly need terminology that will enable us to eliminate the clumsy improvisations of "he/she," "his/her," and also the awkward substitution of "person" for "man" in so many traditional terms (chairman, postman, journeyman, foreman, assemblyman, congressman, etc.) especially when we are speaking impersonally and do not need to specify if we mean to refer to man or woman.

Certainly a major aspect of the future of language has to do with the growing requirement for an international, intercultural linguistic medium. There have been several such, originating in the Mediterranean basin, that were widely adopted by the elite, if not the general population, of many different ethnic/linguistic groups. In the small circa-Mediterranean world preceding the Christian era, Greek came close to becoming a "universal" language because of the conquests of Alexander and the spread of Hellenistic culture. Following this, the growth of the Roman Empire put Latin on the tongues of people from Caesar's Britain to Antony's Egypt.

Latin—in increasingly degraded forms—continued to be the principal international/intercultural medium of the literate minority (as the language of the Roman Catholic Church and as the working language used by many scholars, lawyers, and scientists until the last few centuries).

With the cultural grandeur of France in the seventeenth, eighteenth, and nineteenth centuries, French became the language of the Western European elite and of diplomacy. Meanwhile, language followed empire; the major languages of Europe were exported to their colonies. That, and the commercial prominence and maritime activity of England, made English the most widely used language around the world. After World War I, with the major debut of the United States into European affairs and with the worldwide distribution of the products of Hollywood, the English language (and especially the American variants) invaded Continental Europe and Asia as it never had before.

The growing importance of America in commerce, finance, and culture, and the global spread of American-controlled enterprise, pushed English ever further ahead; and since World War II, it seems inevitable that English is to become the principal second language in all lands where it is not the mother tongue. As such, it will surely affect all other languages—as it has wherever it has been adopted to any degree. And, of course, English itself will be affected in many ways, as it undergoes all sorts of transforming combinations with the traditional languages of other cultures.

Since English is most likely to be utilized by the more educated elements in the non-English-speaking lands, some of the more "powerful" local expressions are likely to be preserved and carried over into English (as has already happened so often), along with those terms that have no equivalent in English. The ultimate effect will probably be to enrich our language with an inflow of new and pungent vocabulary, figures of speech, and even adaptive patterns and constructions, which will spread to the extent that they add useful resources.

An alert monitor of up-to-date English—at least as spoken by the more cosmopolitan among us—will find increasing enrichment and modification; and much of it will spread and be lasting.

This discussion would be incomplete without reference to certain age-old means of communication that have supplemented, paralleled, or even—in some cultures—replaced the spoken word. Here we refer to:

- The use of gestures and "body language." Deaf mutes, practitioners of traditional Hindu dance, North American Indians, and some other cultures or subcultures are or were able to communicate a very wide range of meanings through their gesture languages. Many ethnic groups enrich verbal language or even substitute for it with highly expressive gestures. Considerable popular interest has developed in recent years in "body language"—both deliberate and involuntary.
- Some languages are written in alphabets that are not phonetic. Japanese and Chinese, for instance, are not written in what we call letters, but in symbols called ideographs or logographs, which represent whole words: meanings, not sounds. This, of course, requires a rather large set of characters (which do not, strictly speaking, constitute an alphabet). The effects on the requirements for printing-type fonts and typewriters are obvious.

But the ultimate value of such systems for communication purposes, and their long-range effects on the intellectual development of individuals, have yet to be fully evaluated. A careful exploration of the potentials of logographic or ideographic representation might well indicate the desirability of at least a partial adaptation, where particularly advantageous for certain special applications.

- While some actors do wonders with the English language—and many non-professionals adorn or orchestrate it effectively with all sorts of more-or-less expressive tones, inflections, emphases, etc.—spoken English can be generally understood when enunciated in a perfectly flat way. But this is not true of some other languages, which make essential use of and depend upon tone, rising or falling inflections, and/or other voiced supplements to the bare phonemes of the verbal symbols. Undoubtedly, this "solo duet"—this duality of utterance—can provide a superior degree of communication, of some kinds, which may have considerable value for some purposes. Again, a competent study should indicate whether we could gain some benefits by introducing a certain codified tonal or pitch counterpoint into our speech.

The paragraphs immediately above are intended only to suggest certain possibilities for the enrichment of our language, and for its improvement as our primary means of communication. These possibilities already exist within the many linguistic resources that we do not use, and they are effectively exploited in other cultures.

The twenty-first century will make other, unprecedented demands on our language, some of which are already felt—with others vaguely anticipated. For example:

- A tremendous acceleration in communication technology and services is virtually revolutionizing the transmission resources of originators, the accessibility of recipients, the versatility, quality, and range of transmissions, the availability of alternative modes, the effectiveness of presentational techniques, the near-universal facility and convenience of involvement, the international and intercultural impacts of transmissions, and many other aspects of our working, governmental, cultural, recreational, and home environments. Inevitably, this is exerting many different kinds of effects on language. Such effects include these:

1. The languages of the major originators of communication materials directed at public audiences are invading the linguistic territories of the recipients of such transmissions. This will have the effect of aggrandizing the linguistic territory of the exported language and diminishing the territory of the domestic language.

2. The characteristics of the means of transmission will exert effects upon the language transmitted; limitations of cost, clarity, range, etc., will impose special requirements on the language involved; while new advantages and features will stimulate linguistic exploitation of the opportunities presented.

3. The inherent characteristics of transmissions—apart from content—will affect "the way people think." For instance, as the proportion of presentational impact shifts from verbal to visual, there will be a corresponding cultural shift toward more visually oriented conceptualization. This will have consequences of many kinds for language—probably generally unfavorable, but with some partially compensating developments of an adaptive kind.

Artificial speech is already with us (this refers to the simulation of human speech by robots or other mechanisms, initiated in response to spoken queries or commands, or to the effects of sensors or other inputs, or to report the results of their own performances). Also, voice-controlled mechanisms will be extensively utilized; and two-way verbal interchanges between operator and machine will become routine. Presumably, then:

• Some new languages, or some modification of an existing language, will be developed to provide optimum practicality and efficiency for such developments. We should be thinking about what may be the most desirable characteristics for such a language; what languages may be best adapted; and how English measures up to such considerations.

• When a special language (or modifications of an existing language) is developed for optimum operational effectiveness with, for, and by voice-operated and vocal equipment, what should be learned from such language—or from such modifications—that can be advantageously adapted to English, to improve its value for its traditional usages in communcication and in internal processing?

• There have been many attempts to create a "universal language." Esperanto and Ido come to mind. While none of these has won widespread acceptance, it is still true that each one represents an impressive amount of informed, objective consideration of the merits and demerits, advantages and disadvantages of various characteristics of languages currently in use—and a deliberate effort to create a new language superior to any of these, and better adapted to intercultural use.

Surely, a collaboration among modern linguists, philologists, etymologists, grammarians, lexicographers, syntacticians, systems analysts, programmers, computer specialists, speech pathologists, child development specialists, psychologists specialized in learning processes, and General Semanticists should be able to synthesize a language, or specify modifications of (an) existing language(s), that would accomplish all that the authors of these earlier efforts hoped (and more), meeting also such needs and opportunities as they could not have anticipated but that we can now foresee.

• In the earlier days of computer development, special "languages" were created for programming and for instructing the computer. As computers and computer programming advanced, progressively simpler ("user friendly") "languages"—that is, differing progressively less from "normal English"—came into use. Surely this experience—this history of learning how to provide progressive simplicity and effectiveness in quasi-linguistic man-machine linkage—should be inherently rich in lessons for us on how to upgrade the structural functionality of the language we use for other purposes. We must and will learn much from this, and benefit accordingly—whether it be in the language we use, or in the "programming" of ourselves (by education, training, habituation, conditioning, etc.) to process linguistic inputs with greater precision, comprehension, recognition of intended significance, and potential for appropriate response.

• Meanwhile, an exciting new visual medium is developing rapidly. Computer graphics create, and provide electronically controlled apparent motion to, what have hitherto been, at best, the static products of draftsmen. The communication values inherent in, and yet to be fully realized from, this development are apparent—since language can scarcely convey equivalent meaning and can even approach such a standard only quite laboriously. A new vocabularly of visual symbols and signs will surely follow the fuller development of the new set of potential significances thus emerging from the cathode ray tube, and will most certainly impact our linguistic practices.

• There is still another aspect of the future of language, in a direction that offers no present clues. This is related to the view that "intelligent life" exists elsewhere than on this planet, and that we should explore the (assumed) possibilities for "extraterrestrial" communication. The principle endeavor along this line, so far, has been nonlinguistic, emphasizing visual displays illustrative of such "universal truths" as the Pythagorean demonstration (consisting of squares on the sides of a right triangle), which intelligent beings are expected to recognize, understand, and react to responsively. (Some people, however, appear to believe that "visitors from outer space" are already with us, and have the ability to deal with our languages—presumably through superior intelligence or technology).

The perspective of communicating, over vast distances, with beings of superior intelligence, but of unguessed cultural orientation, is a challenging one and can stimulate ideas that may benefit our linguistic developments for use here, on Mother Earth. The challenge to the imagination is as unlimited as that of the unforeseeable life-forms that may exist on remote planets of distant suns.

For instance, assuming they exist, and that they communicate with one another, we must face the possibility that their sensory capabilities do not include vision and hearing (upon which our own communication capabilities depend), but, instead, involve entirely different means of conveying and receiving meaning or thought. Such means might be non-linguistic—even non-symbolic—as by "thought transference" over distance, or by conductive contact. It is probably futile—however provocative—to speculate on such matters; but if contact is ever made and communication established with intelligent life-forms on other worlds, the consequences for the future of language—as we know it—may be drastic indeed.

The twentieth century saw important developments in many fields of knowledge, with major effects—immediate and long-term—on language (and perhaps especially on English). Among these developments:

a. Renewed and more pragmatic concern for epistemological processes (Whitehead, Northrop, Wittgenstein, et al.)

b. Symbolic Logic (Russell, Carnap, Langer, et al.)

c. Cybernetics (Wiener)

d. Research into special efficiencies of primitive languages (Whorf, Sweet, Boas, Bloomfield, Sapir, et al.)

e. Philological research (Jesperson, Saussure, et al.)

f. Psychiatry (Gardner Murphy's "field theory"; W. A. White, et al.)

g. Psychology (William James, John Dewey, Bentley, et al.)

h. Physiology, biology (Pavlov, Sinnott; neurological discoveries, etc.)

i. Semiotics (Charles Morris, I. A. Richards, C. S. Peirce, et al.)

j. Mathematical and statistical analyses (Shannon, Weaver, MacKay, Cherry; also Thorndike, Lorge, Flesch, et al.)

k. Major advances in linguistics, etymology, lexicography, etc.

• In 1933, a new linguistic and epistemological discipline was born. This was General Semantics, and it originated with the publication of *Science and Sanity*, by Alfred Korzybski.

Korzybski was an engineer and a mathematician, and he had a deep appreciation of the precision and specificity of the "language" of mathematics and of the physical sciences. But he was only too well aware of the imprecision—and the often misleading effects—inherent in ordinary languages (of which he spoke at least four). And he knew that this kind of linguistic deficiency was reflected in much of the "unsane" behavior of people—who derived much of their perceptions of "the real world" via imperfect language, and who used and relied on often deceptive language in their efforts to deal with "the real world."

Korzybski suggested the "map-territory" relationship as a parallel to the relationship between linguistic communication and the "reality" it is intended to communicate; and he provided an acute analysis of the considerations that govern this relationship.

He also emphasized the essential distinction between communications that clearly relate or refer to or identify an element of reality (extensional), and those that are unspecific or vague because they refer to subjective values (intentional), or to generalizations (high-order abstractions), where the "receiver" cannot "know" what "reality" is actually involved.

Korzybski's work dealt in detail with the deficiencies of language; but it also presented constructive ideas and "devices" for minimizing or countering those deficiencies. Some of these devices are in regular use today, by people who have no idea of their actual origin.

Those not yet familiar with General Semantics should certainly become so; but the purpose of referring to this invaluable discipline, in this paper, is to suggest the value and magnitude of its potential future contribution to our language. A thorough-going evaluation and elaboration of General Semantics could greatly help to point the way to a general overhauling and retooling of English, which should substantially improve both its clarity and its efficiency.

This would be invaluably reflected in our improved perception and handling of reality, and in our more functional orientation to life situations generally—a culture-wide gain beyond any calculation.

Clearly, we who look forward to the twenty-first century must recognize that changes in language are now occurring at a greatly accelerating pace—and will, in the future, accelerate and accumulate exponentially. All the factors known to contribute to such changes are increasing and intensifying:

• Scientific discoveries and developments of all kinds are becoming commonplace; and many of them, along with the terminology they occasion, are increasingly popularized.

• Technology is booming, along with an insatiable popular interest in its applications and implications; and this brings many additions to general and specialized vocabularies.

• The media are increasingly pervasive and are able to convert a word, an expression, a neologism, a quotation, or any other verbal or quasi-verbal symbol into a popular cliché virtually overnight.

• The diversity of our national culture, and the personal popularity and success, in various aspects of our media, of individuals of widely differing cultural backgrounds, result in the constant enrichment of the popular vocabulary.

• International/intercultural factors are increasingly prevalent. Two-way travel, tourism, and trade; imported cultural phenomena (books, motion pictures, singers, plays); news from abroad—all contribute to our linguistic wealth.

• The internationalization of business, with multinational corporations operating in and sending employees to and receiving them from many lands, is a major—and rapidly growing—disseminator of linguistic changes.

• Language is transmitted by many different means; and each means of conveying linguistic interchange exerts its own effects upon the forms and usage of language. The telegraph imposed its own restrictions upon the messages it carried, as does any other cost-per-word means of transmission—and, indeed as do those other means that spell out each message, letter by letter (semaphore, blinker, heliograph, etc.). The telephone has had its influence on our language—and so have radio, the motion pictures, and television.

• But communication can be and often is effected through media other than the spoken or written word; and experience of such communication can have considerable influence on language, and on the ways it is used. The development of audiovisual technology has introduced advanced adjuncts to language supplements, or even more effective replacements. The advancing frontier of this technology, and its progressively more effective applications, exert increasingly marked influence on pedagogy, instruction, information, persuasion, etc., of many kinds. And the outlook is for more of the same.

For all such reasons we should expect that all sorts of changes—some major, many minor—will be developing more and more rapidly. And we should also anticipate that such changes will occur variously, without plan or coordinate occasion; for different reasons; from differing causes; in different segments of our society; and in different cultural connections.

The processes of communication, and of thought, depend upon the elicitation, by verbal symbols and syntactical structures, of "associations" stored in the memory, which provide the "meanings" (values) we attach to what we hear or read. Surely the current state of English is not the ultimate in potential excellence for optimizing the probability of the most precisely appropriate—not to say felicitous—association.

Those of us who have learned a language in childhood may never become sufficiently adept in any other to make learning it, for the purpose of improvement in functional communication, worthwhile. And any substantial departure from our linguistic heritage would involve some degree of sacrifice of the literary treasures of our culture.

We must address such questions as these:

What is the purpose, or what are the purposes, of language? (Surely, specific purposes change with changing or new needs, conditions, applications, uses, and possibilities.)

What are, or what are becoming, or what will become, the needs, conditions, applications, uses, and possibilities of and for language in the future?

When we face the long history of linguistic change, and acknowledge its continuing inevitability, should we be satisfied to leave it so? Should we sit back, virtually unconscious of the heterogeneous, helter-skelter, useful and worthless, lasting and faddish, totally unplanned and uncoordinated—but absolutely inevitable—changes in our language, which we know will occur at an exponentially accelerating rate?

Shall we passively allow our language to undergo change in the uncontrolled, unpredictable, haphazard way in which it has undergone change in the past?

Should we not take full and hopeful charge of this tool—as that most essential to our basic need to communicate? And should we not shape it to fit and match—fully as well as possible—those coming needs, conditions, applications, uses, and possibilities, to meet which we must so greatly depend upon the future of this imperfect but indispensable resource—our language.

Shall we not act to assure the brightest potential for the future of communication by forging—for its indispensable handmaiden and tool—the best and most useful language we can possibly create?

Acknowledgement

Grateful acknowledgement is hereby made for the invaluable comments and suggestions of Doctors A.W. Read, P. Norden, and C. Leilhacar.

A Common Second Language: GLOSSA

by

Robin F. Gaskell

We live in an era when those of us wishing the world well need to unite in our efforts; we need to consult together to find the best possible path to our future. The verb *to communicate* is the key to this future. It is not just a passive talking and chewing over of ideas; if we consult a Latin dictionary, we find "communico" listed to mean much more than that. It is "to make common, to unite; to communicate, impart, give a share in, grant; to inform, take counsel with, confer with."

Now we know what we are talking about. And, if we extend this original Latin meaning into communication, we find that it is an active process: the sharing of the material benefits of life as well as of ideas. It also means the consultation between people to create unity. Of course, now that we have the means of sharing with and consulting with the whole of mankind, "communication," from the '80s on, implies a world unity through the sharing of knowledge and resources.

Most of us probably see improvements in communications as faster and more extensive ways of conducting debate and argument, which are the established means of social intercourse. However, even the most high-speed computer networks and the most widespread global television link-ups will not ensure us the classical "communico" until we have a change of heart.

In this paper, I wish to describe progress in written and spoken communication. However, the subject described might appear to be just another technical innovation if it is not made plain that this work implies a change in our attitude towards communication. While computers and satellites represent sales of hardware and the marketing of copyright software, they provide communication only for the affluent. If, on the other hand, you believe that communication should be for everybody, take heart; there is a social innovation that provides for the common counseling and sharing of information that creates World Community. "Communico" is not hardware; it is a living process in which all participate.

All this . . . just to inform you that an international auxiliary language is needed—and now! The World Future Society can play a significant part by

Robin F. Gaskell, a teacher, writer, and linguist, lives in Balmain East, New South Wales, Australia.

stating the problem. It can create a global awareness of the difficulties caused by the national languages, and it can point to the possibility of finding a solution to the language problem. Arthur C. Clarke, in his book *Future World*, places the adoption of a world auxiliary language around the year 2050. Possibly this is because he feels that we aren't ready to talk to one another yet, or perhaps that intelligence, machine or human, is still not up to the task. A solution exists today!

As futurists, we must know that there is a need for one language that all can use. Also, we must realize that events will force mankind to agree on the use of a common tongue for the purpose of sharing, conferring, uniting—for communicating.

Sadly, we are also "pastists" as well. We fear the release of energy that will follow the freeing of information; we are concerned that a truly communicating world will bring a future that is too different. Moreover, we are loath to give up our status and position, which depend, in large part, on the cultural isolation that is afforded by our national languages.

Before anyone can think rationally about the possibility of their children learning a second language that is being taught to all other children around the globe, they must come to terms with an almost universal abhorrence of the idea. An uncultural, world new-speak? Ugh!

But does Arthur C. Clarke really expect us to wait until 2050 A.D. to adopt English as the language of global intercourse? No, he's too shrewd. English is a minority language, with about one-tenth of us having it as our first language and, say, another one-tenth speaking it with varying degrees of competence. Getting that remaining four-fifths of the world's population over the hump is the hard part: it would involve tremendous difficulties in learning, owing to irregularities and strangeness of use; but, worse than that, it would involve insoluble difficulties at the political level.

Despite all this, Robert D. Hamrin (*The Futurist*, August 1981) sees a time, in America, when "the Library of Congress is available to anyone on a personal computer." Will these books be available only in English; and will the pre-eminence of the English-speaking countries impose this language as the only one available via computer networks? Alternatively, might non-English-speaking owners of microcomputers be able to network into the Library of Congress and into networks of Russian, French, Italian, German, Chinese, and Japanese information as well?

There is another way of rationalizing information flow without the cost of multiple translations or the drudgery of learning five or more foreign languages. All information need be translated only once—into an *interlingua* that is learnt by all. Such a language must, of course, convey meaning perfectly and be easy to learn and use. UNESCO sought this kind of "metalanguage," and was still hopeful of finding one when it printed the 1971 report entitled "UNISIST: An Attempt to Find an International Language for Science."

Although, a decade later, the committees of UNESCO have accepted failure in their task, the past 10 years were not entirely wasted. In the same year that the report was issued, working independently and in ignorance of UNESCO's efforts, Ron Clark, in England, began on a parallel task, single-handed; during the decade, Wendy Ashby joined Clark in the work of designing a language. Neither of these names appears in the academic literature; notwithstanding, the language, "Glossa," that they created is presented not only as a holding language for science, but also as a means of communication for all people.

Whether or not the language they produced is suitable for English-speakers and the other four-fifths of the world's population remains to be seen. But, a measure of the effectiveness of Glossa, Esperanto, English, or any other possible auxiliary language will only be found when future-minded people, who are actively watching the situation, conduct objective tests.

Is the World Future Society interested in communication—the communication of sharing? Are members interested enough in the future, and in the sharing of information, to product-test possible auxiliary languages? The Esperantists made the mistake of attempting to mobilize establishment support through members of Parliament and education authorities. As a result of promotion at the League of Nations, Esperanto training programs were set up in many countries, but these received a severe setback with the advent of the Second World War, and the language has made no further progress since then. Esperanto's inherent difficulties have, however, contributed greatly to its continued stagnation. In the light of this knowledge, it appears that the progress of any language toward world adoption depends on its linguistic qualities and on the popular support it receives. At present, English is the language adopted by many multinational companies and international representative bodies, and individuals from all over the world are choosing to learn English because it gives them an opportunity to enter the Western economy. However, this steady progress of English is by default—owing to the absence of any suitable alternative—rather than due to the outstanding qualities of English as a second language.

The World Future Society could establish a subcommittee on auxiliary languages that would look into the criteria for evaluating languages—both designed and national. It could also act as an agency for the collection and evaluation of auxiliary languages. The languages collected could be checked against the various lists of criteria for auxiliary languages. Such an exercise would be worthwhile only if periodic reports were printed in *The Futurist*, and if the subcommittee were totally objective and open-minded.

As an extension of the auxiliary language subcommittee idea, individual members of the World Future Society could learn different auxiliary languages on file; progress reports from members testing and using the languages would give a valuable check of the qualities of the different languages, and would comprise the basis of a recommendation, were such to be made.

Other objections to the adoption of an international auxiliary language exist, and should also be dispelled. While English appears to be taking over as the world's second language, it is alien to both Asians and Arabic-speakers. Will a neutral, European-based language that uses the Roman alphabet be any less objectionable to people outside the Indo-European language tradition? Quite simply, this is a case for inspired decision-making by the world's leaders. It is fairly evident that the Roman alphabet is the most widespread throughout world culture, and it is also clear that keyboards with Arabic and Chinese characters will not be adopted by the West.

27

We could find that, after all of the evidence has been collected, English, or a language that is some form of English, will be the most adoptable, on a world basis. The Glossa language can be seen, in a number of ways, as "some form of English." Although its vocabulary is the currently-used classical roots, and its pronunciation is Italian, its sentence construction and grammatical pattern are very similar to English.

Quite apart from its wide usage in the West, English has definite linguistic features in its favor. Through gradual change, owing to usage rather than decree, English has lost most of its complicated grammar—with only about five declensions remaining. It has also developed a word order that appears to correspond with the deep structure of language: there seems to be an inherent logic in a word order where each word modifies the next. Much of the grammar of English is achieved through the order and emphasis of its words, with punctuation defining this grammatical emphasis when the language is written.

It is highly unlikely that the English language will be reformed to regularize its grammar and usage, even though such rationalization would be necessary to make it attractive to the non-English-speaking majority. However, such a change would be objected to from both sides: English-speakers would never agree to having the foundation stone of their culture so eroded; and learners would still have to learn a vocabulary that was very different from those of the rest of Europe.

The obvious thing to do is to forget about the national languages, and to find, or derive, an easily learnable neutral language. By comparing all of these languages against a checklist of criteria, many would be eliminated. However, a small list of finalists would emerge as being the most preferred; these would be the designed languages that satisfied a majority of the criteria.

This collection and checking of possible auxiliary languages is a task that we, as futurists, can accept. Not wishing to suggest an empty exercise, I present Glossa as one neutral, designed language to start the collection. I feel that an objective assessment will place Glossa among the finalists of possible languages currently available. Perhaps something even more suitable will emerge in time, but let us, as interested futurists, start the discourse, now. If the future holds an ideally adoptable interlingua, an active seeking by the World Future Society should encourage it to appear; if, on the other hand, the most adoptable "second language for all" is already in existence, such efforts will expedite its general use.

Appended to this paper is a list of criteria for an international auxiliary language. To give you a look at Glossa, two more appendices are included; they are "The Rules of Glossa" and a translation example.

In conclusion, I urge futurists to make a list of future projections that will benefit from, or are dependent on, the use of a world auxiliary language; and then, on the other side of the page, to make a list of future projections that will be harmed through the adoption of an interlingua by which all can communicate. The author will be pleased to receive your lists and/or other comments: Robin F. Gaskell, 11 Paul Street, Balmain East 2041, Australia.

References

Ron Clark & Wendy Ashby, *Glossa Dictionary*, 29 Pandora Road, London NW6 1TS, England, 1981.

B. Russel, *!Suma: A Neutral Universal Language*, Third Edition, B. Russel, 202 Terminal Drive, Plainview, New York, 1966.

League of Nations, Report of the General Secretariat of the League of Nations, Adopted by the Third Assembly, "Esperanto As an International Language," League of Nations, 1922.

John Cresswell and John Hartley, *Teach Yourself Esperanto*, EUP, 1957.

Appendix 1

Criteria of Glossa

Glossa was designed, from first principles, to be a second language for all. During the language's development, a number of criteria emerged.

• The vocabulary is the most widely known around the globe: it is the international vocabulary of science. The Greek and Latin roots that are the foundation of science's terminology are also common throughout all European languages.

• Each word conveys a concept. There are no parts of speech, but words used as nouns can be labeled with a terminal letter.

• Words are selected for clarity and efficiency. Shorter words have been preferred, and unwanted similarities in pronunciation and spelling avoided.

• Word order is logical. Meaning is conveyed by word order and context, according to the standard subject-verb-object structure of English; a word is modified by its precedent.

• The essentials of grammar are achieved with a minimum of fuss. There are no declensions, and words do not change because of grammar; fifteen small particles cover all grammatical needs.

• Sentence construction is bound by few rules. There are about 10 rules for language construction; for ease of learning and freedom of expression, a rigid set of rules has been avoided.

• Meaning if conveyed clearly. This is achieved through context, word order, and the semantic power of the classical languages; the lack of idiom combines with the essential grammar to ensure that meaning is conveyed directly.

• The Roman alphabet is used. These letters are recognized around the world, and are found on the majority of typewriters and computer keyboards; scientific terminology is expressed in this alphabet, which is also the medium used for the machine handling of information.

• Spelling is regular. This is assured through the limitation of vocabulary to the two classical languages; spelling is recognizable as the same as that in the roots used in technical terminology and in the national languages of Europe.

• Pronunciation is regular. When sounded in Italian, each consonant is sounded and each vowel has only one pronunciation; this makes good sense, considering that the Italian language derives from Latin.

• The language is pleasant sounding. Italian pronunciation, which is one of the most musical, assures this; practically, this is essential for ease of speaking and listening.

• The language is easily learned. With few rules, little grammar, recognizable vocabulary, and sensible word order, the language is easy to learn and use.

• The language has the broadest possible base to avoid national bias. While the vocabulary harks back to the Indo-European stem language, national elements (English word order, Italian pronunciation) are included because they are best in that respect.

Rules of Glossa

1. Words represent concepts, and can be denoted as either things (with optional -a) or, descriptions or actions (with optional -o).

u droma	a run
dromo	to run, running

2. Meaning is given by context and syntax; word order is logical with subject-verb-object sentence structure.

Un andra fo batto u cana.

The man hits the dog hard.

3. One word modifies the next: so, descriptions precede objects; and modifiers precede actions.

u rubo capella	the red hat
u cellero dromo feli	the quickly running cat
An forto dico ad an ama.	He speaks loudly to his friend.

4. Tense is given by particles placed before the action. These are: *pa* (did), *fu* (will), *nu* (now), *du* (continues), *pra* (had), *fu-pa* (will have).

Fe pa ito ad u theca.	She went to the shop.
Tem mi pa-du dromo, mi pa cado.	While I was running, I fell.
An pra voro pre an arriva.	He had eaten before his arrival.

5. Essential grammar is achieved through the use of a minimum number of particles that modify the action, and (as in English) by the use of intonation and punctuation. No word changes for reasons of grammar. These particles are: *posso* (may), *poto* (can), *lasso* (let), *sio . . . si* (would . . . if), *geno* (get, got), *ge-* (-ed).

John posso ki ad u doma.	John may go home.
Lass u puera util u valuta.	Let the boy spend the money.
An fu sio voro id si . . .	He could eat it if . . .
U camina pa geno dono ad an.	The shirt was given to him.
Fe pa veno dia u ge-fracto fenestra.	She came through the broken window.

6. Plurality is indicated in either of two ways: normally, the article is converted to its plural form *plu*; but if the article is not wanted, a terminal *s* is used. Where plurality is clearly indicated, neither the article nor the *s* is used.

u bruno puera	a brown boy
plu bruno puera	the brown boys
tri bruno puera	three brown boys
Bruno Pueras Voro Fructa	Brown Boys Eat Fruit

7. Pronunciation is with the normal European consonant sounds, and with the vowels sounded as in Italian.

s soft, *g* soft (except for *geno* and *ge-*), *y* similar to *i*,

r sounded slightly rolled, *q* as "kw,"

a past, *e* cafe, *i* machine, *o* hope, *u* plume

8. Within a word, stress is usually on the penultimate syllable.

9. Within a sentence, stress and punctuation are used grammatically, as in English.

Following is the English version of the World Future Society's welcoming letter to new members, followed by a translation into Glossa.

World Future Society

Dear Fellow Futurist:

I would like to welcome you personally to the World Future Society. You are joining an association of forward-looking men and women who recognize the importance of knowing about possible developments in the future in order to make wiser decisions in the present.

Your first copy of the Society's journal, THE FUTURIST, is on its way to you under separate cover. Besides informing you about important forecasts and trends, THE FUTURIST will tell you about other benefits of your membership in our Society. We are also sending you other information about the Society.

On behalf of the staff, let me say that we are looking forward to serving you in this exciting and important enterprise.

Sincerely,
Edward S. Cornish
President

Mundo Futura Societa

Caro Companio Futurista:

Mi auto vo beneveno tu in u Mundo Futura Societa. Tu jugo un associa de plu avanto-scopo andra e gyna, qui cogno u grava de scio de plu posso developa in u futura te faco ma sopho decidias tem u presenta.

Tu primo copia de u Societa journala, 'U Futurista,' du veno a tu per separo posta. Pluso informo tu de plu gravo predica e kia, 'U Futurista' fu informo tu de plu hetero benefica de tu membria in na Societa.

Ex plu na ergo-pe, lasso mi dico que na du spero servo tu con u-ci stimulo e gravo adventia.

Cordialo,
Edward S. Cornish
Presidenta

The Golden International: Communication Triumph and Breakdown

by

Bertram Gross and Kusum Singh

Few things are as obvious as recent and ongoing changes in communications and information technology. Much less obvious are the more significant and confusing changes in the societal systems that have given birth to—and are being shaped by—these new technologies.

A hundred or so years ago the new means and contrivances of communications were seen by reformers and revolutionaries as factors that might bring the workers of the world together. What really came together much more powerfully were the varied organizations of private business and the government agencies that made corporate profitability possible.

During the decades since the end of World War II, this continuing process had produced a veritable transformation in industrial capitalism. Some observers have sought the essence of this change through the concepts of "post-industrialism," "the service society," "the technocratic era," "super-industrialism" or, as in Alvin Toffler's latest book, "the third wave." These concepts offer useful insights. Yet they distract attention from one momentous fact: *industrial capitalism has transcended its previously national boundaries by bringing into being a transnational mode of production that encompasses both the "developed" and the "developing" countries of the so-called "Free World."*

This new transnational mode of production is rooted in networks of communication that by many standards have been miraculously successful. Yet the side effects of this success are two deadly perils that loom ahead during the remaining decades of this century:

• The drift among the countries of constitutional capitalism toward a Big Business-Big Government partnership with enormous capabilities for manipulation, repression, and subversion of democratic freedoms.

• A cold, or possibly hot, war breakdown of communication between the united countries of a shrinking capitalism and the divided countries of ex-

Bertram Gross is Distinguished Professor Emeritus at Hunter College, City University of New York, and visiting professor at St. Mary's College of California, Moraga, California. Kusum Singh is an associate professor of communications at St. Mary's College of California, Moraga, California.

32

panding socialism.

The first of these dangers can best be termed "friendly fascism," a social formation quite different from classic fascism in the era of Hitler, Mussolini, and the Japanese oligarchs. The book *Friendly Fascism: The New Face of Power in America* (M. Evans, New York, 1980), while spelling out these differences, also notes the common element of Big Business-Big Government partnership. The second peril suggests a future in which unfriendly fascism without war could become the major alternative to the mass suicide of nuclear, chemical, bacteriological, or so-called "conventional" warfare.

Marx's Punctured Dream

The ever expanding union of the workers . . . is helped on by the improved means of communication that are created by modern industry and that place the workers of different localities in contact with one another . . . And that union, to attain which the burghers of the Middle Ages with their miserable highways required centuries, the proletarians, thanks to railways, achieve in a few years.

These are the words of two young men, Karl Marx and Frederick Engels, in *The Communist Manifesto* of February 1848. The major conclusion was that, thus united, the proletariat of the most advanced countries would "win the battle of democracy," "raise itself to the position of ruling class," and "centralize all instruments of production in the hands of the State."

The justification for their view was everywhere to be seen during the rest of that momentous year. Urban revolutions, riots, and uprisings took place in almost every country of Europe. In 1848, writes the British historian A.J.P. Taylor, "For the first time news of a revolution passed from one town to another by telegraph; it no longer needed to filter through, and so to affect, the countryside. The revolutionaries traveled by train from one country to the next." Sometimes they arrived at a revolution—which they would quickly join, try to lead, or endeavor to spread—by pure accident. The aim of the newly-formed Communist League, formerly called League of the Just, was to provide communication links between the working people of all countries. These links were shattered when, as counter-revolution triumphed throughout Europe, the League was dissolved in 1852.

In 1864, the International Workingmen's Association—often called the First International—held its first meetings in London. By that time, the telegraph and the railroads were even more in use. Full-powered twin-screw steamers were already ploughing the seas. The penny press had already become popular in London. In his inaugural address to the new association, Karl Marx—who in the meantime had helped support himself by writing steadily for Horace Greeley's *New York Tribune*—looked back on events between 1848 and 1864. But this time he was strangely silent on the "improved means of communication" that were supposed to bring the working people of the world together. His only mention of the subject was its inclusion in this resonant sentence:

. . . no improvement of machinery, no application of science to production, *no contrivances of communication*, no new colonies, no emigration, no opening up of new markets, no free trade, nor all these things put together, will do away with the miseries of the industrious masses. . . . (our italics: BG/KS)

33

And in 1871, seven years later, when Marx formulated general rules for the first International he dropped all references to means or contrivances of communication. Instead, he lamented lack of union among workers in each country and among workers of different countries. As a remedy, he urged the association to "form an international agency between the national and local groups of the Association, so that the working men in one country be constantly informed of the movements of their class in every other country." But the association was already too disunited to do anything of the sort. A little later, the association itself fell apart. Although new proletarian "internationals" were formed in subsequent years, none of them lasted very long or achieved the kind of unity Marx envisaged.

In sharp contrast, however, the bourgeoisie of the late nineteenth century and the first of the twentieth century built large-scale organizations that outdistanced in size and power all the churches, armies, bureaucracies, and other large organizations of the past. Each of these organizations—in Chester Barnard's terms—was a system of communication that wove together the activities of stockholders, creditors, managers, technicians, suppliers, workers, distributors, and consumers. The more successful organizations became enormously large, operating over vast geographical expanses. They used—and promoted—not only the railroad and the telegraph but also the typewriter, telephone, radio, elevators, automobiles, trucks, high-speed highways, oil-fueled ships, and airplanes. They organized and used a vast array of liaison specialists, national and international trade associations, specialized information services, public relations firms, news agencies, and the many media of elite and mass communication. It was thus possible to build huge industrial markets and empires and powerful nation-states to foster industrial interests and protect corporate enterprise against the menace of "cutthroat competition." On this latter score, business did a lot for itself by inventing new modes of imperfect competition, price leadership, administered prices, cartels, commodity agreements, and all the other forms of capitalist communion often referred to by the rather clumsy term "monopoly capitalism."

Labor, in turn, was increasingly fragmented by the capitalist mode of production. The "large socialized workplaces" that were supposed to generate the "gravediggers of capitalism" became, in the words of John and Barbara Ehrenreich, "the gravediggers for human energy and aspirations." Work became more and more specialized and subdivided, with each subdivision separating workers from each other. When they united in trade unions or labor parties, these organizations tended to quarrel among themselves or, when they won small victories, to be absorbed into the junior ranks of the capitalist establishment.

During the period before World War II, however, big capital was also fragmented. The major capitalist powers were continuously at odds with each other. Their conflicts were accentuated by the violent capitalist business cycle and an age-long proclivity to escape internal crisis by external belligerence. In 1914 and again in 1939—a mere quarter of a century later—this belligerence burst out into general wars of unprecedented savagery. The first of these wars triggered the Russian revolution of 1917, the second a whole series of communist successes in both Eastern Europe and Asia. By mid-century, a divided capitalist world seemed to confront a return to the "boom and bust" business cycle, a crumbling of the old colonial empires, and a united revolutionary movement orchestrated from Moscow and Peking.

The Internationalization of Capital

From the earlier days of industrial capitalism, large corporations and cartels tended to work together across national boundaries and form what Nikolai Bukharin in 1915 called "a Golden International." But this tendency was countered by fierce nationalist conflict among the capitalist powers.

By the end of World War II, this situation changed. Through massive economic aid and military expansion, the leaders of the United States bolstered economic growth in Western Europe and Japan, filled many of the vacuums left by the departing colonial rulers, and contained (if sometimes only temporarily) communist expansion. There thus came into being the loose alliance of constitutional democracies, military dictatorships, authoritarian regimes, and feudal autocracies called the "Free World."

This alliance is rooted in an intricate network of regional organizations that brought the leaders of First World governments into continuous contact at many levels: The Marshall Plan, the European Economic Community, NATO, the OECD, and many others. With the help of the World Bank, the International Monetary Fund, and other international agencies, the United States, Western Europe, and Japan re-won, consolidated, or extended profitable economic influence over the majority of Third World countries in Africa, Asia, West Asia, Latin America, and the Caribbean.

In turn, this network of governmental communication and cooperation is rooted in a development of much greater importance: *the internationalization of capital through the growth of transnational corporations that, although home based each in a host country, operate on a global scale.* By 1972, in a pathmark journal article, Stephen Hymer pointed out that the transnationals in banking and services as well as industry "are unifying world capital and world labor into an interlocking system of cross penetration that completely changes the system of national economics that characterized world capitalism for the past three hundred years." In this new system, the transnationals easily vault over trade and tariff barriers (formerly the prelude to economic and then military warfare) by using subsidiaries—often with both equity and debt capital from host countries. They also transcend dependence upon any particular products or sectors by going conglomerate in a big way. Thus the large oil transnationals have been moving not only into other forms of energy (coal, gas, nuclear, "synfuel," solar, etc.) but also into machinery, office equipment, computers, word processors, and data transmitters. Transnational conglomerates like ITT and Gulf & Western are into mining, sugar, insurance, transportation, hotels, professional athletics, book publishing, radio, TV, and cinemas.

Strangely, most observers have ignored the fact that no transnational is an island unto itself. Each operates as a complex, central message center at the heart of a far-flung network of concentric and, eventually, overlapping circles:

- *Clusters* of closely-related suppliers, distributors, research organizations, and the firms providing banking, accounting, managerial, advertising,

35

and public relations services.

- Larger *constellations* of cooperating clusters that compete with each other up to a certain point but also cooperate closely through consortia, groups, commodity agreements, or cartels.

- Still larger and more flexible *complexes* of clusters, constellations, and supporting government agencies, such as the "industrial-military complex," the "auto-trucking-highway-petroleum complex," agribusiness, the radio-TV-cable complex, etc.

- Loose, flexible national *establishments* (or complexes of complexes) through which the leaders of corporate and government institutions negotiate their strategic and tactical differences and guide the operations of a many-tiered power structure with communication links to every problem area in the society.

- A variety of supra-governmental *interlockings* such as the Trilateral Commission, the Bilderberg conference, and other less publicized, or even highly secret, systems of formal and informal communication among First World power elites and their more dependable allies.

Thus, unlike the First International or the International Chamber of Commerce, the Golden International has no single headquarters, central committee, or general rules. Its enormous strength, rather, derives from looseness, flexibility, redundancy, and its capability—despite unending conflicts among its many components—to mobilize and deploy remarkable intellectual, cultural, economic, political, and military resources.

Breakthrough and Breakdown

Judged by the standard of previous experience over the centuries, First World capitalism has achieved miraculous breakthroughs.

First of all, since the end of World War II, there has been no catastrophic depression. A new word, recession, had to be invented to describe the short and shallow declines or slowdowns that have interrupted the longer-term processes of growth and technological innovation.

Second, although capitalist prosperity has been fueled by military (as well as welfare) spending, no war or near-war among the great capitalist powers has occurred. Whatever wars have taken place have involved different contestants and were geographically limited. And since Nagasaki, the growing stockpile of nuclear weapons has never been used.

Third, First World establishments have maintained political and cultural hegemony at home. Part of this is due to the influence of business-supported policy groups, research institutions, and mass media. Credit must also be given to the structural superiority of transnational conglomerates *vis à vis* organized labor. No trade union has ever been able to organize all employees of, initiate collective bargaining with, or call a strike against any transnational conglomerate as a whole.

Fourth, the First World establishments have won and maintained remarkable influence—if not hegemony—over the great majority of Third World countries. Even OPEC (the most conspicuous example of apparent opposition to the First World) has been able to push oil prices up and keep production down only because its policies have been enforced by the Western oil companies.

Finally, the major capitalist countries have done much to tone down the so-called cold war by detente with both the Soviet Union and China. In so doing, they have bolstered their own economies through growing and profitable business with the communists, have drawn various communist regimes further into the capitalist world economy, and have laid the basis for the possible conversion of some communist-led societies to state capitalism. Above all, they have done this in a way that divides the two communist giants and nurtures the conflict between them, thereby slowing down communist and anti-capitalist movements in other countries.

All these successes, however, have obvious side effects, which result more from methods used than from original intentions: pollution, resource shortages, over-dependence on capital-intensive production and on petroleum, racial and ethnic conflicts, the frustration of rising aspirations, social fragmentation and alienation. The most obvious side effect has been stagflation, the two-misery combination of recurring stagnation and persistent inflation, a combination that goes further than many other factors in nurturing frustration and alienation.

Still more significant, however, have been two communication breakdowns with potentially disastrous implications.

The first is a breakdown of communication between the majority of the people and a minority of quarreling decision-makers. Although the constitutional machinery of electoral democracy still creaks on, every voter knows that he or she—in Giovanni Sartori's words—has "but a powerless fraction of power." Persons, families, neighborhood or village groups, and even university departments, labor unions, and ordinary legislators are but pygmies in comparison with the huge private and public bureaucracies and globe-spanning clusters, constellations, complexes, and establishments that dominate most of the planet. People are increasingly objects to be studied, polled, influenced, encouraged to quarrel among themselves, and, in some cases, co-opted or drawn into ritualistic dramas of fraudulent participation. The drift in this direction is even justified on the ground that freedom can only be saved by having less of it. This is the friendly fascist road toward the silent subversion of constitutional democracy.

The second is the breakdown of detente between the two superpowers, the United States and the Soviet Union. This breakdown has been crystallized in the sidetracking of the SALT II treaty and the rupture of commercial, scientific, technological, and cultural interchange between the two countries. It has resulted not only from the expansion of communist regimes into some areas (including the movement of Soviet troops into Afghanistan) but also from the belief in some First World circles that the capitalist order can best be preserved by expanding their own military power and interventionism. "I can think of no period in modern history," wrote George Kennan, "in which such a breakdown of political communication and such a triumph of restrained military suspicions as now marks Soviet-American relations has not led in the end to armed conflict." John K. Galbraith adds this to Kennan's analysis: "Wars, let us remember, come when men, single-minded in certainty and righteousness, lose the ability to communicate with each other."

Despite many prophecies of apocalyptic doom, there is still time to repair what has been breaking down. Indeed, there is an alternative logic working on both fronts.

The alternative to friendly (or unfriendly) fascism is a more genuine democracy—and its logic is grounded in humankind's long history of resistance to unjustified privilege. It is also grounded in the daily activities of innumerable groups throughout America and the entire First World who seek the opportunity for more persons to cooperate and communicate with each other —both directly and indirectly—in making decisions that affect themselves, others, and the larger communities of which they are a part.

The alternative to renewed—and hotter—cold war is an improved detente. As Galbraith has cogently pointed out, this requires on the part of Americans "active communication—diplomatic, economic, scientific, cultural, above all on arms control—with our Russian counterparts." To this we add our own comment: A new detente should not be limited to the two superpowers. It should include the NATO and Warsaw Pact countries and also provide for a role by Third World countries.

This too is being sought by many concerned citizens, including corporation executives, some anti-war groups, and some political leaders, in the United States, Western Europe, and Japan. It is a major demand of the non-aligned movement.

Although neither of these efforts is given much attention in the mass media, they are nonetheless making some headway. If they should succeed in counteracting the present communication breakdowns, they could herald still greater triumphs than those of the Golden International—a breakthrough from creeping authoritarianism toward more genuine democracy and from a fragmented world to a more civilized international order.

Information Technology and the Flowering of Enterprise

by

William E. Halal

It is amazing to realize that, about 25 years ago when the digital computer was being born, IBM estimated the market potential for the entire United States to be less than 10 computers. These original machines cost millions of dollars per unit, and they were so bulky and complex that special "computer rooms" were built to house them. The new generation of microcomputers features brands like the "Osborne," which is more powerful than the early computers but costs less than $2,000, including disk storage and software, and can be carried in a portable case about the size of a typewriter.

Just as these predictions were so wrong that they now seem ridiculous and quaint, so too is the prevailing gloom about the economy. Opinion polls show that the majority of people believe that the high point of prosperity is over; that the future will require personal sacrifice and accepting a frugal lifestyle. There is serious concern that a severe economic depression is imminent. Many people are also fearful that capitalism will grow into an authoritarian system ruled by a few megacorporations that create a world of mindless work, pollution, and bureaucracy.

But the revolution now underway toward an information society is transforming business into a more mature, enlightened institution that should transcend the original vision that Adam Smith and others saw only dimly. Before this century ends, I suspect that modern economies are likely to see the growth of large numbers of small, innovative, constantly changing enterprises offering an endless variety of sophisticated goods and services. Also, corporations are likely to be governed in a fairly democratic manner that will reconcile the benefits of material consumption, the needs of employees, the impact on the environment, and other social considerations. This transformation will probably require many years of difficult institutional change and economic disruption, and there will always be some authoritarian and exploitative organizations. But over the long term, the relentless growth of information technology should cause the free enterprise system as a whole to

---

William E. Halal is a professor of management at The George Washington University in Washington, D.C. This article is adapted from his forthcoming book, which is tentatively titled Strategic Power: The Principles of Democratic Free Enterprise, *to be published by John Wiley & Sons. Copyright © 1982 by William E. Halal.*

bloom into full flower as a responsible and vastly more productive form of economy.

The Growth of Competition

There are several major forces at work that seem likely to bring this transformation about. One such trend is the worldwide increase in competition that is encouraging innovation and responsiveness to changing social needs. This has become clearly apparent largely because of the entry of Japanese and European business into American markets in automobiles, steel, electronics, and many other industries that were once controlled by U.S. firms. And now that Korea, Taiwan, Mexico, South American countries, and other less developed nations are also entering the industrial race, competition should heighten even further.

This intense new competition has been made possible by the rapid growth of global information systems that are necessary for the operation of international business. For example, the new Satellite Business Systems Corporation is now providing worldwide telecommunications satellites for business use that will transmit 6 billion bits per second, about 1 million times more than the average land line. Such systems are rapidly creating a global "central nervous system" that is essential to an integrated world economy. International trade now accounts for about one-third of world GNP and is growing twice as fast as national economies.

This international competition has now reached a critical economic shakeout period. The early stage of this difficult adjustment has been marked by the failure of many corporations to provide products that are able to compete in the global marketplace. This is the underlying cause of the malaise that is now affecting the economies of the U.S., the United Kingdom, and other nations. Only a dozen or so multinational corporations are likely to survive in each industry, so the competition is fierce, and it will get much tougher.

In addition to the growth of competition from abroad, competition is also growing from below. The number of new businesses formed increased from 43,000 per year in 1950 to 600,000 per year in 1980. In contrast, roughly half of the Fortune 500 firms listed in 1950 had disappeared by 1980 as a result of mergers, failures, and other causes. The vitality of small business ventures can be seen in the fact that almost all new job formations have come from small firms rather than the large corporations in established industries.

The number of small enterprises is increasing so dramatically because information technology does not usually require the massive capital investment and large production facilities needed in heavy industrial manufacturing. Providing services, developing software, R&D, information handling, and other "soft" technologies all lend themselves to small-scale ventures. So the growth opportunities of the future may not lie with General Motors, Exxon, or even IBM, but with the countless small new information-related firms like Apple, Genentec, and Wang.

Managing Organic Networks

Not only has the revolution in information technology fostered this growth of more responsive competition from abroad and from below, it is also changing corporations from within. A recent survey indicates that 85% of the For-

40

tune 500 firms are starting to implement office automation systems that will provide computerized data-files, teleconferencing, electronic mail, and other such features. Texas Instruments, for example, has installed a system that links 50 plants in 19 countries in a corporate-wide network that sends 100,000 messages a day at an average cost of 8 cents in less than 10 seconds each. Ford Motor Company recently held a video conference to show its new car models to 18,000 dealers and sales people at 38 sites around the country.

As this growth of office information technology continues, and as assembly lines are replaced by automated machinery and robots, modern corporations themselves will increasingly be thought of as complex information systems rather than manufacturing systems or social systems. The old hierarchical chain-of-command that worked well in an industrial era is now cumbersome and inefficient because it is no longer able to respond quickly to the demands of a more competitive and rapidly changing marketplace. Consequently, corporations are increasingly structured more like multidimensional matrices of overlapping subsystems responsible for different products, business functions, geographic regions, and the like. This new form of corporate structure creates fluid organizational systems that encourage decentralized decision-making by a large number of small, self-autonomous business units that are better adapted to change and diversity.

The net effect is to bring the market system *inside* the corporation to replace bureaucratic structures and offer the advantages that business has always attributed to free enterprise. Individual employees could then behave as semi-independent entrepreneurs, unleashing the frustrated talents of the me generation that often yearns for freedom and challenge. At 3M Company, for instance, employees are encouraged to form new projects and to start small business ventures. These possibilities are going to be further enhanced as the electronic-cottage concept permits large numbers of people to work from their homes. Alvin Toffler estimates that half of the present work force could do so now.

Democratic Governance

A particularly interesting and crucial possibility is that corporations seem likely to become more democratic, socially oriented institutions. The need to improve productivity has become so apparent that the principle of employee participation has become commonly accepted and almost all industries are starting innovative programs to introduce some form of participation.

Once the concept of participation is shown to be feasible, it may only be a short step to extend the idea to other aspects of corporate life. Corporate goals, information systems, policy-making, and other key functions are likely to be expanded to include the interests of employees, customers, the public, and other business constituencies to form a "soft corporation" of the future that creates "social wealth" as well as profit. Many organizations will continue to be managed traditionally because some situations require authoritarian, financially focused control, and there will always be many people who prefer this old form of "tough" leadership. But participative and democratic forms of governance should grow and thrive as a viable alternative simply because they are considered more civilized by most people and because in

41

many situations they will prove to be more effective in reaching complex decisions and gaining support.

The Economic Transformation

These changes will probably require at least a decade or two, and they should take a rich variety of forms in the U.S. and other parts of the world. But if present trends continue, and if a major depression or other calamities can be avoided, business corporations should create a vastly more productive and more humane economy—not out of benevolence, although that might be a sufficient reason, but because information technology is encouraging this more sophisticated form of business behavior. Economists are fond of pointing out the conditions that are required to produce orderly, effective market competition: a large number of competing enterprises, accurate information for buyers and sellers, and the freedom to choose among alternatives. The growth of information technology is providing these conditions, thereby causing the evolution of capitalism into a more benign and powerful form that I like to think of as "Democratic Free Enterprise."

From an institutional viewpoint, this transformation is likely to meet considerable resistance and it will require great leadership. Persons in positions of responsibility in business, government, labor, and other sectors will be sorely challenged by these deep and disturbing changes. The history of business is a long story of resistance to social change, and the rate and type of change is now especially severe because it involves a transformation from one era to another—a paradigm shift. But we can be hopeful that visionary leaders will emerge—leaders who understand these unusual opportunities and are able to create new institutional structures and political coalitions.

As individuals, we will continue to be severely tested as we redefine our personal and professional identities in this shifting landscape. The relationships between superior-subordinate, student-teacher, buyer-seller, labor-management, and other roles that frame our lives have been changing for years, and I suspect that the biggest changes are yet to come, possibly during the 1980s. One of the most common problems all people face today is the limited freedom to exercise initiative and self-responsibility because of the hierarchical control imposed from above in almost all institutions. New institutional structures are needed to overcome these obstacles, but at a deeper level we will have to revise the psychological structures that govern how we use and respond to authority. We may then be free to fulfill our own goals, but at the cost of facing the messy, uncertain, and risky complexity that authority has shielded us from.

Although these will be formidable challenges, at another level we really need do nothing exceptional or heroic to bring this transformation about. The inexorable power of information technology is silently driving social evolution in these directions. It seems to me that Adam Smith and other proponents of free enterprise were basically correct in their belief that *enlightened* self-interest is a powerful motivating force for progress. As our information-rich environment provides us with more accurate information, greater knowledge, increased power, and heightened awareness, we will contribute still more to the forces acting on business firms to work for progressive social change.

42

The Future of Instructional Technology

by

Fred F. Harcleroad

Predicting the future of instructional technology and the learning resources field poses genuine problems. It is so easy to be wrong! For example, just one week before the Wright brothers made their first flight at Kitty Hawk, the *New York Times* carried a story ridiculing the idea of human flight. Futurists can be both too conservative or too far out. Nevertheless, estimates of future social and technological developments are vital today in all phases of life, in business, health, social relationships, and government. And, nowhere is it more important than in the uses of technology in education.

Striking social and technological changes in the past quarter century have affected education in significant ways and provide some basis for judging the future. In the United States, for example, the "baby boom" of the 1950s and 1960s brought a great wave of additional students progressively through elementary schools, secondary schools, and postsecondary education. Modified social attitudes about sizes of families plus new laws about abortion resulted in the "baby bust" of the 1970s and 1980s—with major effects on all phases of education. Second, major changes in types of work to be done and in the composition of the work force itself have affected education. Perhaps its most dramatic result is the increased need for lifelong learning and recurrent education for people of all ages. As a third illustration, the Space Age of the last quarter century contributed spectacular technological achievements that have resulted in personal microcomputers, worldwide television programming by satellite transmission, miniaturized videotape cameras with good fidelity and instant playback, lasers, and holograms. These three examples illustrate rather well the need to study and plan for the future.

Similar scientific breakthroughs and significant social adaptations undoubtedly will come about in the next decades. Quite possibly, they may come at an even faster rate.

The innovative devices and procedures of the 1990s and 2000s are even now being developed to help people to communicate and learn better. Today, in laboratories and classrooms all over the world, revised modes of instruction based on applications of new technology are being developed. Conceiv-

Fred F. Harcleroad is professor of higher education, Center for the Study of Higher Education, College of Education, University of Arizona.

ably, one of these innovations could exert as significant an impact upon education and society as did the printing press, film, television, or computers.

A few of the most critical trends that will influence education and training include (1) changes in populations, (2) developments in science and technology, (3) the information explosion, and (4) the changing nature of education. The effect of these possible trends on the availability and uses of all forms of media can be very significant.

Changes In Population

In recent decades, world population growth has been explosive. Currently, it is expected to reach a total of six and one-half billion by the year 2000 and possibly 10-12 billion by 2075. A high proportion of the increase is in the less developed countries, which therefore need to greatly expand their educational services. The population of the United States, close to 230 million in 1981, is estimated to exceed 260 million in 2000, approximately 4% of the total world population at that time.

Twenty-five years ago, with 6% of the world's population, the United States used over 40% of the world's production of natural resources; in 1970, with approximately 5%, it was using around 30% of the world's production. As uses by other nations increase dramatically, the share available to the United States shrinks proportionally even though the level of production is far greater. If it decreases further by 1990 and scarcity of additional key raw materials becomes a problem, further limits may appear to constrain economic and technological growth. Joint business ventures required by other countries may well restrict the wealth available in the United States. The positive hope in the resource field lies with new scientific techniques to locate new reserves of raw materials such as remote sensing, isotope measurements, and radiometric dating, plus such valuable programs as reforestation and recycling of critical materials. Future funding available for desirable social programs, including media in all phases of education, will depend on the strength of the economy and the importance given to each social "good."

Meanwhile, population patterns in the United States have gone through three great shifts since World War II. First, the baby boom lasted from 1946 to the early 1960s, with annual births finally exceeding four million a year. This huge wave reached the most productive age bracket (25-45) in the 1980s, increasing it by 25%. Second, the baby bust of the 1960s and 1970s followed immediately thereafter. Birth fertility rates fell rapidly from 3.8 to 1.8, while abortions rose to well over one million a year. Third, the elderly became an increasing proportion of the total population. Since 1950, the number of persons 65 and older has doubled to almost 25 million (approximately 11% of the 1981 totals), and will reach close to 30 million by 1990 (12.2%, almost one-eighth of the whole population).

Enrollments in public and private elementary and secondary schools by 1988 are estimated to drop over 5% in a decade, to a total of 45 million. Enrollments in higher education similarly are estimated to drop by 1988, to a total of 11 million. At the same time, a relatively small increase in teachers (41,000) is estimated (less than 2%), with a small proportional increase in funding for elementary and secondary schools (14.6% in 10 years to 114.6 billion dollars) and for higher education (10.4% to 60.7 billion).

44

The effects of these changes on education are very important. Since persons in the U.S. work force hold an average of 10 different positions in a work lifetime, and retraining usually is needed in several of them, the educational systems will have great responsibilities for both initial training and retraining of this larger and older population. Although births increased in the early 1980s, resulting in increased elementary school enrollments in the late 1980s, the number in that age group (5-13) in 1990 will still be 10% less than in 1970. Thus, emphasis on efficiency and accountability will be a continuing characteristic of the society. Educational expenditures will be limited in the main to proven, cost-effective media that contribute significantly to learning.

Developments in Science and Technology

The United States in 1981 provided more than a third of the basic research going on in the world, according to the National Research Council. Some startling new technologies and major improvements in existing ones are projected for the late 1980s and 1990s. Major areas of emphasis include biotechnology, solid-state electronics, optical computers, and improved materials and fibers.

In biotechnology, the hereditary characteristics of bacteria have been modified to produce improved drugs and chemicals. For example, a bacterium has been identified that will improve crude oil by removing sulfur, a major pollutant. Genetic engineering already has produced improved insulin, a human growth hormone, and interferon. Although still in early stages of development, biotechnology could effect fundamental changes in food production, health care, pollution control, and possibly in production of energy.

Solid-State Electronics

Already in the 1980s, optical fiber technology has expanded the potential for communication improvements. Each of the tiny hairlike fibers can carry several thousand voice channels or five or six TV channels. Microengineering currently produces, commercially, thumbnail-sized silicon chips with 64,000 bits of data. By 1990, using super-focused electron, X-ray, or ion beams, chips of the same size could hold one million bits and a basketball-sized main-frame computer could exceed current large computers in capacity. Even beyond these developments are hybrid electro-optical chips, followed probably in the 1990s and 2000s by optical chips made with circuitry based on transparent light guides. Current computers already can control advanced communication systems and assist significantly in diagnosing certain types of disease. At a much simpler level, home computers with increasingly larger memories constantly become more available and cheaper. Coupled with video discs, video tapes, satellite transmission of sound motion pictures, and working on an interactive basis by keyboard, voice, or light pen, they can have increasing impact in the very near future.

The Information Explosion

The expansion of knowledge and the increased availability of sophisticated equipment to transmit sound motion pictures have created an existing communication revolution. In the years since 1960, television has become the principal source of news and information. Its use has progressed steadily, with average daily viewing of over three hours and with children spending more hours watching television than in school attendance. Over 10 million television sets are sold each year in the United States alone, and many of the future developments in information distribution revolve around differing ways to use the home television screen on an interactive basis. Coupling television screens with microcomputers to digitize data elements and with satellites to eliminate most distance transmission problems, the boundaries break down between print and electronic media—and between work, education, and leisure activities.

The information and knowledge industry now includes around half of the total labor force, according to the U.S. Labor Department. Growing at a rate of around 2% a year, it accounts for almost half of the gross national product. In most industries that were once labor-intensive, improved equipment has made each worker more productive—and the industries have become capital-intensive rather than labor-intensive. For example, American factory workers use equipment averaging $25,000 per worker. Even homes are more capital-intensive, and the resulting time efficiencies have contributed significantly to the two-worker family. Two major labor-intensive areas still remaining are offices of all types and teaching in schools and colleges. Serious proposals for a "paperless office" estimate that up to 40% of current office work can be automated. In addition, some work (such as programming, word processing, or selling) can be carried on from home with minimal office contact and a saving of travel time and energy costs. Currently, teachers make only limited use of media to improve instruction, mostly to provide expert approaches to particular content or to provide varied types of learning experiences for students. Whether the major new types of technology will create great changes in schools and colleges or result in new ways to organize education for lifelong learning is a major question yet to be resolved!

Changing Nature of Education

All of these social trends affect education in many varied ways. Schooling mainly for children and adolescents (from 5-18), with post-secondary education for a third of them (from 18-23), is no longer sufficient. Truly, the United States has become a "learning society," with close to 40% of the population in some organized learning situation all of the time. However, close to half of the total is provided by training and educational programs in business corporations, government agencies, and voluntary organizations. Regular public and private schools no longer monopolize either basic, liberal, vocational, or professional education. Thus, if the society's educational needs are not met adequately by traditional forms others are available and ready to meet them.

Along with this major change there are a number of other allied trends. Proprietary educational institutions offer vocational, and sometimes liberal or basic, education to several million students a year. Improved communication systems make "distance" education possible so that students can learn or be retrained without moving or giving up salaried jobs. Older students, often retired, have more leisure time and funds to pay for hobby, interest, or liberal/civic education. Currently, much of our current information and affective/emotional education comes through television. Potential improvements in "home learning" centered around the television screen (such as the interactive Qube system operating in Columbus, Ohio), accompanied by home selling, ordering, and financial processing, could greatly expand the impact of television on education, with a diminished role for regular schooling.

Within the regular education system the decreases in enrollment, accompanied by voter-imposed limits on taxation and resultant funding shortages, have caused budget and morale problems for professional and technical personnel. Reductions in force are common, and salaries for those remaining take a larger portion of the budget than during past decades. Thus, other expenditure areas, including media, must exist on a smaller portion of the budget—and funds for new, relatively expensive capital equipment are hard to obtain. Funding may even revert to the methods of the early development of media, when parents at individual schools bought equipment they thought desirable for their own children in their own school.

These changes raise a number of other questions regarding organized education and use of media. New media technology serves four major markets: (1) business and industry (including business training), (2) home consumers, (3) military services, and (4) other government agencies (especially the Department of Education). Business and industry can try out technology, depreciate it, and go on to new technology. As an example, General Motors bought over 10,000 MCA videodisc players in 1978 and created their own selling and educational programs. The military services have large sums to use to educate and train personnel to defend the country. Much of the original miniaturization and use of microcomputers and satellites has resulted from these large expenditures. The mass consumer market brings costs down if a particular technology is broadly accepted—and then it becomes more likely to appear in educational budgets. For example, videotape recorders reached 60% saturation of the consumer market before achieving a significant education market. Having reached this stage, and being usable for both production and viewing activities, videotape recorders may have great effect on the amount of future use of competing videodisc players by schools and colleges.

Education in the late 1980s and 1990s, thus, faces many critical questions, all of which affect the uses of instructional technology. How will the demand for basics and competency be met by "schooling"? Will some current offerings (such as driver training) be turned over to other agencies? Will uninterested adolescent students be educated by business and industry, with tax support? Will liberal education be targeted at real-world social needs that students of all ages will appreciate? Will increasing world interdependence and instantaneous communication systems broaden our concepts of basic or liberal education? The gradual development of answers to these questions will determine the need for media with new content materials and the uses of instructional technology to improve their availability for learning.

Utopia:
We Can Get There from Here
—By Computer

by

Lane Jennings

The sad truth about Utopia is that one man's heaven is almost sure to be another's hell. To make matters worse, individuals not only disagree with one another about what makes a society ideal, they keep changing their own minds as their knowledge and interests change. A five-year-old's utopia would be a very different place from a utopia designed by teenagers or senior citizens. To be truly ideal, then, a utopia must be self-designed by each of its inhabitants, and always be capable of changing to reflect changes in the designer's values and desires.

Does this sound impossible? Certainly, it has always been so in the past. The very word *utopia* may be traced from two Greek roots with conflicting meanings: *eutopos* ("good place") and *outopos* ("no place"). This basic conflict, between perfection and inaccessibility, has persisted in utopian thinking down through the centuries.

But now, for the first time in history, a possible answer to the utopian dilemma is emerging. By applying new technology and adopting a new perspective, we may at last be able to achieve a way of life that is personal yet communal, secure yet flexible, practical yet spiritually fulfilling. The "new technology" I mean is the computer—specifically, the small "personal" or "home" computer; and the "new perspective" I have in mind is simply to "think small."

Utopias Unlimited

Edward Cornish, president of the World Future Society, has suggested that, instead of striving for one universal way of life—one big Utopia—people should develop thousands, perhaps millions, of little utopias—diverse communities, each with its own way of life, existing simultaneously all over the earth, which individuals would be free to join, remain in, or leave at any time.

The freedom of movement implied in this concept may seem daunting at first glance, but only because we have traditionally conceived of communi-

Lane Jennings is research director of the World Future Society and editor of the Society's professional journal, the World Future Society Bulletin.

ties exclusively in physical terms.

Although we often speak in more abstract terms of "the community of learned individuals" or the "business community" without implying any physical proximity among community members, utopian writers and reformers of the past have universally focused on the concept of community as a "place."

Embracing utopia has typically meant breaking with the past as quickly and completely as possible. Possessions, pastimes, material comforts, old job skills, friends, and family ties have all had to go. In their place, utopian pioneers have generally tried to build up complete new physical, economic, and social structures for their communities starting from scratch—often with little organization, less practical knowledge, and no money.

No wonder so many of these utopian communities have failed. The real wonder is that some few have managed to survive—however short of their ideal vision—for a time.

Computer Conferencing

As soon as we drop the "place" restriction and conceive of utopia as a state of existence, not a physical location, the problem of creating and sustaining an ideal community becomes enormously simpler. Using an existing communications network (the telephone system), it is already possible to link individuals—however widely scattered—with one another and with a common mechanism for storing and processing information (i.e., a large central computer and any number of "personal" or "home" computers) to create what is known as a "computer conference." To date, most computer conferences have been set up to address short-term problems of limited scope. But the same techniques and electronic networks could be used for the express purpose of pooling knowledge and skills to achieve utopian objectives.

Specific advantages of an "electronic community" as utopia compared to a "geographic community" at a fixed place include:

• **Ease of Access.** Any member can participate in the activities of the community (work, discussion, decision-making, etc.) from any place in the world that offers electricity, telephone service, and a computer terminal.

• **Maximum Personal Freedom (and Responsibility).** Participation in community life cannot be coerced, so attendance at any meeting or contributions to any collective effort are always voluntary. By the same token, those who fail to participate have no one to blame but themselves if a decision is reached or an action taken that they object to. The electronic community only exists through participation. Thus it is indeed "no-place," yet it can be anyplace.

• **Nature of Participation Can Vary As Needs or Interests Change.** For certain projects (surveys of opinion, for example), community members could make comments using pseudonyms or even anonymously. This helps encourage honesty without the risk of making or deepening personal enmities. (I wonder how many intentional communities over the years have broken up simply because their members lacked some way to express or respond to criticism anonymously?)

• **Novelty Combined with Continuity.** The number and identities of people "on-line" will vary from moment to moment during a computer conference,

49

but the conferencing technique is always the same. Translated into utopian community terms, computer conferencing offers opportunities for new meetings and chance encounters that keep relationships fresh, while also maintaining a "tradition" (the computer network access protocols) that helps people feel secure. Moreover, having a permanent transcript of all communications on file in the central computer preserves the history of the community, and assures that early contributions are not forgotten and that ideas discussed and rejected at one time remain available for future re-consideration.

• **Supportive But Not Confining.** Being a member of one computer conference or "community" does not prevent you, or even discourage you, from joining others. The only travel time between communities is the time it takes your fingers to dial a new telephone number or punch a few keys. In utopian terms, this means that while you contribute to the life of a given community by your involvement, you need not depend exclusively on the members of that one community to satisfy all your needs and interests. In effect, you design your own utopia by opting to contribute your time and effort to the particular communities that want or need your talents and by enjoying the companionship and benefits of those communities that offer what *you* want and need. As your needs and interests change, you can "remodel" your utopia at any time by becoming more active in some communities and less active in (or dependent on) others.

• **Evolutionary, Not Revolutionary.** The decision to join a computer conference does not require abruptly abandoning your present life. You can enter gradually, contributing and sharing more as you gain experience and confidence. You can keep your job in the "real world" as long as you wish to—though you may find ways to earn your living within the computer network. Research, editing, clerical work, and, of course, computer programming are all jobs that are easily performed from remote locations using a computer today. As computers become more commonplace, and the number of programs for using them increases, it may become possible to perform practically any job—from factory work to farming—at the console of a computer.

• **Visitors Are Welcome.** Unlike most intentional communities, part-timers will be welcome in Computopia. There are no borders to guard against intruders; no workshops or fields where onlookers would be in the way; and visitors' questions never disrupt the work in progress since all messages are simply stored in the "in" box of the person they are addressed to, and remain there until the addressee has the time and inclination to read them. Anyone is welcome to enter the conference/community, stay as long as he likes, and contribute as much or as little as desired. (Freeloaders and curiosity-seekers can carry off nothing but knowledge—the one commodity that is not lost by being shared.)

• **An Adventure, Not an Escape.** Finally, instead of seeking to run away from the problems of their present lives—and, in the process, giving up the good things with the bad—the members of an electronic utopian community will be adding to what they already have. They need not try to duplicate the real achievements of technological civilization (sanitation, public libraries, modern medicine, electricity, etc.) in a remote setting. Nor must they renounce these benefits to pursue "more spiritual values" at the cost of physical discomfort and exhausting labor. Instead, Computopians will stay where they are physically, but concentrate their attention on improving the *quality* of life for themselves and others in their electronic community by focusing on those areas where community efforts are most likely to succeed: e.g., providing mutual support, encouragement, and stimulation; sharing knowledge; and exchanging tools.

This aspect of Computopia has an important side benefit for civilization as a whole. Unlike some rural communitarian groups, Computopians can never be misled by their apparent isolation. Since an electronic community so obviously depends on modern industry, the electric power grid, and the global telephone system for its very existence, its members always have a real stake in the fate of the nation where they live and the planet as a whole that services these systems. Computopia will be a fine and private place—but it will always have its roots in the soil, the oceans, and the air of the earth (and eventually other planets). We must never forget that we live in a world of rising population, limited resources, and growing discontent—a world, in short, where the welfare of every community, however isolated, depends on somehow promoting the welfare of all. Problems we choose not to concern ourselves with can still hurt us. People to whom we mean no harm will not hesitate to harm *us* if we stand in their way too long. Ecological disasters we did not bother to foresee can overwhelm us all the same. Even in utopia, there will be no place to hide from the twenty-first century.

Toward Computopia

The road to Computopia is open and inviting; but there are dangerous curves and crossings along the way. The same technology that can help bring humanity closer together, that can stimulate cooperation and creativity, can also be used to impose the will of a powerful few on an uninformed, and therefore weak, majority.

For Computopia to come into existence, it must first be recognized as possible, and then made credible through fictional accounts and actual experiments in communitarian computing. I want to emphasize the point that experiments in actual computer use will not be enough by themselves. Creating Computopia is a job that must engage the imagination as well as the intellect.

Many people today distrust computers and regard most applications of "high" technology as more likely to destroy humane communities than to help establish them. This fear and distrust of computers has developed from two sources. One is the way that computers have been used by governments and large business organizations (till recently the only groups with access to the costly and elaborate computer hardware) to standardize and complicate once simple and personalized activities. The other is the stereotyped images of machines in general, and of computers in particular, that have grown up in literature and popular culture. Computers in science fiction (almost, by definition, the only form of literature in which they appear at all) have most often been depicted either as all-powerful monsters, or as magic boxes that solve problems with minimal interference from humans. Neither image is very flattering—or very accurate.

Experiments by humanistic computer users and groups can do much to dispel the myth that computers are by nature tools for dehumanization. But

51

to make the computer less than monster or mechanical god, a new set of "images" must be created, too. One way to accomplish this might be through good entertaining stories, set in a future where electronic communities of people who use computers humanely and unself-consciously are the norm. In time, such stories could make human/computer cooperation appear as natural as the idea of antagonism between man and machine does today.

First Steps

Practical experiments in computer networking are already well underway. In particular, three computer networks aimed at small computer users have emerged in the last few years.

The first of these, the Electronic Information Exchange System (EIES), developed by Murray Turoff and others at the New Jersey Institute of Technology, is specifically designed for computer conferencing. Many conferences have been held on the EIES network, and it remains a major source of innovative work on the potentials of electronic communication.

The second computer network aimed at small computer users is THE SOURCE, founded in 1979, and now a subsidiary of Reader's Digest, Inc. THE SOURCE offers a wide variety of data bases and a very detailed user's manual, which even explains how users can set up their own data bases and make these directly available to fellow users. This capability, discovered and first publicized by users of THE SOURCE network, has led to the creation of computer "magazines" and other innovative programs undreamed of when the network was first founded.

The third small computer network, CompuServe, offers services similar to those on THE SOURCE, and is now marketed through the chain of Radio Shack electronics stores.

Several U.S. newspapers, including the *Washington Post*, the *San Francisco Chronicle* and the *St. Louis Post Dispatch*, publish "electronic editions" on CompuServe. If this service proves popular enough to be widely adopted, it may soon be possible to stay as well informed about issues and events in another city as it is to keep up to date on what is reported in local news media. Thus, someone who came from Los Angeles say, and moved to Detroit, might choose to maintain ties of loyalty and interest with his old city by reading its newspaper and watching its TV stations (via cable or satellite) rather than those offered locally. In effect, such a person could be more truly a "citizen" of Los Angeles than a Detroiter. Ultimately, recognition of such "electronic citizens" might be formalized by permitting them to vote and pay taxes in their electronic community, not their geographic one.

This brief discussion barely begins to explore the many ramifications of electronic communities. But in fact, the story of Computopia is still to be written. I hope to do some of that writing myself. But I invite any interested readers to join the work—and the fun—of bringing Computopia to reality. In the words of computer systems analyst James Martin, "The potential of human intelligence combined with the best capabilities of computer networks will take decades to understand fully, let alone exploit. But of all technological advances it may be the one which brings the most change to society."

Twice As Natural: Speculations on the Emerging Information Culture

by

William Kuhns

"What—is—this?" he said at last.
"This is a child!" Haigha replied eagerly, coming in front of Alice
to introduce her, and spreading out both his hands toward her in an
Anglo-Saxon attitude. "We only found it today. It's as large as life,
and twice as natural!"

—Lewis Carroll, *Through the Looking Glass*

If our sudden new world of all-pervasive, instantaneous information could be embraced in a single metaphor, it might be Alice's leap through the looking glass. We still inhabit a physical world created by the industrial revolution, but less and less are our jobs or pastimes or perceptions or imaginations really shaped or governed by that world; increasingly, it's by the world of another revolution, in which a striker's face in Poland is visible in California before the word he speaks has passed from his mouth, and in which the entire arcana of a distant specialized library can be summoned in a few dozen rappings at a keyboard.

Call it an emerging information culture. Surely one keynote of such a culture is that our image of the world is formed less and less by direct experience, increasingly by media-generated—or "mediated"—experience. Since the bards who sang the Homeric poems, this has always been the case with culture. What makes ours different is the erosion of implicit authority in the sources of that mediation. With TV and now minicomputers, cassettes, two-way cable, and satellites—and the barely glimpsed technologies of the future, like holography—we have the opportunity, unknown in history, to shape our own mediated experiences of the world.

The industrial revolution acted upon the physical world, recasting landscapes and cities, speeding transportation, and creating an awesome new ar-

---

William Kuhns is professor of communications, University of Ottawa, Ottawa, Ontario, Canada. He is currently doing research for a book, also to be entitled Twice As Natural, *that will expand on the ideas presented in this paper.*

ray of material goods. It accomplished this by three processes to which everything, nonorganic and organic, was applied: mechanization, quantification, and consolidation. The information revolution acts on our senses, our psyches, our collective knowledge of the world and of ourselves. Its processes are applied with equal rigor to everything in its reach, but the nature of these processes is quite different from the industrial revolution. I propose them as *mediation* (the ever-expanding role of the actively interpreting and describing the world to us); *simulation* (the effort—scarcely limited to information technologies but spearheaded by them—to recreate the perceptible world, and all natural experience, with increasingly heightened fidelity); and finally *circularity* (in which the mediated version and real events whip round like the poles of a spinning magneto, charging and changing history).

Of the Ambition of the Holographers

At an international holography conference recently, hundreds of young holographers—the contemporary equivalent of photographers circa 1829—stood in awe at one exhibit, by a Russian holographer. A lion's head was projected in a glass cube, so vividly that one could see the burnish colors of the underhair stiffening on its mane: "as large as life and twice as natural." This achievement—a tremendous leap beyond the exhibited state-of-the-art in North American holography—achieves something of the dream of today's pioneering holographers: to reproduce the visual world with an uncanny, "twice as natural" fidelity. To speak with these pioneers is to taste their excitement, to be touched by their dream. Yet what of that dream, and the future it portends?

In "The Machine Stops," a mordant short story by E. M. Forster, written some 20 years before commercial television, the world's inhabitants all reside in tiny, private cells where all interpersonal contact is made through the ubiquitous and godlike Machine. The physical body has atrophied to sluglike indifference; curiosity, passion, and adventure are unknown; people mostly lecture or ingest others' lectures on subjects that have been stripped of any contamination by direct experience. When the machine stops, humanity's collective breath immediately expires.

Already television has made Forster's story seem disturbingly prescient, and the systems now appearing on the market such as two-way cable and video-computer hookups will certainly encourage major shifts of habit and movement; as the industrial revolution created modern travel, the information revolution conceivably might extinguish it. Of course, the questions being raised by this revolution—ranging from education and politics to the scariest scenarios of the science-fiction writers—will often themselves seem laughably obsolete in a five- or ten-year generation. It's important to phrase these questions in a context that doesn't depict these technologies as absolutely unique in history, or anywise more fatalistic than the printing press—in effect, to see them in the light of their own tradition.

Toward a History of Information

It was Josef Goebbels who said, "We speak not to express ourselves but to elicit a desired response." With bold exactness, this remark conveys the psychology of the propagandist: whether of a P. T. Barnum or a Madison Avenue copywriter or an idealogue press writer—and not only of these, but of a wider, grayer shading of publicists, newscasters, filmmakers, etc. "Media bias" has come to mean things more universal, and more intransigent, than the old notion of "propaganda": from problems of distortion in the broadcasting of a news story to the effects of American television shows being broadcast in developing nations.

One could chart a tradition, with roots in the seventeenth century penny press and, more recently, figures like Barnum, Hearst, even Mencken: a tradition of the conscious uses of the newspaper to sway or create opinion: a tradition that in the twentieth century has exploded with the volatility of the media themselves. Yet in the history of controlling and engineering information, this tradition is merely the most conspicuous. Call it the explicit tradition. What's more significant is the implicit tradition of the bias in the innate structure and nature of the medium.

The implicit tradition has roots in the very earliest techniques of recorded language, in the Babylonian reed stylus and clay tablet, in the Greek alphabet set to papyrus with pen. The best chronicler of this implicit tradition was McLuhan's mentor Harold Adams Innis, the Canadian economic historian, who showed that different media of communication could wield profound psychic and dislocating institutional effects in the cultures in which they appeared. He argued, for example, that Gutenberg's press undermined the authority of the Papacy—and of the medieval dynasties interlinked with the Church—by stealing the Church's real thunder: its "monopoly of knowledge." The authority of the Latin-reading *cognoscenti*, the priests, was transferred in a stroke (and only tangentially by a Calvin or a Luther) to the authority of the printed and vernacular pages of the Bible.

Others have contributed to our understanding of this implicit tradition. William Ivins, for example, has argued that certain peculiarities in the etching techniques of printmaking in the shops of eighteenth-century engravers created a "convention of vision" in which the picture of the outer world that most Europeans carried in their heads was dominated by certain notions of musculature, or carriage, promoted unconsciously by an engraving technique. The examples, through photography and even the motion picture, can be multiplied; no medium escapes the inherent bias of its very structure, portability, and idiom.

In Pulses of the Phantom Electron

We perceive them ubiquitously, almost interchangeably; yet a television "picture" is as unlike a photograph as Chicago's circuitry of rails, circa 1920, was to the hitching posts that lined its widest streets 50 years before. The phantom electron has transformed not only our media of information but the nature of information itself. Previously all recorded knowledge existed, one way or other, in transcription; the phantom electron has made information an act. In television, it's the act of an ever-reassembling picture, formed by 50 scanning beams a second; in the computer, it's the act of endless binary yes-no "decisions" through a shuttle of a thousand or a thousand million circuits; in both cases we're recipients of a process that's invisible and in some ways, like electricity, still inscrutable.

One could argue, as McLuhan and Ong and others have, that there have been three critical stages in the evolution of information: the original re-corded alphabet; the printing press; and the electronic media. (Ong has even paralleled these stages, fascinatingly, to the Freudian oral-anal-genital stages.) In the alphabet, the supply of information was restricted to the hand; in the printing press, to the mechanical devices of the time. With electronics all restrictions lay outside the media; the processing potentialities of inter-linked cable/TV and computer introduce a threshold past which we can scarcely imagine other thresholds—in effect, a concept of the infinite.

Histories of the industrial revolution by Mumford, Giedion, and others have emphasized the ubiquitous application of mechanized labor, inter-changeable parts, quantification of space and time and energy, etc.; in effect, drawn a line from the earliest steam engines to the robotizing effects of the time-motion studies of such assembly-line designers as Frederick Winslow Taylor, a century later. Theorists like Jacques Ellul, and several generations of science-fiction writers, have even speculated about an inherent, semi-de-monic soul to mechanization: its urge to consume everything in its path, to turn it into its own image. Clearly, mechanization has its own implicit logic, by which its evolution can be traced. Might the same be said of the electronic revolution? The discussions that follow offer speculations along these lines.

The New Celestial Dome: Mediation

In the New Orleans Superdome, it is not only possible to neglect the pres-ence of an entire football game on the field below by watching the game on screens above: it's encouraged. Huge theater-sized screens hang over the field, showing the action in televised closeup, with instant replay and no com-mercials. In walking round the perimeter of the second tier, I noticed that far more eyes were focused on the great screens where colossi in red and white jerseys clashed than on the scrabblings of red and white antlike figures on the distant field below. In this dome where sun and sky are replaced by vast banks of lights and a roof of such immensity it becomes oddly invisible, the real conquest isn't of one team over another, but of one manner of experience over another. Here we accept, even welcome, the mediated version of the event before our eyes.

It's a principle of mediation that invariably, when given the choice, people do prefer the mediated version. The novelist Jerzy Kosinski once conducted an experiment in a classroom: while being videotaped before his class—he stood near the door, the monitor stood by a window—an accomplice, un-known to the students, stepped into the room and began beating up on Kosin-ski. The students watched the beating over the monitor; no one intervened.

Already, in a generation and a half, television has profoundly mediated our experience of the world and become, itself, the most widely shared ex-perience in our culture. It has also made mediation itself as indispensable to us as mechanization was to the Victorians.

Anthropologists would argue that there is no such thing as unmediated experience: that culture by definition mediates. Linguists would say the same of language, and indeed, the hypothesis of two linguists, Benjamin Whorf and Edward Sapir, that we can know only as much as a language is capable of expressing in its grammar, isn't a bad metaphor for the discreet constraints imposed by any medium. But previous media, including culture or language, didn't so actively and tenaciously expand their mediating roles as television has, and as it promises to do more so. And although we inhabit a world of various mediating forms, from long-playing records to newspaper photographs, television is the cutting edge and dominating technology of mediation, as the computer is of simulation.

Like mechanization, mediation has its own implicit structure, its own (frequently paradoxical) logic. The structure and logic can be explored in five tenets, which I wish to develop. Very briefly:

1. Mediation is self-sufficient. The mediated version is always enough: never does a mediated experience prompt us beyond itself; rather, invariably, toward the acceptance of more, and wider, mediated experience.

2. Mediation is actively constructive. Everything that television, for example, transmits, it also "reconstructs" in both elementary and sophisticated ways, implicitly creating its own picture of the world.

3. Mediation is palatable. We welcome it, for its streamlining of complex, unwieldy experience, as much as for the safeguards it seems to offer.

4. Mediation is unbreachable. With two-way video, for example, it's possible to bank, shop, or pray over the TV; but it's always according to fixed rules that amount to a kind of "media etiquette." The rules of that etiquette are inflexible and unbreachable.

5. Mediation is all-encompassing. Potentially nothing lies outside its reach and the future uses of two-way video, for example, might best be conceived in terms of those activities and functions that until now have appeared most invulnerable to the encroachments of TV.

Sight of the Promised Land: Simulation

Imagine, six or eight years from now, dialing the telephone and speaking to a voice that may or may not be the voice of a computer. Would it simply not matter, or prompt one to question the voice (surely, if a computer, programmed to disguise its origin) to discern who or what one is speaking with? This classic conundrum was articulated first by Alan Turing, and called the Turing Test; when computers can pass that test, Turing said (as they already have in specialized areas, such as chess), the computer will have come of age.

The industrial revolution was built of machines that performed physical labor—in short, which expanded man's muscle power to incredible reaches. The computer revolution expands the power of the brain, and soon we'll be witnessing those reaches—with pocket-sized computers common and cheap as calculators that carry whole libraries in microchip; with robots capable of responding to aural commands; with simulation games of such engulfing "real" presence that skills of flying, driving, ballplaying, etc., can be learned largely through the simulations.

As television is the cutting edge of the technologies of mediation, the computer is the cutting edge of the technologies of simulation. On a score of levels, our world is rapidly being shaped to a world of simulations: in plastics, for example; in the growing science of flavor extracts and artificial foods; in the fabrics of rayon, polyester, etc.; in such not-so-far-off developments as live holography, or bioengineering techniques such as cloning. The technologies of simulation may be the most important shaping feature of our time, and what we see on the near horizon represents only feeble clues of a movement with almost unimaginable dimensions. What early promoter of plastic surgery, for example, would have guessed at the present uses of plastic surgery by rock singers to have their faces "cloned" to the faces of dead rock stars like Elvis Presley, Janis Joplin, or Jim Croce? Or what young holographer might guess at the uses of holography in replacing and duplicating whole museums, or creating palpable records of what cannot endure—from demolished architecture to a new waxwork of statesmen, filmstars, and criminals?

In the computer, in bioengineering, and in holography, the potential for ultimate simulation—whether Turing's test or cloned animals or "twice as natural" holographic images—seems already present, eventually inevitable: we're entering a world where the ability to discern between simulated and unsimulated becomes a form of specialized knowledge. In nature, we know, there are severe limits to man's simulations: a beekeeper in Ohio, for example, planted his fields in a high-grade hybrid flower with an accentuated (or "simulated") scent, to speed up the bees' honey-making; the bees distrusted or ignored the scent, and turned to the wildflowers at the edges of the field. But the bees, so to speak, have been programmed to resist the simulated version; increasingly, we find the simulation not only more attractive (or economical or safer or available) than the original but also more satisfying. In Britain, on July 29th, 1981, more people watched a soap opera wedding on BBC-2 than watched the royal wedding on BBC-1, as though the simulated version—both a sendup of the real one and a part of the ongoing story—had more to offer (which, in a sense, it did).

Like mediation, simulation has its own structure and logic, already discernible in the developments centered on the computer and the field of artificial intelligence. Some tenets of simulation and their implications, briefly:

- **Perhaps Not Original, But Real.** The "ambition," so to speak, of simulation isn't toward originality but an exact and real simulacrum *of* an original: either in appearance (holography) or "deep function" as computer people call it, of intelligence (computer) or even complete organic existence (cloning). Nonetheless, as with adaptive programming in computers, simulations are capable of at least minimal divergence from their original models.
- **Infinitely Reproducible.** Walter Benjamin's observations about art in his essay "The Work of Art in the Age of Mechanical Reproduction" offer some hints about what we might expect in endlessly reproduced "real" simulations. The recent history of xerography offers other hints.
- **The Thrust to Work and Play.** Simulation marks a threshold in the history of information: from recording to actively participating in all forms of man's work and play. Industrial holography, automation, and simulation gaming are early examples of a process in which increasingly we'll be actively involved with simulated experiences in work, play, and education.
- **The Thrust to Absolute Fidelity.** Simulation seeks an ever-heightening quality of reproduction, or faithfulness to the original, even if the technique varies as drastically as electronic circuitry and neural circuitry. R. L. Gregory: "As time goes on things (computers) get less and less like the human being but still carry out the deep logical functions by a different mechanical means. I think this is a very good way to look at artificial intelligence. It doesn't have to look like a human being but deep down the function should

be similar."

• **The Thrust to Improve on the Original.** Jack Good, an early computer designer, coined the phrase "Ultra-Intelligent Machine," meaning a computer that would dwarf human minds by comparison. In virtually any sphere of simulation, the effort to match the original is abetted by an effort to improve on the original: accentuating the felt effect in simulation training, for example. (The test pilot who stepped from Boeing's simulation chamber: "Glad I never had to fly like that.") The history of prosthetic devices and the recent history of bionics (fast replacing prosthetics) offer some clues to this evolution.

The Loom of History and Media: Circularity

In *Die Nibelungen*, the film version of the great German saga (1924), Fritz Lang portrayed young Siegfried walking through endless rows of standing soldiers, using his camera to accentuate the merging of architecture and troops, of monumental spaces and the lone warrior's stride. One great devotee of the film, Adolph Hitler, later instructed an architect to design a stadium modeled partially on the enormous mosaic that Lang and a set designer had rigged 10 years earlier in a studio. On September 4th, 1934, at a Nazi party rally in that stadium, now known as the Luitpold Hall, Hitler marched down the naked aisle while 30,000 hands were raised in the Nazi salute. The triumphal march was filmed by Leni Riefenstahl and became one of the most stirring scenes in her propaganda masterwork *Triumph of the Will*, a film that "translated" the mythic narrative of Siegfried into the contemporary mythos of the Third Reich. Some 42 years later, a young Hollywood filmmaker, searching for a conclusion to his own mythic science-fiction epic, literally "lifted" the triumphal march of Hitler from Riefenstahl's film, replicating it shot for shot in Luke Skywalker's final march in *Star Wars*. Siegfried's march had come full circle, and in the meantime history had been transformed.

Circularity is the process by which history and media accent and affect one another. If the phrase "life imitates art" seems overworn in recent times, we have circularity to blame: it has speeded up its magneto-like whipping action enormously since television. When President Reagan (himself an ex-movie star) was shot outside a Washington hotel in March 1981, the world learned that his would-be assassin, John Hinckley, was making his attempt to secure the attention of a teenage movie star, Jodie Foster, who'd played one major role in her career: as a young prostitute who'd attracted the attention of a lone, psychotic cabbie who spends his days preparing to assassinate a political figure. Circularity begins when the world steps through its looking glass.

Consider Sproul Plaza in Dallas, on November 22, 1980. On one side of the street, some dozen mourners had collected to remember the assassination of John F. Kennedy, in that plaza, 17 years before. Across the street, hundreds crowded into a bar to celebrate an "event" of such seeming unlikelihood that one begins wondering what they found in it to celebrate: learning that Kristin, the scorned lover, had been the one to shoot J. R. in a previous spring episode of the hit TV show *Dallas*. The AP release that described this discrepant scene—mourners of one shooting in Dallas across the street from the celebrants who bolted down their drinks in learning the assassin of another shooting in Dallas—made no ironic overtones; but then, it didn't need to. If there is a logic to circularity, it's the logic of dipolar spin, the magneto that whirls from its positive and negative charges. Consider that for the first shooting in Dallas, the assassin's identity was never absolutely proven—at least, according to Roper polls, to the satisfaction of some 78% of the American population. Might that dissatisfaction, stewing over 17 years, have prompted the importance of *knowing*, absolutely, who held the smoking gun after that other shooting in Dallas?

Leslie Fiedler, the literary critic, coined the term "circularity" to describe what we might expect of future artists and writers and (perhaps especially) filmmakers who've grown up in a world where media experiences far overtake their own: in effect, an increasing reliance on older movies, TV, etc., as the source and origins of their work. His remark was certainly astute: in Hollywood in recent years, the dominating "style"—if one can call it that— has been remaking old genre pieces with no real original touches but rather a celebration of what fun and joy those movies really were. In *Star Wars* or *Raiders of the Lost Ark*, we're transported back to early adolescent selves, and the serials and genre thrillers that we craved and enjoyed then; but these films—like De Palma's xeroxing of Hitchcock—offer nothing really fresh, distinctive, or original. They're narrowly, even consciously, circular: old, fondly remembered films remade on a lavish budget, in 70 millimeter, with Dolby stereo.

But circularity can mean more than a process by which filmmakers draw solely and exuberantly on older films: it's the process by which mediated experience itself comes to shape real experience, or history. Certain recent events suggest an indigenous consciousness of circularity. When the Symbionese Liberation Army kidnapped Patty Hearst, for example, they were paying grandfather Hearst the sincerest possible form of respect, even as they sent him writhing in his grave. It's said that Adolph Hitler created the famed salute of an outflung arm and the "Heil Hitler!" after seeing an American newsreel depicting the cheerleaders at a Yale football game.

As Large As Life, And Twice As Natural

In the songs and publications and the lurid styles of the movement variously known as "Punk" and "New Wave" and other off-shoot names, one finds a pop nihilism that both celebrates and disdains every object before it, and sees the world with a mad collagist sensibility reminiscent of Dada—but bleaker than Dada, and without Dada's exhilaration in trashing the bourgeois forms that held cultural authority. There seems no center to the New Wave's perception of things: in a mock tribute to a TV celebrity's newest hairdo in one magazine, the writing gushed with grandiose metaphors; in the retouched photograph, the woman's hairdo resembled a nuclear mushroom cloud. Is this meant to be satire, slander, or some intentionally confusing admixture of both?

Harold Adams Innis described certain periods in history—when the authority of an older medium was being subverted by a new, untried medium— as tremendously precipitous and invariably transforming. What was changing hands wasn't merely the dominant medium of information but the "monopoly of knowledge" maintained by the dominant medium. We're undergoing the pressures of such a change right now; and perhaps not even in the generations that followed Gutenberg were the pressures so intense. With the oncome of cheap portable computers no larger than present hand-held calculators, and with two-way video systems of virtually infinite possibility, the monopolies of knowledge maintained by institutions such as the schools and professions such as medicine and law will begin eroding. Indeed, all authority with vested control maintained by reason of its specialized knowledge will lose some of that authority. The most distinctive feature of the coming information culture is the absence of authority in the mediation of knowledge: we can all control, to some extent, the world we'll learn about through television and the computer.

The prospect is somehow unsettling: how do we know these technologies won't further contribute to the splintering of interests and forms of knowledge, and create thousands of tiny specialized "tribes," interlinked electronically and perhaps faceless to one another, sharing a private language, private interests, and all the time becoming more solitary and introverted? An eminent computer pioneer, Joseph Weizenbaum, has argued that research into artificial intelligence should be curtailed or even abandoned, because of the unsettling questions just now beginning to emerge: perhaps most alarming is his depiction of the brightest (invariably the brightest) computer students who become obsessively involved with a computer, to the detriment of everything—grades, family, sex life—other than their growing, oddly passionate knowledge of a computer.

In New Wave songs and writings, the breakdown of reliable tradition and authority seems complete; even the point of view shifts erratically, tellingly. Perhaps such a breakdown, so total it seems a kind of annihilation, is required before a new sense of the world, itself engendered by the processes of mediation, simulation, and circularity, can emerge. If one looks to the explosive growth of fundamentalist "video churches," or to the work of video and computer artists, there are glimpses—equally frought with hope and menace—of just what may emerge.

Non-Communication and the Future

by

Michael Marien

Communication is an idealism. When we use the verb "communicate," we hope to pass along information that is received and understood. The nouns "communicator" and "communications" reflect our predisposition to emphasize the positive,[1] assuming that communication does indeed largely take place. Similarly, we assume that learning takes place where there is teaching, and that educators and education educate.

Alas, this is not always so for either communication or education, which is a major form of communication. In our seemingly well-educated society, ignorance—the gap between what we know and what we ought to know—is widespread. And so is non-communication, which I define as the multitude of instances where full communication ought to occur but does not.

My basic argument here is that such non-communication is widespread, and that we cannot begin to seriously understand the present and thus the future of communications unless we take a holistic stance: looking at non-communication as the hidden hemisphere of the communications moon.

Information Society or Age of Infoglut?

It is particularly important to recognize that the idealism in the concept of communication is reflected in the notion of the information society. Modern societies have in fact evolved into service societies, with the majority of the labor force employed in services, and most of these services can be defined as informational in nature.[2] Thus we have an "information society," and this trend is likely to be amplified by new communication technologies such as computers, satellites, and cable television. Such a society is presumed by its proponents to be both viable and desirable. But the argument has yet to be made for either viability or desirability.

The unexamined presumptions of information society proponents are taken to a utopian extreme by Yoneji Masuda,[3] who envisions a global computopolis, the mass production of knowledge, the intellectual industries as the major sector in the economy, a synergetic economy and a participatory democracy, an open educational environment enabling lifetime education, information utilities enabling anyone to get any information easily and

---

Michael Marien is editor of Future Survey, *a monthly publication of the World Future Society. The views expressed herein are his own and do not necessarily reflect those of the Society.*

cheaply, and "computopia" as the global futurization society where everyone actualizes one's own needs in multi-centered voluntary communities with freedom of decision, equality of opportunity, and voluntary management replacing bureaucracy.

Such heady idealism, reminiscent of the global-freedom-enabled-by-comprehensive-automation preached for many years by R. Buckminster Fuller,[4] may well serve to bolster spirits at a time when the world is facing the prospects of nuclear war, economic collapse, life-threatening pollution, and/or destruction of irreplaceable resources—matters that proponents of the information society frequently neglect. Or such idealism may be an adolescent escape from investing our energies in fully addressing these serious concerns. I am not arguing against idealism, which is very important to cultivate. But we should encourage a synergy of idealism and realism—and we should not confuse the two by indulging in the widespread delusion of equating ideals with evolutionary trends if not actual attainments. All of the ideals articulated by Masuda are obviously desirable. Who could argue against lifelong learning, participatory democracy, and information as a virtually free good? Still, we must not be so swept away by this cosmic humanism[5] that we ignore present conditions and negative future possibilities.

A useful antidote to the overt idealism of Masuda and the crypto-idealism of others such as Daniel Bell is provided by the extremely pessimistic view of Jeremy Rifkin,[6] who views entropic disorder resulting from virtually all activities of modern industrialized societies. According to Rifkin, the massive increase in information has translated into a massive expenditure of energy, mounting disorders, increasing centralization, and more specialization. Superficially, the computer appears to use less energy and to open up informational access for all; but the total overall effect of the computer revolution has been a dramatic, worldwide increase in entropy. The computerized society is becoming increasingly complex, and with complexity comes the real potential for breakdown. Paradoxically, as more information is made available to us, we become less well-informed and decisions become harder to make. A similar but more restrained argument is made by sociologist Orrin Klapp,[7] who draws together much social science literature in describing information overload as the crisis of noise in modern society, and as an avalanche of bits and signals creating an "endless jigsaw puzzle." Jean-Pierre Dupuy argues that the more we "communicate" the way we do, the more we create a hellish world; ours is a world about which we pretend to have more and more information, yet one that is increasingly devoid of meaning.[8]

Advocates of an information society, such as Masuda, do consider the possibility of a controlled society or an automated state.[9] But they do not consider the far more fundamental problem that non-communication is already dangerously widespread, and that the new information technologies inadvertently aggravate this condition by increasing our technologically-induced hubris, while adding to our infoglut and ignorance. Indeed, it is notably ironic that information society proponents are so alienated from their critics that, apparently, they do not even recognize the criticisms that have been made.

Therefore, as a matter of caution, as well as truthfulness, I think it far more appropriate to label our era the Age of Infoglut, rather than an Information Era or Information Society. It is essential to encourage a focus not on the central trait of our information abundance, but on our central problem of failing to make constructive use of this information. Perhaps the Age of Infoglut will prove to be an interim period leading to Masuda's computopia, or, more modestly, the communications era advocated by Robert Theobald for many years.[10] But we must not allow our enthusiasms for the future to distort our understanding of the present.

Complex Societies and Non-Communication

In a simple society, a single language and a few modes of communication can suffice for satisfactory human communications. Modernity makes the task far more difficult. Advances in communication and transportation have created an interlinked, multi-level global community, where the affairs of neighborhood, city or town, county, region, state or province, nation, continent, and planet are all intertwined. (If contact with extraterrestrial intelligence is made, a further dimension will be added.) Individual human contact has the simplicity of McLuhan's global village, but the managerial reality for this complex social system is that of Doxiadis's ecumenopolis. Complicating this tangle of communities is a greater number of people on our planet and a greater proportion of these people spending much of their time in informational activities. This complexity forces more and more specialization, which in turn creates further problems in communication. According to James Martin, electronic media are necessary to manage the "information deluge of our age."[11] But we must insure that such media do not encourage the deluge, much as new freeways have inadvertently encouraged highway traffic.

Despite the great advances in computers and television, with concomitant promises that we will be better informed, social malaise is spreading, and it is increasingly difficult to manage our societies and control onorous technologies such as nuclear weapons. The most fundamental issues about the course of modern societies lack any serious discussion. There has never been a dialogue between the proponents of further industrial growth via an information society and those who argue that we must aim for a more humane and sustainable society. Nor has there been any serious interchange between those who seek to increase American military capability in response to the perceived growth of Soviet might and those who seek arms control and disarmament. Both sides of these two critical issues appear unwilling and/or unable to listen, and there is no cultural mechanism to make them listen and to respond to each other. As documented in *Future Survey* and *Future Survey Annual*,[12] every other problem area is also approached in this fragmented fashion. The blind men describing the shape of the elephant now seem deaf to each other's partial views. Will the new technologies help us to better understand and manage our modern societies? Computers cannot help us if we are unwilling or unable to take a broader view, nor can they facilitate dialogue and cross-cultural understanding unless we seek such dialogue and understanding.

A more specific focus on non-communication might entail at least four general categories:

1. Failed Communication: Message of importance not sent (information withheld; a book not published) or message not received (lost mail; a purchased book that isn't read; a potential reader who does not know of a message addressed to his or her needs).

2. Flawed Communication: Wrong message sent as a result of unintentional error or intentional lying or distortion (government explanations of events; citizen income tax returns).

3. Miscommunication: Message received, but not understood or believed, or it results in an unintended effect.

4. Junk Communication: Message received and understood, but of no importance (most advertising); time involved with such trivia detracts from time that could be spent with more important communication.

All of these forms of non-communication grow out of the complexities of modern societies, and are likely to persist and perhaps even worsen. A fully wired society does offer the potential of non-failure in communication, for, ideally, one can have access to all that is known or thought about a subject. But whether one can do so at little or no cost, and be able to deal with all that is known or thought about any subject, is quite problematic. The fruits of industrial productivity are not distributed freely to consumers, nor should we expect the fruits of telematic society to be free. Furthermore, reading and writing skills have been declining,[13] and a recent synthesis of data warns that the quality of our human capital has deteriorated as a result of environmental influences.[14] Thus, despite the potential of the tools that may be at our command, there is no reason to expect any decrease in flawed communications and miscommunication. And in a society raised on junk foods, there could very well be an increase in junk communications—the brain candy of an over-indulged generation.

An Inventory of Human Nexuses

To fully understand the potentials for both communication and non-communication, it is useful to employ a framework for examining the full range of human nexuses. If communication is the basis for human civilization,[15] we should look at *all* communicating situations and ask whether communications have been improving in each area—and whether they are likely to improve or worsen with the advent of new technologies.

A possible framework for such an inventory of human nexuses might be divided into four basic categories: economic, civic, cultural, and personal. A few sample prospects are listed below for each nexus:

A. Economic

1. Employers and Employees: Industrial automation (robotization) and "office of the future" will probably result in considerable labor force displacement; computerized homes and "electronic cottages" may allow some decentralization of work.

2. Sellers and Buyers: Computers will enable better inventory control; customers will have better information on alternatives by "teleshopping" and various information systems.

3. Landlords and Tenants: Landlords are now developing a computerized listing of problem tenants; tenants may do same for problem landlords and have better access to information about alternative housing.

4. Doctors and Patients: Medical personnel will have better access to pa-

tient records (probably with loss-of-privacy problems); patients will have better access to medical information enabling a greater degree of self-care, as well as electronic devices to monitor body processes and perhaps even computers as therapists.

B. Civic

5. Government and Citizens: Enhanced government potential for invasion of privacy through connection of various data banks; potential for enhanced citizen participation and better knowledge of representatives and public issues (perhaps even instant polls and plebiscites)—but these could be superficial "sandbox" exercises.

6. Intergovernmental Communication: Local and state governments worldwide might have better access to ideas being tried in other jurisdictions.

7. International Communication: Possible improvement in intercultural understanding (especially with automatic language translators), but Western culture may increase dominance.

C. Cultural

8. Teachers and Students: Better access of both teachers and students to alternative learning materials; learning by computer may risk loss of human contact.

9. Entertainers and Audiences: More audience access to wider range of sports and culture, but at a loss of live-performance experience and more cultural fragmentation.

D. Personal

10. Men and Women, Husbands and Wives: Less interaction to the degree that the sexes are involved in other communications, especially entertainment.

11. Parents and Children: Same as above.

12. Neighbor and Neighbor: Same as above, although theater-in-the-home might increase neighborliness; less shared culture, however, will probably harden barriers between racial, ethnic, and religious groups.

The positive and negative possibilities for each of these 12 human nexuses should of course be studied in far greater detail than that provided here. A brief and very preliminary analysis indicates that considerable changes might be expected in the economic and cultural areas, and these changes should for the most part be positive—if the major problems of unemployment and social inequality can be dealt with. The new communications offer a great potential for enhancing civic communications, but, at a time when citizen alienation and non-participation is increasing, there is no indication that this potential will be realized. Nor is there any indication that personal relations will be improved: notwithstanding the togetherness potential of mom, dad, and kids all playing video games, it seems far more likely that the sum of the new technologies will increase alienation on the personal level. After all, we must remember that the new technologies are not designed to improve human communication, but to capture markets and consumer dollars.

Toward Improving Human Communications

Are there any reasonable possibilities for improving human communication? I doubt that any serious improvement will come about if we expect salvation from technology alone. Rather, we will begin to improve human communications when we decide to make some effort to do so. Such an effort must involve an exploration of non-communication, and such matters as the extent of information overload, who lacks literacy in what modes of communication, and how we can improve the capability of both adults and children to deal wisely with the large amounts of information that will potentially be available.

From such studies, we may begin to shape new policies aimed at managing information, building human capacity, reducing trivial information, and bringing people together. Self-restraint, or voluntary simplicity in communication,[16] may become a desirable cultural norm. Knowledge institutions may shift their reward systems away from quantity and towards the recognition of quality. To overcome our fragmentation, we may see a greater emphasis on integrative studies, and on information bridges and brokers. And perhaps new structures might be developed to promote serious dialogue. Future studies, of course, is one such way to bring information and people together into more meaningful frameworks.

In sum, communication will always remain as an ideal. If we recognize this ideal, study the incidence of non-communication, and act on our findings, we may begin to realize genuine communication.

Notes

1. Many psychological studies have shown the distorting human tendency to stress the positive. This is summarized as "The Pollyanna Principle" by Margaret Matlin and David Stang, *Psychology Today*, March 1978, and in *The Pollyanna Principle: Selectivity in Language, Memory, and Thought* (Cambridge, MA: Schenkman, 1978).

2. The major argument for the service society is provided by Daniel Bell, *The Coming of Post-Industrial Society* (New York: Basic Books, 1973). The major document for the explication of an information society is Marc Uri Porat, *The Information Economy: Definition and Measurement* (Washington: U.S. Dept. of Commerce, Office of Telecommunications, 1977, 9 vols.). For a brief history of service society and anti-service society thinking, see Michael Marien, "The Two Visions of Post-Industrial Society," *FUTURES*, 9:5, Oct 1977.

3. Yoneji Masuda, *The Information Society As Post-Industrial Society* (Washington: World Future Society, 1981).

4. For example, R. Buckminster Fuller, *Utopia or Oblivion: The Prospects for Humanity* (NY: Bantam Books, 1969).

5. In addition to Fuller, globalistic-humanistic thinking is exemplified by Oliver L. Reiser, *Cosmic Humanism* (Cambridge, MA: Schenkman, 1966). Especially see sections on the World Sensorium and the World Brain, the latter idea first proposed by H. G. Wells in *World Brain* (New York: Doubleday, Doran, 1938).

6. Jeremy Rifkin, *Entropy: A New World View* (New York: Viking, 1980).

7. Orrin K. Klapp, *Opening and Closing: Strategies of Information Adaptation in Society* (NY: Cambridge University Press, 1978).

8. Jean-Pierre Dupuy in Kathleen Woodward (ed), *The Myths of Information: Technology and Post-Industrial Culture* (Madison, WI: Coda Press, 1980).

9. For example, see the "Tout-Etat" scenario postulated by Simon Nora and

Alain Minc, *The Computerization of Society: A Report to the President of France* (Cambridge, MA: MIT Press, 1980); or John Wicklein, *Electronic Nightmare: The New Communications and Freedom* (New York: Viking, 1981).

10. Robert Theobald, *Habit and Habitat* (Englewood Cliffs, NJ: Prentice-Hall, 1972). The entire book is structured around the concept of the end of the industrial era and the coming of the communications era, with its necessary patterns of systemic thinking (which, of course, are still far from widespread).

11. James Martin, *Telematic Society: A Challenge for Tomorrow* (Englewood Cliffs, NJ: Prentice-Hall, 1981; first published in 1978 as *The Wired Society*). "Telematic" is an Americanization of the French "télématique," a common European term for the integration of telecommunications and computing.

12. Michael Marien (ed), *Future Survey Annual 1980-81* (Washington: World Future Society, 1982). Also see *Future Survey Annual 1979*. Both annuals should amply demonstrate the utter chaos in contemporary thinking about the future.

13. Paul Copperman, "The Decline of Literacy," *Journal of Communication*, 30:1, Winter 1980.

14. Bernard Rimland and Gerald E. Larson, "The Manpower Quality Decline: An Ecological Perspective," *Armed Forces and Society*, 8:1, Fall 1981.

15. Frank Snowden Hopkins, "Communication: The Civilizing Force," *The Futurist*, XV:2, April 1981.

16. Duane Elgin, *Voluntary Simplicity* (New York: Morrow, 1981).

The Information Civilization:
The Challenging Upward Trail
for Humanity

by

Yoneji Masuda

Introduction

The human race is on the threshold of a new emerging civilization: the information civilization. It is an extension of and successor to the agricultural and industrial civilizations that have determined our social structure until now.

There are two aspects to the character of this new era: The first is that for its physical functioning in information production, it will depend on computer and communications technologies; the second is that its qualitative character will reach its peak in the high level of knowledge creation. This contrasts sharply with the high mass consumption character of the industrial civilization.

Because these are its basic characteristics, the successful attainment of the information civilization will depend in the main upon the rising level of human ability and character.

Agricultural and Industrial Civilizations

Civilization can be defined as "the integration of various cultures brought about by the improvement of societal productivity." The characteristics and structure of each civilization are molded strictly by the technological structure and nature of societal productivity.

In the history of mankind, there have been in broad terms two kinds of civilization: agricultural and industrial. Agricultural civilization was the first to take concrete shape. It was established broadly in fertile alluvial areas in the Middle East from the stabilization of agricultural production. This development of agricultural production not only assured the survival of great numbers of *Homo sapiens*, but also led to the accumulation of large amounts of social surplus. The increasing dependence of agricultural productivity on the sun and manual labor led to the development of two social aspects: a religion of sun worship and a system of agricultural slave labor. Out of this there

Yoneji Masuda, one of the early pioneers of computerization in Japan, is president of the Institute for the Information Society and the author of The Information Society As Post-Industrial Society.

emerged the class society of feudal lords and priests ruling over serf-bound labor.

The grand legacy of pyramids and temples has remained as historical monuments of that agricultural civilization.

Industrial productivity provided the means by which industrial civilization flourished. Its origins lay in the natural sciences, and the machinery of the industrial revolution made this possible thousands of years after the agricultural age. New societal systems emerged, with the free competition of private business, commodity markets, parliamentary democracy, and the emergence of the management class and labor unions. The historical monuments of this industrial civilization are our giant modern factories and skyscrapers.

Invisible Civilization Based on Information Productivity

The information civilization, successor to the agricultural and industrial civilizations, will be unique, never before having been experienced by humanity; its foundation will be information productivity that uses computer communication technologies. This is in contrast to the two earlier civilizations, the existence of which depended on material productivity.

What are the basic characteristics of the information civilization? First, it is invisible. In the agricultural and industrial civilizations, the products were material goods, visible to people's eyes in the form of huge harvests of food, and a million kinds of industrial goods.

But the products of the information civilization will consist of signals, symbols, and images. This is already seen in the processing of information by computers, which is put together by a combination of electronic signals, 0 and 1, and stored on tapes or disks.

Note that the existence of the agricultural and industrial civilizations depended on the fulfillment of material needs, the production and consumption of material goods being the typical activities of these civilizations. These activities are visible to everyone, because the processes are based on physical functions.

The genesis of the information civilization, on the other hand, is the need to realize self-actualization and fulfill goal-achievement needs by the proper use of information. Computers produce sophisticated cognitive information and eliminate uncertainties; they optimize action selection and improve goal-achievement ability for everyone.

It should be stressed that the goal-achievement process can be explained objectively as situational reform to change the existing situation, to bring about a more desirable and feasible situation.

For example, suppose one sets the goal of becoming a doctor, and then goes on to achieve this goal. Objectively, this means a change from the specific situation of being a student at a medical university to the new situation of being a medical doctor. This process is invisible.

The historical monuments of the information civilization will be found in a few one-inch-square chips in a small box. But this box will be the repository of many historical records, and if human wisdom succeeds in raising the level of life, these historical records will tell how four billion world citizens overcame the energy crisis and the population explosion; how they achieved the abolition of nuclear weapons and complete disarmament; how illiteracy and hunger and deprivation were conquered. What can this be called but an invisible civilization.

Global Civilization Crosses National Barriers

The second basic characteristic of the information civilization is that it is global. The agricultural civilization that emerged along the lower reaches of big rivers where the overlay of fertile soil was deposited could be called a river civilization because of this. The industrial civilization is a metropolitan civilization, which flourished in metropolitan areas where millions of people and thousands of tall buildings were crowded together.

But the information civilization will truly be a global civilization, because it will spread all over the world in unified form. The global character of the information civilization will come about from two main factors, the first of which is the concept of globalism arising from the deep consciousness of the human crisis caused by shortages of natural resources, environmental disruption, etc.

The second is the expansion and improvement of computer and satellite communications technologies. In the highest stage of the dawning information society, a Global Information Utility Network will make its appearance, and ordinary citizens all over the world will have easy access to such a network and be able to exchange information and ideas relating to global problems. Then the mutual understanding and global thinking of citizens will override national interests, with the deepening of different cultures. In the course of these processes, the sprouts of a global culture will grow and an Informational Global Community (IGC) will come into being. One special characteristic of this IGC will be freedom from ties to the local place and the bonds of national barriers. The fundamental bond that will bring citizens together will be the growth of a common philosophy and common goals in day-to-day living and on global issues. It is the emergence of this IGC that will provide the foundation of the global civilization.

Sublation of Oriental and Occidental Civilizations

The third basic characteristic of the information civilization will be the sublation of both oriental and occidental civilizations. There is a fundamental contrast between these two civilizations—oriental civilization being fundamentally spiritual and intuitive, whereas occidental civilization is rational and materialistic, a fundamental difference deriving from differences in value thinking and attitudes toward the natural environment.

In oriental civilization, as seen in the practice of Yoga and Zen, the system of value thinking is meditative, passion mortifying, the goal being to maintain spiritual peace and attain nirvana; and toward the natural environment the aim is to live in harmony with nature. By contrast, the occidental civilization has a physiological value system, passion-filled, aggressive, with the goal of fully enjoying life's pleasures; and toward the natural environment the aim is to subdue and control nature by the application of the natural sciences and technology.

The future information civilization will bring about the sublation of these civilizations. (By this Hegelian term we mean "unifying them at a higher level.") The information civilization being fundamentally a humanistic civilization, it will bring about the unification of the present spiritual and materialistic civilizations.

Firstly, its value system will become a process of self-actualization, elevated from spiritual or material consumption needs to goal-achievement needs.

Secondly, the human attitude toward the natural environment will change from subduing and controlling it to synergetic coexistence with it.

The special invisible and global characteristics of the information civilization will become powerful factors in achieving these two goals. Here we may refer to the synergetic character of information. Information has the unique character of being nonconsumable, nontransferable, indivisible, and accumulative, its most effective processing and distributing system being seen in synergetic production and shared utilization. This unique characteristic of information, combined with the spirit of globalism, will contribute to actualizing the synergetic coexistence of mankind with nature.

The ultimate goal of the information civilization will be the rebirth of theological synergism of man and the supreme being, or if one so prefers to call it, the ultimate life force, terms that have relevant meaning to those of both religious and nonreligious faith. Mankind can live and work with nature. Put in another way, man approaches the universal super life, man and God acting as one.

Global Intelligence As Essential Personality Development

However, it will be a long and difficult trail to reach the heights of the information civilization. Human beings will have to challenge and overcome two steep paths, both subjective and objective.

The subjective path for humanity is the development of global intelligence as a new human characteristic. In industrial civilization, the trail for human personality is relatively not so severe, because the development of industrial productivity depends completely upon manufacturing technology based on natural science, and consumption needs belong in the realm of social instincts. Once human beings have mastered scientific knowledge and technology, the problems of production are resolved. Useful goods can readily be produced from natural resources. The one thing that matters is how the purchasing power of consumers can be improved.

By contrast, in the information civilization human beings must develop intelligence of a truly human character. Intelligence means the ability to make optimum action selection by the use of information and knowledge and positive adaptation to the changing social environment.

It is intelligence rooted in and acquired from the accumulation of knowledge and many experiences of failure and success. So intelligence is basically the capability of rational selection of human action in solving problems.

Intelligence starts at the personal level and is leveled up to group intelligence, the higher and wider level. Among a group, personal intelligence will be combined and harmonized toward the common goal of changing the social environment. That is social intelligence.

The ultimate developmental stage of intelligence would be global intelligence. If ordinary citizens living in different stages and belonging to different cultures can take the same manner and action to resolve a specific global problem, this will be the application of global intelligence. Unless human beings succeed in developing global intelligence, the solution of global problems will be impossible. This is why I emphasize that global intelligence is the most critical subjective trail that must be taken for the information civilization.

Information Democracy As the Foundation of a New Civilization

Another severe test for humanity is how to establish information democracy as the essential objective condition. It is the need to avoid Orwell's *"1984,"* and to enable the desirable information civilization to take shape.

Information democracy is the essential basic right in the information civilization, consisting of four developmental components of the information right. The first essential to information democracy is the protection of privacy. The nature of this is negative, viz, the human right to keep one's private life private from others. The second level is the right to know. This is more positive and it guarantees the right of citizens to know all kinds of governmental confidential information such as would seriously affect the citizens. The third level is the right of use. This means that every citizen can freely utilize all information utilities and data banks, at low cost and from any place, at any time. The fourth level is the highest level of information democracy, viz, the right to participate directly in the management of the information infrastructure, such as the information utility, a global watchdog institute, and critical decision-making at all levels—global, governmental, and local.

The successful establishment of these four information rights could pave the way to the most favorable environment for citizens to solve social and global issues voluntarily, and to enlarge their own opportunity for the potential future of each person.

The emphasis on the importance of global intelligence and information democracy cannot be too great, if we are to realize the future desirable and feasible information civilization.

The Future of Global Satellite Communications: Space Odyssey 2000

by

Joseph N. Pelton

In 1956, the world's first submarine telephone cable was laid across the North Atlantic. Up until that time, voice communications were provided by high-frequency and short-wave radio, which was subject to fading and interference, particularly due to sunspot activity and atmospheric disturbances. In 1965, when INTELSAT launched the world's first operational communications satellite ("Early Bird"), with a capacity of some 240 telephone circuits or a black-and-white television channel, the total global network of telephone interconnection across the oceans was only a few hundred circuits. Early Bird, in effect, doubled the communications capacity crossing the North Atlantic and made live television interconnection between the continents a possibility for the first time in man's history.

INTELSAT II was launched in 1967 largely to support communications requirements needed for the NASA manned space program, GEMINI. In 1968, INTELSAT III, with a capacity of some 1,200 voice circuits or up to four color TV channels, was launched. By 1969, just a few weeks before Neil Armstrong landed on the moon, a complete global network of satellites interconnecting the Indian, Pacific, and Atlantic Ocean regions was established, and thus it was that some 500 million people, the largest television audience in the history of mankind, was able to watch the moon landing.

In 1971, the large INTELSAT IV satellite, standing some two and one-half stories tall, was launched with a capacity of some 4,000 telephone circuits, or 12 television channels. This was followed, in 1975, with INTELSAT IV-A satellites with a capacity of 6,000 voice circuits, or 20 TV channels. In 1981, the INTELSAT V satellite, with a total capacity of 12,000 voice circuits, or 40 color TV channels, was launched over the Atlantic Ocean. By 1984, a network of INTELSAT V and V-A satellites (V-A's have a capacity of 15,000 circuits) will be launched into earth orbit, to provide the most sophisticated global communications network ever devised by man—a network whose capacity will be 825 times greater than that represented by Early

Joseph N. Pelton, who has been involved in satellite applications since 1965, is currently the executive assistant to the director general of INTELSAT in Washington, D.C. The views expressed in this article are the personal views of the author and do not intend to reflect the views of the INTELSAT organization.

Bird, the communications satellite that started the era of space communications less than 17 years ago. If the same rate of growth were to continue until 2025, we would find a global satellite network capable of transmitting 130 billion telephone calls all at the same time. Since the earth's population should be no more than 12 billion by that time, we will either see a slackening of growth or, perhaps more likely, dramatic new demands for telecommunications services that require many times the capacity of a telephone circuit, such as videoconferencing, high-resolution TV, or perhaps, alternatively, three-dimensional television.

Just one INTELSAT V satellite, such as those now operational over the Atlantic Ocean region, if configured in an all-digital mode, can today send 1 billion bits (one gigabit) of information per second. At that rate, the equivalent of the *Encyclopaedia Britannica* can be sent across the Atlantic Ocean some six times a minute.

By 1986, INTELSAT will begin launching its INTELSAT VI satellites, which will provide some 33,000 voice circuits, or the equivalent of 120 TV circuits. As many as 12 of these INTELSAT VI satellites will be launched and, together with launch vehicle costs, will represent a capital investment of perhaps $3 billion. This global network would be able to send the equivalent of some 36 billion bits of information per second or, to continue the earlier analogy, the *Encyclopaedia Britannica* some three times every second.

Despite the impressive gain in ever increasing transmission capacity, there is a parallel onrushing demand for new services, such as videoconferencing, packet-switched computer communications networks for facsimile, electronic mail, and other business services—these almost seem to know no bounds. Contractor studies, conducted under NASA's auspices, have shown that there is a potential demand in the U.S. domestic market alone for millions of telephone circuits, thousands of videoconferencing circuits, and a fantastic demand for communications services to support emerging computer communications networks, high-speed facsimile, and electronic mail. Already, today's satellites and submarine cables relay some $5 trillion in international electronic fund transfers on the Eurodollar and Asiadollar money markets. The world economy depends heavily on the vast global communications networks that encompass the whole world. INTELSAT not only has 106 member countries, but it provides services to over 150 countries, territories, and independent possessions.

In light of the proliferation of communications satellite systems, with over 100 systems now either in operation or planned for deployment by the mid-1980s, new approaches to satellite communications will be needed by the late-1990s and certainly by the early twenty-first century. Two of the principal concepts under study are clusters of satellites and space platforms. Clusters would be an interlinked network of satellites, up to 10 in number, in a so-called "halo" orbit around a single nodal point in geosynchronous orbit. Space platforms, or Orbital Antenna Farms, would combine a number of frequency bands and communications requirements on a single large structure in space. Space platforms allow a single large antenna reflector to be used with a large number of multiple-feed elements. This produces a large number of antenna beams that can reuse the same frequencies perhaps 100 to 200 times. Such beams could theoretically be focused even on individual earth stations. The INTELSAT V satellite, by comparison, is able to use the same frequency twice through geographic separation and then twice again through the use of polarization techniques. The space platforms of the twenty-first century would use the same techniques, but many times over, to use radio frequencies perhaps 50 to 100 times more efficiently than today's satellites.

Furthermore, such platforms could achieve very high power levels sufficient to work to very small antennas—perhaps down to tiny antennas for wristwatch radio transceivers, à la Dick Tracy. Even more far-ranging studies, such as those recently completed by General Dynamics under NASA contract, suggest that, if there is a demand for a large number of hugh space platforms in geosynchronous orbit, it could be cost-effective to establish a lunar base for material processing that would manufacture the space platforms on the moon's surface and then, in effect, lower these platforms down to geosynchronous orbit. This would be—if I can use the term in the context of billions of dollars—cheaper than paying to launch them into orbit from the earth's surface. These studies, however, assume the economies of conventional launch vehicle technology will continue into the future.

There are other advanced concepts that might provide alternative answers for the long-range future. I would like to briefly share two such advanced concepts with you. One of these is Arthur Clarke's concept of the space funicular.

Clarke recently presented a technical paper showing how a very long, high-tensile-strength cable of a suitable material (a diamond, unfortunately, being among a very few materials that might today potentially so qualify) could be launched into geosynchronous orbit. The tapered cable would then be lowered to the earth's surface below. If another section of cable were also extended spaceward, this could be done in such a way to counterbalance gravitational and angular momentum forces so as to create a "dynamically stable system" that would allow the deployed cable system to serve as a sort of space elevator. Two baskets, operating as a two-way funicular, could then serve to raise or lower mass from Clarke's orbit at an energy expenditure rate thousands of times less than conventional mechanical combustion launch vehicle systems such as are used today. Despite the hoopla, the space shuttle is probably more accurately a space Rolls Royce, rather than a space truck, and it only gets mass into low earth orbit, only 1% of the way to the Clarke orbit. Such a space funicular system would be hundreds of times more cost-efficient than even advanced systems currently under study, such as ion thrusters that may be developed for launching applications satellites in the 1990s. Although there are practical difficulties with this exotic concept, it does show that today's launch systems are hundreds of times less efficient than the theoretical possibilities.

Another system that might be developed in coming decades is known under the term "Spider Sat." This concept, developed by physicist Paul Csonka of the University of Oregon, is based on the idea of using a high-powered photon or microwave beam that would transmit power to a small, active communications antenna, stabilizing it in low earth orbit in such a way that, with its active electronics, it could relay messages from one point on the earth to another. It should be noted in this respect that a microwave tower to effectively relay messages across the Atlantic only needs to be about 465 miles tall. Although we are still a long way from developing either SPIDERSAT or space funicular technology at a practical level, the future is always difficult to predict. Already there are serious studies under way of using microwave or photon beams not only to stabilize various types of application satellites or platforms in low earth orbit, but even to power aircraft. Indeed, we some day might reverse such a process and use solar-energy satellites to power and stabilize low-orbit satellites.

The potential of space telecommunications for the twenty-first century is awesome. Global television, three-dimensional television, satellite broadcasting, Dick Tracy radios for firemen and security personnel, global library access, telecommuting to work, affordable rural communications for developing countries, a better standard of living in remote areas, etc.—the economic, societal, cultural, and political implications are awesome. Thoughtful and wise developmental policies will be needed to ensure that such powerful technology is used to benefit mankind and avoid undesirable applications. The proper use of technology is certainly not a new challenge to mankind but, because of the influence of "future compression," we face perhaps the most difficult challenges of any time since the beginning of man's civilization. Phase Three of man's development (the cybernetic age) is clearly a new beginning, just as Phase One (the birth of the city and farming around 8000 B.C.) and Phase Two (the birth of scientific research and the Renaissance in the thirteenth century) were many centuries ago. The tolerance for error is small, but the potential benefits are large. Let's hope that man can find the proper scale between these "large" and "small" dimensions and between the often conflicting values of "survival" and "progress."

Global Talk and the World of Telecomputerenergetics

by

Joseph N. Pelton

In case you hadn't noticed, times are changing. In fact, the extent and nature of change is enormous. If one compares the top 50 corporations in the United States today and those back at the turn of the century, one finds that only about 20% are still on the list. Steel, mining, rubber, and meat packing have slipped badly. Oil, telecommunications, automobile manufacturing, computers, merchandisers, and financial institutions have made gains while chemicals, foods, and electrical manufacturing have held even. The place at the top is slippery, as today's oil companies and auto industries may find in coming years.

Figure 1 illustrates the dramatic shift in employment patterns in the United States over the last 150 years. During that time, agriculture as an employment activity has peaked and declined; manufacturing has peaked and declined; and today services are still increasing as a total percentage of employment activities. A recent study, conducted by Professor Marc Uri Porat, has formally verified that over 50% of the employed personnel within the United States are engaged in the obtaining, organization, distribution, processing, or use of information. In truth, we live in a society that spends more time studying how, why, when, and whether we should do things than actually doing them. Technology—particularly information technology—has radically transformed the way we live.

At the turn of the century in the United States, 20% of the population lived in towns and cities; 20% in suburbs; and 60% lived in rural areas. At that time, there were 16-million households in the United States, with an average size of 4.8 members per household. Today, we find a totally different situation. As the population has grown from 76 million to 230 million, we see major demographic shifts occurring. The size of a typical household in the United States has decreased from 4.8 members to close to 2.5. Today, over three-fourths of the American population lives in urban or suburban areas.

Modern transportation and communications systems have contributed in

Joseph N. Pelton is the executive assistant to the director general of INTELSAT. His book Global Talk, *published in 1981, has been nominated for the Pulitzer Prize for distinguished nonfiction by an American author. The views expressed in this article are the personal views of the author and do not intend to reflect the views of the INTELSAT organization.*

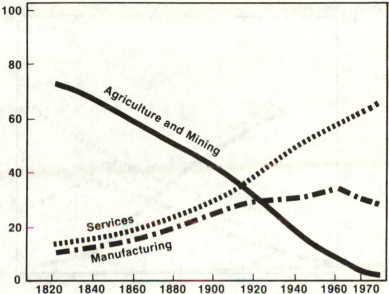

Figure 1

U.S. LABOR COMPOSITION, 1820-1970

Percent Labor Force

Agriculture and Mining

Services

Manufacturing

Sources: de Souza and Foust, *World Space Economy,* 1979.
U.S. Bureau of the Census.

Copyright permission, Oxford University Press.

large part to the breakdown of the extended family community, the dispersion of populations, and the reshaping of job markets, not only in the United States but in other information societies around the world. Indeed, it is interesting to contrast employment patterns that exist in various countries around the world on the basis of GNP per capita. (See Figure 2.) As income increases, the employment patterns radically shift within a society. Some would say this is in vice-versa fashion.

The relationship between computers and communications has been increasingly recognized in the United States, as AT&T and IBM have increasingly found themselves competing for the same market. It is probably surprising to few that AT&T and IBM are respectively number one and number three in profitability among all corporations in the U.S. The computer and communications industries have both shown astonishing technological growth in recent decades, with progress being made so rapidly that equipment that is five years old is often obsolete.

There are increasing indications, however, that these two highly technological and "intelligent" industries will be joined by similar high-technology, "intelligent" industries in the 1980s and the 1990s. In particular, the lead

79

Figure 2

WORLD LABOR AS A FUNCTION OF PER CAPITA GNP
TRANSFORMATION OF LABOR

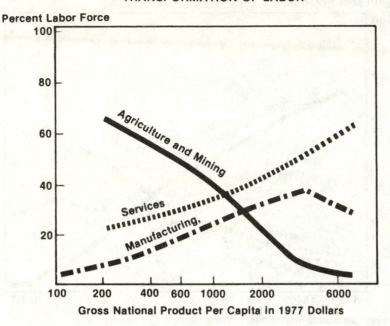

Sources: **The World Bank, *World Development Report.***
Chenery & Syrquin, *Patterns of Development, 1978.*

industries, in terms of stimulating economic productivity, are likely to include telecommunications, space applications, computers, cybernetics, robotics, alternative energy sources, and genetic engineering. The merger of these enterprises will arise from many sources. These forces include: (a) the need for large research laboratories; (b) a heavy reliance on semiconductor materials research (particularly in the area of silicon and gallium arsenide chips); (c) the importance of artificial intelligence and cybernetics to continuing market success; (d) the need to obtain new technology, often through acquisition of small "think tank" corporations; (e) a combination of economies of scope, economies of scale, and the associated ability to make heavy capital expenditures; (f) the need for rapid amortization of new plants and materials; (g) the need for concentration of highly skilled human resources in the form of scientists, engineers, and microbiologists; and (h) international competitive pressures among the information society's high-technology megacorporations.

Already, one can see the emergence of what I called (in my new book *Global Talk*) the telecomputerenergetics industries, as represented by such organizations as Hughes Aircraft Company, TRW, EXXON, Volkswagen, and others. It will perhaps come as a surprise to some that EXXON, for instance, is not only heavily involved in traditional energy extraction and marketing in the form of petroenergy but is also heavily involved in solar energy, ocean thermal energy conversion, geothermal energy production, information systems, telecommunications and computer processing equipment, and electrical vehicle development. Further, there are a number of other activities on the EXXON horizon, such as robotics production. These are all emerging activities of a corporation with sales revenues over $100 billion per year. Mitsubishi Corporation of Japan, with sales of $55 billion (number five on a global scale) is, likewise, moving into a diversity of tele-computerenergetics activities. Today, advanced communications systems allow global transborder data flow. International electronic funds transfers today take place at a rate of $5 trillion per year. There is instantaneous access to information resources from all parts of the world. Figure 3 shows the likeli-

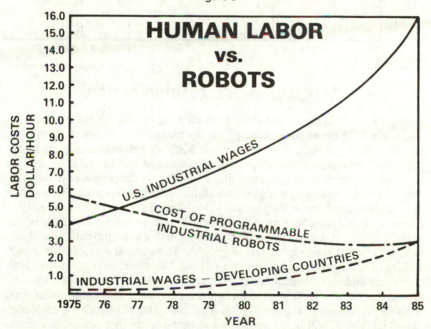

Figure 3

hood that robotics devices will, within 10 years, be the most cost-effective means of large-scale mass production regardless of the domestic labor market. These factors, taken together, portend a world economy and employment patterns significantly different from what we know today. These changes will, in turn, affect our transportation systems, our urban planning, our social and cultural activities, etc.

This background is simply to emphasize the fact that the future of telecommunications is more than simply an isolated aspect of the future development of our global society. Indeed, it could be argued that telecommunications is, in large part, the determiner of our future.

Let's then look at telecommunications in terms of where it has been and where it is going. If one looks back over the last 200 years, one finds that

81

Figure 4

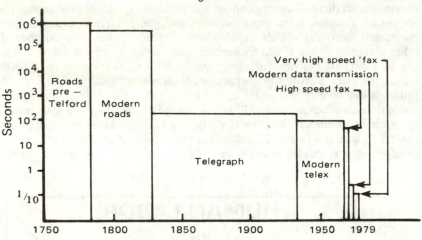

PROGRESS IN TELECOMMUNICATIONS

within this time span the speed with which a single page of information can be transmitted over a long distance has decreased by a factor of 10 million. (See Figure 4.) Again, if we look at the history of digital communications since the invention of the telegraph by Samuel Morse in 1832, we find an increase in transmission rate capabilities, as well as development of new service demands that require higher and higher transmission rates. As Figure 5 shows, there has been on the average a doubling of transmission capability at intervals of less than once every four years. There have been in the history of mankind no similar long-term technological developments that have achieved such a remarkable rate of growth. The computer revolution is only a third of a century old. It is not too radical, therefore, to suggest that both computer and communications growth trends will continue at least into the twenty-first century. New service requirements, such as videoconferencing, high-speed facsimile, high-resolution television, and ultimately three-dimensional television, will likely generate a demand for higher and higher transmission capabilities that is well beyond those that we know today.

A fiber optic laser system using laser communications, or an advanced satellite such as the INTELSAT V, can now transmit up to a billion bits of information per second. This transmission capability is the equivalent of sending the *Encyclopaedia Britannica* across the Atlantic Ocean some six times a minute. By the end of the century, however, it is not unreasonable to project satellite and laser communications capabilities to as high as 100-billion bits of information per second. Space platforms or satellite clusters in geosynchronous orbit utilizing 100-fold frequency reuse, together with eight to sixteen kilobit voice processing and other digital compression techniques, will be able to achieve a 100-fold increase above today's capabilities. Certainly, by the year 2010 these speeds should be possible. Similar progress with fiber optics and laser communications can also be anticipated. Infrared

82

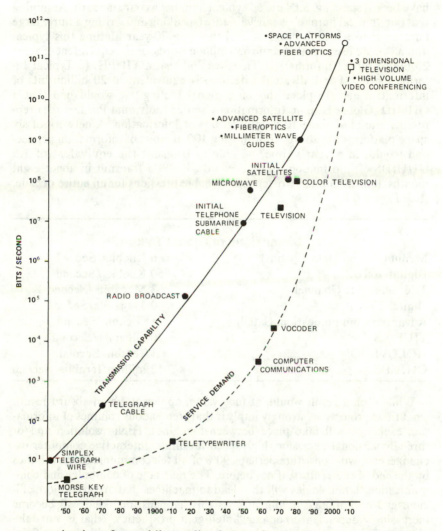

Figure 5
150 YEAR LOOK AT DEVELOPMENT OF TELECOMMUNICATIONS
(Service Demand vs. Transmission Capability)

communications for mobile applications and wristwatch transceivers may also unplug us from our wired cities.

One of the implications of continued communications development will be the fact that most communications transmissions will not be from one person to another, but will involve largely human-to-machine, machine-to-human, or machine-to-machine communications. The most powerful reason why this is likely to be so is simply that humans will be too slow in their mental processing capabilities to deal with the high volume of information rates that will develop by the twenty-first century. Communications systems that operate at the rate of 100 gigabits per second or above are much too fast to be the result

83

of human communications requirements at the level of telexes, telephone calls, etc.

To calibrate the scale of advanced communications systems such as we have been discussing, let's use a "typical human" as our standard. Assuming that our "typical human" is fairly literate (speaking and writing a fairly large number of words each day), we find that in a 70-year lifetime this typical human would use a total of some 650 million words, or the equivalent of some 20 billion bits of information. Thus, we find that a TIUPIL (a Typical Information Use Per Individual Lifetime) is equivalent to 20 billion bits of information and, to place this on a global footing, we would find that a GHUID (Global Human Information Use Per Individual Per Decade) represents a total of some 12 quintillion bits of information. A network of six space platforms capable of transmitting 100 gigabits of information per second would, in a year's time, be able to transmit the equivalent of 1.5 GHUIDS of information. In other words, it could transmit in about eight months' time all human written and verbal expressions for an entire decade. (See Figure 6.)

Figure 6
Dimensions of Global Talk

Medium-Speed Data Channel	9.6 Kilobits/Second
Digital Voice	50 Kilobits/Second
Teleconference Channel	3 Megabits/Second
Digital TV	40 Megabits/Second
Advanced Communications Satellite	1 Gigabit/Second
TIUPILS	20 Gigabits/Second
HOLOVISION	1 Terabit/Second
GHIUDS	12 million Terabits/Second

While such a result would, at face value, appear to be an absurd result, what these projections strongly imply is that tremendous volumes of information exchange will take place between machines. High-resolution and/or three-dimensional television, high-speed facsimile, interactive computer exchange, etc., will constitute perhaps 90% of all telecommunications volumes by the end of the century, if not before. The marriage of computer and communications technologies will thus lead to machines that are even more efficient and ever more "intelligent." As this happens, mankind will become increasingly dependent upon our "intelligent prosthetics," that is, our telephones, our computers, our robotics devices and, if you will, our artificial intelligence. We will need these intellectual prosthetics not only to extend our capabilities but, if you will, to maintain a parity with the machines we have invented.

John B. Calhoun of the National Institute of Mental Health has forecast that the greatest race of the twentieth century will be the race to speed up man's evolution by artificial means, in order to keep man at least on a level of parity with our machines. As Professor Anthony Oettinger of Harvard University, has said: "Man must adapt and adapt rapidly or we as a species will perhaps stand in danger of dancing the dance of the dinosaurs." There is no doubt that the rapid evolution of communications technology poses many issues—such as information overload, information privacy, totalitarian political abuses in the use of information and communications devices for control, and, conceivably, the military use of advanced technological devices such as laser and particle beam systems, together with sophisticated computer and communications networks, as instruments of war.

Figure 7

Counter-Inflationary Trends in Global Satellite Communications

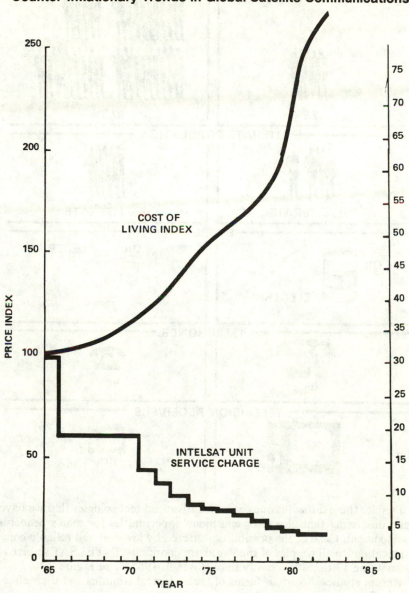

Figure 8

GLOBAL VILLAGE
1981

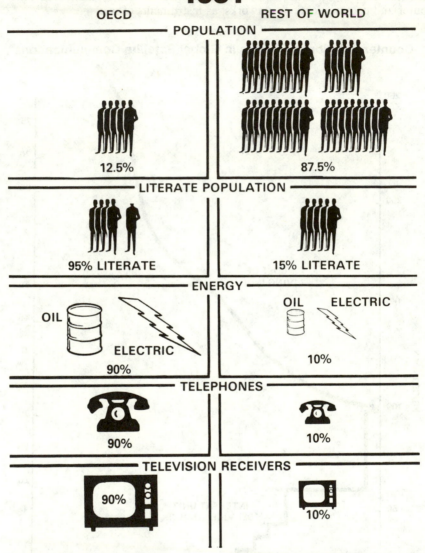

OECD   REST OF WORLD

POPULATION

12.5%   87.5%

LITERATE POPULATION

95% LITERATE   15% LITERATE

ENERGY

OIL   OIL   ELECTRIC

ELECTRIC   10%

90%

TELEPHONES

90%   10%

TELEVISION RECEIVERS

90%   10%

Despite these difficult issues, it is the advanced technologies that we have been discussing that also offer enormous opportunities for man's peaceful development. Clearly, the possibilities offered by low-cost and reliable communications to all peoples of the world are enormous. INTELSAT service is today some 17 times less costly than it was in 1965. (See Figure 7.)

Recent studies of various forms of technological stimulus and their effectiveness in achieving economic development have shown telecommunications to be extremely powerful in this respect. However, Figure 8 shows the world as a global village, wherein access to communications is quite unequally distributed. The challenge of next year's World Communications Year is to begin in earnest to advance the availability of communications services to all peoples of the world, particularly those in developing countries.

Ultimately, this rapid advance in communications may even allow us to communicate with other intelligent beings from other star systems. It would seem that the evolution of advanced telecommunications systems is almost inescapable and that, once man has joined the race to space and the race to discover the secrets of our universe, there can be no turning back. We must, therefore, face the future bravely and intelligently seek to use our powerful communications technology as a beacon—a beacon to be used with caution and respect for our global cultures, but also a beacon that seeks to spread knowledge and a better quality of life for all mankind.

An Assessment of Japan As an Information Society in the 1980s

by

Jerry L. Salvaggio

On July 8, 1853, Commodore Matthew Perry guided four ships into Uraga Bay and successfully opened relations with Japan. Since then Yedo, now known as Tokyo, has not been the same. Prior to that eventful year, the rulers of Japan had isolated the country from foreign influence for more than 200 years. Under the Tokugawa rulers, Japan had virtually been a closed country during a period when the Western world was making tremendous advances in technology.

Centuries of unique isolation from the rest of the world had both positive and negative effects. By avoiding contact with other countries, Japan was able to develop a unique culture and a nationalism unparalleled in the modern world. On the other hand, this isolation was responsible for Japan finding itself centuries behind Germany, the United States, and numerous other advanced countries that had made major technical and social advances between the seventeenth and nineteenth centuries.

Thanks to Commodore Perry, today Japan is a land of high technology where the samurai sword is a valued treasure and the computer a necessity. Since the Meiji Restoration, Japan has evolved into what Herman Kahn and others call a "super state."

If Japan does indeed have a uniquely homogeneous culture and a nationalism that verges on fanaticism, what does this portend for Japan as an information society? Is Japan on the threshold of becoming the first wired nation? And is there any reason to believe that Japan will not only be one of the most informationalized countries in the future but will take a leadership role in developing new forms of communication technology?

The answer to all these questions is, I suggest, an unqualified yes. Barring any major catastrophe, I feel fairly safe in making the prognosis that by the year 2000 Japan will be the most informationalized society on earth and will have pulled ahead of the United States and other developed countries in the systematic development of communications technology. In what follows, I shall describe the present status of the communications industry in Japan and then attempt to support my hypothesis by outlining those features of

Jerry L. Salvaggio is an associate professor in the School of Communication, University of Houston, Houston, Texas.

Japanese culture, government, and economy that will enable Japan to realize its goals.

Projects Underway in the Computer and Telecommunication Fields

At the metacenter of future communication systems will be computer and telecommunication systems, a merging of two technologies that Anthony Oettinger of Harvard University has termed "compunications." The success of future information societies is dependent on the efficiency and sophistication of systems that integrate computers and telecommunications. One can therefore logically assume that leadership in compunications will mean leadership in the communications arena.

The computer industry. Since 1946, when Mauchly and Eckert turned on ENIAC, the first large-scale computer, the field has been dominated by the United States. Even today, Japan's share of the computer market worldwide is a paltry 10% to 15% compared to IBM's 50% holdings. I suggest that this will soon change and possibly be reversed in years to come. I say this because the goal of Japan's Ministry of International Trade and Industry (MITI) is to win a 30% share of the world market and an 18% share of the American market by 1990.

How will Japan accomplish this feat? Basically, with a heavy financial investment from the government and cooperative strategic planning by industry. Between 1975 and 1985, the Japanese government will have injected approximately 70 billion dollars into the computer industry. According to Christopher Evans, a noted computer scientist, Japan will spend in the neighborhood of 3 billion dollars a year in computer training and teaching. It can be expected, then, that the design, manufacturing, and exporting of computers, as well as their integration into communication systems, will undergo rapid increases in the next decade. Without doubt, the healthy infusion of financial resources into the computer industry will serve as a catalyst for the development of communication systems.

Use of mainframe computers in future communication systems. Information societies of the future will be dependent on mainframe computers for storing large data banks. These data banks will be used by industry, government, and the public for accessing needed information. Many individuals will use dumb terminals to tap into these mainframes—allowing the latter to do their computing. Mainframe computers will also be used to scan the homes of individuals subscribing to interactive systems, such as the experimental Hi-Ovis Project in Japan. In this latter function, the computer scans each home once every seven seconds, tabulating data and monitoring the home's burglar and fire alarm systems. In the case of Hi-Ovis, the computer is also capable of responding to the individual's personal request for a particular movie.

Use of microcomputers. Microcomputers will form the outer strands of a huge communications web allowing individuals to send and receive information to and from the mainframes. Since they were first introduced by Digital Equipment Corporation in 1965, microcomputers have become essential components in information networks. Jack Tramiel of Commodore International predicts there will be as many as 50 million personal computers in use worldwide by 1985. While Tramiel's estimate may be overly optimistic, there is little doubt that microcomputers will be widely used in Japan by the end of the decade.

Fundamental to microcomputers becoming integral units in communication networks for the general public is a lower unit cost and greater portability. The average micro today sells for a minimum of $1,500 and is too large to carry around. The leading contender in the race for inexpensive, portable micros seems to be Japan's Sharp. According to *Business Week*, Sharp may have the edge due to its enormous investment in C-MOS chips. Sharp's pocket computer is already being sold through Radio Shack, and future micros capable of accessing videotext systems may be only slightly larger.

Computers and voice-recognition systems. It is generally agreed that if computers were able to understand the human voice rather than only being able to accept typed commands, large-scale use by the general public would be assured. Presently, computers with voice-recognition capabilities have limited vocabularies and cost in excess of $60,000. It is only a matter of time, however, before computers are able to input and output voice commands. Bell Labs, IBM, and Nippon Electric of Japan are among those experimenting with continuous-speech voice-recognition systems. The Japanese system uses a procedure called "nonlinear time-warping" and already has a fairly large vocabulary. By the late 1980s, the voice-recognition component of a computer will be detachable and will probably resemble a tape recorder. This will allow individuals to record information while away from the computer and input it at a later time. In all likelihood, this development will spur public use of computers and computer communication.

Intelligent computers. A new concept, developed with the backing of the Japanese government viz. the MITI, has been dubbed "fifth generation" computers. Fifth-generation computers are expected to be much more humanlike than previous ones and will have the ability to use stored reservoirs of knowledge to make judgments and decisions. Users will be able to communicate with the computers orally through a voice-recognition system, and researchers are predicting that they will be used as "intelligent assistants." In the office, for example, they would be able to accept spoken requests and use stored knowledge to decide which information was most relevant to the decision at hand.

The field of artificial intelligence is certainly going to play an important role in future communication systems, as it will make the computer friendlier and easier for the layman to use. While the United States presently has the lead in AI development, Japan has made a concerted effort to lead the way in the commercialization of the concept.

Developments in the Telecommunications Industry

In addition to investing heavily in the computer field, the Japanese have made a major commitment to developing telecommunication systems that will become part of large information networks. Following the lead of England, they have both a viewdata and a teletext system in the experimental stage.

Viewdata. CAPTAIN (Character and Pattern Telephone Access Information Network System) is an interactive (two-way) videotext system that is expected to be put into operation next year. Approximately 190 information providers will supply information and news to users by means of a keypad interface unit attached to the television set. CAPTAIN is similar to Britain's "Prestel" and, like most interactive videotext systems, offers patrons information on virtually any subject that would ordinarily be found in encyclopedias or in books on library shelves. As an example of its application, electronic messages, mail, the local news, airline schedules, weather, and encyclopedic information could be made available to the traveler simply by plugging into the hotel's electric outlet.

Teletext. In addition to CAPTAIN, Japan is developing a national one-way information system simply known as TELETEXT. As an advanced system for accessing data bases, CAPTAIN will be rather expensive due to its interactive capabilities and its need for wire transmission. A one-way system would be more cost effective for the public. For this reason, Japan will broadcast TELETEXT via satellite in the near future.

Data facsimile terminals. Japan is looking toward the day when the cost of lumber, transportation, and labor will make home delivery of newspapers and mail prohibitive. Perhaps anticipating that the public might not be receptive to "reading the newspaper off of a TV screen," Japanese researchers began very early developing "home" facsimile terminals. By 1988, Japan is expected to have invested well over 500 billion yen (two billion dollars) in the production of facsimile equipment. At the present time, Japan uses a facsimile system known as "Subscription Fax." The unit costs approximately $600 and each sheet of paper recorded one-and-a-half cents. Further development by NTT is being done on a new system the Japanese are calling "Lensless Fax," which is expected to be even more advanced and less expensive.

Flat-panel displays. Japan is also making significant strides in the field of flat-panel displays and miniature TVs. Franklin Meyer has recently pointed to Japanese firms that are experimenting with both gas plasmas and liquid crystals in an attempt to build miniature video terminals. Meyer further notes that the Japan Broadcasting Corporation has already succeeded in developing a DC gas plasma color TV display.

The development and large-scale marketing of flat-panel displays that can be hung from the wall of an office or home is likely to answer the question of whether or not consumers will be willing to use TV sets for hours of reading textual material. Development of wall-sized TV sets and miniature sets that can be placed in every room will certainly serve a catalytic function in making home information systems a reality.

Speculating on Future Developments

Having examined Japan's computer and telecommunication industries and experimental communication projects, what can we conclude in regard to the future? I suspect that, on the surface, Japanese communication systems will look very similar to those in other information societies. In time there will be telebanking, telecourses, telegames, telecommuting, and electronic newspapers. Individuals will use personal computers, tap into large data banks, watch television programs from other parts of the world via small home antennas, interact verbally and visually with friends and relatives through the TV set, and many will work from their homes.

What is significant about the development of communication systems in Japan is that they are being developed through long-range planning. The Japanese evidently believe that communication systems are too important to leave to the whims of the marketplace. They have correctly determined that the national economy will be dependent on a national communication system. In many countries, most notably the United States, new forms of communication technology are integrated into society only to the extent that private industry can extract a profit. Interactive cable is the best example. To this day, the development of cable systems is left to the industry and the regulation of cable is left to the local governments.

My first prediction, then, is that Japan will make a decision on which particular form of communication technology to implement on a national level after assessing the viability of all the systems they have been observing around the world. A quick glance at the *Report on the Present State of Communications in Japan*, published by the MPT (Ministry of Post and Telecommunications) shows the extent to which Japan studies the systems of other countries prior to investing in new forms of technology themselves. By basing their decisions on a thorough study of all available systems rather than depending on private industry, Japan should end up with a communication system that will serve its needs for the next two decades. This further means that communications technology will be integrated into Japanese society in a predetermined manner rather than on an ad hoc basis. Unfortunately, an examination of the development of communication systems on an international level indicates that this is the exception rather than the norm.

My second prediction is that Japan will be the leading nation in the world in designing, manufacturing, and exporting communications technology. Joseph Pelton of Intelsat has noted that at the present time Japan and the United States lead the world in the development of "transistors, microcircuitry, large-scale integration; holographic and bubble memories; laser-optical fiber communications; digital modulation and processing techniques; and video cassette recorders—to name but just a few examples." The Japanese will probably surpass the United States in this area due to their experience in the field of electronics. A recent study, for example, by the United States General Accounting Office, found that electronic subassemblies made by Fujitsu America had 10 times as many defects as identical parts made by Fujitsu in Japan. Productivity is likely to increase in the future as Japan continues to forge further into the field of robotics.

Thirdly, I expect that Japan will be the first nation to make a national information system available to the entire country at a cost that will make it a viable operating system for the masses rather than an optional status symbol for the middle class. By 1984, at least one system will be in operation transmitting the *Asahi Shimbun* and other newspapers via satellite. By the late 1980s, consumers will have the option of reading information directly from a flat-display screen or a miniature TV set using TELETEXT or of making a hard copy with a small data-facsimile terminal. During the 1980s, Japan's national information system is likely to be strictly a one-way form of communication emanating from a satellite. Because of Japan's crowded cities, and the high cost of transportation and paper products, the public is almost certain to make greater use of the system than members of other cultures.

My fourth prediction is that two-way video and audio communication will become available in parts of Japan in the 1990s. The experimental Hi-Ovis project has shown the capability of fiber optic information systems. It can be expected that areas of high information usage, such as Tokyo and Osaka, will be wired with fiber optics as a prelude to the wiring of the entire country. Two-way communication systems, in turn, will facilitate the move to a cottage industry, as more and more information workers in Japan commute to work only occasionally.

Finally, there will clearly be certain adverse social consequences as Japan becomes one vast information network. I have attempted to make the case that Japan will lead the world in the development of communications technology. If this turns out to be the case, then it would logically follow that Japan will be the first to experience the social effects of being highly informationalized. The primary side-effects are likely to be in the areas of government censorship, information overload, psychological dependence on video, computer piracy, and invasion of privacy.

Rationale for the Above Speculations

Though I could cite a dozen or more reasons in support of my basic hypothesis that Japan will lead the world in communications technology, I shall avoid prolixity and cite only four reasons.

Japan realized the importance of information flow in the early 1960s. Since 1973, the Ministry of Posts and Telecommunications (analogous to the FCC, though with considerably more authority) has conducted a comprehensive survey of the level of information dissemination in Japan. The objective of the MPT survey is to provide a quantitative analysis of the annual flow of information. This will facilitate the analysis of development trends for each medium, and at the same time, produce indices for gauging the degree of "informatization." Based on this information, the MPT can make policy decisions regarding the development of new communications technology. Few countries in the Western world have taken the concept of informatization so seriously.

Perhaps even more important than the study of information flow is the design of experimental projects on a large-scale basis. Japan has already completed two projects that required the combined resources of industry, public corporations, and government.

The Tama New Town experiment, known as CCIS, began in 1976 and at its completion was able to offer 10 unique services, including a form of videotext, two-way cable, pay-TV, program origination, still pictures, request service, and regular TV programming. Perhaps Tama New Town's most interesting service was "memo copy," which allowed users to exchange handwritten messages among themselves and with central control.

Hi-Ovis, a far more sophisticated project, took place from 1979 to 1981 and used fiber optics to provide two-way communication to 158 homes. Among the many services it offered were a videotext-type system with headline information, theater reservations, burglar alarms, access to still pictures, videocassette programs originating from the control center, and local program origination. The one element that gave Hi-Ovis its claim to fame was the installation of a small TV camera above the TV set aimed at the home viewer. This permitted the viewer to switch in and join the conversation in the case of locally originated programs.

Both of the above systems were designed for what the Japanese call "a service-oriented society" as opposed to a consumer-oriented society. Furthermore, both systems were built at a cost far exceeding what a single government or industry could afford. Only through a cooperative agreement between the government, public corporations, and private industry could these advanced information systems be developed. In my opinion, though, the most significant aspect of these two experiments and that of CAPTAIN and TELETEXT is their holistic approach to solving communication problems. Similar experiments being conducted by CBS and AT&T are designed to determine the extent to which a profit can be made. These experiments, on the other hand, involve educational programs, library access, health care, and other social programs. If these prototypes are any indication of the way in which the national information systems will be built, then the chances of success are likely to be far higher since they will offer indispensable services.

A third reason for my optimistic outlook for new communications technology in Japan has to do with the infrastructure of Japan's regulatory system. We might break national forms of communications into four categories for the sake of simplicity: mail, telephone, print publications, and broadcasting. In Japan, all of the above (with the exception of the print media) fall under the jurisdiction of the MPT. Having a single regulatory body that makes extensive use of advisory boards and has the authority to set up sophisticated experiments based on the advice of the boards facilitates the implementation of advanced communications systems. In the United States, the FCC has neither the scope nor the authority, not to mention the financial resources, of the MPT.

Finally, the infrastructure of industry in Japan is unique in its ability to cooperate on extremely large projects. The largest conglomerates, generally known as the "zaibatsu" (zai meaning wealth and batsu meaning clique), get together regularly to discuss matters affecting all the companies in the group. Willard Price notes that while conglomerates with as many subordinate companies as the zaibatsu would be accused of collusion in the United States, they make sense in Japan. Developing a viable national information system that will utilize satellites and data-facsimile terminals and would offer newspapers and a college degree is an example of a communication system that could not be accomplished without cooperation among various companies involved in computers, satellites, print publishing, etc.

In summary, I am impressed with Japan's early realization of the importance of measuring information, its commitment to designing experimental projects, its regulatory infrastructure, and its willingness to allow large corporations to work closely together to solve national problems. While I may be overly impressed and may be omitting in this paper certain problems that Japan faces in the next decade, I remain convinced that Japan will lead the world in developing and implementing communications technology in the years ahead.

Acknowledgement

I would like to acknowledge two individuals who were instrumental in one or more aspects of this study: Ryuzo Ogasawara of the *Asahi Shimbun* and Helen Simon of Louisiana State University.

Leapfrog Strategy
in the Information Age

by

Kimon Valaskakis

The principal thesis of this article may be stated in the following terms:
- The information revolution is ushering in a pattern of non-linear technological growth featuring *short* and *explosive* life-cycles for particular technologies. Although this pattern is not new and has some roots in history, the very nature of information technology compounds this explosive characteristic and makes it dominant.
- The successful forecasting and harnessing of a particular technology life-cycle yields enormous dividends in terms of industrial leadership for a firm or a country as a whole. Failure to harness the cycle leads to severe penalties. At the present time, the center of global industrialization is subtly shifting from the Atlantic economy to the South-East Asia triangle of Japan, the four "Mini-Japans," and China. The threat of severe and involuntary de-industrialization looms over the West.
- The optimum strategy in the new information age is to look for the *leapfrog*, an approach fully explained below.
- Interestingly enough, the predominance of the leapfrog as a strategic principle leads to a desirable global order where whoever is *behind* may now leapfrog ahead. The last shall be first and the first last. This proposition, if true, could be a great source of hope for the Third World and for all backward countries.

The rest of the paper is an elaboration of these four key points.

The Nature of the Information Revolution

The information revolution is much more than a communication revolution and should not be perceived in a narrow sectoral sense. It is primarily a technological revolution where two hitherto separate fields are now merging: computer science and telecommunications. The advent of the microprocessor in the middle seventies revolutionized computer science by dramatically altering the cost/performance and volume/performance ratios. Microelec-

Kimon Valaskakis is professor of economics at the University of Montreal and founding director of the GAMMA Group, a futurist think tank sponsored by the University of Montreal and McGill University, Montreal, Quebec, Canada.

tronics has since been blessed with a unique anti-inflationary bias with cascading costs coupled with increased performance and miniaturization. Some experts even propose the following rule of thumb: double the money investment in a microelectronic system and you multiply tenfold the computing power. At the same time, parallel inventions and innovations in telecommunications (satellites, telephony, cable, fibre optics, etc.) have extended a sort of "electronic highway" to the microprocessor, allowing multiple long-distance usage and greatly decentralized production patterns.

All this is (or should be) well known. What is less known is that the information revolution is as much a *process* as a *product* revolution. Although there are hundreds of new communication products being developed every year, the process of *conventional* production is also changing, as are lifestyles and values. The most important of the process changes are robotics and bureautics. Factory-automation and office-automation are substantially reducing production costs and creating comparative advantages for those who adopt them.

In the final analysis, the microelectronic revolution is transforming the mode of production in a manner at least as profound as the steam engine two centuries ago. In both cases we have a process of automation (capital/labor substitution)—but with a difference. Whereas in the earlier industrial phases, energy capital was replacing labor, in the contemporary phase, information-capital in the form of computers is replacing human labor.

The Paramount Importance of Technology Life-Cycles

If we take the point of view that technology is applied science, then a particular technology has a definite life-cycle, going through discrete stages of growth, maturity, and eventually decline.

A standard or reference technology life-cycle is characterized, in our view, by the following stages: (1) discovery, (2) invention, (3) innovation, (4) na-

---

Table 1

Life-Cycle of a Technology Generation

Stage 1: **Discovery**
This stage features the discovery either of a scientific principle or law of nature or a natural resource (e.g., electricity).

Stage 2: **Invention**
The application of the scientific principle or law to a specific purpose, leading to the invention of a particular machine (e.g., the microprocessor).

Stage 3: **Innovation**
Commercial use and marketing of the particular invention (e.g., incorporation of a microprocessor in a pocket calculator).

Stage 4: **National dissemination**
The technology spreads throughout the land.

Stage 5: **International dissemination**
International marketing of the innovation.

Stage 6: **Decline**
The particular technology is in decline due to the rise of alternate technologies.

Stage 7: **Obsolescence**
The technology is replaced by newer ones.

---

tional dissemination, (5) international dissemination, (6) decline, and (7) obsolescence. (See table 1.) This seven-stage progression constitutes a technology generation. For each specific invention or group of inventions, there exists a corresponding technology generation. The concept itself is somewhat elastic since, in some cases, a finished product may be the object of a technology life-cycle (i.e., a car) and in other cases a component of a product (electronic fuel injection systems).

The technology life-cycles are not linear in that certain phases are subject to sharp acceleration and others slow down considerably. The most probable shape of the technology life-cycle is the ubiquitous S-shaped curve: initial slow growth followed by an exponential phase of rapid growth ending with a logistic phase of peaking and decline.

A careful study of leading technological countries in the contemporary period will show that their leadership comes from successful mastery and control of the technology cycle and in particular the use of the "leapfrog" principle. This means either skipping a stage within a technology generation (which we call a minor leapfrog) or skipping an entire generation to arrive on the ground floor of the next one before anyone else (major leapfrog). Japan's technology strategy since the second world war has been implicitly based on this idea and to some degree France's current strategy in this area is also characterized by this approach. These two countries—even more than any other—have identified the enormous potential of information technologies—not just in the communication field but throughout the economy—and adapted their strategic orientation accordingly. The result is that they are redeploying their industrial structure to make full use of the new technologies while their competitors, including the U.S., are much slower in harnessing them. Carried to its logical conclusions, the Japanese thrust will result in the transfer of economic and (ultimately) political power from the Atlantic economy to the South-East Asia triangle of Japan, China, and the four mini-Japans. What Japan was unable to achieve by military means it is now realizing by carefully planned technological leapfrogs centered on microelectronics and its various applications.

As explained in Table 2, a minor leapfrog aims at skipping a stage within a technology generation. In the case of the earlier stages of discovery and invention, they can be skipped by one or more of the following ways:
- Purchase of patents.
- Importing the inventors (brain drain).
- Industrial espionage.

In the case of the later stages of innovation and dissemination, the appropriate policies are:
- Adopt and adapt policies.
- Marketing strategies.

In both these latter cases, speed is of the essence since slowness in execution means the loss of the comparative advantage.

Throughout the sixties and early seventies (indeed since the Meiji restoration), Japan has purchased patents, conducted amiable industrial espionage, and in some cases imported inventors. The Japanese have also made superb use of the adopt and adapt idea and have consistently marketed their products before their competitors. Here are some illustrative examples:

Table 2

The Leapfrog Principle As a Technology Strategy

General Type	Purpose	Appropriate Policies
Minor Leapfrog (Skip a stage within a technology genera-tion.)	1. Leapfrog discovery or invention stage.	1. Purchase of patents. 2. Import the inventors. 3. Industrial espionage.
	2. Leapfrog innova-tion/dissemination phases.	1. Adopt and adapt. 2. National and interna-tional marketing strategies.
Major Leap Frog (Skip an entire technol-ogy generation.)	1. Arrive first at the next technology genera-tion.	1. Medium-term forecast-ing of technology. 2. Medium-term economic forecasting. 3. Medium-term socio-psy-chological forecasting.
	2. Skip the next tech-nology generation and arrive first at the one af-ter that.	1. Long-term technology forecasting. 2. Long-term economic forecasting. 3. Long-term socio-psy-chological forecasting. 4. Basic research.

• The Japanese optical and audio industries have developed using West-ern technology and (in the early stages) Western components.

• Japanese industry sat out the black-and-white-television stage, prefer-ring to adopt and adapt foreign inventions and then come in strong with their color television sets and dominate the market. 217433

• France's videotex system Antiope-Titan borrows heavily in technology and system architecture from its rival, the British Prestel system.

Major Leapfrogs in the Information Field

The major leapfrog, which involves skipping an entire technology genera-tion (either the present or a future one), stands and falls on the basis of one key element: the accuracy and comprehensiveness of the forecasting in tech-nology, economics, and social psychology. Technology cycles must be accu-rately forecast—and in particular the gestation times (period between stages of the same technology generation) and transition times (period between the beginning of one technology generation and the next one). Three elements are crucial here: the technical element, the economic element (will the prod-uct be profitable?), and the social-psychological element (will the public ac-cept or reject the new product?). Failure to consider carefully all three, and their interdependencies, will lead to great industrial failures.

Here are some examples of successful major leapfrogs.

• The Japanese digital watch industry has completely upstaged and de-throned the Swiss watch industry, traditionally the undisputed leader.

- In 1979, U.S. dominance in microchip production of 16K RAM chips was complete. In 1982, Japan is rapidly effecting a stranglehold on the 64K RAM chip and is also preparing to corner the market of very large scale integration chips of 256K ram.
- France's telephone system is moving in one fell swoop from the most antiquated in Europe to the best in the world (using fibre optics and videotex technology).
- Canada's videotex TELIDON is one generation ahead of its British and French rivals. It may, however, be counterleapfrogged by a U.S. or Japanese entry in the near future.

Here, on the other hand, are examples of unsuccessful leapfrogs.

- Quadraphonic sound in the mid-seventies (due to consumer rejection).
- The much touted picture-phone (due to perhaps temporary consumer resistance).
- Polaroid's intant movie Polavision (due to inaccurate assessment of competing technologies).
- The Franco-British supersonic Concorde (due to failure to forecast the energy crisis, the power of the environmental lobby, and the efficiency of the Concorde's competitor, the jumbo jets).

The Leapfrog Principle As Great Equalizer

There is, interestingly enough, a surprising morality to the leapfrog principle: it is the weapon of the underdog, the also-ran, the follower. In fact, the leader or pioneer is constantly exposing himself to leapfrogging and, as a result, if the principle is valid it becomes a great equalizer, a weapon for the weak and not for the strong. Inherent in information technology is the fact that information in all its forms is very difficult to protect because it can be copied with impunity. The great danger of the information society is the threat to privacy. The other side of the same coin, however, is the fact that information cannot be hoarded by information-capitalists and used to subjugate others. The leapfrog principle takes care of that.

Ultimately, the leapfrog principle inherent in microelectronic technology presents the single most potent source of hope for the weak of this world and if applied universally may well guarantee that no single country remains in a leadership position indefinitely. Japan was, after all, once a Third World country. The New Japans, the newly-industrializing countries of the Third World, are also in the leapfrog business. In fact, as Jean-Jacques Servan-Schreiber and others have pointed out, the new microelectronic revolution may allow the most gigantic of all leapfrogs: skipping the entire stage of traditional Western industrialization (with the Third World adopting, right away, the newest technologies). Seen in this light, the present and next decade will be an interesting period of leapfrogs and counterleapfrogs conferring temporary advantages to all the players as long as they can successfully effect the particular leapfrog they are planning. This will by no means come automatically and requires more and more accurate forecasting. Future studies, then, will be seen increasingly as not just for utopian dreamers, but as a key to survival itself.

This article is based on GAMMA's on-going multi-client program on the Human and Economic Impacts of the Information Revolution. All inquiries concerning this program should be addressed to GAMMA, University of Montreal, 3535 Queen Mary, Suite 210, Montreal H3V IH8, Quebec, Canada.

Doing the Traditional Untraditionally

by

Frederick Williams

As we move well into the decade of the 1980s, there is no paucity of attention given to the so-called "new technologies" of communication. In the centripetal view, at the heart of most of these innovations are the digital microprocessor ("chip"), telecommunications advances, or the combination of the two. In a centrifugal view, these technologies mostly refer to the wide variety of contemporary and visible "hardware" (i.e., equipment) innovations—for example, satellites, video tape and disc, large ("mainframe") and small ("personal," "home," "micro-") computers, hand-held and arcade electronic games (specialized computers), giant-screen television sets, and the further panoply of home entertainment and office electronic devices.

Despite the increasing attention given to this virtual explosion in technologies, we have hardly begun to explore their deeper social consequences.

On the one hand, our daily press tells us of new and expanded uses of television, including pay-TV, video cassette or disc, and TV cable services offering everything from pornography to armchair grocery shopping. We read of miniature computers entering our lives as electronic hand-held games, appliances that we can turn on and off by talking to them, and units that will both balance our checkbooks and turn off our sprinklers. Business publications abound in descriptions of management information systems, electronic mail, teleconferencing, and the worlds of "CAD-CAM" (computer-assisted design, computer-assisted management). So popular has been the arrival of the new technologies into the organization environment that the so-called "office of the future" is already a cliché.

At the other extreme, we have the prophetic visions of our future as conjured up by Marshall McLuhan, Buckminister Fuller, Isaac Asimov, Gerard K. O'Neill, and others. We can add to these the more down to earth, yet sweeping forecasts of "post-industrialism," "the age of discontinuity," "century of mismatch," "information society," and even the entrance of the "knowledge worker."

Is there a middle view between these two extremes—a focus for study of social consequences that momentarily disconnects us from our television sets

Frederick Williams is professor of communication and former dean (1972-80) of the Annenberg School of Communications at the University of Southern California.

or arcade games, yet does not propel us into galactic revelations of our human destiny?

One middle-ground approach to investigation of the social impacts of the new technologies is to examine their effects collectively upon many of our traditional institutions and services. What are their consequences, for example, upon leisure or transportation? Such examinations—a few summary observations of which are on the following pages—may lead us to conclude that the so-called "communications revolution" is not about to come crashing down upon us in one massive "third wave." Instead, we may sense that it has already permeated many of our traditional ways of carrying out everyday life. We are already doing some of the traditional untraditionally.

Following are brief summaries of observations in the areas of transportation, politics, health care, work, and leisure.

Transportation

For most of the first three-quarters of the twentieth century, transportation was one of the largest growth areas of the American economy and a topic seldom treated in crisis terms. All of this came to an abrupt end in 1973 with the Arab oil embargo, the shortages six years later, and the 1000% rise of crude oil prices over a decade.

In the 1980s, we are witnessing many changes in our petroleum-based transportation system, including its replacement in some cases with communication systems. In research circles, these are called communication-transportation trade-offs. Certainly we already have many existing examples of communication-transportation trade-offs, but we seldom think of them as a substitution of electronic movement for people work. For example, we have been letting "our fingers do the walking" for some time now when we have shopped in the *Yellow Pages*. All types of home entertainment that have evolved in the present century are in a sense transportation trade-offs because they are bringing the entertainment or the performance to our home rather than transporting us to it.

In some respects, we can look at the growth of communication-transportation trade-offs in terms of information network services that are deliverable to the home. For example, a study by Herbert Dordick and his associates (*The Emerging Marketplace*, Ablex, 1981) predicted that banking and entertainment services will be used in roughly 50% of all households in the U.S. by 1995. Other projections of adoption of nontraditional ways of receiving traditional services include (percentage of adopting out of total households):

- Information such as addresses, numbers, calendar of events: 45%.
- Home security such as fire and police alarms: 40%.
- Shopping by catalog: 30%.
- Directory of goods and services: 30%.
- Personal message systems: 30%.
- Games: 30%.
- Public information such as zoning regulations, elections, law making: 25%.
  - Library services: 20%.

"Teleconferencing" in all of its forms is another example of a communication-transportation trade-off. Usually, when we think of teleconferencing, business applications come up first. Of course, there are some ways in which teleconferencing may be relatively less desirable than our traditional way of attending a national or regional business meeting. Travel is often considered as a perk, so perhaps one cannot directly substitute teleconferencing as this type of reward. There is also the problem of people's fear of adapting to the new technologies. It is increasingly obvious that participation in a video conference is not something that comes naturally to us. Teleconferencing may alter the desired power structure in certain situations, giving advantages to people who have better command in audio and visual mode, or to participants who have the superior equipment or control over that equipment. Nonetheless, teleconferencing seems to be rapidly becoming a fact of life in business and governmental worlds. As networks become more accessible and less expensive, and as fuel costs continue to rise, we can certainly expect teleconferencing to increase.

The business environment, however, is not the only application of teleconferencing. In a sense, telecommunications as used in education can represent a form of teleconferencing. Consider the Instructional Television Fixed Service facilities where students are seated in a classroom that is relatively normal except for the existence of two or three remotely operated television cameras. These cameras capture the image of the instructor, or images of any charts or graphs that are to be presented. The captured images and sounds are then transmitted into remote classrooms where students are seated before small television receivers. At different points in the lecture it is possible to "raise one's hand" electronically be pressing a buzzer that will sound in the master classroom and the student's question can be transmitted "upstream" as a radio signal.

Studies of the use of teleconferencing with the Instructional Television Fixed Service facilities indicate a number of advantages. One is that many students say that they are taking advanced work that they might not ever take had they not had the opportunity to do it on-site in their company. Also, there are the added advantages of reduced costs, savings of time from commuting, and the like.

Still another fascinating application of the telecommunications infrastructure is in the concept of the "new rural society" as envisaged by the late Peter C. Goldmark. In describing his strategies for developing the rural society, Goldmark drew upon results of British research that indicated that the greatest single problem in urban decentralization was likely to be "reduction in operating efficiency due to the stretching of communications links." The key then would be to devise ways of stretching, and for this Goldmark proposed a system of new community communications networks.

The main network would be a substantial extension of the telephone system so as to include videophone and computer linkages for data transmission. The objective would be to interconnect as fully as possible everybody in the community. This would be just as critical as the streets, electricity, and other utilities are to a modern city. Stretching was to be accomplished by having all homes just as connected as if they were in physical proximity, perhaps even more so. There would be further layers to this network, including radio and television broadcasting, two-way cable communications systems, videotext services, and networks linking the operating components of community government, emergency services, travel services, schools, libraries, and health-type services. In all, the strategy would be to try to maintain most of the communications advantages of the urban environment, but to do this in such a way that the community would be relatively free of the type of congestion typically found in the great cities.

By the same token, the traditional concept of community takes on quite different physical forms when we think of communities as they are formed on communication networks. Too often we think of community in physical terms, but for us humans it can just as well refer to community of interests. The freedom from geographic and transportation factors that communications provides is a basis for new types of communities, ones assembled via communications networks.

Politics

Political systems and communication systems are two sides of the same coin. For most of history, we can see how the limits of political influence were defined by the limits of the communication system, which itself was configured by geographic and transportation factors. It is not difficult to see how the spread of most civilizations until the nineteenth century was limited by the extent of the transportation system.

What marked the nineteenth century? With the invention of the telegraph, the communications networks of nations were able to transcend transportation ones. Further advances in communications such as the telephone and the radio in the late nineteenth and early twentieth centuries made possible changes in political orders heretofore restricted by geographic and transportation limits. The rise to world power in the mid twentieth century of such geographically dispersed nations as the United States and the Soviet Union would have been impossible under a political system where the communications and transportation infrastructures were necessarily synonymous.

Now, as we are witnessing the communications technological innovations of our times and are about to enter the twenty-first century, there are many signs that changes in the communications infrastructure are bringing about changes in how we operate the political structure.

We can see this internationally, for example, in debates over the "new world information order." As Third World nations are potentially threatened by a form of "electronic colonialism," they are arguing for a greater access to, and control over, the world's communication infrastructure.

There are many examples even closer to home of change driven by communications technology. For example, our election campaigns are increasingly taking on the characteristics of "media blitzes." Nor is this to overlook the consequences of televised presidential debates. Another potentially fascinating example of change is in the capability for instant polling, or "dial in" voting, as the U.S. becomes wired with two-way interactive cable systems. Finally, to return to the national scene, we have seen the rise of electronic diplomacy in our time, as meetings between heads of state (Begin and Sadat, for example) were prompted in part by the questions and challenges of TV news commentators. As heads of state appear directly on television, or, for that matter, as revolutionaries—as in the case of the Iranian hostage crisis—

appear directly on TV news shows, the normal channels of international diplomacy are bypassed altogether.

Since the Vietnam War, we have seen a tightening loop between the occurrence of world events, their near instantaneous transmission to us, our reaction to them, and then our reactions to our reaction. Most citizens of the world followed World War II in terms of morning headlines (with adjacent maps of battle fronts), radio news flashes, newsreels, and magazine reports. There was a technically imposed communications lag between the event and public perception of it. This lag often made it possible for presidential commentary to accompany the news of the event, thus shaping public interpretation of it. International negotiations were reported mostly in terms of what diplomats wanted the public to think, coupled with whatever scraps of additional news reporters could uncover.

Certainly, for the United States at least, television in the Vietnam War marked a turning point in coverage of international crises. On-the-spot reporting was delivered so directly and quickly to the nation's living room each evening that it was difficult to interpret Lyndon Johnson's policy announcements. The direct message of the devastation of war was already digested by the public. The pronouncements of the president came *after* citizens' personal opinions were formed. We could see this also a decade later when President Carter was reduced to being a TV bystander like ourselves during the hostage crisis in Iran. Iranian revolutionaries cleverly bypassed diplomatic channels altogether, even appearing on interview programs. On several occasions when Jimmy Carter was asked his opinions of the latest Iranian position, he was forced to preface his remarks with "Well, I watched that program, too."

Further, we might even ask ourselves: Is democracy obsolete? The world of the eighteenth century in which the United States Constitution was written differs far more from the world of the impending twenty-first century than it does from the birthplace of democratic theory in the Athenian world of the fourth century B.C. A citizen of ancient Athens would be less challenged to understand the workings of democracy and revolutionary meetings in Boston's Faneuil Hall in the 1770s than would an American patriot transported two-and-a-quarter centuries later into the midst of Washington, D.C.

In the time since the American Revolution, we have transformed the speed of communications from the speed of a transportation system to the speed of light. Through computers we are automating the storage, manipulation, and retrieval of potentially infinite amounts of political information. With the merger of telecommunication and computer technologies, our power over information makes possible a communications infrastructure instantaneously and totally incorporating all citizens. No longer is a political event limited by the distances voice can be heard, nor a political unit limited to the distance we can travel in one day. No longer are political perceptions delayed by the times necessary for transportation systems to deliver the news. No longer does government perception of news reaction depend upon flow from citizens via elected representatives to the central government. The political order of nations is rapidly being transformed from the written document and spoken word to an electronic communications network enveloping all.

The new political order is the communications infrastructure. Such a transformation would probably be incomprehensible to the citizen of eighteenth-century Boston, including the writers of the U.S. Constitution, under which we are daily governed.

Ideally, however, the new communications technologies offer an opportunity for citizen information participation undreamed of by our founding fathers. We are faced with a challenge of adjusting our democracy away from the constraints of the eighteenth century and toward the advantages of the twenty-first. Democracy is not dead, but some of our ways of practicing it are rapidly becoming obsolete.

Health Care

Medicine is traditionally a high adopter of technology. As might be expected, the applications of communications technologies in medicine are growing. All of these are set against a context of changes in the delivery of health care. For example, we are now faced with the increasingly specialized physician. Specialization brings with it the problem of distribution. To some degree, this provides a context for the implementation of telecommunications networks for the distribution of specialized services to remote paramedics, or so-called "telemedicine."

We have also seen the growth of medical information systems, at least among larger institutions that can share the costs of the network and that also need the access to very diverse information.

Perhaps one of the most fascinating speculations on doing the traditional untraditionally in medicine comes from Jerrold S. Maxmen's book *The Post-Physician Era* (John Wiley, 1976). Maxmen predicts that in 50 years the computer will replace the physician as a primary agent of health care. Fewer highly specialized physician-researchers could monitor and constantly improve the automated medical decision systems. The necessary "human" link between the computer and the patient would be a health-care professional selected for talents in interpersonal communication and sensitivity toward the ill. Simple medical advice would be dispensed directly by the computer to the patient. After all, computers and physicians do share a number of characteristics. Both depend on memory, or a "knowledge base," for many types of problem-solving. Both have strategies for evaluating problems against their knowledge base. Physicians have medical history forms, their routines, and questions that by the process of elimination narrow down to identification and analysis of the specific problem at hand. Computers have "branching" program procedures, which take input data and attempt to assess them in successive steps. Both physician and computer use procedures whereby data can be evaluated in alternative ways for comparative purposes.

Whether Maxmen's prediction is eventually realized or not, it is an intriguing thought to imagine the utility of regional, national, if not international data bases that assemble the collective experiences of a great variety of diagnostic instances. These assemblages, by including rare and exceptional cases, could increase the diagnostic power of medicine itself. Not only would such systems provide a basis for pooling the collective experiences of experts, but could continually add on-going diagnostic experiences as well. If this system were a network of computers in remote diagnostic stations, we could

107

have a system of almost unlimited growth and coverage.

Because great amounts of a physician's time are devoted to diagnostic procedures that can be conducted by a single human mind with access to reference books, it is not likely that physicians as we know them will pass soon from the scene, let alone be replaced totally by computers. Nonetheless, we are already experiencing the growth of computer applications in medicine. A more conservative prediction is that just as the computer has not replaced the designer or manager, it will not replace the physician. However, we may expect a "computer-assisted medicine" to evolve in ways not dissimilar to computer-aided design (CAD) or computer-assisted management (CAM).

"Telemedicine" is not all that new. However, with the coming of the telecommunications infrastructure aided by satellite as well as stand-alone disc and tape technologies, we can expect telemedicine to grow. Most of us already know of successful experimentation with the use of satellite communications to link remote areas with centralized medical facilities (e.g., the ATS-6 projects).

As research has revealed, medical personnel, patients, and researchers are generally satisfied with the results of the experiments, which include regular "telemedical" diagnoses and treatments of individuals in remote locations. Human adaptation to telecommunications systems has been demonstrated as feasible and practical. Costs are high, but there is promise that the investment can be amortized over a reasonable period of service. It is also concluded that other services simultaneously provided by the telecommunications infrastructure (TV broadcasting, education, navigation, business data links) will significantly reduce the cost for medical (or telemedical) applications.

As in most applications of new technologies, we can expect attitudinal barriers to their adoption. Potential users often have quite fixed attitudes from prior experiences with different technologies in everyday life. Television, for example, is thought of only as an entertainment medium, as is videocassette technology. It is rarely considered how television might be used for educational or two-way educational purposes. Radio is often considered as simple "background noise" for home, car, or office, rather than a potentially useful communications medium for dissemination of information. Many potential users of sophisticated applications of telephone service, such as conferencing or facsimile transmission, are unaware of such services. Computers are often considered excessively "complex and uncontrollable."

Although there is much emphasis upon computers and telecommunication networks in consideration of communications technology in medicine, there is still another very relevant dimension. This is the public image of medicine and health care that are created in our mass media, particularly in entertainment television. A decade or so ago, for example, we had *Dr. Kildare* and *Ben Casey*, then later *Marcus Welby*, and then *Medical Center, Emergency, General Hospital*, and the ever popular reruns of *M*A*S*H*. Much of the public attitude regarding medical issues is open to conditioning by both the show business treatments and the sensationalist news coverage we have seen of such weighty issues as birth control, abortion, genetic counseling, patients' right to use certain unapproved medicines (laetrile), test-tube babies, and the recent popular exploitations of genetic manipulation.

If all these issues have not already taken their toll in challenges to individuals in our society, they pose a monumental challenge to our abilities to generate value-based judgments in a democracy. We have not used our national media to alert society sufficiently to these issues in order to provide a forum for full and balanced deliberation. Somehow, we must use the new communications technologies, especially their interactive potential, to facilitate social awareness of biomedical techniques that may soon have the power to alter human life itself.

Perhaps there is an even more basic use of our communications technologies: to promote a positive public attitude about health itself. Too often we consider "health" as only the opposite of "disease" rather than a positive goal to be sought in everyday living. If we were to invest as much in our national media for a campaign to build highly positive attitudes toward physical and psychological health as we do for patent medicines, sugar cereals, and deodorants, it might accomplish as much toward prevention of disease as we do with all other communications technologies used in the curing of same.

Work

Nobody seems to be quibbling these days about whether we are entering an era of post-industrialism. What is of greater concern are the details of our changing economy, work force, and potential areas of growth. All of this is set against a visible change in the nation's work force. The average age of workers is increasing as health care becomes more effective and as retirement age is boosted. More special interest groups are demanding employment rights, as reflected in the rising visibility of ethnic minorities in the '60s, women in the early '70s, homosexual groups in the late '70s, as well as the current push by handicapped and elderly groups. The average educational level of the work force is steadily increasing, a reflection of not only the educational system but the demands of the workplace. The educated worker is demanding more control over the workplace (thus the rise of "participatory management"). If Daniel Bell (*The Coming of Post-Industrial Society*) is correct, the shifting values of the work force and the workplace will carry over to society as a whole.

Because so much is written elsewhere, little need be said here about the growth of telecommunications or computer-related industries and services. One need only to look to the classified ads for job opportunities in any of our major papers to see evidence of rapidly expanding employment opportunities in such areas as computer-assisted management, electronic funds management, as well as in the design and manufacture of all the hardware and software necessary to perform these services.

Although executives are not yet, nor will they probably ever be, living in absolutely paperless offices, there is hardly a manager who has not been affected by the necessity for adoption and implementation of office technologies. This is not only the usual automation of accounting systems, but now word processing, electronic mail, and other technologies that generally fall under the term of "computer-assisted management." The traditional tasks of an office in records-keeping, information gathering and dissemination, product or services monitoring, and general coordination are all being influenced by the communications technology revolution.

There are many good reasons to anticipate that the communications revolution will have as significant a qualitative as quantitative impact upon occupations. One focus is upon characteristics of the so-called "knowledge worker," the individual involved in the acquisition and manipulation of information or knowledge. Engineers and physicians, teachers, managers of data systems, financial analysts, and individuals in research and development are a few examples of this occupational area. What is important is not the detailed definition of this occupation, but that the number of clearly knowledge-based occupations is increasing rapidly in our society. An even more important point is that these occupations are qualitatively different from others in several important characteristics.

Productivity is difficult to gauge in knowledge work. In agriculture, productivity is easily defined as how much one person, or family, plus a horse or mule could grow and harvest in one season. That is, what was achieved (output) relative to what was invested (input)?

How is the productivity of research in an engineering manufacturing organization to be gauged? Research investments (particularly in basic research) might not have visible payoffs for years to come, certainly outdistancing the span of control of any cost-accounting system. How is productivity to be gauged when a governmental office goes "on-line" with a new computer system? (Witness our own experiences with attempts of universities to devise professor "workload" formulas.) Certainly it is theoretically possible for productivity to be assessed, but the practical steps for such assessment are still a matter of considerable dispute. For the most part, if we were to accommodate what is theoretically possible for assessing productivity of many types of information, the costs of making such assessments might themselves be so high as to be "unproductive." The answers to nontraditional assessments of productivity are complex.

Leisure

Mention leisure to someone and you are apt to find yourself in a discussion of one of the least understood social-psychological concepts of the twentieth century. For a type of activity that we all like to spend some time in each day and that business sees as one of the largest growth areas in our post-industrial economy, it is paradoxical that we know so little about the basics of it. Often in Western civilization, particularly where the Puritan work ethic dominates, we tend to view leisure in terms of a narrow definition of that which is not "work." Our modern challenge is to broaden the concept of leisure, to see it as a necessary and fulfilling part of life and most of all to learn how to use it. Leisure is not just nonwork; it is recovery from fatigue, deliverance from boredom, and personal growth.

How do Americans spend their leisure time? Although going to sports events, pursuing hobbies, or exercising might come to mind, studies show that watching television is the number one leisure-time activity. We spend roughly 40% of our free time with television, and all indications are that this figure will increase as the work week reduces and as the new communications technologies transform our environment. Most television sets in the U.S. are now on over six hours a day, tuned into what adds up to about five

110

million hours of programming annually from over 700 stations.

What kind of leisure is television? One generalization that has emerged in 25 years of social research is that most people watch TV simply as a means to relax. Although program tastes and the resulting TV rating systems are evidence of the importance of particular programs or types of programs to viewers, there is good evidence that as often as not the decision is simply one of watching TV rather than planning for a detailed schedule of shows. Accordingly, we will seldom turn on our television sets for information or for quality entertainment, but simply for purposes of distraction, much the way staring into a campfire is relaxing to us.

There is also the television we watch simply for arousal, such as the "T&A" or "jiggling t-shirt" shows of the 1978-79 season. (Can you remember any plot from Charlie's Angels?) This is "junk food TV." It gives immediate satisfaction, but it has no long-range value. From the TV business side of things, it gets big prime-time ratings, and that is why there is so much of it.

Unfortunately, we spend little leisure time with quality television, such as with the imports from the British Broadcasting Corporation (*Civilisation, America, Ascent of Man*) and even occasional breakthroughs in American programs (e.g., *Cosmos*). These programs are persuasive evidence that leisure hours spent with television can be enlightening, if not instructive, in a pleasant sort of way. We have even seen this type of television emerge on the commercial channels (as in the dramatization of Alex Haley's novel *Roots*, or later miniseries such as *Holocaust* and *Roots, The Next Generation*). These programs have literary value. They are interpretive, creative, humane, have an excellence of form, and contribute ideas of lasting value.

All of the contemporary forecasts of new delivery technologies (tape, disc, direct-broadcast satellite, cable and pay cable) project a vast increase in TV fare. One forecast is "television will be like radio," or another analogy is the transition from the mass magazine of two decades ago to the specialized magazines of today. Despite the emergence of art and cultural programming channels and sports alternatives now offered via the new technologies, there is still no firm basis for believing that we will have an improved type of TV leisure in our future.

New technologies are exceedingly expensive, and so that investors may get a return for their money, it is not improbable that mass marketing techniques will spill over into the programming of many of these technologies. As a matter of fact, they already have in terms of current disc and tape sales, as well as pay TV program purchases.

As long ago as 1959, we were warned that it is not what television does to us that counts, but what we do with television. The communications technology revolution is transforming the television marketplace. Perhaps before mass marketing takes its toll in moving our current program mediocrity from one set of technologies to another, we could take advantage of this transformation to use television for more varied and constructive types of leisure.

The Shaping of Things to Come

Given the foregoing observations on the communications technology revolution relative to transportation, politics, health care, work, and leisure, what further, and longer-range, consequences should merit our concern? Let me speculate on the likely direction of answers to this first question with a series of further ones.

1. How can we better understand the transformations that the new technologies bring to our traditional institutions and services? Are there common phenomena, variables, constructs, processes, or effects among these applications? For example, can an understanding of computer-assisted management in business contribute to computer-assisted medicine? Can adoption of innovations in medicine aid us in accelerating adoption of new technologies in education? Is there a general theory of "communication technology impact?" What are its parameters?

2. If we do gain a deeper, more theoretical understanding of the consequences of communications technologies upon institutions and services, can we use this theory to maximize desired effects? What are these desired effects and how do we accommodate a balance between goals of efficiency and social benefits? How can applications be directed toward solving such global problems as the threat of nuclear holocaust, the population explosion, food shortages, drought, pollution, or resource conservation?

3. How does political context affect the growth and applications of the new technologies? For example, will the current deregulation of communications technologies in the U.S. further stratify the "information rich" and the "poor?" In a climate of deregulation, how can programs with "sociologizing" goals be implemented? On the other hand, how much and what kinds of control will stifle efforts for growth toward "economizing" goals? What are the interactions between communications technology growth in communist as against free enterprise political and economic contexts?

4. What of the management of these technologies? If we understand their impacts and can define goals, how can we insure that we are promoting optimum applications? Are contemporary theories of management sufficient to aid us in this direction? How can the technologies themselves assist their management? What new types and training of managers are implied?

5. What are the prospects of going beyond the "traditional" in the applications of communications technologies? Is there theory that will aid us in creative speculations? (For example, are we capable of creating de Chardin's "noosphere"?) Can we go beyond the applications of communications technology for information, education, management, entertainment, or persuasion? What about enlightenment?

These questions present us with a fundamental and concrete option. We can be the shaper or the shaped of tomorrow's social consequences of the new technologies.

The choice is ours.

Portions of this paper are adapted by permission from the author's *The Communications Revolution* (Sage, Beverly Hills, California, 1982).

Communication Education
for the
Twenty-First Century

by

William Work

Daniel Bell's observation about the evolution of communication is to the point. Said he, "Human societies have seen four distinct revolutions in the character of social interchange: in speech, in writing, in printing, and now in telecommunications." Each of these revolutions has added to available communication options; each has increased the demands on the capabilities of individual communicators. None of the communication innovations has made any of its predecessors obsolete. Reading and writing did not outmode speech, nor did television make either the printing press or radio obsolete. Daniel Bell's inventory of communication revolutions will grow—at an increasingly rapid pace. Some say that computer-assisted communications constitute a new communications-revolution-in-the-making. Others, looking farther down the road, foresee new kinds of human relationships growing out of genetic and biochemical experimentation and even, eventually, direct brain-to-brain communication. One implication is clear: citizens of the future will need to understand and be able to use a rapidly growing array of new technologies—technologies that extend the individual's and society's communicative capacities.

Two fundamental questions need to be addressed. What are the social and technological developments—now in progress or anticipated during this century—that have important implications for the communication education needs of tomorrow's citizenry? In the light of these developments, what communication competencies will be needed in the twenty-first century?

These are global questions. My responses will inevitably be limited by the biases and parochialisms of my own cultural heritage. I must, of necessity, use the United States as my frame of reference; I hope that my observations have some usefulness for persons with other orientations.

At the outset, let us agree that today's communication education has achieved only limited success. John and Jane, all too frequently, lack real proficiency in such basics as reading, writing, speaking, listening, and critical

William Work is executive secretary, Speech Communications Association Annandale, Virginia.

viewing. College aptitude test scores have been declining; the goal of conquering illiteracy—even in America's privileged society—has only been partially met. Worldwide, the literacy battle is being lost. So, as we look toward the educational needs of the future, we must acknowledge that we have not adequately met the educational needs of the present. What, then, are the currents in society that will help determine the communication competencies that individuals will need through the twilight of the twentieth century and the dawning of the twenty-first?

There is a consensus that America has entered what Daniel Bell calls a "post-industrial," "information" society. Already, more than half of America's work force and Gross National Product are in such "information industries" as telecommunications, data processing, publishing, and education itself.[1] As Peter Drucker has pointed out, "Knowledge has already become the primary industry, the industry that supplies the economy the essential and central resources of production."[2]

But knowledge that is not communicated and translated into action remains largely impotent. Robert Theobald prefers to call the post-industrial age "the communications era." In his words, "We have entered the communications era . . . partly because so much of the society is now engaged in communications activities and partly because the survival of the world now depends on our ability to listen to each other and to learn from the experience of others. . . . The need to create more effective intercommunication is the second, more critical, implication of the communications era."[3]

The emergence of the communications era, like all revolutions, means that, along with promises to be fulfilled, there are problems to be solved. Jan Henrik Nyheim, a Norwegian publisher, put it well when he wrote:

> The information society embraces every action, process and piece of equipment, all personnel, every institution and resource involved in the collection, production, storing, distribution and use of information. It may be visualized as an expanding universe, in which overall density and pressure increases all the time. This illustration suggests why greater information output tends to clog the information channels and highways, why it seems more difficult to get the facts while at the same time more facts are getting more available every day, why many people tend to get more confused and frustrated instead of better informed and relaxed. And it suggests why paper-based information is expanding everywhere, in spite of the fact that armies of experts for many years have insisted that paper-based information is dying.[4]

Communication overload in an increasingly complex communication environment challenges the communication capabilities of us all. The proliferation of information leads to greater fragmentation of information, and fragmentation creates islands of expertise not easily bridged. Robert Maynard Hutchins identified a growing dilemma when he observed, more than a quarter of a century ago, that the *intelligibility* of our messages has declined while the *means* of communication have improved.[5] And all of this is happening within a context of social change that seems to be accelerating out of control.

Consider the computer. The capacity of computers to store, organize, and manage large quantities of information strains the human computer, the mind. The dramatic growth in computer speed and capacity and the dra-

114

matic reduction in computer costs continues, seemingly, unabated. In the industrialized world, computers are already commonplace in the world of work; they will soon be as commonplace in our homes as the telephone and the television set. Clearly, computer literacy is an emerging educational mandate of our time. The concept of a computer for every learner—whether in a formal school setting or elsewhere—is gaining acceptance. Stephen Willoughby put it this way:

> Ideally, every high school graduate should have learned at least one computer language and should have plenty of opportunity and incentive to use a computer to solve problems relating to science, social science, mathematics, language, and other fields of thought. With the reduction in cost of small computers and computer terminals, this is not an unrealistic prospect now and it will become even more reasonable with each passing year. Certainly in the future, educated adults will be expected to have at least this much knowledge and experience with computers.[6]

Today's computers, marvelous though they are, will seem primitive in comparison with the computers now on the drawing board in this and other countries. Computers that are user-friendly and that produce and respond to "natural speech" are under development and will soon be a reality. Further, according to Lewis M. Branscomb of IBM, current trends "will ultimately completely obscure technical distinctions between information technologies. Typewriters, television, movies, telephones, and even radio, records, and tapes will become interrelated and interchangeable."[7]

Let us consider one specific example. The voice-activated typewriter (VAT), we are now told, will be available commercially as early as 1983. Ultimately, it has been predicted, more than a million typists and secretaries in America will in some measure be displaced by this new application of computer science. As early as 1990, the value of VATs produced will exceed the value of conventional typewriters produced.[8] Consider the implications of this one technological development for education in communication through speech.

The computer is, of course, only one of many communication-related technologies that are changing the nature and scope of human communications. Of particular concern here are those technologies that are interactive—that allow individuals to create and send messages or images as well as receive them. Our traditional media of mass communication—books, magazines, newspapers, television, radio—have tended to be one-way. These media have linked professional communicators with passive, lay audiences, audiences with only limited opportunities to respond. To these traditional media now are added two-way, interactive cable television, as well as inexpensive photocopiers and audio and video cassette recorders—all of which provide opportunities for the nonprofessional—the ordinary citizen—to create and disseminate communications to others.[9]

John Ciampa of the American Video Institute projects a stunning array of user options for videodisc technology. These range from the simple option of selecting a particular disc on a particular subject to view at a particular time to interpolating user responses—verbal or graphic—into the content of a disc for display, transmission, or re-recording. Exercising such options, Ciampa points out, is a far cry from the almost nonexistent options offered by network television. Says Ciampa, "The Nielsen ratings are like studying whether addicts prefer heroin in a tinted or a clear bag."[10] Full participation in the communication-rich environment of the future will demand communication competencies much more sophisticated than those needed for the consumption of prime-time commercial television.

There are a number of implications for communication education that derive from the fact that spaceship earth continues to shrink. Jet travel, satellite communications, and a growing worldwide direct-dial telephone network have facilitated communication between the peoples of many lands. The emergence of multinational corporations has been a prime factor in the growth of communications across national boundaries. Threats to the common well-being—overpopulation, food and energy shortages, resource depletion, pollution of air and water, and the possibilities of nuclear holocaust— have served to demonstrate the essential interdependence of all peoples of the world. Fortunately, communication is almost universally recognized as a preferable alternative to violence as a means for resolving or reducing conflicts. In the international arena, effective communication is truly a survival skill. The study of communication across cultures is still in its infancy, but we're beginning to learn to understand our own cultural biases and blinders, and we're beginning to learn to adapt to the biases and blinders of other cultures. Languages themselves are, of course, culturally biased. Furthermore, living languages, like all living things, change constantly, although often subtly. It is hard enough to "get a message across" with members of one's own culture; it is doubly difficult with persons whose histories, beliefs, and value systems are different.[11]

Someday, free and open communications among the world's cultures may reduce cultural dissonance to a level of insignificance. Someday, the world may enjoy the benefits of a universal language understood by all. Until that time, we will be well-advised to strive as best we can to transcend the barriers that our cultural diversities impose upon us.

The best efforts of pollsters and social-science researchers notwithstanding, it is difficult to identify emerging social movements, especially when in the midst of an ongoing social revolution. Those who have the temerity to describe our todays and predict our tomorrows project two alternatives for humankind: either we will develop the skills of a true participatory democracy, or we will surely slide into the abyss of autocracy and dictatorship. In the light of the apparent unwillingness of increasing numbers of Americans to exercise their rights at the polls, one can only hope that the present era represents the deep darkness before the dawn. Citizens can participate effectively in their own governance only if (1) they are informed; (2) they are encouraged to share in decision-making on matters that affect their own destinies; (3) they understand the need for accommodation between their own needs and the needs of others; and (4) they have the analytical and forensic skills needed to arrive at a position and advance it persuasively.[12]

Advocates of true participatory democracy see it as the successor to representative government. Theodore Clevenger, Jr., then president of the Speech Communication Association, said in 1972:

It is . . . awareness of individual helplessness which lies at the core of our

116

problem. What we confront is nothing less than the impending breakdown of representative government. Sometime before the year 2000, it will have become technologically obsolete. By that date, I predict that certain provisions of our Federal Constitution will have been rewritten, or else the Constitution and the Republic will have passed into history. During the last quarter of this century, we will move inexorably toward either dictatorship or paticipatory democracy.[13]

John Deethardt has set forth in some detail the conditions and educational requirements that will have to be met if direct, electronic participatory democracy is to become a reality.[14] True participatory democracy will require levels of skill in information management, analysis of data, decision-making, and persuasion demanded only of the governing elites in our present form of representative democracy.

We may now ask what kinds of educational programs will be required if the challenges implied in the social movements are to be met? Put another way, we may ask what communication competencies will citizens of tomorrow need in order to deal with the stresses and capitalize on the opportunities that the future promises? What are the communication "coping" skills for the communication era? What will be the characteristics of the "compleat communicator" in the year 2000?

Education itself, of course, is in flux. This is remarkable when one considers its traditional resistance to change. Of all our social institutions, education has been particularly prone to that part of the law of inertia that says, "A body at rest will stay at rest." Nevertheless, there is a consensus that teaching and learning will indeed be different in the twenty-first century. There will be more individualized, computer-assisted instruction; life-long learning will be firmly established; the distinctions between formal education and work-related experience will become blurred; learning in the home and in other non-classroom environments will increase; the individual learner will be a more proactive participant in the learning process; information embodied in a wide range of sight/sound learning resources will be available almost instantaneously and at low cost. Since education is itself essentially a communication process, we can expect both its efficiency and its palatability to improve as a result of the communication-era resources available to it.

Communication education programs of the future will, of course, continue to reflect the special and sometimes parochial needs and interests of the learners and of those who manage their learning environments. The attempt here will be to describe educational outcomes that will be of value to most citizens. We are *not* talking here about knowledge and skills that will be needed by communication professionals, by graduate-school professors of communication, or by the framers of communication policies. We *are* talking about competencies that will be needed by all members of society who want to maximize the personal and social rewards and minimize the personal and social hazards of the communications/information era.

1. The citizens of tomorrow will require, at the very least, the basic communication skills (in their native language) that continue to elude many today, namely, the skills of effective reading, writing, speaking, and listening. They will need what a former United States Commissioner of Education has called "comprehensive literacy." As I have written elsewhere,

"Comprehensive literacy" suggests that an individual has the full repertory of knowledge, skills, attitudes, and experiences needed to function effectively and comfortably in most communication situations. It suggests that in the process the individual develops and maintains a sense of self-confidence and self-sufficiency. It suggests the achievement of a reasonable mastery over one's symbolic environment—both the internal environment of thinking and conceptualizing, and the external environment of verbal and nonverbal messages received *from* and directed *to* others.[15]

2. The demands and opportunities of the twenty-first century will require a higher order of competency than we ordinarily associate with "basic skills." Thinking abilities and communication abilities are inextricably linked—developmentally and functionally. The communication era requires the acquisition of such higher-level cognitive capacities as: information-processing, concept-formation, problem-solving, conflict management, issues analysis, and creative thinking.

3. Communication literacy must be drawn from the full spectrum of the communication arts, sciences, and technologies. As noted, a functional understanding of computers—their capacities and limitations in home, learning, and vocational settings—will be required. Tomorrow's citizens should also be conversant with such emerging communication technologies as: teletext, videotex, interactive cable television, satellite communications, videodiscs, and the whole range of audio/video data recording technologies, not to mention such established technologies as telephony, radio, television, and photography. Our "compleat communicator" of the twenty-first century will need also to understand and be critically responsive to the communication dimensions of the fine arts and will need to understand the relationships between and among nonverbal, visual, and mathematical symbol systems.

4. Assuming that democracy and civilization survive, it seems likely that the twenty-first century will offer individuals unprecedented opportunities to participate in decisions that affect their own lives. Much of today's communication is what John Ciampa characterizes as "downhill" communication: communication from a powerful source set above and apart from the targeted receivers. As Ciampa says, "We set the stage for downhill communication in every aspect of our culture: education, media, theater, corporate structure."[16] There are signs that the passive reader/listener/viewer wants to change unidirectional monologue to bidirectional dialogue. The protests of the '60s and '70s represented people "talking back" to the authorities; employees are gaining the right to participate in management decisions; even such seemingly trivial cultural phenomena as citizens band (CB) radio and radio talk shows confirm an apparently growing need and desire for more dialogue. More widespread availability of such interactive media as cable television will multiply opportunities for human interaction. Fortunately, the interpersonal skills needed for constructive social intercourse can be learned.

5. Ecology, as most schoolchildren now know, has to do with interactions between an organism and its environment. Human beings are only beginning to become aware of and sensitized to their communication environments. We have taken communication for granted—much as, until recently, we took clean air, clean water, and unlimited supplies of petrochemicals for granted. Reflected in the unfolding of the communications revolution is a heightened

realization that communication is the very matrix of our civilization. We are also learning that our communication environment is becoming more complex, that it is shackled by myths from the past that have outlived their usefulness, and that it, like the physical environment, is vulnerable to a whole spectrum of special-interest assaults.

Ecology deals with *reciprocal* influences between inhabitants and environment. Just as we are beginning to learn of the effects of environmental pollution on our physical well-being, so we are beginning to understand the effects of the communication technologies and systems that we have created on the way we view ourselves and others. Edward Ploman, now with UNESCO, expressed it well when he wrote:

> In overall cultural terms, we are dealing with the emergence of a new communications and information environment. We introduced new time-scales of slow-motion and ultra-rapid, we changed the spatial scale by picturing the infinitely small and the outer reaches of cosmic space. We are beginning to perceive that changes in the modalities of communication are crucial in their impact on cultural forms and identities. New technologies reshape the information content of societies. Their larger impact is on the symbol systems which sustain all cultures and our images of the world. Through the new communications systems, we are dealing with the signals and messages which change us as well as those through which we act upon our environment.[17]

Twenty-first century communicators will function in a communication environment replete with both opportunities to be realized and difficulties to be overcome. It will be a communication-rich environment, offering a bewildering array of communication options. Information overload will be a continuing and, doubtless, growing problem. Coping with cultural barriers that have been sustained for centuries by ethnocentricity and militant nationalism will constitute a serious impediment to constructive international communications until we learn to focus more on our commonalities and less on our differences. The pen and the larynx and the cathode ray tube either are or are not mightier than the sword. Violence as the ultimate arbiter of human conflict has held sway throughout human history. Settling differences through the available means of communication—persuasion, negotiation, conciliation, compromise—is surely the most viable alternative to violence. Whether, in this age of communication, communication will triumph over terrorism, intimidation, threat, and violence remains to be demonstrated.

Notes

1. N. B. Hannay, "An Information Society," *Vital Speeches*, 46 (May 15, 1980), p. 461.

2. Ibid.

3. Robert Theobald, *Beyond Despair*, Revised Edition (Cabin John, MD: Seven Locks Press, Inc., 1981), p. 5.

4. Jan Henrik Nyheim, "The Age of Doubt," *Intermedia*, 9 (March, 1981), p. 10.

5. Quoted in Harold G. Shane, "Social Change and Educational Outcomes: 1980-2000," in Kathleen M. Redd and Arthur M. Harkins, Eds., *Education: A Time For Decisions*, (Washington, D.C.: World Future Society, 1980), p. 33.

6. Stephen S. Willoughby, "Teaching Mathematics: What is Basic?," (Washington, D.C.: Council for Basic Education: Occasional Paper 31, 1981), p. 39.

7. Lewis M. Branscomb, "Information: The Ultimate Frontier," *Science*, 203 (12 January 1979), p. 145.

8. News release for September 8, 1980, issued by International Resource Development Inc., Norwalk, CT.

9. Alvin Toffler, "A New Kind of Man in the Making," *New York Times Magazine*, March 9, 1981, p. 24 ff.

10. John Ciampa, "Video Discs Suggest a New Theory of Interactive Media," *Intermedia*, 9 (September, 1981), p. 46.

11. See Lane Jennings, "FUTURECOM: The Human Future in Communications," in Frank Feather, Ed., *Through the '80s*, (Washington, D.C.: World Future Society, 1980) pp. 302-307.

12. See Yoneji Masuda, "A Global Voluntary Information Network: The Most Hopeful Global Collective Means," in Frank Feather, op. cit., pp. 312-316.

13. Theodore Clevenger, Jr., "Communication and the Survival of Democracy," *Spectra*, 9 (February, 1973), p. 4.

14. John F. Deethardt, "Education and Electronically Mediated Democracy," in Redd and Harkins, op. cit., pp. 122-131.

15. William Work, "Toward Comprehensive Communication Literacy," *Communication Education*, 27 (November, 1978), p. 337.

16. John Ciampa, op. cit., p. 45.

17. Edward Ploman, "The Communications Revolution," *Intermedia*, 9 (September, 1981), p. 11.

Promises

Videotex:
Blessing or Bane
for the "Boob Tube"?

by

Stephen K. Badzik

Videotex—a generic term applied to a new, consumer-oriented group of electronic distribution services—has yet to become a household word. As a term, it is about at the same recognition level as the word *television* was in 1947. In fact, videotex employs a television set to display transmitted signals in recognizable words and graphic images much like the video games played over modified "boob tubes" in homes and commercial establishments across the country.

Beyond these intriguing toys are countless applications envisioned by proponents who marvel at the innovative convergence of computer, electronic, and telecommunications technology that produced videotex. By 1990, advocates predict that videotex will be the basis for a young but significant industry that links eight million American homes with a dazzling array of computerized information data banks.

Commercial videotex systems are already operating in Europe and Japan, with field trials of the new technology underway in the United States and Canada. Apparently, the time to discuss the fundamental question of whether or not videotex systems should be developed at all has already passed. John G. Madden, director general of Special Research Programs in the Canadian Department of Communications, says, "Only a deliberate renunciation of a pluralist system and its substitution with a highly centralized government could prevent videotex development."

Since videotex development and deployment are inevitable, what are some of the basic concerns surrounding the utilization of this modern technology, which promises to bring many changes in life-styles for millions of people around the world? This paper seeks to identify some of the sociocultural issues that should be considered not only by commercial and governmental policy-makers but by individual consumers, whose future may be radically affected by videotex—perhaps the vanguard for the revolution that will take us from the industrial to the information society.

Stephen K. Badzik is manager of advertising, Office of Public Relations, George Washington University, Washington, D.C.

Glossary

Before proceeding with a discussion of the issues facing videotex, it is helpful to present the following definitions:

Videotex is a two-way, interactive, easy-to-operate medium linking computer data bases to television monitors.

Teletext is a one-way, noninteractive medium transmitting information via regular or cable television broadcast signals. Teletext makes use of the vertical blanking interval (VBI), the unused scanning lines of all television broadcast signals. Use of the VBI limits the amount of information that can be captured by a user, since the entire number of information frames must be sequentially broadcast over a fixed period of time (for example, the television signal transmits a total of 300 frames of information in a minute and then repeats the same coded transmission every minute).

Viewdata is a videotex system that generally uses an internally modified or externally adapted television set to display text and graphics. The public telephone network is usually the link to a host computer activated by the user requesting specific information from on-line data bases associated with the system. Viewdata services are typically designed for personal use rather than for professional or academic use, and are paid for by the individual user. School and business applications are being explored. Relative ease of use and low cost are characteristic of viewdata systems, traits that distinguish them from commercial time-sharing or information-retrieval services. (Teletext advocates point out that a teletext system is less costly than viewdata, although they admit teletext does not have the versatility or information capacity of a viewdata system.)

Telidon is an advanced, graphic communications system that enables text and high-quality animated images to be transmitted directly to TV sets. It is often called second-generation videotex (along with the British Prestel system). According to its developers, scientists in the Communications Research Centre of the Canadian Department of Communications, "The Telidon system has been designed to be as flexible as possible and immune to obsolescence. As related technologies develop, existing Telidon equipment will be able to perform new functions and carry improved images."

Currently, the Telidon system can be applied in videotex (interactive), teletext (one-way), and audiovisual systems. Telidon's graphic images are a considerable improvement over those made by the British Prestel and French Antiope systems because Telidon employs a sophisticated alphageometric coding scheme known as its Picture Description Instructions (PDI). Both French and British systems rely on an alphamosaic PDI that can only draw diagonal lines in a steplike fashion, requiring images to be built up from a mosaic of colored squares that do not allow natural lines and curves and often must be drawn in an order dictated by a computer rather than by the artist. Telidon's alphageometric PDI, however, allows the artist to use the natural language of drawing to create circles, rectangles, lines, and polygons.

The first international trial of a Telidon-based consumer information system is presently being conducted in Washington, D.C., by the Alternate Media Center of the New York University School of the Arts. Sixty terminals are being used in this Telidon trial, operating in the teletext mode. The test is

124

sponsored by the National Science Foundation, the National Telecommunications and Information Administration (NTIA) of the U.S. Commerce Department, and the U.S. Education Department, with the assistance of the Canadian Department of Communications. The terminals are located in homes and offices throughout the area and receive signals broadcast in the VBI of the regular transmissions from public television station WETA. WETA is broadcasting some 300 pages of constantly updated information provided by the *Washington Post*, District of Columbia Public Libraries, several federal agencies, and a number of consumer and business information groups.

Home and Family Life

Videotex systems may either draw a family together or further erode this basic unit of society. In a field test of the viewdata system called Channel 2000, sponsored by the Online Computer Library Center, Inc. (OCLC) and Banc One of Columbus, Ohio, 15% of the users felt that they spent less time watching television programming during the three-month test period. Among the 200 test homes, 8% of the respondents to the final survey also indicated that they spent more time talking with their children as a result of having Channel 2000. Although the OCLC researchers note that statistical confidence cannot be attributed to these finds, they suggest that a positive behavioral effect may be inherent in viewdata technology.

Potential uses of videotex systems for home teleshopping (seeing a product or service on the screen, ordering it, and charging it by appropriate credit-card input), banking, financial services, and link-ups to home security and home energy control systems may cause considerable changes in family living patterns. It could mean that families would be able to spend less time on the road shopping, conduct personal business in the privacy of their homes, feel safer, and live more comfortably and economically.

Parents may be able to work in their homes via a videotex system that connects them to their place of business. This would allow more interaction with pre-school children who are now often left in child-care centers that usually lack the amount of personal attention that a full-time parent can provide.

Children may be able to learn at home through videotex systems operated by school systems or private companies. It is possible that, with videotex, families may spend so much time at home that they will be on each others' nerves and need places away from home to which they can escape. Another problem will arise when family members begin to compete for use of the videotex terminal. A costly solution to the resulting squabbles would be purchasing additional terminals and hook-ups (as in the case with today's multiple telephone and television households).

Due to the possibilities that videotex presents for the development of home-based or "cottage" industries, the country may experience an acceleration of "deurbanization" foreseen by some sociologists in the current population boom of small towns. If parents can perform their work at home and children can have access to a vast storehouse of information that city educational and library centers provide, then there is a good chance that many families will choose to move out of the megalopolis into rural and small-town environments. Such an exodus would have additional impetus from the growing number of young couples who are finding themselves priced out of the housing market in metropolitan regions. Less expensive and better housing values are to be found in nonmetropolitan areas that frequently cannot attract young couples (which are unions of "baby boom" children—the largest population segment in the U.S.) because they do not have enough job opportunities. A handy home videotex terminal can solve the job problem, since young couples will be able to create their own money-making opportunities or at least plug into networks as employees of public or private industry.

The changes in national living patterns that videotex may strongly influence are beginning to emerge in what pollster Daniel Yankelovich calls a "search for community" based on a new "ethic of commitment." Although evidence for Yankelovich's assertions may not be solid, several social scientists at the Catholic University of America in Washington, D.C., believe that the "me" generation of the '70s will be replaced by the "we" generation of the '80s. "As people are pushed down by their circumstances," explains Monica Kyc, a faculty member of the Catholic University School of Social Service, "they have nowhere to turn but to each other."

Mary J. Flynn, also of the social service faculty at Catholic University, adds that "when the full impact of the media and computers is felt, people will have to cooperate in new ways." She points out that parents are beginning to reflect this trend already. "At one time it was their pride and joy to raise their children to be independent, but now they are starting to raise them to be interdependent," she says. The catalyst for such interdependence, according to Flynn, is the ever-increasing amount of information to be acquired in any one field of knowledge. "In the future, people will each have to rely on the expertise of others, since no individual can come close to knowing everything," notes Flynn.

People of the future may have a tremendous tool for tapping the expertise of others if videotex meets the expectations of its champions. Videotex may become the cement for the foundation of the "we" generation.

Education

Individuals will have greater learning opportunities with interactive videotex than ever achieved with educational television. With educational television as we know it, there is a delay in response time (if there is a response at all) between teacher and student. With videotex as designers envision it, the teacher (which can be a computer programmed for instruction) will be able to respond directly to a pupil who keys into the system.

In remote areas, and in countries with burgeoning populations, videotex may be the device that brings education to the people. A videotex system allows for home learning, which saves the cost of on-site education and retaining large numbers of teaching and support personnel. Parents could be more intimately involved with their children's education, which would be a return to the traditional learning system employed by Western society prior to the late nineteenth century.

Some will argue against home education for children because it will eliminate peer-group interaction. Others, such as Fritz Machlup, have argued that much of what goes on under the guise of social interaction is really wasted time better spent on learning activities. If parents truly desire social activities for their children, there is no reason that church and community groups cannot provide such opportunities. Most observers would also point out that kids are usually quite adept at finding outlets for social interaction in their own neighborhoods. Whatever case may arise, videotex home education may kindle a new spirit of neighborliness among young and old alike who are spending more time around the house because they are not away at school or at work.

Specialized schools to accommodate the needs of mentally and physically handicapped children would still have a place if videotex-inspired home education becomes widespread. But even in specialized schools, as well as in school systems currently operating, videotex holds great promise as a supplemental learning tool for both classroom and home use.

The entire system of higher education could also be greatly influenced by the introduction of videotex-based education. Interactive videotex, such as Telidon, can put teachers and students in direct two-way contact even when they are far apart. The teacher will be able to visit the work space of each student and can direct him to research and background material that will be immediately available from the data bank accessible by videotex. Physical components of universities could change considerably, since students may no longer need to congregate in classrooms, and the need for many other university facilities—dining rooms, dormitories, and recreational buildings—may be diminished.

When videotex and videodisc (an audiovisual system that records sound and images in a digital format) technologies are married at some point in the future, students (along with almost everyone else) can have some fascinating learning experiences. The day may come when the greatest teachers will sell themselves to the highest bidder (like today's free agents in sports) because they could easily present their lessons to a large number of students through the combined videotex/videodisc system.

Adults interested in continuing their education could look to videotex. An exciting array of both academic and pleasurable pursuits could be provided to videotex users by non-profit and profit-oriented educational institutions—from classical Greek literature to computer programming to bridge lessons. Easy and enjoyable learning programs through videotex technology may not only serve adults who have increasing amounts of leisure time but also help them gain new skills to meet the constantly changing conditions of the working world.

In theory, all the information in the Library of Congress (or the British Museum or the French Bibliothèque Nationale) could be put into data banks and made available to videotex users at home. Even though this may be a possibility, most videotex proponents still see a role for libraries.

Herb Bown, director of data systems research and development at the Canadian Department of Communications, thinks that there will always be people who will use traditional libraries but may find that videotex provides much more information than they are accustomed to getting at home. "Primarily, though, the people who can benefit most from this new technology are those who currently do not go to libraries," says Bown.

Jean Paul Emard, vice-president of Online, Inc., and former analyst in information sciences for the Library of Congress's Congressional Research Service, says that "Information in the home will not replace the library down the street. In fact, it may augment the library's role by making it the local teletext/videotex 'tavern' or access center."

Librarians involved in a field test of the British Prestel system that was installed in their reference departments ranked the system's advantages in the following order: it provides up-to-date information to library patrons; it draws more people to the library; it fills gaps in existing information coverage; it provides a quick way to retrieve data; it broadens means by which information is available, presenting it in a novel manner of interest to those turned off by books; and it has the potential to relieve the staff work-load.

These same librarians said Prestel's disadvantages included the potential to take too much time from staffers who must help inexperienced users; its costs; its space needs; and the "hubbub" it often creates.

Gus Hauser, chief executive officer of Warner Amex Cable Communications—the Warner Communications subsidiary that operates the commercial two-way television system Qube in Columbus, Ohio—thinks that the definition of a library may change when home electronic information systems become more widespread. "Maybe, the library will become a data bank people will access from the home," he says.

Bradley University journalism professor Paul B. Snider predicts that "the familiar community library may be nothing more than an electronic relay station—a means of sending requests to other collection centers and relaying responses to the questioner."

In contrast with this mechanistic forecast for libraries is the more humanistic viewpoint of Kathleen Criner, former program manager for home information technology at NTIA and now director of telecommunications affairs at the American Newspaper Publishers Association (ANPA). She believes that "The library has the role of introducing people to these (videotex) services." Library benefits of videotex, outlined by Criner, include: reducing costs of in-house and interbranch communications because of paper elimination; gaining a new medium to publicize services, new acquisitions, and programs that would cost less than direct mail literature; and providing an aid in answering reference questions and in expediting orders for services such as books by mail.

Ray Vondran, associate dean of the School of Library and Information Science at the Catholic University of America in Washington, D.C., points out that "you can't lie down with a computer terminal, and it doesn't cost you anything to stop and think about what the author has written when you're reading a book. I think it will probably be two centuries before we replace books with a video display terminal."

However, researchers at OCLC explain that books and printed material will play an "ever-diminishing role in the generation and dissemination of 'hot' ephemeral information, the continuously changing day-to-day information we rely on to live in our fast-paced society. Just as books and other direct-perception media are eminently suitable for long-term storage, computer systems, with their capabilities for rapid update and communication of information, prove ideal for serving topical, timely information needs."

128

The OCLC Channel 2000 report concludes that the results from the trial of the OCLC viewdata system were positive. Authors of this report propose that "Libraries stand on the threshold of great opportunities. Emerging electronic technologies provide the potential for a new age of community service in which the library can command new attention and financial support as an information resource serving the survival, growth, and recreational needs of Everyman."

Apparently, librarians are gaining an awareness that they must take a leadership position in the home information race spearheaded by videotex or else face becoming an irrelevant institution. Videotex also threatens to displace many individuals employed in other segments of America's educational enterprise. They, too, may be gearing up for this eventuality, but current rates of professional dissatisfaction and job "burnout" indicate that many teachers might be glad to leave the classroom if a videotex machine can do their job. Think of all the financially strapped school boards across the country who might joyfully consider videotex replacements for teachers. After all, machines cannot unionize, demand higher salaries, or go on strike—at least not yet.

Perhaps, educators can feel a sense of security in the face of technological advances if they believe Andrew R. Molnar when he says, "In an information society, human capital is the wealth of a nation and education is the process for refining the resource."

Leisure Activities

Videotex is entering the American marketplace on the path forged by video games, which were introduced by Atari in the 1970s. The growing leisure-time industry that propels video games to a top entertainment choice among a wide variety of consumers will undoubtedly spur interest in videotex. Videotex can provide the consumer not only with video games but a broad spectrum of activities that can occupy those increasing hours of leisure, some of which may be the result of videotex applications that reduced the time spent working.

For the person who does not have time or interest in reading newspapers or magazines, the videotex machine can provide regularly updated news items. Sports fanatics can get scores before they are announced on radio or television. People who like to go out for dining or enjoyment will be able to access videotex information about restaurants, movies, plays, special events, places to go, as well as transportation schedules to get there; but beyond this information they may be able to make reservations or purchase tickets for a selected activity through their videotex terminal.

Herbert Bown believes that it will be possible to transmit live and stored entertainment through the Telidon system in the relatively near future. "We're initiating a program of research to expand image coding. Now we can code alphanumerics, geometrics and slow scan images (photographic facsimiles). We want to move into the television area and do coding schemes for moving pictures. That's a good 10 years off," he says.

When people purchase an information-provider terminal, they can create their own graphic images using a specially designed drawing stylus that instructs the computer to draw the picture conceived by the artist. Videotex and its link to a computer may provide artists with a fascinating new medium for expression that could be recorded with an electronic storage device on cassette tape or floppy disk, or with a paper printout terminal.

Perhaps it is the videotex potential to provide such a broad range of entertainment that interests both newspapers and TV stations in videotex.

Kathleen Criner of ANPA says, "Overall, newspapers are among the major videotex experimenters in the country. They are taking a variety of roles—from systems providers to information brokers." By 1982, newspapers will have invested more than $20 million on videotex trials, according to an estimate by Mark Plakius, director of videotex research for Link Resources Corporation.

Most observers feel that newspapers will still be part of our leisure-time activities but may be in a different form. Robert M. Johnson, vice-president and general manager of Dispatch Printing Company, which publishes the *Columbus Dispatch*, believes that newspapers will be smaller and have less detail. Tom Dozier of Knight-Ridder Newspapers, which is conducting a viewdata trial in Coral Gables, Florida, with AT&T, thinks that videotex systems "complement print and may actually increase and stimulate readership. They will draw people to their paper to read the whole story leisurely." Tactile stimulation and other uses (like wrapping china or garbage) will also keep people turning to newsprint, according to Harnish at OCLC.

In order to remain competitive, television stations will probably be more than willing to offer teletext over their VBI transmission. If consumers are using their television sets to pick up videotex, they cannot be watching the shows broadcast by stations, so broadcasters feel that they should try to get in on the action with their own teletext service that could be a source for ad revenue lost due to diminished audience size.

Jerry Borrell, research assistant in information policy and technology for the Congressional Research Service at the Library of Congress, does not feel that videotex and teletext serve the same market as television. "I watch television for entertainment," he says, "and in my more selective moments I seek out informed entertainment. Inasmuch as television news is more entertaining than reading, I watch the evening news."

David M. Simons, president of Digital Video Corporation, a New York-based consulting firm, points out that "while videotex may be appealing as a means of providing around-the-clock headlines in countries with only two or three television stations that carry less than an hour of news programming a day, it may not sell when it is used this way in the United States," which has both network and local news programs plus the 24-hour, live, full-video, full-color news programming of the Cable News Network (CNN). He adds that "unless videotex graphics make an important integral contribution to the utility the videotex service provides, they may simply be perceived as falling short of U.S. video standards." The April 1981 cancellation of Newstime—UPI's continuous audio service accompanied by still photographs and offered to cable television systems—was blamed on the competition from CNN's live video programming. Simons notes, "The expensive and lush quality of U.S. commercial television programming and its abundance have had a powerful conditioning effect on Americans."

Despite the handicaps cited by Simons, videotex can present an entertainment outlet that may send some segments of the leisure-time industry scurrying for Excedrin®. Newspaper owners and television broadcasters will be joined by book publishers, film and record producers, and individual entertainers who may feel threatened if videotex catches on with the American public. However, these headache sufferers can find comfort in history, which demonstrates that the introduction of new entertainment forms does not always lead to the demise of established entertainment activities. Recall that movies did not bring the final curtain down upon live stage shows, television did not keep radios turned off forever, and telephones did not reach out to completely eliminate letter-writing.

The faddish nature of entertainment choices may not be much consolation to those whose livelihoods may suffer because of videotex competition, yet competition may serve the public if older formats improve their acts in order to regain patrons. Those lost patrons will probably return anyway as they tire of playing "Space Invaders" and reading flashing headlines on their televisions. It is unlikely that videotex will someday suffer the fate of the once popular hoola-hoop or disco dance; videotex's destiny will be as a viable alternative to—not a replacement for—today's leisure activities.

Conclusion

The technological innovations of the past 50 years far surpass the total sum of innovations made during the previous 5,000 years of man's history. Despite such an extraordinary record, today's citizen of the world seems to readily accept and adapt to the countless developments and improvements spawned by modern science and technology.

Widespread utilization of videotex will probably cause barely a ripple in the everyday lives of people who have grown accustomed to the relentless tide of technological change. Undoubtedly, videotex has the potential for significant if not radical impact upon humans and their social and cultural institutions. Since recent history indicates that mankind has a tremendous capacity for ameliorating the effects of the ongoing technological revolution, I suspect that serious sociocultural disruption due to videotex will be minimal and will only be another step on the earth's speedy journey into the twenty-first century.

Bibliography

Badzik, Stephen K., "Home Computers Predicted As Part of 21st Century's Information Revolution," Washington, D.C., The Catholic University of America Office of Public Information, February 1981.

Bloom, L. R., A. G. Hanson, R. F. Linfield, and D. R. Wortendyke, *VIDEOTEX Systems and Services*, Washington, D.C., U.S. Department of Commerce, National Telecommunications and Information Administration, 1980.

Borrell, Jerry, "The State of Videotex," *ASIS Bulletin*, June 1981, p. 26.

Channel 2000 Project Report—Description and Findings of a Viewdata Test Conducted by OCLC in Columbus, Ohio, October-December 1980, Dublin, Ohio, Research Department of OCLC Online Computer Library Center, Inc., April, 1981.

Cherry, Susan Spaeth, "The New TV Information Systems," *Video Involvement for Libraries*, Chicago, American Libraries Association, 1 June 1981, pp. 57-75.

Kelly, Tom, "Waves of the Eighties," *Canada Today*, March 1980, pp. 1-11.

Lapides, Julie D., "First the 'Me' Generation And Now the 'We' Generation," Washington, D.C., The Catholic University of America Office of Public Information, 12 January 1981.

Madden, John G., *Videotex in Canada*, Ottawa, Canada, Minister of Supply and Services, 1979.

Simons, David M., "Cable Courts Videotex—Programs Will Shape Videotex Services," *ASIS Bulletin*, June 1981, p. 32.

Telidon Today, Ottawa, Canada, Canadian Department of Communications, 1981.

"Window on the World—The Home Information Revolution," *Business Week*, 29 June 1981, pp. 74-77, 80, 83.

"Reverse Negotiation": A New Conflict Management Tool

by

Michael Blinick

It's often been said that "better communication" is the answer to many, if not most, of our disputes and disagreements, both private and public. But, by itself, it may merely make the parties realize that the chasm between them is even deeper than they had thought.

Furthermore, the actual issues may be very different from what seems to be the case. It may even be possible for the parties, although they are bitter enemies, to share the same appraisal of what the issues are—and to be totally incorrect!

"Reverse negotiation" is a new approach to negotiation and conflict resolution, designed to clarify issues and values, as well as ends and means, and help the parties agree on which elements of "rightness" may exist in all sides of the dispute.

Reverse negotiation is a new framework—a standardized process—to aid the parties in conflict situations. Its purpose is to assist the parties in discovering, analyzing, and accommodating all legitimate interests concerned, thus avoiding the all-too-familiar outcomes of failed negotiation: confrontation (and sometimes violence), litigation, stalemate, or a decision that hindsight later shows to be wrong.

Let's look at the components of this improved approach:

Reversing the Traditional Rituals of Negotiation

It can truly be said that if the parties to a dispute are willing to sit down and talk with each other at all, they should consider themselves fortunate. However, reverse negotiation changes the classic ways of doing this.

In fact, it actually inverts the standard bargaining process. Normally, in the standard method, each side first makes demands and counter-demands, which it then compromises in return for concessions from its opponents. But if we look closely at these demands, we will see that they are really means to reach certain goals, or to protect some interest. In many cases, they are arrived at by "putting the cart before the horse" and advocating a particular

Michael Blinick, who practices law in New York City, is completing a book on a new approach to conflict resolution, embracing both negotiation and advocacy. His articles have appeared in various legal and lay periodicals.

"solution" without having first defined the problem. Often, even the ends sought are not properly defined, except perhaps in the most short-range terms.

Suppose that the different sides have different goals in mind. If so, the solutions they advocate may be contradictory. Even if they share a common goal, the solutions favored by one (or all) parties may not be effective, may cause unanticipated new problems for the parties or others, or may even worsen the original problem. So the parties should refrain from advocating particular solutions until each side has stated and explained: (1) just what it thinks the problem is, (2) what it thinks the legitimate interests of *each* party are (with respect to the conflict and whatever has brought about the conflict), and (3) where relevant, what goals it is trying to achieve both in solving the conflict and in related contexts. The parties may agree with each other on some of these points, and may jointly decide to reformulate some of their views so as to enlarge the area of agreement. Only after these matters have been articulated and worked out should thought be given to the best methods of accommodating the legitimate interests (hereafter abbreviated as "LIs") and reaching the goals. In doing so, the precise manner in which each element of a possible solution or reform would protect all LIs, or help attain one or more desired goals, should be made clear. Then, an accord on the best solution can be reached and a consensus of support for it can be established. Finally, any conflicts concerning the means of implementing the agreed-on solution can be settled—if necessary—in the same manner as the original dispute.

It may be that one or more parties may be hesitant to "put their cards on the table" by revealing just what their goals or other views are. If so, such an obstacle can be overcome by having the parties do so in writing, privately, and then exchange documents, so that neither side will have to recite its position first. Or, the process can be carried on through a mediator or other party, who can assist in the efforts to reconcile the factions.

Thus, instead of starting out by arguing about what road to take, the parties begin by trying to see if they can agree on a common destination. Once they have one, they can work together to find a road that will lead both (or all) of them there. In more situations than we may realize, a community of interests, based on mutual needs and wants, and on shared beliefs, exists among those who are at loggerheads. Instead of merely compromising in order to settle disputes, we can use this approach to help us decide what should or should not be compromised, and why. It aids us in determining whether each demand is fair or not. It encourages all sides to regard changes in their positions not as compromises made due to weakness but as desirable alterations that make their viewpoints just and proper.

Actually, reverse negotiation is very well suited to formulating one's position in the first place, before it hardens into "demands" and before one meets with other parties. That is because it shows how to be sure that one's wants are fair and justifiable, and are being sought in a fair and justifiable way, *before* fastening on any specific means to reach whatever is wanted.

Furthermore, potential adversaries who are *not* current opponents could meet for preventive sessions of reverse negotiation, to help keep open conflict from arising.

134

An Illustrative Example

Before we go any further, the following brief notes may help to convey a concrete picture of the actual procedure. Due to lack of space, it is necessarily oversimplifed.

The particular conflict, let us say, concerns a type of police-community relations problem that occurs in many neighborhoods, regardless of racial composition. Young people complain that the police are "hassling" them with "stop and frisk" tactics, checking drivers and occupants of cars and forcing the youths to move off street corners. They feel that "There's no point in obeying the law, since they try to bust you anyway."

Older people in the area say that the problem is, rather, that large and disorderly bands of youngsters are roving aimlessly and sometimes bullying younger children and even adults. Other youths cruise around in cars, often drinking at the same time, and indulge in speeding, drag-racing, "cutting off" other cars, and similar dangerous acts. They add that many muggings, store holdups, and burglaries are probably being committed by some of these same juveniles. They add that while they don't want innocent kids mistreated, they want these "packs" controlled, and insist that the current police tactics don't go far enough.

The police, as usual, feel caught in the middle between the demands of different groups. A reverse-negotiation analysis of this kind of situation should bring in representatives of the mayor's office and government and private human service agencies, since their presence may lead to the adoption of constructive measures outside the province of the police (e.g., better recreation programs, counseling services, and job training projects).

What are some of the LIs here? The youths have LIs in being able to meet with their friends peacefully without being harassed and humiliated. But so do the older people, who are often treated in the same way by these "kids," some of whom are pretty big. The police have LIs in protecting themselves when interrogating anyone (thus the frisking), and those citizens whose cars have been stolen have an LI in recovering them (thus the "car stops" by the police). So it's obvious that the people here share at least one goal: personal security from being "hassled," whether by officious policemen or unruly youths. (Even the police complain of being "sassed" by these groups of juveniles while on patrol.) An earnest teen-ager protests: "At least if some kids are bothering you, you can call the cops. But if the cops are bothering me, what can I do? Who's going to listen to me, or believe me?"

In addition, the residents all have an LI in preventing the more serious offenses from occurring so frequently in the neighborhood, and the youngsters have an LI in securing better recreational facilities and training in meaningful jobs. This enumeration is not exhaustive, of course.

Instead of continuing their destructive form of interaction, the parties should work together to accommodate all the LIs concerned. Many specific suggestions could be extracted from the reports of the National Advisory Commission on Criminal Justice Standards and Goals. Any textbook on police-community relations or police work with juveniles could supply detailed information on successful steps taken by other localities, such as the institution of "neighborhood team policing." The use of outside resources can be

135

the key factor that infuses new hope into what may seem like an endless "vicious cycle." We should always be on the alert for this kind of aid, and never assume that we know all the possible answers ourselves.

A Question of Values

Reverse negotiation is a considerable departure from what others have urged in regard to "conflict resolution." They have recommended better techniques of communication, more willingness to compromise, understanding the other parties' background and feelings, and improving the human relationships involved. Indeed, all those ideas are extremely important and useful. But in many cases they simply don't do the job of solving the conflict. So we need something more: a way of deciding what's fair and right in a conflict situation—a way that respects all LIs.

How can we do that? Doesn't somebody have to win or lose? Not necessarily. In many conflicts, solutions can be worked out so that all sides gain. And, in a wide range of disputes, we have common interests whether we know it or not. That is, there may be no actual conflict between the LIs of the parties, even though there may be a "false conflict" between what each side thinks it wants, needs, and deserves.

However, when conflicts are based on what seem to be hopelessly opposed interests, they can often be settled by using another reverse-negotiation approach—the same technique we should use whenever we can't get agreement at some stage in the process described previously. It's based on a fact that underlies all these steps: defining the problem, analyzing LIs, examining goals, and finally agreeing on a solution in both theory and practice. *They all involve questions of values*. And reverse negotiation can help us to communicate about values. Public policy questions (unlike certain purely economic matters such as some labor relations disputes) cannot be settled without making value judgments (for example, decisions about which values deserve more priority than others, and how values are to be institutionalized or enforced).

In order to make such judgments, we should be quite explicit about just what our values are. But we usually are not. To illustrate this, let's take a value that would seem to be the most essential one of all, and that would deserve priority over other values when a clash is inevitable: the protection of human life, health, and safety. Surely, this is one point on which those occupying all sides of the political, economic, and social spectra should be able to agree. What could be more basic? Yet we hear, all the time, spokesmen for government and industry alike talking blithely about "trade-offs," "interest-balancing," and "cost-benefit analysis" with respect to environmental protection, occupational health, product safety, auto speed limits, aircraft and airport safety, chemicals in food—just to mention a few. But it is "trade-offs" of human lives that they're talking about. It is "costs" of severe, often irreparable impairment to the health of millions.

Some may say that any principle so obvious and elementary is amply institutionalized by existing laws and universally held attitudes. But where are these laws and attitudes when we need them at the air disasters, at the nursing homes where patients are cruelly mistreated, at the construction sites where asbestos, a known carcinogen, was sprayed, and at countless other places where convenience or pursuit of profit are the values that count most? And if human life, health, and safety are so disregarded, what kind of reception can we expect for other fundamental values?

If we are open about our own key values, we will find that we share many of them with our adversaries. We should also join with our opponents, however, by means of reverse negotiation, to construct a *hierarchy of values* for the purpose of solving the particular conflict that divides us. This will bring us several advantages:

1. It will enable us to avoid the recurring and difficult question of how to establish a hard-and-fast definition of "the public interest"—by giving us instead a method of reaching accord on what it would be in specific given situations.

2. It will help promote a consensus on what constitutes a fair solution. This is important, for a "solution" where one side "wins big" and the other "loses big" is inherently unstable due to the bitterness and desires for revenge that it creates. Thus, the best answer, and the one most likely to succeed, is one that is thought fair by all parties.

3. It will help us cope with the value-analysis problems posed by today's management practices, decision-making techniques, and technological developments. Disputes about criminal justice, social welfare, or health services bring modern systems-analysis practices into sharp clashes with understandable emotionalism about critical decisions. Arguments over zoning, other land-use problems, and capital budgets cause urban planning theories to collide with many people's needs and wants. (How many times have we heard the sentiment "That 'halfway house' is a great idea, but not in *my* neighborhood!" voiced in opposition to community-based facilities for ex-addicts, released mental patients, former prisoners, the mentally retarded, or other unpopular minorities?) And fights over the nature and allocation of new mass transportation facilities, and their interface with private car usage, force economic and engineering decisions to be made in a highly charged atmosphere. All these situations—and many others in areas such as housing, public employment and manpower training—call for the kind of specifically value-conscious approach facilitated by reverse negotiation.

4. It will help mend ideological cleavages between such opposed factions as "liberals" and "conservatives," because it concentrates on discovering, and building on, a core of beliefs shared by most Americans. The ideological differences that divide us are largely rooted in the different emphases and priorities we place on certain values, goals, and interests that most of us nonetheless hold in common to some extent. But as long as protection is given to whatever is most important to us, we will tend not to object to others receiving what they want. The "either-or" situations where one side must triumph and the other be defeated are not as frequent as might be supposed, although they often seem to exist because one or both sides have:

(a) analyzed the issues improperly,

(b) allowed polarization to develop unnecessarily,

(c) do not know what their opponents are really seeking, or

(d) are ignorant of options and alternatives—some rooted in recent social science or technological research, others contained in little-known leg-

islation or proven by long experience in other places or contexts—that
could solve their own difficulties.

The framework set forth here helps to overcome all these barriers and to
eliminate what might be called the destructive interaction so frequently occurring between those of different philosophies, backgrounds, life-styles, and
generations.

There are other points to bear in mind during the reverse-negotiation process:

- **No legitimate interest (LI) may be left unprotected.** It is not acceptable to
say, when some opponent raises a valid point, "That's *your* problem!" While
the matter may indeed be his legal and moral responsibility, it is really your
problem too, insofar as you can help him to protect his LIs and fulfill his
responsibilities. He, of course, has a reciprocal responsibility with respect to
helping you to do what you must, and what you desire to do, in a way that
violates no one's LIs. Both of you have this duty with respect to the interests
of others who are not represented at the particular bargaining table. This is
really an application of the Golden Rule. But it also has a distinct practical
value. When you try to help the other fellow solve his problems, and protect
him from any negative side effects of whatever it is you want, getting what
you want from him becomes much easier.

- **Always prepare the other side's case along with your own.** Many experienced attorneys, in readying themselves for a trial or hearing, devote some
time to imagining what they would say and do if they were representing the
adverse party. This exercise helps them to do a better job for their own client.
You, too, should make use of it in preparing for a confrontation; it will enable
you to see whatever merit is in the other party's position, and anticipate his
statements.

- **Concentrate on avoiding negatives rather than on seeking positives.** It's
easier to agree on what is unjust, or on what constitutes bad faith, than on
what is just, or what constitutes good faith. This is because the positive virtues tend to be abstract ideals, whereas the lack of these virtues appears to us
in concrete and readily grasped instances that arouse a strong response.

- **Don't worry about being unable to solve all aspects of a problem at once.**
Once a large amount of a conflict is resolved, it will no longer be the same
situation. Instead, there will be a smaller set of difficulties to cope with,
which can then be retackled from a different stance, using the resources
newly freed as a result of the prior successes. Furthermore, changes that
people would veto now will be agreeable to them after they are reassured by
the favorable outcome of less drastic reforms.

- **Analyze on the basis of individuals, not groups or entities.** To avoid polarization, injustice, and just plain sloppy thinking, don't automatically assume that groups, institutions, agencies, corporations, governmental units,
and other collective bodies have LIs. While they may possess "rights" en-
forceable in the courts, it would be well, while participating in the reverse-
negotiation process, to keep individuals, alone or standing together, as the
criterion of judgment. Thus, the people in a city, not the city itself, would
have LIs. In a school, people (such as teachers, administrators, pupils, parents, and the individuals in the community at large) would all have LIs, but
the school itself, and the entire school system, would probably not. If you

analyze carefully enough, you will see that what would appear to be the LIs of the school are actually those of people for whose benefit the school was established, or who are linked to it in some way. The same goes for a business firm, whose shareholders or proprietors would have LIs, rather than the company itself. Even racial and ethnic groups, which are usually thought of as monolithic units, would be less often misperceived if their members were viewed as individuals, with widely differing characteristics and needs.

A corollary of this guideline was suggested by the legal philosopher Edmond Cahn. He said that the justice or "rightness" of an act or policy should be assessed from the standpoint of the individuals affected by it, not from that of the government or "society." Rather than talk about the rights of society versus the rights of the individual, it might be more illuminating, and more correct, to speak of the rights of one individual versus the rights of other individuals. "Society" is an abstraction symbolizing all of us, viewed collectively; the government, regardless of agency, level, or branch, should be required to represent the LIs of individuals. If we cannot articulate precisely what LIs are being protected by particular governmental action or inaction, or by some claimed "right of society," we had better take a much closer look. Illegitimate interests can wrap themselves in a false cloak of outward propriety.

In summary, reverse negotiation is an important addition to the previously available techniques of negotiation and advocacy. It can make a major contribution to discussions and debates, meetings and conferences, and in all our efforts to solve problems in both the public and private sectors.

Synthesized Speech: A Communication Breakthrough

by

Clarence A. Bowman and Linda S. Althoff

In a vivid essay about brain-injured patients, Howard Gardner wrote that the loss of language abilities in the otherwise normal adult is tragic, and the consequences are as devastating as those of blindness, deafness, or paralysis. Deprived of the power to communicate through language, the individual is cut off from the world of meaning. Although the loss of language is relatively rare among young persons, it becomes increasingly common with age. About 250,000 individuals suffer language impairment each year. Those who lose language as a consequence of damage to the brain are victims of a condition called aphasia. Brain damage such as the kind that produces aphasia creates an anarchical array of symptoms. Instead of all parts of the brain, and every human skill, becoming equally impaired, damage is highly selective. One region of the brain may be completely devastated, while others remain intact.

A large percentage of brain-injured patients lose the ability to generate spoken language while retaining their mental and intellectual functions. These patients are unable to coordinate and sequence movements in the 14,000 muscle fibers used to produce speech. The need for an adequate alternate communication system is critical, and until recently only writing and sign language were available. In a technologically advanced twentieth-century society, the inability to communicate through vocal language essentially isolates the individual from an enormous range of human experiences. Advances in computer technology and related fields have resulted in the development of the Phonic Mirror Handi Voice, a portable electronic voice synthesizer that can communicate verbally any word in the English language. The synthesizer weighs only 5½ pounds, measures 11 by 7 inches, and costs approximately $2,195. It is pre-programmed with 893 commonly used words, 16 short phrases, and the 26 letters of the alphabet. With the 45 speech sounds of English also available, it is possible for the synthesizer to produce any word in the language. The device is manufactured for HC Electronics Incorporated by the Votrax Company of Troy, Michigan.

Clarence A. Bowman is an assistant professor of speech pathology at Illinois State University, Normal, Illinois. Linda S. Althoff is a research assistant in the Department of Speech Pathology and Audiology at Illinois State University.

The significance of a voice synthesizer to an individual previously denied the opportunity to communicate with his peers is beyond comprehension. It can, and in many cases does, signal the beginning of a new and more meaningful relationship with family and friends. As an educational tool, the voice synthesizer greatly enhances opportunities for deriving maximum gains, since teacher-client interaction can more closely approximate "real world" communication.

At the Illinois State University Speech and Hearing Clinic, speech pathologists are using voice synthesizers to teach language skills to severely disabled cerebral palsied children. These youngsters, while retaining normal intelligence, are victims of underdeveloped and abnormal muscular systems. In a sense, they are locked inside their own bodies, unable to communicate with the outside world.

Voice synthesizers are also being used by adults. These individuals led normal lives until an injury, such as a stroke or traumatic head injury, impaired their ability to initiate and sustain muscle movement patterns. When oral muscle patterns are damaged, a condition known as apraxia of speech prevents the patient from coordinating and sequencing vocal movements. Although intelligence is usually normal in these patients, vocal communication is severely limited. The behavioral changes that have been observed in these adults using the voice synthesizer are significant enough to warrant a formal presentation of the findings.

Rabidoux, Florance, and McCauslin (1981) reported that the voice synthesizer was being used with selected apraxic patients at St. Anthony Hospital in Columbus, Ohio. These patients will serve to represent the thousands of human brains that are injured every year. Apraxia of speech is difficult to treat, and only a small percentage of patients ever fully recover. The case history of Patient CB is typical. At the age of 68 years, she suffered a stroke in the left dominant side of the brain and presented symptoms of paralysis on the right side, poor fine motor coordination, and a severe oral speech deficit. Even with extensive brain damage, her intellectual skills remained intact and virtually unaffected by the injury. The loss of oral communication in this patient was devastating. Speech therapy was prescribed for Patient CB, and treatment focused on reestablishing voluntary control of vocal activity with the goal of teaching her to speak in short phrases. Treatment was unsuccessful. Several alternative communication systems were attempted, including sign language and writing, but due to poor fine motor control these systems also failed.

Following careful analysis, it was determined that CB was a good candidate for the voice synthesizer. An initial treatment plan was designed to familiarize her with the device and allow her to memorize the location of vocabulary items. Further treatment focused on increasing speed of programming. During a series of one-hour sessions, structured artificial conversations were conducted with a speech pathologist. The family was encouraged to participate in similar conversations at home. Following successful completion of training, environmental impact of the ability to use synthesized speech was evaluated. It was reported that "she has assumed an active role within her family, is able to complete domestic responsibilities, manage family meals including grocery shopping and food preparation, and pursue social activities outside of her home with family and friends."

The next patient exemplifies a disorder that is all too frequently encountered in acute-care hospitals and rehabilitation centers throughout the country. Patient DC was the victim of an automobile accident and suffered traumatic head injury. In spite of widespread damage to the brain and the resultant physical disabilities, DC retained normal intellectual skills. Oral communication was severely impaired. Again, traditional speech therapy treatment failed to improve motor speech ability, and a training program with the voice synthesizer was developed. This program included both the family and a home health nurse, and within 12 weeks a functional vocabulary was acquired. Success of the program was revealed through the patient's ability to "interact with individuals in his community, to use the phone independently, and to participate with relative freedom within his home."

Development of the voice synthesizer represents a significant advancement in the treatment of non-vocal individuals. It allows many children with severe developmental disabilities to acquire communication skills, and adults can reestablish contact with family, friends, and society. The voice synthesizer offers a greatly needed alternate communication system, and we are only beginning to discover its wide range of possible applications. To the degree that language defines our human character, the loss of language in the otherwise normal adult represents a disability of unparalleled proportion. For these patients, the voice synthesizer offers the opportunity to once again become a useful and productive member of society.

Telecommunications: The Next Generation

by

Jean M. Ciano and E. Bryan Carne

In the 1830s, the first practical application of electricity and magnetism produced the electric telegraph. Using it, trained operators could exchange coded messages over the copper wires that began to march over the countryside in the company of the railroads. In the 1880s, people started talking to one another over ever-increasing distances. Soon, the cities were being buried under strands of wire strung on taller and taller poles as the telephone network took shape. By the beginning of the twentieth century, wireless communication became possible and, in the 1920s, a proliferation of radio stations brought entertainment, news, and eyewitness descriptions of far-off events to everyone who wished to listen. In the 1940s, sight was added to sound—television was born. For many, it opened a window on the world for the first time; and, in the 1960s, that window was filled with living color. Shortly thereafter, satellites made it possible to span the oceans, and the space program soon extended our vision to the Moon and to the planets. Truly, Marshall McLuhan (in his book *Understanding Media*) captured the essence of the telecommunications revolution when he said: " . . . in the electric age, we wear all mankind as our skin. . . ."

In the 1950s, the computer emerged from universities and research institutes into the realm of commerce and industry. As well as being a tool to perform complex calculations, it was perceived to have the added promise of data processing. By the 1960s, remote terminals needed to be connected to a central processor, and processors needed to exchange information, giving rise to data communications. What many now call the information society has produced a proliferation of new facilities and specialized networks devoted to the transportation of data. Continuing advances in computer and communications technology have encouraged new forms of media such as electronic mail, information retrieval services known as teletext and viewdata, video conferencing and computer conferencing, and Interactive CATV. Combined

Jean M. Ciano is a technical research analyst for the Communications Product Technology Center, GTE Laboratories, Waltham, Massachusetts. E. Bryan Carne is director of the Communications Product Technology Center and director of the Computer Center at GTE Laboratories, Waltham, Massachusetts.

with enhancements of existing media, the opportunities afforded by these new media have produced concepts of the automated office and the wired household. In 1960, it would have been difficult to project the technology-rich environment of the 1980s. In the 1980s, the task of projecting technical developments in the remaining years of the twentieth century is no easier. What is certain is that the next generation of services that will be supported by these new media will be shaped by consumer demand, provider reward, the need to conserve resources, and the opportunities provided by the coming together of telephony, data processing, television, satellites, optical fibers, and integrated circuits.

Present and Future Communications Media

Pervasive telecommunications exist in many parts of the developed world. In the United States, a federal policy encourages competition among communications providers. In most of the rest of the world, telecommunications is a closely regulated function of government, with the result that the spectrum of available services and options is considerably narrowed. Nevertheless, innovative services have been introduced in Europe and Japan.

Today's real-time communications media* are an essential ingredient of the infrastructure of modern society. Without them, governments, institutions, corporations, and organizations would find it impossible to operate. They have the following attributes:

Telephone: facilitates two-way messages to accomplish person-to-person aural communication. A real-time medium that delivers a continuous stream of information as it is generated. Telephone offers an easy-to-use extension of private audio-space over any distance, providing a flexible link between members of an increasingly mobile world. From coast-to-coast (or around the world), Telephone makes it possible to obtain information on demand, summon assistance in time of trouble, appeal unfavorable decisions, and maintain intimate contacts.

Data Communications: transports messages to accomplish machine-to-machine communications. A real-time medium that delivers a continuous stream of information as it is generated, Data Communications is used predominantly by business. It offers an extension of private data-space over any distance, making big government, big institutions, and big corporations possible through the sharing of information. By facilitating the flow of records within and between organizations, Data Communications contributes in a major way to the survival of the sophisticated economies of developed countries.

Radio: delivers one-way messages to accomplish one-to-many aural communication. Radio is a true mass-communications medium that extends public audio-space to great distances, allowing one person to be heard by millions of his fellows simultaneously. It delivers a continuous stream of information

---

* To distinguish between media and facilities, technology, etc., capital letters are used. Thus: Telephone (with a capital T) denotes the medium that employs two-way voice to accomplish person-to-person communications, whereas telephone (small t) qualifies facilities, equipment, technology, and services generally understood to be associated with the telephone network.

that informs, educates, or entertains. Irrespective of where they are, or what they are doing, users have a wide spectrum of programs to choose from, which can be listened to attentively or allowed to fill in the background and provide (artificial) company.

Television: delivers one-way video messages to accomplish one-to-many visual communication. A real-time medium that transports a continuous stream of information as it is generated, Television is a true mass-communications medium that extends public audio-visual space to great distances, allowing one person to be seen and heard by millions of his fellows simultaneously. Television delivers a continuous stream of information that informs, educates, or entertains. However, unlike Radio, it will not stay in the background but presents a changing image that occupies the visual sense and demands attention.

Communications media under development have the following attributes:

Videotex: based on Data Communications, facilitates two-way messages to accomplish information retrieval and display. Videotex is implemented in two ways—as Viewdata and Teletext. (At present, there is no universally-agreed-upon nomenclature for these media. Some authors use Videotex to denote what we call Viewdata.)

Viewdata is a two-way, interactive system that uses a video display (often a television receiver), local processing, and a remote data base accessible through the public telephone network. Pages of information, each enough to fill the video screen, are stored in the data base—ready to be accessed through a search protocol that allows the user to page to increasing levels of detail. The data base can embrace a large number of subjects; for this reason, the medium has been likened to an electronic encyclopedia. Its contents are derived from books and newspapers, and it includes some of the functions of Data Communications. Public service is now available in Great Britain (PRESTEL). Test systems have been installed in France (TELETEL), Canada (TELIDON), Japan (CAPTAIN), and other countries. In the U.S., experimental activities and/or technology trials are being pursued by several telecommunications and electronics organizations. AT&T has announced a technical standard that is compatible with TELIDON and with modified versions of TELETEL and PRESTEL.

Teletext is a one-way information system that employs unused lines in the broadcast television signal to transport data to modified television receivers without interfering with the normal program. A sequence of pages of information is sent repetitively. On the average, the user must wait for several seconds until the page he seeks is transmitted and his receiver has captured and displayed it. To make this time acceptable, the number of pages in the sequence is limited to no more than a few hundred. Thus, the detail of Viewdata is not possible, and the service is often described as an electronic magazine. Its contents are derived from magazines and newspapers, and much of what Teletext contains may be included in Viewdata. Public service is available in Great Britain (CEEFAX, ORACLE). In France (ANTIOPE), and several other countries, limited service is available or technology trials and/or experiments are in progress. In Great Britain and France, where viewdata and teletext services are offered concurrently, the format and data encoding are compatible so as to allow both services to use the same information and to permit the use of a common signal processor at the display. In the U.S., experimental signals have been broadcast, and system standardization is being advocated by broadcasters and others. The technique of inserting data on lines in the television signal is used for data display over CATV and for providing captions for deaf viewers of programs over broadcast television.

Electronic Mail: based on Data Communications, allows messages to be exchanged between many persons using terminals communicating through a common memory under the control of a modest computer. Text messages addressed to a specific recipient, or group of recipients, are stored until the recipient logs on, identifies himself, and requests his messages. Usually, the recipient can review a list of the originators and the subjects, and is able to elect to read the messages in order of interest to him. Most systems also provide answering, forwarding, and filing functions. Other systems handle voice messages. Because they can be accessed from a touch-tone telephone and do not require a special terminal, it is possible to use voice-message services from many locations. Both systems have the advantage over telephone that messages are stored until the intended recipients are ready to receive them (no one need be there to answer), and over normal mail that delivery is made at electronic speed.

Teleconferencing: provides an interactive electronic meeting space and the opportunity to substitute telecommunications for travel. The effect of limiting the dimensions of the exchange between the participants by introducing electronic constraints is far from understood. The richness of the medium employed, the degree of familiarity of the participants with each other, the complexity of the topics discussed, and the number of persons and/or locations involved all affect the outcome. For routine discussions between peers who know each other well, good quality audio channels may suffice. For unique discussions between several levels of management in several locations, full-color video may be insufficient. For complex discussions between technical persons, computer conferencing may be ideal. In the U.S., several major companies maintain facilities for teleconferencing that employ leased and/or dial-up connections. Many telephone companies offer voice-conferencing terminals for lease, and AT&T provides public videoconference facilities between major cities. Most major telecommunications entities in the world offer similar services on a limited basis.

Interactive CATV: provides a wideband, one-to-many, downstream connection together with limited bandwidth, one-to-one, upstream connection. Information can be sent to central (head-end) facilities for direct use by the system operator, or for relay to centers maintained by value-added service companies (e.g., security, information, meter reading). In the U.S., several systems provide security monitoring and a few afford the opportunity for answerback to the head-end.

The interrelation between existing record media, existing real-time media, and the experimental media described is shown in Figure 1.

Market, Technical, and Financial Forces

Markets develop through the interaction of user needs that produce demands, supplier rewards that depend primarily on anticipated profits, and the availability of technology. For products and services that use available

Figure 1

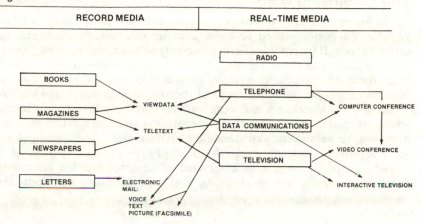

New communications media based on record and real-time media.

technology and are designed to fill an existing need, demand can be assessed, production costs can be calculated, profit can be projected, the probability of a successful outcome can be estimated, and the attractiveness of the market (market pull) to any particular supplier can be determined. For products and services designed to demonstrate the application of new technology in the hope of stimulating demand (technology push), it is virtually impossible to project the probability of a successful outcome. However, statistical evidence suggests that innovation to fill a need is several times more successful than innovation to exploit a technical development.

In the U.S., using advanced technology in an increasingly competitive environment, new carriers are challenging existing telecommunications providers. For regulated suppliers, the functional obsolescence of in-place equipment poses a serious dilemma: replacing the existing equipment so as to provide competitive performance requires writing off the present book value (original investment less accumulated depreciation), an action that increases operating expenses and must result in either increased charges or decreased profits.

With integrated circuit density doubling about every three years, the swing to digital electronics practically guarantees that the next generation of telecommunications equipment will be smaller, more reliable, perform more tasks, and cost less. If this cost reduction is dramatic enough, the book value of in-place equipment may be higher than the cost of new equipment that performs the same functions. This effect is known as value erosion. Again, correcting the overvaluation will result in increased charges or decreased profits. Functional obsolescence and value erosion will provide a disincentive for regulated carriers to upgrade facilities as long as the pace of technical innovation is greater than the rate at which these facilities can be depreciated.

147

The Automated Office

The automated office is a concept produced by the combination of a burgeoning, information-based economy and the communications media described above. It incorporates: data processing services such as word processing, facsimile, and electronic files to achieve desk-to-desk transfer of text, data, and image information as easily as voice information is now transferred over the telephone; computer services to accomplish the design and drafting of complex products and to control and support manufacturing; administrative programs that automate the preparation and coordination of calendars, provide reminders, and schedule activities; and communications services to provide electronic mail, information retrieval, and conferencing.

The stylized elements of an automated office devoted to the generating, handling, storing, retrieving, utilizing, and communicating of information

Figure 2

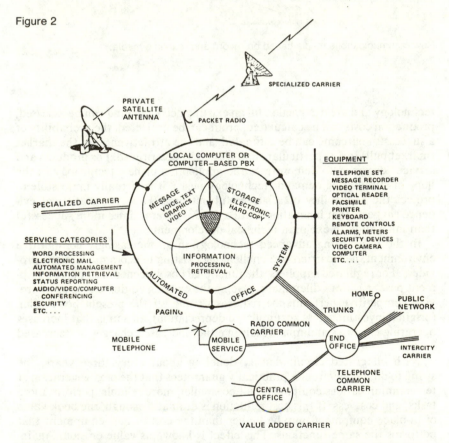

The elements of Automated Office. Communications within the office facilitate the application of advanced technology to improving the productivity of functions. They can be provided on twisted pair, coaxial cable, optical fibers, or electromagnetic and infrared radiation. Communications outside the office may be supplied by several carriers. Electronic Mail, Teleconferencing, and Viewdata have applications in this environment.

148

consist of: diverse terminals (including integrated work stations); message, information, and storage sub-systems based on a local computer or an advanced PBX; and communications over local and long-distance connections. In part, the communications requirement will be voice connections between individual work stations in the office and between work stations in the office and others outside. In part, the communications requirement will be data connections between individual work stations and the local computer; between work stations and remote computers; and between local computers and remote computers. In part, the communications requirement may be video connections between a limited number of local and remote terminals for videoconferencing, and from a central location to a larger number of local terminals for information and training purposes.

Within the office, signals may be carried on twisted pair, coaxial cable, or optical fibers; in star, tree, ring, or bus arrangements; or broadcast using sonic, electromagnetic, or optical energy. Configurations will depend on the bandwidths to be provided, the functions to be performed, and the distances to be covered, as well as the degree to which future computing and communicating equipment is merged. Signals may be analog or digital, and the same medium may employ both. Outside the office, signals may be transported over private networks or over facilities of: common carriers, specialized carriers, value-added carriers, or other common carriers. Voice signals may be compressed to reduce long-distance transmission costs; they may also be packetized and handled with data. Video signals that must be transported over terrestrial radio and satellite links will be digitized, compressed, and probably encrypted.

For organizations operating in markets in which shares and margins are established by competition, there is a continuing need to reduce expenses, to function more efficiently—to improve productivity. In combination with computers and electronic data banks, telecommunications can instantly transport information to wherever it is required and return instructions and new information to be processed and acted on. Insofar as these functions replace people and/or speed up operations, they improve productivity. Insofar as they make other functions possible, increase the amount of information handled, etc., they increase the sophistication of the operation, which may provide opportunities both for savings and for increased output. For any operating improvement that has an expectation of a reasonable return on investment, there will be an innovator ready to introduce it, and for changes that demonstrate a continuing return, there will be a market. Thus, new telecommunications media that contribute positively to productivity improvement will be adopted. For this reason, telecommunications facilities that support data processing, information retrieval, electronic message distribution, and the like are being incorporated into the fabric of the business sector.

The Wired Household

The Wired Household is an idea made feasible by the evolution of home computers, the availability of enhanced communications, and new information sources. It incorporates microcomputer-based entertainment and data processing functions; residential communications media such as Telephone, Radio, and Television; and can take advantage of the new communications

Figure 3

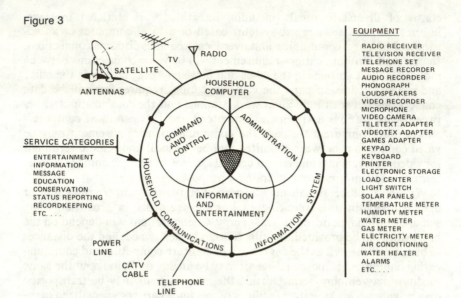

EQUIPMENT

RADIO RECEIVER
TELEVISION RECEIVER
TELEPHONE SET
MESSAGE RECORDER
AUDIO RECORDER
PHONOGRAPH
LOUDSPEAKERS
VIDEO RECORDER
MICROPHONE
VIDEO CAMERA
TELETEXT ADAPTER
VIDEOTEX ADAPTER
GAMES ADAPTER
KEYPAD
KEYBOARD
PRINTER
ELECTRONIC STORAGE
LOAD CENTER
LIGHT SWITCH
SOLAR PANELS
TEMPERATURE METER
HUMIDITY METER
WATER METER
GAS METER
ELECTRICITY METER
AIR CONDITIONING
WATER HEATER
ALARMS
ETC. . . .

The elements of Wired Household, a concept that includes home computer, enhanced communications, and new information sources to provide an environment in which entertainment, information, and personal communications are readily available, and administrative, security, and conservation functions can be performed automatically. Teletex, Viewdata, and Interactive CATV have applications in this environment.

media described earlier to provide an environment in which entertainment, information, and personal communications are readily available and administrative, security, and conservation functions can be performed automatically. Many of the applications will require development of specialized infrastructures (e.g., networks, data bases, administrative centers) that will have a social or commercial basis.

The stylized elements of a wired household arrangement in which security, entertainment, control, and communications functions are performed include: a broad spectrum of household devices; information and entertainment, command and control, and administration subsystems based on a household computer; and local communications facilities. This concept makes use of communications connections that may be supplied by the telephone carrier over wires or fibers, the CATV company over cables or fibers, and perhaps the electric utility, as well as antennas that receive transmissions from local radio and television broadcasting stations and television signals broadcast directly from space by satellite. Connections within the household may be made by wire or cable, coded messages on the power wiring, or wireless links using sonic, electromagnetic, or infrared energy.

In varying degrees, imaginative integration of facilities (ranging from almost none to total integration) may reduce the cost of mixed services distribution systems serving wired households. The degree of integration that is appropriate in a specific situation depends on many factors, not the least of which is the state of existing facilities. For instance, a straightforward approach to providing limited mixed services when telephone and CATV already exist might be to use a common signaling system that coordinates activity on the two distribution systems. If a pole line exists carrying telephone cable, integration may mean attaching CATV cable to the same poles, topology permitting. If new cables must be laid for both telephone and CATV, the cost of trenches or poles can be shared.

A higher level of integration involves the sharing of local transmission facilities, so that all signals enter the household by the same route. This integration of local transmission media implies more than a common electrical or optical pathway. It also includes multiplex and demultiplex equipment, as well as perhaps a strategy for sharing some terminal capabilities. For short distances (a few hundred meters), twisted pair may be used for a limited amount of video and voice. For long distances, coaxial cable or glass fibers must be employed.

Integration of central office and head-end facilities may only be practical to a limited extent. Certainly, the physical facilities may be shared to advantage, as may signaling and transmission. However, differences in holding time and fan-out requirements, as well as bandwidth of voice, audio, and video traffic, are too diverse to make a common switch feasible. Nevertheless, if a switched video distribution strategy is adopted, coordinated control of the separate voice, video, and data switches may be necessary. Integration beyond the local office is also conceivable. The provision of mixed services by satellite to an isolated community served by an integrated local office and common transmission medium is a case in point, although such instances may be rare.

The dilemma posed by the distribution of mixed services is to provide what can be a large number of one-to-many, one-way video channels in combination with a limited number of point-to-point, one-way video channels and a larger number of point-to-point, two-way voice channels. To some degree, the number of video channels devoted to entertainment and general information (one-to-many channels) affects the transmission media that can be employed. The topology, however, will be determined by the need to provide personal video channels (one-way, point-to-point). If many subscribers are to have one or two personal video channels (moderate or high level of mixed services), the capacity of tree and ring structures will be exceeded very rapidly. The provision of personal video channels, then, virtually dictates that a star topology be employed.

A star network for the distribution of personal video makes it possible to consider a switched distribution system that includes entertainment and information video. Such an arrangement can reduce the transmission requirement to each household to the number of channels actually needed and allows total integration of the final transmission path to the household. However, the ability of twisted pair, coaxial cable, or optical fiber to carry video signals is limited to something less than the distance present pairs carry voice. Since it is unlikely that repeaters would be used extensively in local distribution, this implies the introduction of local centers. Here, one-to-one and one-to-many circuits can be separated and the entertainment and information channels amalgamated in a tree or ring. Such an installation is

Figure 4

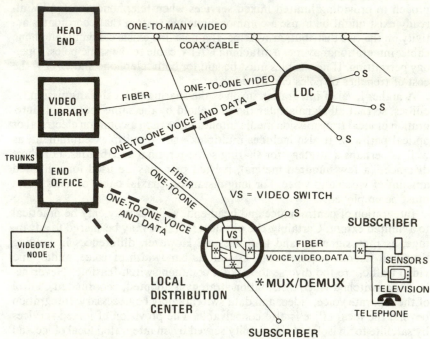

The distribution of television, telephone, and other services using a single fiber to each subscriber. Services are supplied to local distribution centers by a combination of star and tree systems. A video switch is used to provide only those services requested (and paid for) by the subscriber.

sketched in Figure 4. In this way, the best distribution topologies for the different services that comprise a high level of mixed services can be combined to advantage.

For a moderate level of mixed services, the number of one-to-many video channels is relatively small and they can be injected into the final distribution path without switching. Indeed, if the average demand for personal video channels is small, large numbers of subscribers might be served by an overlay of a ring (or tree) audio and video system and a star connected voice system.

Because it is affected by personal factors, residential demand is more difficult to characterize and estimate than business demand. While most consumers expect new services to effect a gain, economic advantage is only one of many important parameters. Personal gratification, enhancing self-respect, raising mutual esteem, reinforcing sense of community, and similar factors provide powerful motivations whose priorities change with time and personal circumstances. Services that contribute to survival may have great appeal in the presence of growing social violence and an aging population. Fire alarms, burglar alarms, medical alerts, and companion services for the elderly are important for segments of the residential community. Resource conservation (if it saves money), education (if it is relevant), and information retrieval (if it is convenient) may also receive support.

Discussion

An explosion can be defined as "a large-scale, rapid, and spectacular expansion, outbreak, or upheaval." Today's information explosion is aptly named. In many offices, an ever-increasing percentage of time is spent in collecting, processing, writing about, or verbalizing information. Effective handling of this explosion demands increased productivity—which can be achieved by the application of available technology to the office environment. Automated Offices can employ all of the established and emerging telecommunications media—and significant amounts of data processing and computer support besides—to assist in providing an environment in which resources are conserved, the reliability and consistency of the product is improved, and productivity is increased.

Market pull drives the development of the Automated Office. Minimizing costs requires the application of technology to office functions to achieve desired results. However, the common interest that exists in business—people making decisions to conserve funds—does not apply in the home. The Wired Household is presently driven by technology push. Its adoption will not keep pace with the development of the Automated Office, although the

Figure 5

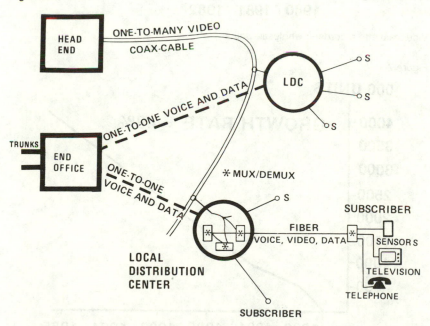

The distribution of a moderate level of mixed services can be achieved with a combination of star and ring systems, without a video switch.

familiarity with advanced telecommunications services and equipment that is developed at the office will lay the groundwork for acceptance in the home. As Marshall McLuhan stated, "Automation affects not just production, but every phase of consumption and marketing; for the consumer becomes producer in the automation circuit." Such involvement will not be confined to the limits of the office environment. Penetration into the home will start gradually, and large-scale penetration of the home is likely to follow large-scale penetration into business by half a decade.

In consumer telecommunications, a host of people spend relatively small amounts of money to support and improve their standard of living. In aggre-

Figure 6

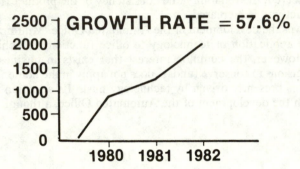

000 UNITS

Videocassette recorders: wholesale sales.

Figure 7

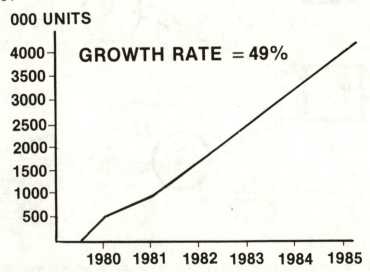

000 UNITS

Personal and home computer sales.

154

gate, the potential revenues are enormous. Prices for electronic products are falling slowly. Products now used for business will transfer to consumer markets when the price becomes enticing. This trend is evidenced in certain markets today. Consumer demand for videocassette recorders is running ahead of supply, and the demand for personal computers is beyond expectation.

Market pull for the Wired Household will evolve as developing technology meets consumer need. Some companies are already preparing for that day. Recently, a Home Bus Standards Association has been established, with Matsushita, Sony, and Texas Instruments among its members. Concurrently, Philips has published a proposal for a Domestic Digital Bus aimed at defining interconnect standards for TVs, VCRs, videodiscs, and stereo audio equipment. Clearly, these companies believe in the market for advanced telecommunications services in the home.

By projecting the trends that have developed in metropolitan living, a National Research Council Committee found that by 1985 there will be approximately 60 million households in the metropolitan areas of the United States. Of these, approximately 60% will be headed by a man and a woman (with or without children), another 10% will be headed by one person (usually a woman with children), and the remaining 30% will be units maintained by individuals living alone. During the day, when schools are in session, perhaps only 30% of the family dwellings will be inhabited. There will be about as many units occupied by nonworking wives with children. If present trends continue into the '90s, there will be shift toward more units occupied by the elderly as the number of elderly people continues to increase.

A current rise in the birthrate, especially among women over 30, may mean a slight increase in the number of households occupied during the day. Furthermore, if these women have careers, they may choose to continue working at home after the birth of their children. This could be accomplished readily through the use of several of the developing media described, together with equipment such as an advanced personal computer.

For the households headed by one person, for households maintained by individuals living alone, and for dwelling units unoccupied during the working day, there will be an increasing demand for security monitoring and for preprogrammed and remotely controlled household services. As resources become more scarce and more costly, the working head of a household will find it economically advantageous to turn off heating or cooling devices while the dwelling is unoccupied, and to turn them on automatically or by a device that is called remotely before the occupants return. In households of the elderly, there will be rising concern for services that contribute to personal security, emergency assistance, and socialization.

A recent study of the *middle generation*, those persons between the ages of 25 and 49, by Doyle Dane Bernbach reveals major market opportunities for home entertainment and telecommunications services. This group constitutes one-third of the U.S. population and accounts for 55% of its income. Among the middle generation, the survey finds "a widespread underlying concern about social isolation, rejection, and happiness." The survey also indicates that these consumers have a strong desire for human contact and concludes that things such as games and telecommunications that enhance direct communication between people have a bright future. A need is evident

Figure 8

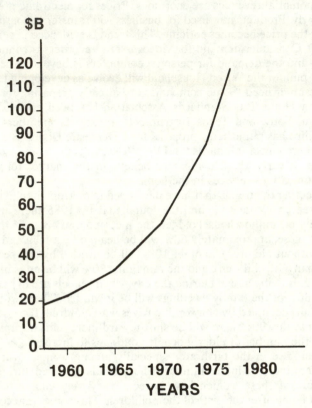

U.S. private consumption expenditure: recreation, entertainment, educational and cultural services.

for social surrogates, things that allow a person who is alone to feel he is not. Video games, home computers, and voice or video communications can fulfill this demand.

Despite their economic concerns, the middle generation is very interested in leisure and recreation. Private consumption expenditures have risen dramatically over the last 20 years. With office automation providing even more leisure time in the future, the development of demand for the services available in the Wired Household is potentially explosive. If pricing trends and social tendencies continue in their current directions, a strong market for the Wired Household could develop.

Technology Is Not Enough

by

Audrey Clayton

Technology developed and applied over the last quarter-century has led to a bewildering variety of emerging information services involving electronic communication. Examples include electronic mail, videotex, airline reservations, hospital records, electronic funds transfer, communicating text/data processors, computerized numeric data bases, and computer conferencing. The most recent and exciting of these to capture attention are videotex, teletext, and related services designed for use in the home.

Businesses and individuals alike are being urged to use these services, but such an undertaking could involve major investments in terms of money, time, effort, and restructuring of established procedures and behavior patterns. This decision should be preceded by consideration not only of the anticipated impacts of on-line systems, but also of factors other than technology that will affect their future evolution. It is the latter aspect that will be emphasized in this paper.

In this relatively new, fast-growing field, the term "on-line system" is freely used but rarely defined. Briefly, it implies the linkage of a communications channel with computer processing and storage capability. Computer terminals or other input devices are used to enter information, or query information already input by this or other means, and selected responsive information is output in some form appropriate to user needs. On-line services offer so many capabilities, and derive from so many different origins, that their future development is vulnerable to a wide variety of forces. It is important that we understand the resulting complex of both opportunities and problems if we are to exert any influence on the extent to which the evolving services actually do meet our needs.

My own experience has been primarily with the use of on-line services for the delivery of scientific and technical information. However, one of the clearest evolutionary trends (Table 1) is the loss of distinction between different types of information in terms both of location, and of the systems and services used for its delivery. Scientific and technical information is no longer stored separately in dedicated files, but is likely to be found in the same data base with social, environmental, regulatory, or other information.

The *equipment* used for on-line access may also no longer be dedicated to

Audrey Clayton is vice president of Forecasting International, Ltd., Arlington, Virginia.

Evolutionary Trends in On-Line Services

- Increase in non-dedicated data bases
- Increase in multi-purpose equipment
- Increase in user-friendly systems
- Increase in diversity of services
- Increase in availability of access points
- Increase in capability for simultaneous use

one particular function. Computer conferencing networks, for example, are already used not only for keeping up with ongoing research, but for political discussions, comparison of schedules to set up future face-to-face meetings, and even the exchange of recipes. A home information center could be used by different family members, or by the same person at different times, to place a bet, review family tax records, scan the local news, play a game, or consult an encyclopedia.

Most of the examples to be cited here refer to the consulting of machine-readable data bases of bibliographic information. These are prepared by many different data-base producers—frequently the abstracting and indexing services who also publish printed reference materials—and made available for on-line access either directly or through vendors who act as retailers for a large number of data bases. In the United States, there are currently three such major commercial information retrieval services—DIALOG, BRS, and SDC-ORBIT.

Historic Evolution and Current Status

There is no consensus on the total number of machine-readable data bases in government, industry, and the commercial sector, but it is generally agreed that there has been an order-of-magnitude increase over the past 10 years. The number of *commercially available* data bases accessible on-line has grown from less than 20 in 1965 to over 300 in 1979—and at a very conservative estimate will be greater than 800 by the year 2000. It should be emphasized, in connection with all such projections relating to recent innovative services, that to forecast 20 years into the future based on only 15 years of historic data does not generate a high degree of confidence in specific numbers; however, the overall trend is undisputed.

It is difficult to make a realistic assessment of the quantity of *information* thus made accessible on-line because of an undetermined degree of duplication, but the number of *records* in these U.S. data bases increased from less than 1 million in 1965 to 58 million in 1977, and is projected to reach 165 million by the year 2000.

Factual and numeric (as well as bibliographic) information is available on-line, covering a broad spectrum of topics, usually organized by discipline (such as engineering or agriculture) or by format (magazines, newspapers, or congressional reports).

An estimated 2 million on-line searches were performed in 1977, and based on growth rates prior to that time, 12.5 million would be conducted in the year 2000. We are currently running a little ahead of this trend, with about 4 million searches completed in 1979. It is true that "number of searches" may no longer be a meaningful concept in the future, in view of the growing lack of distinction between information delivery systems. Nevertheless, it is certain that on-line searching will increase due to the influence of a number of factors (Table 2): it is more cost-effective in many applications,

---

Table 2

Reasons for Increased On-Line Searching

- Frequently more cost-effective
- More available terminals
- More communications networks
- Increasing applicability to needs of small users
- Qualitative superiority over manual searches
- Increasing costs of NOT using on-line services

---

and more and more people are able to access the needed equipment and communications channels. Terminals are becoming more readily available, and the existence of commercial time-sharing networks, as well as government and private lines, makes communication with the data bases both simple and inexpensive. More than 25% of the scientific and technical community now has access to an appropriate interactive terminal—and essentially all of its members are expected to do so by 1990.

Increased use will also result from the growing capabilities of on-line services and their qualitative superiority over manual searches in many instances, together with the costs of *not* using them in an increasingly information-oriented society.

Current users of on-line information come from almost every sector of business, academia, government, and industry. Most of them now obtain access to on-line services by equipment located at their place of business, or through an information broker. However, with the growth of the personal computer market, the infiltration of terminals into libraries, and innovations in the entertainment and consumer service industries, this situation is bound to change.

The future thus seems to offer a continued increase in the availability and utilization of on-line services. New users are being trained, by just one of the three major vendors, at the rate of almost 10,000 a year. A substantial portion of the increase in usage is expected to come from small users, thus aggravating problems due to inexperience, infrequent use, and inaccessibility of support structures.

What will these users pay for the services? Reliable cost data for on-line searching are hard to obtain because of the highly competitive environment and the lack of uniformity in measurement. Search costs are currently estimated to range between $1.50 and $75 per search, with most of them falling

159

between \$10 and \$15. Dramatic improvement in cost-performance in the computer and communications industries will tend to decrease the real costs to the user of searching his own or privately owned files. However, the cost of accessing *commercial* data bases is almost certain to rise, as royalty charges approach a more realistic level and data-base producers seek a pricing structure more appropriate to their mix of printed and on-line products and reflecting increasing labor costs.

Factors Affecting User Satisfaction

We can identify three groups of forces that will influence the evolution of on-line services (see Table 3). The first group, situational factors, includes

---

Table 3

Forces Influencing Future Information Services

Situational Factors
- Technological advance
- Existing momentum of on-line services
- Information explosion

Reactive Policies
- Management and policy
- Government practices
- Legislation and regulation

Externalities
- Financial/economic context
- Social attitudes
- Leisure and entertainment industry

---

technologies as well as the existing momentum of various segments of the information industry. The category of reactive policies includes government legislation and regulation, and both government and private-sector decisions directly related to evolving information services. The final group encompasses the externalities—social, economic, and political elements that determine the future context in which such services must function. Not all the factors that should concern us fall neatly into just one of these categories, but it is a convenient basis for discussion.

Starting with the situational factors (Table 4), we see that advances in hard technology are tending to decrease costs and increase the capabilities of on-line services. However, there may be hidden penalties. These advances—which make on-line services faster, more comprehensive, more flexible, and in some instances cheaper to use than their manual alternatives—further stimulate the already dramatic growth in usage, which threatens the quality of service.

The size of individual data bases is also increasing. Assuming member statistics provided by the National Federation of Abstracting and Indexing

160

Table 4

Situational Factor Impacts: Technology

Technological Advances:
- Increased speed
- Increased comprehensiveness
- Increased flexibility
- Selective decrease in cost

IMPLY

Increased Usage:
- Increased waiting time
- Increased response time

Services are typical of the industry, the average data base will increase in size by more than 70% between 1980 and the year 2000.

The larger the data base, the more comparisons have to be made by the computer, in searching, to determine whether or not each record meets the selection criteria specified by the user (Table 5). Even with very fast hard-

---

Table 5

Situational Factor Impacts: Momentum

Information Explosion:
- Growth in size of data bases

  ### IMPLIES

  - Increased response time
  - Decreased retrieval efficiency

- Growth in number of data bases

  ### IMPLIES

  - Greater difficulty in source selection
  - Increased duplication of records
  - Increased need for standardization
  - Increased need for user education

- Generally:
  - Decreased information currency
  - Increased operating costs
  - Increased incentives for on-line rather than manual searching

---

ware access, more comparisons mean more elapsed time. This problem is being tackled from several angles deriving from so-called "soft technology" research: specification of more appropriate retrieval criteria; construction of inverted files and similar retrieval aids during record entry; alternative built-in search algorithms; and non-traditional record storage formats appropriate to computer *needs* rather than to user *preconceptions*.

However, the rate of progress in these areas is slow and uncertain, lagging far behind the "hard" technologies. Consequently, these growth trends will have negative impacts, at least in the short term, on the on-line services. Response time will increase, and retrieval efficiency will deteriorate. As the *generation* of information (particularly scientific and technical information) continues to escalate, system insertion time will increase, thus decreasing information currency, although this will still remain far superior to that provided by manual systems.

Continued proliferation of data bases will make it harder for the user to select a source, and will increase duplication of records in a multi-source search. Lack of standardization among sources, especially with an expanding population of infrequent and inexperienced users, will make education and training an ever more critical issue.

These examples illustrate some of the problems that arise as a consequence of the combined effects of technological innovation and the continuing growth patterns evidenced by on-line services. The second category of factors identified previously encompasses management decisions, government policies, and industry efforts to solve these problems or circumvent their effects (Table 6). At the individual level, a user may elect to use an intermediary rather than struggle with the diversity of system protocols.

Table 6

Reactive Policies

Individual Users	• Selection of type of service
	• Direct/indirect use
Commercial Users	• Purchase of own equipment
	• Establishment of own files
	• In-house training programs
	• Modification of established procedures
Information Industries	• Standardization efforts
	• Generalized education thrust
Government—As purchaser	• Procurement practices
	• Internal operations
—As controller	• Legislation/regulation
	• International negotiation
—As enhancer	• Funding of research
	• Pilot programs

Commercial users may compile their own private files, either on an in-house computer or through existing vendors, to avoid excessive cost increases. A major effort could be undertaken to provide *generalized* education in on-line searching, rather than the more usual system-specific instruction. *Government* policy options range from funding of essential areas of soft technology to providing greater incentives for the industry to work towards standardization.

In this context, I like to draw a parallel between the movement of information and the movement of people. No one is suggesting that we all utilize mass transit—or purchase Henry Ford's automobile "in any color, provided it's black." However, rules of the road must be established and observed; cars must have a basic similarity to the extent that, having mastered one model, we can reasonably be assumed competent to drive any other passenger vehicle; and government regulation is imposed and accepted regarding clearly-defined issues such as auto safety and emission control.

Translating these limitations in terms of *information*, we all agree that rules are needed to govern the flow in communications channels, avoiding conflict between the rights of way of individual messages. Surely it would also make sense to be able to apply skills acquired in operating *one* information system to the use of a different model, from a different supplier, with only trivial deviations that can be comprehended and compensated for in a few seconds. The appropriate role of government is undoubtedly a more contentious topic, but this is true also for the automobile industry, and there are few *users* who would advocate abolition of *all* government regulations, though I would not say the same of manufacturers. The analogy is far from perfect, and should not be pursued too far. I introduce it here only to point up the importance of issues such as training, standardization, and regulation, in both contexts.

A few examples of what may be termed "externalities" are listed in Table 7. This category includes the power of the labor unions, who will fight the

---

Table 7

Externalities

- Job-related social models
- Broadcast industry
- Public school curricula
- Labor union attitudes
- Leisure-time occupation
- Entertainment industry

---

introduction of automation if jobs appear to be threatened. The broadcast industry has succeeded in slowing down the installation of two-way cable communication, and thus hindered one possible mechanism by which interactive information centers may reach the home. Exposure to home-based systems would contribute a major advance in the familiarization process (which is already well under way, particularly with the younger generation,

163

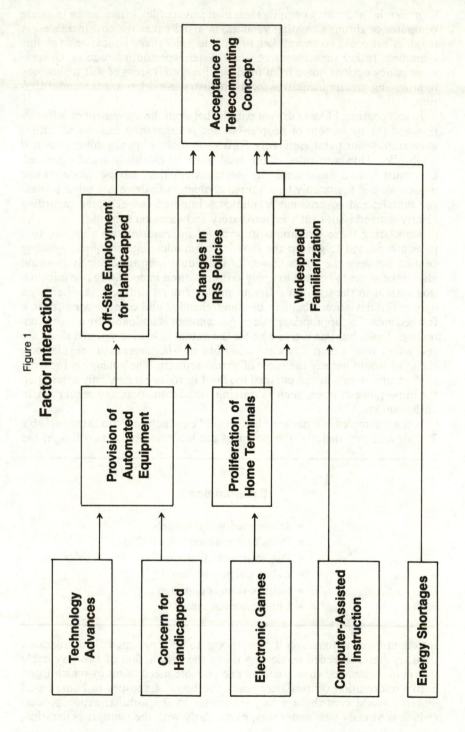

Figure 1
Factor Interaction

Acceptance of Telecommuting Concept

Off-Site Employment for Handicapped

Changes in IRS Policies

Widespread Familiarization

Provision of Automated Equipment

Proliferation of Home Terminals

Technology Advances

Concern for Handicapped

Electronic Games

Computer-Assisted Instruction

Energy Shortages

as a result of exposure to electronic games) and give a boost to computer-assisted instruction. The consequent shift in public attitudes may well be of greater significance than any other single factor in the evolution of on-line services.

Some interesting considerations result from the interactions *between* factors (Figure 1). As an example, concern for disabled veterans and other handicapped individuals may encourage the provision of automated equipment to permit them to work at home or in sheltered-environment "satellite offices." Along these lines, experiments are already underway in the private sector, and the Department of Labor last year reported an experiment with "flexspace"—analogous to flextime—in which a disabled employee uses such a system from her home. The IRS may be persuaded to redefine its regulations as they apply to permissible tax deductions for home terminals. Government policies regarding this "telecommuting" concept for other employee categories may follow. Such developments would tend to increase availability and actual usage of on-line services.

In another example of factor interaction, the introduction of adequate voice-input devices would encourage *direct* user access to on-line services by side-stepping the reluctance of management, whether male or female, to become involved in what is still perceived by many as the "typically female" task of keyboard entry. Touch-sensitive screens may also represent a small step in this direction.

Summary

Such a rapid survey as this can hardly begin to indicate the complexities attending the future evolution of on-line services. Some of these diverse factors will tend to improve the total spectrum of available capabilities. Some will increase complexity and decrease the quality of service. The interaction between differing factors may have consequences that are not apparent from considering any one of them alone.

The boundaries between communications and computer processing are rapidly shifting and will ultimately disappear—and with them the rationale for many of our regulations and restrictions. The publishing, printing, computer, communications, broadcast, entertainment, and leisure industries have become uneasy bedfellows, and must learn the accommodations necessary to avoid conflict. The public must learn the choices available in this time of fluidity if they are to formulate preferences and exert influence toward or away from unification of services.

The future may see a variety of convenient services coordinated and made readily available to us at home, business, or public sites, with access procedures sufficiently simple and uniform for us to use them ourselves, if we choose. At the other extreme, we may continue to be inundated by a variety of information services from different suppliers and different market sectors, accessible by different and incompatible mechanisms and procedures. The choice between efficiency and diversity is a familiar one, and it is likely that the eventual outcome will represent a compromise. The extent to which future services satisfy user needs will depend to a considerable extent on the unanimity and enthusiasm with which all of us, as concerned individuals, make our preferences known.

Acknowledgement

This paper is based on research supported in part by a grant from the National Science Foundation's Division of Information Science and Technology. Any opinions, findings, conclusions, or recommendations are those of the author, and do not necessarily reflect the views of the National Science Foundation.

People Lead Their Leaders in an Information Society

by

Harlan Cleveland

In mounting a program of education for leadership, four attitudes are indispensable for leaders in a complex and interconnected world.

• The notion that crises are normal, tensions are promising, and complexity is fun.

• A realization that paranoia and self-pity are reserved for people who *don't* want to be public executives.

• The conviction that there must be some more upbeat outcome than would result from the sum of available expert advice.

• A sense of personal responsibility for the situation as a whole.

Hubert Humphrey, the great American in whose honor I am now privileged to work, was the very model of a situation-as-a-whole person. He felt personally responsible for growing more food, manufacturing useful goods, making our cities more livable, distributing wealth fairly, creating better jobs, delivering public services, combating inflation, limiting the growth of population, protecting the human environment, ensuring the common defense, and keeping the peace. We need millions more people with a similar sense of responsibility for the whole.

People Lead Their "Leaders"

As I get around the country, I find my fellow Americans not so much overwhelmed by the problems we face as underwhelmed by the leaders who are urging us to face them. I think there is something that those of us who care enough about the future to make it a part of our professional lives can do about this mood.

That isn't because we are wiser than the people at large. It's because the people at large are already beginning to sense that *they* are going to have to lead their leaders out of the wilderness.

The American people have had quite a lot of practice, in the 1970s, getting

---

Harlan Cleveland is director of the University of Minnesota's Hubert H. Humphrey Institute of Public Affairs. Author of* The Future Executive *and several books on international relations, he has served as assistant secretary of state, U.S. ambassador to NATO, and president of the University of Hawaii.*

out ahead of our leaders. The federal government was the last to learn that the war in Vietnam was over. President Nixon and his staff were the last to realize that Nixon was through. The tidal movements of social change in the past 20 years—environmental sensitivity, civil rights for all races, the enhanced status of women, the progress in reducing population growth rates, recognition of the rights of consumers and small investors—were not generated by established leaders, but boiled up from the people at large.

But as we now look down the long murky tunnel of the '80s and '90s, it is clear that the American people (who will continue to make U.S. policy) still have a very long way to go in thinking through the contradictions of population and consumption, inflation and recession, growth and environment, defense and détente, work and welfare, resources and restraints, enterprise and planning. The policy-making general public is going to need help—help in peering into the middle distance, beyond the next election and next year's balance sheet, help in analyzing alternative futures, help in seeing the interconnections of their microproblems with the macroproblem, help in reconciling special interests with the general interest—help, that is to say, in "getting it all together."

Where is the help going to come from? Not, with painfully few exceptions, from the prominent leaders of the great established institutions—the federal government, business, labor, universities, foundations. The most visible leaders are, ironically, too responsible to take the responsibility for change—until the direction of change is widely accepted and it thus becomes more dangerous to stand still than to move on. For the leaders of record, it's just too scary to be the first birds off the telephone wire—until they're sure the rest of the flock will follow.

That's why the new ideas, the practical initiatives, and most of the real leadership in promoting new policies come from activist citizens, managers who know how "to lead by being led," men and women who are not preoccupied with formal power or getting their names in the newspapers—people whose concern exceeds even their confusion. These are the shock troops of the get-it-all-together profession, and the get-it-all-together professionals have to keep getting out ahead of the publicity heroes that *People* magazine still thinks are our leaders.

It's an exhilarating profession, but also a vulnerable one. The first reaction to a new idea may recall that pungent line from a Ring Lardner story: " 'Shut up,' my father explained." The resistance to what's never been done before may remind you of Peter Ustinov's claim that one of his grade-school teachers wrote on his report card, "Peter shows great originality, which must be curbed at all costs." The first birds off the telephone wire need the spunk and persistence of that courageous and original lady who was arrested on a one-way street for going the other way. "Officer," she said, "has it occurred to you that that arrow may be pointing the wrong way?"

Each of us who presumes to this kind of leadership—the kind of leadership that shows but doesn't show off—has to try hard to think about the situation as a whole. I mean that quite literally. None of us can expect to *act* on more than a tiny corner of the great complexity. But in our interrelated society, itself part of an uncompromisingly interdependent world, we have to *think* about all of it in order to act relevantly on any part of it.

168

The Art of Leadership

So the indispensable quality of leadership—the get-it-all-together function in a complex system—has to be breadth. Breadth is a quality of mind, the capacity to relate disparate "facts" to a coherent theory, to fashion tactics that are part of a strategy, to act today in ways that are consistent with a studied view of the future.

People are forever saying that leadership is an art, not a science or technology—a matter of instinct, not the product of thinking. The classroom is indeed an unlikely place to learn charisma. But leadership is the art that determines the social fallout of science and points technology toward human purposes. The information to understand our tools and our purposes, and especially to relate them to each other, is not carried in our genes. It has to be learned. So we educators cannot cop out: Equipping minds for leadership ought to be what's "higher" about higher education.

We have the beginnings of a general theory of leadership, from history and social research and above all from the ruminations of reflective practitioners such as Moses, Pericles, Julius Caesar, Jesus Christ, Martin Luther, Niccolo Machiavelli, James Madison, and in our own time such disparate sources of wisdom as Mahatma Gandhi, V. I. Lenin, Winston Churchill, Charles de Gaulle, Dean Acheson, Mao Tse-tung, Chester Barnard, John Gardner, and Henry Kissinger, who have very little in common except that they have not only been there but tried with some candor to speculate on paper about it.

From folklore and observation, then, we know that leaders are physically strong and abnormally hard workers. They are the strategic thinkers, more inclined than their followers to relate things and people to each other, to project patterns of collective behavior, to keep trying to see the situation as a whole. They are unusually curious about issues and methods outside the specialties in which they got their start. They are more preoccupied with values and purposes than their contemporaries; that is, they are more likely to cut through the forest of how-to questions and ask "Why?" They are the optimists, the visionaries—the people who, confronted by the gloom and reluctance that are the hallmarks of expertise, are most inclined to ask "Why not?"

Where We Are Going

As an exercise in breadth, let's stare for a moment at the macrotransition we are already in. It comprises a variety of changes in beliefs, loyalties, fears, aspirations, doctrines, and assumptions—about personal and national security, personal and national growth, personal and national equity (or "fairness").

"Post-industrial" is what the sociologists call the society we are becoming. I find that too retrospective a tag for so different and exciting a future. Besides, if we are to set our compass by where we have been, each of us could invent any number of equally backward-looking nicknames for the '80s and '90s. We are emerging, for example, into the post-military, post-Keynesian, post-New Deal, post-centralized, and post-scarcity era.

These nicknames tell us where we're coming from. But they also tell us something about where we are going. Briefly, let's try them on for size.

169

Post-military? Strategic theory, based on the primacy of U.S.-Soviet relations and the neglect of "development," doesn't seem to work very well when threats to our security come from the collision of modernization with drives for social justice and the resistance of cultural traditionalists.

Post-Keynesian? In our economic management, we are lost in a foggy no-man's-land strewn with obsolescent theories. Neither Keynesian nor monetarist doctrines seem to be very helpful in dealing with a business cycle that glues inflation and recession together in a dynamic stagnation that may not even by cyclical.

Post-New Deal? The New Deal's central assumption, from Franklin Roosevelt to Lyndon Johnson, was that more social justice required more of the nation's resources to be captured by taxes and spent by government agencies. In the 1970s, and especially in the 1980 election, we the people clarified the premise of the post-New Deal, whatever it is to be called. We said we wanted less government. But we also made clear that we wanted more fairness, more growth, and more defense—the blessings that government was supposed to be securing for us.

Post-centralized? We are moving from doctrines of centralized power to notions of decentralization, devolution, separatism, and broadened participation. Central economic planning, popularized around the world by industrial democracies that do not practice it themselves, is everywhere in disarray. Power is leaking out of national governments to local communities determined to exercise more jurisdiction over their own destinies. The formulation of public policy is increasingly done by nongovernments (profit and nonprofit), which can more easily think farther ahead, and experiment more flexibly, than governments can. And the yen to participate keeps spreading—through what the Communists call collective leadership and the Japanese call consensus and we call committee work—so that the key dilemma of the new era is how to get everybody in on the act and still get some action.

Post-scarcity? We are moving away from our early-seventies preoccupation with "limits to growth," based on an assumption that the world's key resources were nonrenewable, to a much more sanguine attitude about physical scarcities—with a new emphasis on recycling, on biological resources (because they're renewable), and on information, a resource that is not subject to the law of conservation of energy.

Information As a Resource

I will linger for a moment only on the last-mentioned of those interlocked transitions—the prospect of a post-scarcity world—because it has such large and intriguing implications for our capacity to handle our complex destiny.

We have heard many dire warnings, and I take them all very seriously. Yet it is worth noting that the race between world population and world resources will apparently *not* look so scary in the 1980s and 1990s as it did in 1970.

What used to seem an exponential explosion of population is now beginning to resemble the familiar biological S-curve. Only a few years ago, the more earnest believers in catastrophe could attract headlines, sell books, and be taken seriously if they predicted the world's population would grow to 7, or 7.3, or 7.5, or even 8 billion by the year 2000. The current U.N. median projection forecasts a global population of a little over 6 billion by then—and

Philander Claxton has suggested recently a sober scenario that would bring world population below 6 billion by the time we really get to the year 2000.

Why did so many get it so wrong? The forecasters once again committed the original statistical sin of mistaking current trends for human destiny. They were mousetrapped by countervailing trends: development, chemicals, women's instincts, and hope. All proved hard to fit into a computer program.

I don't want to be misunderstood about this. Population growth is still the primary engine of world poverty. Two billion more mouths to feed, three-quarters of a billion jobs to create—these are still massive assignments to tackle in one short generation. But the task might just be manageable. By contrast, the assignment implied by the earlier projections seemed unmanageable—looked so discouraging, in fact, that we were all exposed to those vivid metaphors about lifeboats and *triage*.

On the resources side of the equation, we have also gained in knowledge, insight, and wisdom during the 1970s. The early-seventies panic about limits to growth was a useful wake-up tonic. But it soon became evident that the "problematique," as the Club of Rome called it, was not a shortage of physical resources as such but a shortage of political will to control our human selves in using the biosphere's rich and versatile endowment.

Even nonrenewable resources, the familiar fossil fuels and hard minerals, would present no real supply problem over the next generation—*if* conserving attitudes, research-and-development on petroleum substitutes, and international cooperation don't continue to be in such short supply.

Beyond the nonrenewables lies a hugely underutilized biomass (one-fifth of it microorganisms, an inconceivably numerous army of workers now underemployed in making cheese and sauerkraut and fermenting beer and wine), plus a supply of solar radiation that is for practical purposes infinite. And these renewable resources are disproportionately available in the world's tropical regions, which are home for most of the absolutely poor. If they are still poor in the twenty-first century, that will not be nature's doing; the enemy will be us.

Beyond the physical and biological resources, *information* has in the 1970s come to be regarded as a resource, too. It's not marginal; Peter Drucker says information is now the key resource in our business economy. It's not depletable; John McHale taught us that information expands as it is used. It's not scarce; Lewis Branscomb says information "is in quantitative surplus. To be sure, there are great gaps in human knowledge that have yet to be filled by research and study. But the yawning chasm is between what some have learned, yet others have not yet put to use."

Taken together, the computer, the satellite, and the silicon chip are historically comparable to the invention of steel and the steam engine—or even the invention of the wheel.

The implications of putting more emphasis on bioresources, and on information as a resource, do not leap to the eye. But if you think hard about them, as I have been trying to do, you may conclude (as I have) that, compared with the resources associated with the age of physics and geology, they encourage:

• "Extensive" rather than "intensive" systems ("extensive" in terms of geography, capital, and labor).

- Economic, social, and cultural patterns that make interdependence, not independence, the law of life (for nations, for groups, for individuals).
- The spreading of benefits rather than the concentration of wealth (biomass is more equitably spread around the world than petroleum or uranium).
- The maximization of choice rather than the suppression of diversity (it is harder to regiment farmers and intellectuals than assembly-line factory workers or members of a government bureaucracy).
- The diffusion of individual responsibility rather than hierarchical command and control.

In a world depending less and less on the allocation of scarce (because nonrenewable) resources and more and more on biological and informational (that is, renewable and expandable) resources, management is bound to have a different "feel" to it:

- Cooperation, not coercion.
- More "sharing" transactions and fewer "exchange" transactions.
- More "positive-sum" games and fewer "zero-sum" games.
- Horizontal structures rather than vertical structures.

With nobody in general charge but everybody partly in charge, more participatory decision-making implies a need for much feedback information widely available. That means more openness, less secrecy—not as an ideological preference but as a technological imperative.

In such a management environment, "planning" cannot be done by a few leaders as experts with detailed blueprints. "Planning" has to be dynamic improvisation by the many on a general sense of direction that is announced by "leaders" only after genuine consultation with those who will have to improvise on it. Maybe that's what Donald Straus meant when, with posthumous apologies to Marshall McLuhan, he told us that "the procedure is the prophylaxis."

The Limits of Government

The macrotask ahead of us is to manage a worldwide transition from indiscriminate and wasteful growth to purposeful, efficient, and compassionate growth. We must enhance the human environment within perceived energy and resource constraints, minimize the damaging side effects of development, and guide the growth of the presently richer societies to allow "growth and equity" in the presently poorer societies. This task has to be undertaken in a world where no one race or creed or nation or alliance can (or should) arrogate to itself the function of general management; that is, in a pluralistic world society.

A tidal change of values is already well under way; I have suggested some of its surface manifestations. The main obstacle to converting these new values into policies, practices, and institutions is not limits to physical resources or limits to the capacity of the human brain. It is the limits, even more recently discovered, to government.

If we are going to work out ways of governing ourselves without inflating our governments more and more, those with public responsibility for action are going to need continuous access to the best thinking of those who, because they are not publicly responsible, can more readily convert into suggested public policy the interest of the general public in getting that macrotask performed. And those who are privileged to think freely because they are not burdened with formal responsibility must be the first to widen their perspective and lengthen their view. Thus can the nonresponsibles be partners with the responsibles in the governance of a nobody-in-charge system.

The reactive mode of modern government requires that most new ideas originate outside government. An interesting division of labor results—between nongovernmental experts, thinkers, and advocates on the one hand and government officials and legislators on the other. The nongovernments in our society can do some things better than governments can:

• They can work, ahead of time, on problems that are important but not yet urgent enough to command political attention.

• They can shake loose from conceptual confines and mix up disciplinary methodologies.

• They can think hard, write adventurously, and speak freely about alternative futures and what they imply for public policy today.

• They can generate discussion among people in contending groups, different professional fields, and separate sectors of society who might not otherwise be talking to each other.

• They can organize "dialogue" across local, state, and national frontiers on issues not yet ripe for more official "negotiation."

I do not suggest that nongovernmental organizations are universally or even usually effective in compensating for the rigidities of responsibility. But the opportunity is there, and is reflected in the rapid growth of nongovernmental enterprise working under such rubrics as policy analysis, futures research, humanistic studies, environmental action, population research, public interest law, energy conservation, technology assessment, and (as in my case) "public affairs."

There is even a rough and ready test of relevance for nongovernments: Are they working on issues that are still too vague, too big, too interdisciplinary, or too futuristic for governments that are too busy, too crisis-ridden, and too politically careful to tackle? If not, they should be.

In our enthusiasm—which I share—for more comprehensive ways to pull the agencies of government together, let's not neglect to include the nongovernments in a wider concept of governance. Maybe the key political dilemma of the 1980s can be expressed (like most truth) as a paradox: How are we going to get more governance with less government?

The Chinese, as usual, said it best a long time ago. "Ruling a big country," said Lao-tse, "is like cooking a small fish"—that is, too much handling will spoil it.

Communications Technologies and Education: The Coming Transformation

by

Christopher Dede, Jim Bowman, and Fred Kierstead

Isaac Asimov once wrote that the important thing to predict is not the automobile, but the parking problem; not radio, but soap operas; not the income tax, but expense accounts; not the Bomb, but the arms race. Similarly, the important thing to forecast is not that schools and universities, homes and industries will add videodisks, microcomputers, satellite telecommunications, and interactive "artificial intelligence" simulations to their repertoire of instructional techniques. Rather, the crucial question becomes, "What new 'social inventions' will spring from routine usage of these devices to enhance learning?"

Technology assessors classify impacts of a technological innovation as primary, secondary, or tertiary. Primary effects are intended outcomes of a new technology (automobiles are a faster means of transportation than horses). Secondary effects are largely unexpected by-products of routine technological usage (lead pollution from gasoline replaces fecal pollution from horses). Tertiary and higher-order effects spring from these unintended impacts (lead-free gasoline requires more energy to produce, thus contributing to shortages).

Most discussions of information technology have centered on primary effects. This article will focus on the tertiary and higher-order consequences of the communications revolution in education. To chart these imports, the types of subject matter most likely to be delivered by information technology must be delineated, and the capabilities for instruction that these devices are likely to have by the end of the decade discussed.

What Kinds of Content Will Be Taught by Machines?

A basic and reasonably accurate way to divide concepts, skills, and values into two clumps—things adaptable to being taught by technology at reason-

Christopher Dede is professor of education and studies of the future, University of Houston at Clear Lake City, Houston, Texas. Jim Bowman is co-chairperson, Studies of the Future, University of Houston at Clear Lake City. Fred Kierstead is associate professor of education and studies of the future, University of Houston at Clear Lake City.

able cost and things not adaptable—is to create a differentiation between "training" and "education." Any type of instructional programming will be most effective for subject matter with a limited range of right answers (training), because defining an incorrect learner response and channeling student effort in an appropriate direction are much easier. While creating good "multiple right answer" instructional units (education) is technically possible, the difficulties and costs of doing so are prohibitive compared to using human teachers. Thus, training in subjects such as reading, basic math, accounting, carburetor repair, nuclear power plant operation, and cooking will be done by machines; and education in creative writing, clinical psychology, salesmanship, and executive decision-making will be done by humans.

Most curricula will be a carefully differentiated mixture—with training initially predominant, then ever increasing amounts of education being added. Training is a good approach for learning procedures (such as laboratory methods) and tends to be focused on the lower levels of Bloom's taxonomy of cognitive skills. Cost-effective training is most easily possible in large classes learning low-level subject matter or in small, highly specialized mastery sessions.

In contrast, education tends to be content-based, communicating the interrelationships of words and symbols. These upper levels of Bloom's taxonomy of skills require human instruction, as do rapidly changing subject areas in which training materials would quickly require reformulation to avoid obsolescence. Education will probably continue to be done primarily in schools or their future equivalent; training, in extra-school settings (where its flexibility and individualization can be used to greatest effect).

Shifting to a curriculum with instruction disaggregated into education and training is likely to make possible much greater efficiency in learning. Training is best done on an individual basis in spontaneous, relatively small chunks of time, rather than in classrooms with large numbers of students and a prescheduled, extended block of time to be filled. Moreover, the process of creating an instructional program for subject matter requires enough thought and detailed specification that the resulting product is likely to be a quantum jump ahead of existing materials.

Education, too, will become easier when each of a group of learners has been individually certified to have the requisite skills and knowledge to tackle more advanced subject matter. As a result of efficiency gains in both education and training, the school curriculum may eventually be taught in one-third of the time it takes currently (especially where training is predominant, as in the early primary grades or in the workplace). In turn, this will allow financial savings from students finishing earlier and/or the inclusion of additional material in the curriculum.

Capabilities for Instruction of the Information Technologies

The information technologies will be used in education because they possess certain "functionalities": properties and attributes desirable to the learner. Some of these characteristics will provide ways of delivering instruction at a lower cost than possible with human teachers (thereby helping to solve present problems in financing education). Other capabilities will allow types of instructional interaction not possible before (such as a driving simulation in which the student can turn at any intersection and see the scenery change appropriately, or a nuclear power plant simulation in which the learner can "operate" a reactor).

Several decades may pass before the full range of abilities of devices as powerful and versatile as the information technologies is realized. It will take much longer for educators to master completely how best to use this range (four hundred years after its development, instructional usage of the book is still being refined). Some illustrative functionalities that seem likely to be available by the end of the 1980s are listed below:

Hand-Held Computers
- drill and practice
- presentation of simple material, with questions to test assimilation
- response to student-initiated questions on a specific topic
- simple games that build basic skills (such as spelling)

Microcomputers
- complex games to build higher-order skills (such as advanced math)
- simple interactive simulations (such as modeling lab equipment)
- simple "microworlds" (e.g., what would happen if gravity behaved differently?)
- voice input and output
- computer art and music
- word processing and spelling/grammatical correction
- authoring programs (enabling teachers to create instructional packages)
- computer-managed instruction
- information management, record keeping, and data-retrieval

Mainframe Computers
- complex simulations and microworlds
- complex presentation of data bases (e.g., a 3-D tour through the Animal Kingdom)
- sophisticated electronic library

Computer Networks
- electronic mail
- computer conferencing
- transfer of large data bases

Mass Telecommunications
- instructional delivery to multiple extra-school settings (one-way or interactive)
- dramatic vicarious experience (with corresponding affective overlay)
- simple models of skilled performance (e.g., cooking, welding)

Interactive Videodisc
- complex models of skilled performance (e.g., carburetor repair, surgery)
- surrogate travel (such as a trip through an art museum with the student controlling speed and angle of view).

This list is incomplete, and many of the labels are too narrow to convey the spectrum of capabilities possible. Nonetheless, these sample functionalities illustrate how certain instructional properties and attributes of these devices can be matched to the learning process. As cognitive psychology gains a greater understanding of how people learn, existing functionalities of the information technologies will be reconceptualized and tailored to fit individual thinking styles. Thus, the advent of these devices allows instruction to advance further toward an applied educational science by increasing our knowledge and control of the teaching/learning process.

Social Invention or Social Change?

Thus far, this paper has delineated possible technological inventions pursuant to communications in the future. There are various levels of interrelationship between such technological inventions and the realms of social invention and social change. (An invention is defined here as a creation in which the intent is clearly visible in the result, while change is defined as a created thing or idea that does not clearly establish the intent of its creator.) Even though there are many new developments that are by-products or accidents of intent, the authors of this paper are concerned with invention as a planned matter. For example, if Alexander Graham Bell had shouted at a telephone with the intent of making it type, the result he got we would classify under change rather than invention.

It may be easier to discriminate between technological invention and technological change than to distinguish between social invention and social change. It is less complicated, for example, to establish that a phone can or cannot type than it is to establish that we were born by accident or by intent. However, some deliberate social inventions (such as the Red Cross or Alcoholics Anonymous) can be readily distinguished from haphazard social change.

An example of the tension between invention and change is evidenced by television. The television medium has established itself as a major vehicle for social change worldwide. It influences appearance (clothing, hair styles), language, family (marriage, divorce, child-care), politics, health (food, exercise), religion, and status—to mention only a few areas of impact. This is all accomplished under the pretense of entertainment (as distinguished from education) and a demand-supply theory that assumes that the public gets what it wants. As a result, television assumes little responsibility for its product. This is a subtle form of education (change) that does not acknowledge accountability and even has the appearance of being random.[1]

This brief perspective on television as an agent of social change also establishes an interrelationship between technological invention and social change. Thus, a technological invention such as the television (doing what it was "intended" to do) may result in social change (whereby programs are not accountable for social consequences) rather than social invention. Society needs to begin perceiving the matter of invention as a predictive concern involving both social and technological consequences. The goal of such a shift would be to minimize accidental change by planning paradigms that link social and technological invention under one isomorphism. (Douglas Hofstadter defines an isomorphism as a process whereby "two complex structures can be mapped onto each other, in such a way that to each part of one structure there is a corresponding part in the other structure" and both parts play similar roles in their respective structures.[2])

Invention is neither static nor beyond revision. In looking at societal (or global) good, we may determine that any given social or technological invention should be revised, reconstructed, or abolished. This assumes that individuals and groups are receptive to critical assessment of their work. Historically, this has not been easily achieved, as John Dewey noted in 1927:

> There is a social pathology which works powerfully against effective inquiry into social institutions and conditions. It manifests itself in a thousand ways: in querulousness, in impotent drifting, in uneasy snatching at distractions, in idealization of the long established, in a facile optimism assumed as a cloak, in riotous glorification of things "as they are," in intimidation of all dissenters—ways which depress and dissipate thought all the more effectually because they operate with subtle and unconscious pervasiveness.[3]

Technological Impacts on Education

Educational institutions are currently witnessing a kind of pathology much like that described by Dewey. There is abundant literature designed to promote schools as they "used to be." This perspective offers an essentialist theory premised on "back to basics" and a "market approach" to education (which assumes that learning can best be equated with earning). The orientation is to perceive the school as a basic-literacy/job-mill institution, modeling a kind of common school (from the 1850s) that is present-centered and generally lacking in historical or futures application.

In the midst of a technological revolution, a "common-school" mentality exhibits more than pathology. It results in a paradox in which the pendulum of social change is swinging to a past social invention—the common school—with a simultaneous reluctant acceptance of educational technology necessitated by a need to reduce costs in education. In such an essentialist structure, computers can certainly teach a cognitive, competency-based curriculum. Thus, a group that dislikes computers may paradoxically be dominated by them. As technology becomes less expensive and increasingly available, it may eventually replace teachers (who are becoming more expensive).

As this example illustrates, technological-social isomorphisms are weak in normative applications. Christopher Lasch argues that diminishing economic and psychological returns are creating serious normative problems. He believes that America has created a narcissistic culture, as deferred gratification is less rewarding in an age with an uncertain future. Lasch asserts that this has resulted in individualistic strategies for self-preservation and "the happy hooker stands in place of Horatio Alger as the prototype of personal success."[4] Thus, individuals in a present-centered world struggle for interpersonal advantage through intimidation and seduction of others. Lasch offers an insightful perspective into normative problems. To the extent that Americans are merely reacting to social change, his thesis is useful. Today's middle-class child cannot expect to adopt the same wants/needs as his or her parents. Ownership of single-family dwellings, for example, does not appear to be highly probable for the next generation. This is a cherished want that has been a major form of deferred gratification for a long period of time.

Educational concerns such as these (in the broadest sense) should be addressed through alternative social-technological inventions. This entails anticipatory planning rather than adaptive approaches to planning. James Botkin describes the dilemma as follows:

178

The question is not whether the eighties will usher in learning, but what kind of learning the decade is bringing. Will humanity be taught by shocks, whose lessons entail prohibitive costs and deadly delays, or will people learn how to shape those events which with intelligence and willpower could be controlled?[5]

The technological inventions discussed earlier will have a profound influence upon the answers to Botkin's questions. Equally important will be the social inventions or social changes that interact with technology. The following section will establish educational inventions that transcend a common-school mentality. The view is toward an isomorphism between technological planning and anticipatory learning.

Social Invention in Education

Unfortunately, most discussions about information technologies have centered on their primary effects, and a great deal of what seems to be emphasized in the future for schools is training (competency-based learning) rather than education. Trying to deal with social change without social invention (which provides a human mechanism for planning, deliberating, and choosing alternatives) leaves too much to chance and unplanned consequences. The possibility of educational institutions being outstripped by outside agencies in the dissemination of information seems high, unless educators take an active role in the use and applicability of educational technology. If, however, the technological inventions of the silicon revolution continue to be haphazardly integrated with social institutions, technological needs will continue to replace human needs, learning will still be fixated on earning, and inequality of opportunity between the rich and the poor will be widened.

Most futurists present a convincing argument that, in the emerging "communications era," knowledge will be the value. For social invention to occur at all, there is the need for information exchange. Robert Theobald, John McHale, and Dennis Gabor (to name just a few) have predicted that "use" value will replace "ownership" value in the near future, and access to information will be of chief importance as the data explosion continues.

In the past, educational critics have noted that what goes on in schools is several years behind what is happening in the society. If educators continue to view the information technology available today as too expensive, or if they equate education with dissemination of knowledge, instruction will be even further behind the times as an agency for social invention. There is abject fear by many educators that they will be replaced with computers and word processors. This can only be true if education continues to train rather than educate.

There may be a strong need to reevaluate educational goals, structures, and the meaning of an "educated" person. If educational institutions continue to be transmissive, a great deal of what we learn in schools could be replaced with appropriate technology. But the technology itself has contributed to a redefinition of intelligence from accumulation of knowledge to use of knowledge. An educated person cannot be defined as one who has accumulated knowledge, lest we agree that the computer is "smarter" than we are. Educational goals must reflect higher-order learning and continued evaluation of data received. Social invention must be the driving force of techno-

179

logical invention, rather than the converse.

In order to effect this change in educational goals, the structure of education (itself a social invention) must also be changed. Schools at present support more collection than evaluation of what is learned. In order to establish the importance of evaluation, innovation, planning, and participation in learning, educational institutions must reflect problem-analysis and synergetic planning modes. Finding desirable futures requires normative interpretation of what is learned. Educators will be required to provide very different kinds of learning environments than what is expected today. Education, in the true sense of the word, must be an agency for change and provide a forum for synergetic resolution of problems and possibilities. "Schools" could be replaced with time-free, location-free centers for the resolution of desirable goals.[6]

The present paralysis in education—with competing goals, interest groups, and administrative structures—is blocking any concerted effort to work toward shared visions of the future. Diversity and plurality are needed in a society facing problems of choice at all levels. Merely fitting technology into present educational institutions will not solve the problems of hunger, disease, global domination, or worldwide illiteracy (examples of the kinds of questions that need to be addressed). Having a participatory and informed citizenry who can communicate ideas at all levels is not a luxury, but rather a necessity. Amelioration of the human condition throughout the world will require reinterpretation of values, goals, and educational purposes.

A Defensible Partiality

With the possibility of increased malaise and a continuation of crises on a global scale, the need for an education that transcends present models is evident. The authors of this paper defend the contention that education may be the one social institution that can make a difference in the resolution of these problems. Reliance on "experts" and "technicians" in a communications era will continue to promote a "have"-"have not" orientation—producing a society intent on information denial as a means of power and worth. Education over the years has done its part in the promotion of this kind of thinking, continuing to treat knowledge as a scarce commodity that must be doled out. With the prospect of information technology providing alternative sources of information and with the increased importance of problem-solving skills, educators must change the instructional emphasis to an orientation that is problem-centered and inventive.

If educational institutions in fact were designed to help in the resolution of social problems, "schools" as we know them would disappear. Basic knowledge would be more than just reading, writing, and arithmetic. Computer programming and symbolic logic might be just some of the "basics" added to the curriculum. Integration of outside agencies (business, communications, libraries, information services) with educational institutions would aid in educating the public for participation in decision-making.

There are a number of considerations/prerequisites that must be addressed if, in fact, education rather than training is to occur in educational institutions. Some of them include:
- Decision-makers accept that the future is not predetermined.

180

- Organizational structures (including schools) reflect synergetic models.
- Use of information technology is not considered "education," but rather a tool for further learning.
- Learning becomes lifelong and interdisciplinary.
- The meaning of intelligence changes from the collection of facts to the ability to interpret data for alternative uses.
- Lateral situationally-based thinking and linear, extrapolist thinking are both encouraged. Skills in assessing primary, secondary, and tertiary consequences are taught.
- Policy-setters understand that technological needs must be replaced with human needs.
- Citizens recognize that social invention and planning are important skills for the betterment of humanity.

This is certainly not a complete list, nor is there any order of importance placed on each, but they reflect a defensible partiality on the part of the authors.

Conclusion

Communications devices have the potential to reshape both the delivery systems used to convey instruction and the subject matter of the traditional curriculum. Because of their functionalities, these technologies will expand the pool of educational consumers beyond the traditional student population to include very young children, recipients of industrial or professional training, the aged, adults engaged in non-formal learning activities—in short, virtually everyone in the society. Instructional activities will routinely take place not only in schools and universities, but in homes, the workplace, and communities. The size, method of operation, locus, and content of education will alter dramatically.

As society moves to a knowledge-based economy, increasing numbers of people will use communications technologies as a major tool for learning, whether educators choose to encourage this process or not. If this shift takes place in an unplanned, reactive fashion, a variety of undesirable side effects may occur. On the other hand, a deliberate transformation that maximizes the strengths and minimizes the weaknesses of these tools could greatly improve current educational practice. Hopefully, society will realize the importance of encouraging such a planned transition.

Footnotes

1. This is presented in greater detail in "Mass Media Values and the Future of Education" by John D. Pulliam, Fred Kierstead, and Jim Bowman, in *Needs of Elementary and Secondary Education in the 1980s: A Compendium of Policy Papers,* Subcommitee on Elementary, Secondary, and Vocational Education, Committee on Education and Labor, House of Representatives, Ninety-Sixth Congress, 1980.

2. Douglas R. Hofstadter, *Godel, Escher, Bach: An Eternal Golden Braid.* New York: Basic Books, 1979, p. 49.

3. John Dewey, *The Public and its Problems.* Holt and Company, 1927, pp. 170-171.

4. Christopher Lasch, *The Culture of Narcissism*. New York: W.W. Norton, 1978, p. 53.

5. James W. Botkin, Mahdi Elmandjra, and Mircea Malitza, *No Limits to Learning*. New York: Pergamon Press, 1979, p. 123.

6. See Jim Bowman, et al., *The Far Side of the Future*. Washington, D.C.: World Future Society, 1978, pp. 71-82.

Using Video in Rural Development

by

V.K. Dubey and S.K. Bhanja

Communication research indicates that development takes place in a local context with a decentralized set-up in which people have scope for meaningful participation in controlling their own lives and environment. Unless the content of media originates at the community level and relates to the viewers' world of values and environment, it is bound to be irrelevant and ineffective. In this context, there is increasing consciousness in the present-day world of the need to demystify and democratize media use at the small-community level so that people can present their problems and explore possible solutions in the context of the realities of their situation. Besides increasing message credibility and acceptance, this effort can work equally well to motivate action. Communities thus can derive the strength and confidence to solve their own problems.

Community communication is based on the credo, "of, by, and for the community." The natural choice falls on video as the most suitable medium for generating interaction. Video has the ability to present the community in both moving images and sound for immediate reproduction. Unlike movies, it does not require processing. Video equipment does not require sophisticated training to operate, can be easily handled by illiterate rural folk, and is portable enough to be carried by bullock cart, by camel or horse, or by hand. The color camera, portapack, and monitor all operate on batteries and are not dependent on electric power networks. India is making color monitors and cassettes. Hence, only the camera and recorder need to be imported.

Video in Developing Countries

Experiments with small-gauge videotape have recently interested nonformal-education instructors in the developing countries. Videotape is seen as an ideal medium for promoting audiovisual literacy for motivation, attitudinal change, behavior reinforcement, community participation, and entertainment.

The approach used in the Tanzanian Year 16 project (1971-72) was based on the premise that communication is a necessary prerequisite for social change, that rural populations involved in the process have valuable information and knowledge to transmit, and that video was the right medium to

V.K. Dubey and S.K. Bhanja work for the Division of Dairy Extension, National Dairy Research Institute, Karnal, India.

choose for communicating this.

Video has been used in rural development both as a process and as a product. Its utility as a process was illustrated by the Fogo Island experiment in which the Memorial University of Newfoundland and the National Film Board of Canada participated; film and video screening brought problems of a political and economic nature into the open to be discussed, analyzed, and acted upon.

In Chile, video was used for training thousands of members of farmers' cooperatives. In Thailand, video was used in a National Family Planning Program, where it proved its utility in training rural field health personnel of all types. The uses varied with the context and place of use. Some of the fields and countries associated with video are indicated below:

• Agricultural development: Bangladesh, Gambia, Sri Lanka, Tunisia, Upper Volta, Peru, and Venezuela.

• Child care: Egypt, Gambia, Iran, Jamaica, Philippines, and Thailand.

• Literacy program: Egypt.

• Urban development: Pakistan.

• Generating community consensus and problem-solving with community effort and self-help growth: Alaskan region of U.S. and Newfoundland in Canada.

Video in India

The Indian experience with video as an interactive medium for community development is very limited. There are only a few examples of its use in a community context. The effort made by CENDIT (Centre for the Development of Instructional Technology) in its Saharanpur media experiment brought out vividly the possibility of using video for humanizing the process of communication. A second experience was that of ISRO (Indian Space Research Organization, Ahmadabad), where video was used to produce programs for the local television network on such problems as bonded laborers, untouchability and other such evils, and local development. But the utility of the video medium has been demonstrated in other settings too. Recently, the National Dairy Research Institute, in collaboration with the Memorial University of Newfoundland, Canada, has been engaged in a rural development action research project in the village of Taparana, Karnal, using video extensively in various contexts.

The Taparana Experiment

Taparana is an insignificant entity in the midst of prosperous Haryama Villages. Essentially a village of low socio-economic status groups, Taparana consists of 209 families from seven different castes belonging to low and backward communities. Sixty-four percent of the households are landless agricultural laborers. Only 13.4% of the families—those who own more than two acres of land—are able to live comfortably on agriculture. The average household income is about 250 rupees per month (for a family of three adults and four children). There are only three married women who can read and write and, in all, there are about 45 families with one or more members who can decipher printed letters.

The core component of this action research project (which has already lasted two years) is the faith that the ultimate users of an idea must have control over the what, why, where, and how components of the message, so that it reflects their own reactions and opinion, and are responsible for what they say.

This project is a departure from the conventional aid-oriented government programs made *for* the people. It aims at activating an individual's dormant potential to enable him to better exploit the available possibilities existing around him at a given point in time. The philosophical assumption is that human potential is unlimited and that ignorance of this potential is the basic cause of human suffering. Thus, the developmental efforts must aim at cultivating in the community the creative power to realize and estimate its own latent strength and resources from the perspective of available institutional provisions—and at initiating self-action for growth. This means leading people gently to a gradual realization and assertion of their own hidden abilities and the progressive utilization of these abilities to achieve their desired goals through carefully regulated exercises.

Development from this perspective means fusion of individual and community needs. An order is created whereby emerging individual growth is reinforced through newly created social networks. People join together to produce those resources that are missing but necessary for the well-being of the community. The inaccessible necessary resources are made available through mutual patterns of interaction. Achievement of this goal requires three things: (1) recognizing the importance of the individual; (2) building the community network; (3) creating a decentralized media-use pattern. This amounts to the creation of a new culture. The project emphasizes creating a new order of self-governance. In general, it means cultivating personal and social responsibility, sensitivity to the environment, confidence, mutual trust, knowledge of one's own capabilities and possibilities, and acquiring the skills to manage community affairs. This is achieved by democratization and media control by the people of the community, who are the ultimate beneficiaries of any development program. Thus, interactive media originated by the community should ultimately result in increased initiative, freedom of action, shouldering of responsibility, and acquiring of power to overcome the sense of helplessness. This socio-economic transformation of the individual and his community is the ultimate goal of the effort. Realizing these values in society is a time-consuming and hard-to-measure process. Hence, the usual yardsticks of roads built, hours of voluntary labor contributed, etc., need to be dropped.

The achievement of the above goals demands a new approach and a new outlook. At the same time, it demands patience and faith in the supremacy of human self-affirmation. In discussing the methods being followed in the project, we do not claim that these methods must be used in every situation. Variations are always possible and welcome.

Initiating Community Actualization

This is the process whereby the community identifies its own problems and their causes and explores possible alternatives for their solution. In this process, the individual or community may need help. The role of the media at this stage is to link the isolated individuals, groups, and communities and get them started on the process of positive interaction. To initiate this process, the community worker needs to be acquainted with surrounding realities and to have intimate knowledge of community culture. He should contact people individually and in functional informal group settings and engage in a series of open-ended discussions relating to general problems or topics of interest. Gradually, people can be led to speak out about their concerns. At this stage, the community worker needs to isolate those issues that are easy to solve and are also on the priority list of the individual, group, or community. Such matters then could be videotaped and presented in the community for discussion. Through this process, a few individuals in the community could be identified as "community actualizers." Those are the persons who have a conscious concern for their community and the issues it is facing. There is seldom a community where no such persons are available. They possess a treasury of knowledge for rationally reasoning toward a solution. Such individuals generally have social acceptance, though they may not be from the elite group or ruling segment in the village. Before the taping is done, thorough discussion with the actualizers is a must. Afterwards a final recording can be made. This recording should be presented to the concerned group or community for generating or arriving at a consensus. Interactive community media help to spot the effective leaders.

Democratized media participation plays a major role in the community actualization process. This amounts to completely reversing the role of media from being top-down to being bottom-up. In other words, many of the messages originate at the community level and people have full control of what is presented, how, why, and to whom. This breaks the vicious cycle of dependency, and real power of decision-making and self-governance is achieved by the community.

The Community Worker As Social Animator

The role of the community worker in traditional development programs has been that of an advocate and executor of programs for people. To the community, he is the state personified and a custodian of the people's interest. Such persons often find it difficult to win the confidence and trust of the community, and their motives are always suspected. Even the most concerned development workers find it difficult to identify with the problems faced by the community. Most of the time, their feeling of concern is one of pity and sympathy for people they consider to be inferior, and is marked by a condescending or paternalistic attitude. People sense this condescension and respond by not being responsive, since this hurts their self-respect.

A community worker is expected to be a catalyst to facilitate the development process. His conscious involvement with the villagers' own desires, problems, and suffering identifies him with the community. He no longer remains above, but moves ahead to be *of* and *for* the community. Due to his intimate involvement, he becomes more knowledgeable about the community he serves. He learns how to engage people in constructive interaction and transfers the real power of decision-making to them so that his continued presence does not become a necessary precondition for progress.

In the Taparana community development project, the project workers cultivate a sense of empathy. Since the basic concern of this development project is improving the quality of human life, there is no effort to achieve a predetermined target. The project workers take their time to become *part in* and *part out* of the community. These workers try to identify issues and help in finding solutions by initiating interaction within the community. The community is thus assisted to become involved in problem-solving and to assume responsibility for, and control of, their own action for development. Once the action is begun, the project workers withdraw from it and involve themselves in looking for some other issue.

Introducing Media

In the Taparana project, video is used as the community medium due to the advantages discussed earlier. The following steps for the gradual introduction of media into a community are suggested.

Step 1: Media demystification. The video units (half-inch portapack, camera, and monitor) are carried into the community. Scenes of common community interest, such as their fields, their school playground with children playing, village streets, etc., are recorded; in addition, the work of village artists may be recorded, with their consent. This tape is then played to community members. Care must be taken at this crucial stage not to record any sensitive subjects within the community (such as village girls); community workers must be aware of local cultural values. It is essential that the social animator build a good rapport with the community prior to introducing the new media. At this stage, the community members come close to observe the operation of the video equipment and gradually come to understand media capabilities like instant reproduction, playback, erasing, recording, etc.

Step 2: Recording and playback of an informal community discussion. As a second stage in the process, informal group discussions are recorded and played back instantly. At this stage, the social animator may also participate, engaging the group in constructive and positive discussion. Gradually, the community members come to identify some of their felt and unfelt needs. This could be described as problem identification and sharing by the community. Potential community actualizers are identified during this process.

Step 3: Selection of community actualizers and small-group discussion to identify priority issues. Democratically-selected community actualizers are subsequently engaged in discussion of the broadly identified issues in a general informal group discussion. After viewing a recording of that informal discussion, the social animator must assist the small group to pinpoint some immediate but easy-to-solve issues through general consensus. An action plan is then prepared by the community actualizers. One or more individuals are then selected to help the social animator to video-record a particular issue.

Step 4: Video-recording of a community issue by one community actualizer, and discussion. The issue is discussed with a representative community actualizer. An outline of the issue to be recorded is prepared with his help. Then the issue is video-recorded under his guidance. Time and again it is replayed to this community actualizer for modification. After his approval, the tape is played to the other previously selected community actualizers for their approval. Needed modifications are carried out as desired by the group.

187

Thus, the tape becomes ready for general community viewing to discuss the issue.

Step 5: General community viewing and issue discussion; reediting if desired in cases where the issue must be presented outside the community. At this stage, the videotape is played to different groups in the community in their free time and at a convenient place. Since the community at this stage gets engaged in serious discussion of problem-solving, care must be taken to avoid any outside distractions or disturbances. Children should be kept away at this stage. In this process, the people in the community have begun mutual interaction, and consensus on an action plan commonly emerges.

If the issue involves an official agency or other outsider, the tape, after general community approval, is sent out for presentation to the concerned official. The response of the authority is likewise video-recorded and presented for viewing by the community in small groups. In this way, the community and the authority concerned are joined in mutual problem-solving.

There are many other ways to use video, such as for science education, transfer of technology, community entertainment, etc. Such tapes can be directly recorded by the social animator and may be viewed by the community in small groups.

A Case History: Owning a Rikshaw

Although the project was launched on January 1, 1980, we did not make any headway until April, because we did not know where to start. The community did not trust us; none of us was native to the region, and we were unaware of the cultural orientation of the community. But our repeated visits to the village gradually led to rapport.

The workers were open-minded about village issues. Mostly in informal chats, people used to ask for jobs. Attempts to discuss personal or community problems led to expressions of community helplessness, the blaming of others, and general indifference. Criticism of government (village and state) was a popular topic.

A ray of hope emerged when a rikshaw puller from the village met with one of the team members in the town. During an informal chat while Mr. Rajpal, the rikshaw puller, was pulling his rikshaw with the community worker on it, he asked for help in solving his problem of buying a rikshaw. He said he had been pulling a rikshaw for the past three years and was paying a rental charge of four rupees per day. He had already paid more than the cost of two rikshaws. (A new rikshaw costs about 1,000 rupees.) He wanted to own a rikshaw. The worker came to know that there were a dozen rikshaw pullers in the village. He advised Mr. Rajpal to gather the others for a meeting and discussion. The group gathered one evening at the home of another rikshaw puller. The discussion focused on the modalities of the work and the possible consequences.

A second meeting was held two days later. The details of economics were discussed, and five members of the group were identified as articulators. These were the persons who could present their ideas to others clearly and systematically. The next morning the group was taped, and they presented their problems and possible solutions. The taped message was presented to the group for approval and modification, if necessary. Later the tape was shown to the manager of the Bank of India branch office in a neighboring town.

The bank manager was pleasantly surprised by the rationality of the group's problem analysis and by the alternatives put forth for the solution. The communication of the group convinced him of the rikshaw pullers' ability and willingness to act. The bank manager's response was taped. He expressed his agreement with the suggested terms of repayment for a loan, and gave full details of how he could help. The tape was played back to the group on the next evening and discussions were held. Five rikshaw pullers decided to participate in a loan; they selected a group leader, who was literate, to represent them. His travel expenses to the neighboring town were shared. In this way, the rikshaw pullers were able to acquire ownership of their rikshaws and take a vital step up the economic ladder.

A Word of Caution

Video is a powerful communications tool in the hands of the development worker. But no tool, however powerful it may be, can ever replace the human element. The effectiveness of the tool depends on the people using it. Unless the community worker is committed, motivated, and prepared to play the ever-changing role of empathizer rather than that of preacher, the media alone can never deliver the goods. The support of national and local political authorities, and a conscious desire to solve people's problems, are other prerequisites for the successful use of video.

On the basis of the above discussion, we believe that the community communication approach attempted through the use of videotape-recording and playback offers definite possibilities for building people in relation to their community.

The Future of Public Library Service: A Behavioral View

by

Rosemary Ruhig Du Mont

As we move into the next century, increasing attention is being paid to the variety of ways people use information and the variety of ways it can be distributed to them. Population demands for diverse kinds of information and formats for that information are growing. Yet, at the same time, financial support for traditional information agencies such as public libraries is being reduced. Some critics believe that until public libraries rethink their design and operation, they will continue to fall behind in competition with newer forms of information provision.

> . . . there appears to be a relentlessly spreading indifference, if not hostility, to the public library in the minds of Americans. The American public seems disenchanted with the public library. People no longer see the library as important—at least not in relation to other community services—and public libraries everywhere find themselves in a precarious financial situation as a result. The very existence of the public library appears to be in jeopardy (Harris, 1975, p. 21).

Past library responses to societal change are in part responsible for this current state of affairs, for the historical development of public libraries is replete with ambiguity. This ambiguity is reflected in contradictory goals that on one hand have expressed interest in providing a wide range of services and materials to attract the masses to use the library for education and leisure time pursuits, and on the other hand have reflected the desire to have only the best in literature for those that actually did use library services (Du Mont, 1977, chapter 8). The educational leaders who supported these contradictory goals saw the important stabilizing role of the public library. "It was their conviction that if the common man could be induced to read the best books, he would be more inclined to be conservative, patriotic, devout, and respectful of property." At the same time, "even the most desultory reading of fiction" was preferred by librarians who were trying to distract people from vicious entertainments designed to satisfy the "lower impulses of human nature" (Harris, 1975, p. 11).

This much abbreviated discussion gives one only the most general idea of

Rosemary Ruhig Du Mont is associate director, School of Library Science, University of Oklahoma, Norman, Oklahoma.

the conflicts inherent in goals for public library service. However, it is the basis for conclusions that, if correct, will have a great impact on the possible futures of public library service. A first conclusion is that as a result of the apparent contradiction in goals, public libraries have continually struggled to fill a variety of conflicting needs with limited financial support. They have consistently tried to maintain services to scholars and serious readers, while at the same time attempting to support more popular library programming for leisure-time pursuit. That these variety of approaches have not succeeded in increasing support for public library service has been a continuing source of frustration for public librarians (Harris, 1975, p. 17).

The lack of extensive support for libraries, however, has not caused widespread change in library policy. Michael H. Harris points out that library administrative functions have beome so extensive that librarians have little time for reflection on either clientele or purpose (Harris, 1975, p. 12). Instead, attention is paid to organizational issues, and the goal that has become most prominent is survival (Galvin, 1976, p. 1833).

One way of surviving has been "residuation." To residuate means "to burrow into a fixed, immovable position while maintaining a low profile (Sidney, 1976, p. 13). The verb was created to describe satirically Washington bureaucrats. The term might apply to the development of public library service both in terms of the lack of widely known and identifiable philosophy of service and in the lack of organized responses to the demands of a changing society.

A more telling survival tactic consists of piecemeal attempts to make the library more responsive to the masses. The intent is to get the nonuser into the library by any means possible. A wide variety of library activities have resulted, as the library has wandered from one program to another in attempting to prove utility (Davies, 1974, p. 118).

It can be generally concluded that such programming has failed, if recent surveys and polls are indeed accurate reflections of library use. Libraries have not "gotten through" to those who it is thought have the most need of their services. The findings of two recent polls, by Yankelovich in 1978 and Gallup in 1978, emphasize the lack of interest in public library service by large segments of the American public. The Yankelovich study, sponsored by the Book Industry Study Group, was designed to identify the book consumer and thus it provides secondary information useful to libraries. The Gallup study was designated to focus specifically on library use and reading habits.

The Yankelovich study is based on results of 1,450 interviews conducted in 1978. It reports that 94% of its sample *read*. However, only 25% are described as heavy readers of books (having read 10+ books in the past six months). Thirty percent are light book readers, having read 1-9 books in the past six months. Nonbook readers are 39% of the sample. They state their dislike of books. The heavy book readers, on the other hand, comment on the enjoyment reading gives them. Those who enjoy reading tend to be white, middle class, well educated, female, and young.

The Gallup survey reinforces the above findings. Interviewing 1,515 persons nationwide, Gallup asked questions regarding frequency of library visit, amount of book reading, and knowledge and attitudes about the library. The survey found that 843 persons had visited the library in the past year. The profile of the "heavy" reader supports the Yankelovich study: female, 18-34 years of age, and college educated. The "heavy" library user (one who visits the library about every two weeks) is male, 18-34 years of age, and college educated.

Both polls reinforce earlier studies that show that readers and library users are, for the most part, white, middle class, and college educated. These people have always been the primary users of libraries. Programming to attract other groups into the library has not succeeded in changing this user profile.

> The truth of the matter is that the literature is quite clear on one central point. Most U.S. citizens can be called "hard to reach" communicatively speaking, although the poor are certainly more so. Relatively few people seem to be standing around waiting for our important messages or anxious to gain access to the information we so desperately want to share (Dervin, 1979, p. 3-4).

In response to the lack of interest in libraries and books, library activists have long supported the notion that the library must redirect its attention toward becoming an active information (in all its forms) dissemination center rather than a passive book distribution center (Dowlin, 1978). In spite of this conviction, books have remained the librarian's favorite way of transmitting information, and service can still be characterized as passive (Harris, 1975, p. 20). In essence, libraries appear to be trapped by their historical roots, and they may remain trapped unless a serious effort is made to examine alternative futures. The major question for the future is whether the current emphasis on books will be perpetuated with the aid of technology, or whether technology will be used to create other meaningful alternatives for information and dissemination and communication in libraries.

In considering alternatives that have potential, certain key issues need to be addressed: ease of access, the training of librarians, and the continuing identification of the library with books.

Ease of access will be a significant issue for the library of the future. Literature in the field of communications suggests that individuals seeking information generally operate under an essential law of least effort. That is, when people look for information, they take whatever is easiest or most convenient (Doyle and Grimes, 1976, p. 53). Advances in electronic communications and all the implications and applications inherent in such advances are attractive because new, easily accessible information and entertainment resources can be made readily available to users in their own homes.

Some library systems are trying to respond to these new insights about users. The Online Computer Library Center's Viewtel/Channel 2000, for example, can provide a variety of information services over television in the home. These include: a video catalog of the local public library, a video encyclopedia, home banking, information about public agencies, a calendar of local events, instructional programs in math and reading, and a community bulletin board for the deaf. The project is part of an ongoing effort by OCLC to investigate the development of innovative systems offering library patrons easy and inexpensive home access to library services (*OCLC Newsletter*, 1980, p. 2-3). In providing such services with the use of technology, the library can make a planned and conscious shift from the traditional book supply function to what Dowlin calls "an information and professional advisory function in the service of nonspecialized adults" (Dowlin, 1978, p. 445).

The training of librarians to work in the new technologically oriented public library is a second key issue. A largely justifiable criticism of library education has always been that it is too closely tied to present practices and that it educates for current service rather than for future growth and change (Garrison, 1970, p. 2763). The move toward the development of technological expertise and the understanding of the social changes brought about by technology has been only slowly adopted in library science curriculums. Yet, if one accepts the notion that new, meaningful alternatives to traditional book-oriented public library service are needed, it follows that professional education for public librarians must also change.

Robert Taylor, in a provocative essay on the future of library education, suggests that librarians of the future need to emphasize a variety of new attitudes and skills (Taylor, 1979a, pp. 1871-1875). They need to learn how to select and organize data and information that people will *use*. They need to develop an awareness of the totality of information resources and the appropriate strategies for searching for information in specific situations. They need to become sensitive to use, uses, and users of information, emphasizing service and client-satisfaction goals. To encourage development of such attitudes and skills, Taylor suggests six subject areas as a framework for professional education:

- **Organization of information.** Information in all of its many forms and formats must be considered. The book orientation must be expanded to include alternative media and the ways in which people seek and utilize information from these media.
- **The information environment.** The study of organizations and communities in information terms is required. Examination of societal institutions as they acquire, organize, process, retrieve, and disseminate information is necessary in this regard.
- **The study of information media.** The variety of media channels for the dissemination of information must be considered. Not only physical characteristics but also the functions of different channels for fulfilling different purposes for different audiences must be examined.
- **Systems and Technologies.** The principal focus here is on systems analysis, i.e., the study of the way people, technology, and information combine to make up an information system. A student will not only be able to understand and describe such information systems, but also be able to judge the cost and benefits of various system options.
- **Research methods.** Knowledge in this area will allow students to become "critical consumers" of research results as well as effective researchers in their own right. Assessment of information services and products relies on good research that can adequately measure results obtained.
- **Management.** Management issues relate to all of the other topics so far discussed. Management is concerned with organizational behavior, productivity and accountability, and human motivation in an organizational setting. It is also concerned with organizational politics and power and conflict. Most importantly, it is concerned with decision-making, forecasting, and strategy formation. Any attempt at integration of information systems with

human resources must concern itself with management.

Taylor is convinced that the true potential of librarianship will be recognized through the study of the subjects listed here. They reflect the massive changes taking place in the information environment and the demands of technology and social forces surrounding the library profession (Taylor, 1979b, 364-368).

A third key issue relates to a matter already alluded to: the continuing identification of the library with books. This identification must be broadened to include recognition of the alternative forms and types of information available from libraries. Films, phonograph records, books in large print, books by mail, religious lectures, information on community affairs, and health and emergency services appear to have potential for attracting a wide audience (Hays and Wilson, 1974, p. xiii). Public library information and referral activities appear to have much potential in this regard. Such programming can be offered over television as well as by phone and in person.

Many libraries are offering some of the alternative types of information delivery mentioned here as part of a fragmented service pattern. What is needed is a coherent approach that pulls the many disparate kinds of programming into a unified delivery system.

In addition to responding to the three issues identified here, a new attitude toward programming and delivery in libraries is also needed. This new attitude may be called "communication based."

A communication-based library system involves more than information transfer and the use of communication. It involves making sense of information obtained from the system by asking, answering, comparing, thinking, listening, redefining, repeating, etc. An effective information system in this regard must do more than collect, store, and disseminate information. It must also build into its formal structure procedures for interrogating the system in ways that make sense for individuals (Dervin, 1979, p. 17). In terms of actual design of systems, with the aid of technology, libraries can begin to adopt and use more flexible ways of storing and retrieving information. Manipulation of information arrangement can be more readily accomplished, leading to an infinite variety of arrangement patterns to be created as needed to reflect individual needs.

Libraries can place more emphasis on the acquisition of materials in response to demand. Not only the subject matter of materials but the format in which they can be provided must reflect the ways in which people will use them. A more visually oriented library can be one result, with materials on film or on television a predominant feature.

The utility of information use needs to be measured in people terms rather than in institutional terms. Currently, circulation statistics are still the most common way of measuring library success or failure. Other recently identified performance measures include title fill rate, browsing fill rate, subject information fill rate, response time, reference and information service provision, circulation per capita, in-library use, collection turnover, registration as a percentage of the population, program attendance, number of people using library services, and workload measures (Zweizig, 1981, p. 2). Such statistics tell little about the value of use, since they ignore such vital questions as: How useful is the book to the person who takes it out? How pertinent is the reference service? How adequate is the cataloging process? (Du Mont and Du Mont, 1979, p. 125) More effort should be spent on trying to relate statistics to impact on users and usefulness of materials to them.

Betty Sell, in a study of academic library effectiveness, provides a user-oriented model, which can be used in a public library setting as well (Sell, 1980, p. 296-336). She measures such variables as benefit provided by the library and benefit received by intended users. Other variables measured include relative importance of benefits accrued and level of satisfaction with service. The type of information provided by her research approach is evaluative and basically subjective in nature, and at the same time is quantitative and cognitive. Such a user-oriented approach to measuring library use will enable libraries to identify user needs more accurately and so provide needed materials and services more successfully.

Perhaps most significant for the future is the sensitizing of information practitioners (librarians) so that they can successfully interact with people and machines, and in particular be more accepting of the ways in which people go about finding out things. This means, for example, that librarians need to help people on their own terms and take people's perceptions of how information systems should work as guidelines to how systems need to be manipulated to serve them.

Private for-profit information agencies, of course, are already helping to establish and manipulate machine-oriented information systems. In addition, the "knowledge industry" utilizes radio and television programming, films, records, newspapers, magazines, advertising, sports and entertainment, and teaching machines in what has been estimated to be a fifty-billion-dollar business (Hixon, 1973, p. 190). We are told:

> . . . everybody's into "cable television"—networks, book publishers, newspapers. Cable television is a system for building the best TV antenna in town and then wiring it into everybody's television set—for a fee. . . . But the new technology is such that it has broadcasters and newspaper publishers worried. For the same cable that can bring off-the-air television into the home can also bring programming from the cable operator's studio, or an "electronic newspaper" printed in the home by a facsimile process. Books can be delivered . . . over "television" by using the station's signal—so everybody's hedging their bets—including the telephone company. . . . But at this point it is not at all clear who will have his hand on the switch that controls what comes to the American people over their "telephone wire" a few years hence (Hixon, 1973, p. 101).

The large communications conglomerates have seized a good share of the initiative. The public library does have its own unique role to play, however. It can add a "people perspective" to the development and use of new information technology. Development of new methods of storing, retrieving, and disseminating information has concentrated on the technological aspects of such methods. Librarians can have as their prime focus the people who use these systems and how they interact with them. Ultimately, it will be users who will identify ways such systems can be of help to them, and libraries can help them in this task.

Historical precedents have been discussed that reinforce public library caution in taking on new roles. The growth of a passive "mind set," the evolution of a bureaucratic organizational structure, the adherence to the book as the significant "information package"—these are but a few of the elements identified in this regard. This situation is further compounded by present-day financial contingencies.

> Present organizations that are almost overwhelmed by the sheer demand to provide services on a minimum budget cannot be expected to invent new methods. . . . Sometimes such agencies are not able to adapt sufficiently to accept new social inventions. . . . (Conger, 1973, 0. 156)

To overcome such barriers of past and present seems like a formidable task. Yet recognizing that these barriers exist is the first step in overcoming them. The potential of public librarians in becoming human links between information and communication technology and uses of that technology is so useful and so significant that it certainly is worth the effort and investment to support the changes that will make such a librarian role possible now and in the future.

References

Conger, Stuart. "Social Inventions." *The Futurist*, VII (August, 1973): 149-152.

Davies, D.W. *Public Libraries As Culture and Social Centers: The Origin of the Concept*. Metuchen, N.J.: Scarecrow, 1974.

Dervin, Brenda. "Meeting Individual Informing Needs in the Midst of the Information Explosion of the 1980s." Paper presented in the Colloquium Visiting Lecture Series of the All-University Gerontology Program, Syracuse University, February 1, 1979.

Dowlin, Kenneth E. "The Technological Setting of the Public Library." *The Library Quarterly* 48 (October, 1978): 432-446.

Doyle, James M., and George H. Grimes. *Reference Resources: A Systematic Approach*. Metuchen, N.J.: Scarecrow, 1976.

Du Mont, Rosemary Ruhig. *Reform and Reaction: The Big City Library in American Life*. Westport, Conn: Greenwood Press, 1977.

Du Mont, Rosemary Ruhig, and Paul F. Du Mont. "Measuring Library Effectiveness: A Review and an Assessment." *Advances in Librarianship*, Vol. 9. New York: Academic Press, 1979, p. 104-141.

Gallup Organization, Inc. *Book Reading and Library Usage: A Study of Habit and Perceptions*. Chicago: American Library Assoc., 1978.

Galvin, Thomas J. "Beyond Survival: Library Management for the Future." *Library Journal* 101 (Sept. 15, 1976): 1833-1835.

Garrison, Guy. "Library Education and the Public Library." *Library Journal* 93 (Sept. 1, 1970): 2763-2767.

Harris, Michael H. "The Role of the Public Library in American Life: A Speculative Essay." University of Illinois Graduate School of Library Science, *Occasional Papers* 117 (January 1975).

Hays, Timothy P., and Concepcion S. Wilson. *A Survey of Users & Non-users of Public Libraries in Region 6, North Carolina*. Greensboro, North Carolina: Piedmont Triad Council of Governments, 1974.

Hixson, Richard F. *Mass Media: A Casebook*. New York: Thomas Y. Crowell, 1973.

"OCLC's Viewtel Test Gets Under Way." *OCLC Newsletter* 143 (December 9, 1980): p. 2-3

Sell, Betty. "An Evaluative Holistic and User-Oriented Approach to Assessing and Monitoring Effectiveness of the Academic Library in Its Setting." *Library Ef-*

fectiveness: A State of the Art, ed. by Neal Kaske and William G. Jones. Chicago: LAMA/ALA, 1980, p. 296-336.

Sidney, Hugh. "Danger: Residuators at Work." *Time* 108, November 29, 1976, p. 13.

Taylor, Robert S. "Educational Breakaway." *American Libraries* 10 (June 1979): 364-368. (b)

Taylor, Robert S. "Reminiscing About the Future: Professional Education and the Information Environment." *Library Journal* 104 (Sept. 15, 1979): 1971-1975. (a)

Yankelovich, Skelly and White, Inc. *Consumer Research Study on Reading and Book Purchasing*. New York: Book Industry Study Group, 1978.

Zweizig, Douglas, to Charles Robinson. Typed letter, July 30, 1981.

Communications for Global Development: Closing the Information Gap

by

Frank Feather and Rashmi Mayur

The information-poor are growing poorer while the information-rich are being overwhelmed. Existing communication systems around the world are in a state of chaos, facing catastrophic collapse, thus perpetuating the information gap and economic underdevelopment. A full 60% of the world's people remain illiterate. Out of a global population of 4.3 billion, some 3 billion never read a newspaper or watch a television set and 2 billion never listen to a radio. Yet, the potentials of existing and futuristic modes of communication offer the opportunity for global economic development to occur. In fact, the power of information is economic power, and the realization of a "New World Information and Communications Order" (NWICO) is part and parcel of the "New International Economic Order" (NIEO) called for by leading representatives of the South. Communications is the key tool in developing human potential and well-being on a mass scale.

The Communications/Development Link

In the traditional method of development, communications has been regarded as an outgrowth of economic development. In other words, illiteracy could only be eradicated through education, which, in turn, could only be provided through funds spun off from economic activity. This is a "Catch 22" situation. How can economic activity proceed without education and training? Today, it would seem more appropriate to regard telecommunications as a *pre-condition* for economic development to occur. Indeed, with the massive advances in microelectronic technology, this is the only way to perceive future economic development strategies.

Seymour Papert of MIT has shown that computers impact on illiteracy in two dialectically related ways:

1. Access to the most modern and up-to-date forms of knowledge is avail-

Frank Feather is chairman of the Global Management Bureau (a New York-based consulting firm) and is also president of the Global Futures Network. Rashmi Mayur is director of the Urban Environment Institute, Bombay, India, and vice president of the Global Futures Network. They are co-editors of a new book entitled Optimistic Outlooks.

able by other than written words.

2. Far from increasing illiteracy, computers create conditions whereby people can learn (even how to read and write) with greater ease and at lower cost than previously imagined.

Children who have not yet learned to read and write can command a computer, thereby gaining access to all the power of the electronic age. In this way, sophisticated forms of computer power can be brought to hundreds of millions of illiterate people. Thus, with one stroke on a terminal keyboard, the distribution of knowledge in the world can be changed. With it, standards of living will gradually become similar.

To Save Work or To Make Work?

Of course, introducing the home computer to Asia (or anywhere else) may be akin to introducing the first pair of chopsticks to the West. It is not enough to show potential customers how to use the new tool; they must also be convinced they need it in the first place.

If you speak to Prime Minister Indira Gandhi of India, she will tell you that an enormous number of young people have never been educated—perhaps 200 million of them under 15 years old in India alone. She cannot understand why we should use micro-chip technology to save human labor when her people *need* work.

The information occupations now constitute the largest single category in the work force of most industrialized countries, as typified by the United States. It seems that industrialized economies have a considerable capacity to create new jobs that absorb people displeased by changes in technology.

Unemployment and labor displacement problems in industrialized countries resulting from technological changes are a mere pittance compared to the grave problem of providing meaningful and productive work for the people of developing countries. Confronted with high unemployment and underemployment, these countries seem destined to experience a major equity crisis in the 1980s, marked by a rapidly growing work force, widespread poverty, and unbalanced income distribution.

Developing countries are faced with a dilemma in formulating ways and means to provide productive work for their peoples. Implausible increases in industrial jobs would be required to deal with the present and future population growth. In India, a 22.1% yearly increase in industrial employment would be needed; in Brazil, it would be 16.2%. As a matter of fact, India's employment in the private industrial sector has virtually come to a standstill during the past decade.

The outlook for resolving the dilemma becomes even more gloomy if the labor-absorption possibilities of agriculture are considered. Even under the best circumstances of a favorable cropping and technology mix for providing employment, almost 50% of India's rural population would have to look for some non-farm employment. Although so-called appropriate technology can help to some extent, it is not sufficient to deal with the gigantic problem of generating work for the Third World countries. Concentration on labor-intensive technology would be disastrous to developing countries, because the resulting low productivity would make it even more difficult for them to meet their essential material needs and to provide productive labor for their population.

What Mrs. Gandhi does not grasp, however, is that simply providing jobs will not close the rich-poor gap. India's per capita income is $200 a year. In the developed countries it is $10,000—50 times higher. As Jean-Jacques Servan-Schreiber has pointed out, if the annual economic growth rate could be sustained at 5% a year across the Third World (while the developed countries hold steady at only 2.5% a year), it would take 150 years for the Third World incomes to catch up. The Indian people are patient people, but they are not that patient.

Electronic Speed-Up

Microtechnology now provides the means to speed up this process of economic development so that the poverty gap can be closed—not in 150 years but within a generation or less. This inescapable fact has yet to be grasped by developed and developing countries alike. Above all, we must avoid perpetrating the catastrophic hoax of industrial development on the Third World when post-industrial technology will serve the mutual advantage of all countries within a relatively few years. Microtechnology has a potentially significant role to play in helping poor societies grapple with their equity problems. It may also help them achieve a more autonomous, less dependent role in the international system.

Microtechnology will bring significant productivity gains, for, all other things being equal, it is certainly an advantage of capital-poor developing countries to obtain greater output per unit of capital invested. Other characteristics of microtechnology are also relevant to developing economies—for example, its relative flexibility and the possibilities it offers for greater product differentiation. In principle, this means that developing countries can adapt existing technologies more easily to their own social requirements or raw material availabilities. Possibilities for decentralization of production may enhance development of small-scale, high-productivity industrial enterprises that are physically dispersed and close to consumers, thus diminishing transportation costs and urban concentrations.

Industrialized societies will capture the benefits of microtechnology more readily, of course, because they already have communications, transportation, and technical education infrastructures. The economic and political realities of developing countries cannot be ignored, and the circumstances under which it will make sense to use microtechnology will differ greatly from the industrialized countries. There is a danger that economic and political decision-makers in the Third World, seduced by hardware and software salesmen from the North, will become infatuated with the new technology and apply it indiscriminately.

The increasingly computerized industrial West needs to adopt a course of transferring the new technology to the Third World. It would be ridiculous to expect the developing countries to continue supplying "cheap labor" to outmoded factories whose products can no longer find markets.

The transfer of technology is the matrix of all progress and development. It will occur and impact in a number of ways. We will discuss each in turn.

200

Isolated Radiophiles

On the average, every American has two radios, making the U.S. the only nation on earth with more radios than people. China's 954 million people have only 45 million radios between them—1 for every 22 people. India's 684 million have only 15 million radios—1 for every 45 people. In Ethiopia, there are only 200,000 radios for 30 million people—1 for every 150 people. We could go on.

What, then, is the sense of selling more radios in America? Where is the sense in carrying around the streets of America a 30-pound receiver to listen to punk rock music through a set of private headphones when poverty-stricken people are scratching out a livelihood without the benefits of adequate communication? It is insane! The unemployed American male youth spends his useless dollars to isolate himself from the rest of the world. His hard-working Southern relative has no money and has no choice but to remain isolated from a world with which he is desperate to communicate.

Of particular interest in this North-South context is the Trail and Remote Camp HF/VHF Radio System developed to meet the needs of the Inuit communities of northern Quebec—the "South" within Canada's own borders. This system provides reliable communications within small, dispersed communities, and between such communities and remote sites or outpost camps (for example, hunting parties). Portable VHF and HF radios, operating on batteries, are equipped with telephone dialing facilities that allow remote parties to call the community—and community people to call each other. These radios can be interconnected with the standard telephone network.

The importance of battery operation cannot be underestimated. For example, in a country like Haiti, only 5% of the homes are equipped with electricity. Other countries are in equally poor situations. On the other hand, the linking of radio with the telephone system is easier said than done.

Telephone Telefrustration

In the developed countries, an efficiently functioning telephone system is taken for granted. It is an annoying paradox of the communications era that we can talk instantly and clearly with a person 238,000 miles away on the moon yet we cannot get a simple connection with a Bombay suburb only 25 miles away. A Parisian passing through Bombay recently described Bombay Telephone as "telefrustration." After a full two days of grueling efforts to call from one area of the city to another, he gave up and left the city distraught and disappointed. His experience can be multiplied a thousand times by thousands of telephone users in India and other Third World countries.

It has been estimated that 15% of Bombay's telephones remain out of order on a regular basis. This number reaches 25% during the monsoon period. The percentage of telephones out of order on a single day has been known to reach nearly 70%. Repairs can take hours, days, or months and telephones often go out of order again soon after repair.

Even if you can find a telephone that is working, literally half the time you will have difficulty hearing the other party or will have cross-connected lines. On 40% of your calls, you will either get a wrong number, no dial tone, a dead line, or no connection at all. It has been computed that over 40 man-years of time is wasted every day by the people of Bombay just dialing useless telephone calls. (It is worth noting that less than 1% of New York City's telephones are out of order at any one time.)

If this is not frustrating enough, long-distance telephoning in a large country like India is costly and impractical. Often, it is simply not possible to place a call, even if you can afford it. To call from Bombay to New Delhi is difficult. To call from Bombay to Toronto is almost impossible and can take several hours before a line is obtained. To call from Pakistan to Canada is even worse, and, if a connection is successfully made, the conversation is restricted to three minutes, whereupon the operator will automatically disconnect you in mid-sentence. In Cairo it can take hours, even days, to place a phone call. In Delhi, urgent messages are delivered by bicycle, not by telephone.

Another aspect of telephone systems in the developing countries is poor access. More than 50% of India's telephones are in the main urban centers where only 20% of the total population reside. In some countries, like Argentina, almost 85% of the telephones are in the main cities. In Bombay, there is a shortage of telephones, with close to half the city's population having no access to the system except via a limited number of public telephones—most of which never function.

Almost everyone in countries like Canada and the U.S.A. has a private telephone. Often, there are several telephones in a single dwelling. Canada alone has 16 million telephones for its 24 million population. In India, there are only 2 million telephones among 684 million people. Canadians can buy an extra telephone off the shelf at a telephone store for $40 and take it home and simply plug it in. In India, people have to wait months for a telephone to be installed, only to have it break down immediately thereafter.

At first glance, the obvious solution is to improve the telephone system. Unfortunately, designing and installing a modern telephone system is an enormously expensive undertaking. Bell Canada is presently installing a system in Saudi Arabia at a cost of over $5 billion. Only an oil-rich country can afford such a system. Secondly, to reduce the cost per user requires the addition of as many new users as quickly as possible. The development of this large user base, particularly in rural areas where costs are highest, is a slow process.

Nevertheless, telephones have provided the means for individuals to communicate social and economic information to one another, to call for help in emergencies, and to seek and give advice on matters of mutual concern. Developing countries cannot expect national integration and economic development without this basic means of communication. Most of the world's villages could be interconnected by telephone through space technology within 10 years at reasonable cost. The economic, political, and social impact of this development would be so profound that it is difficult to measure the cost-benefit in financial terms on an up-front cost basis.

The political ramifications have been calculated by Tom Stonier of the U.K.'s Bradford University. He argues that the critical point beyond which a country's autocracy or bureaucracy finds it has to restrain its power is when 20% of its population have telephones. This is reinforced by the fact that whenever a coup d'etat occurs, the new "authorities" quickly try to control telephone and broadcast systems. Person-to-person telephone communication (preferably without telefrustration) across the grass-roots of the social pyramid promotes the open democratic society and free exchange of information that are conducive to economic development.

Tele-Conferencing

The computer-based conferencing system (CBCS), also known as electronic mail or computer messaging, offers the very real possibility of a new means of communication for the Third World. Unfortunately, these networks do not yet reach the Third World.

The International Federation for Information Processing (IFIP), a UNESCO-chartered organization, has a special group looking into CBCS, and particularly at the needs of developing countries, for there is a very real fear that the new technology is developing so fast that the Third World may be left behind if something is not done quickly.

Dr. Ramani, of India's Tata Institute, belongs to this group. He sees the problems in developing countries from a different perspective. Computer-mediated conferencing is uncommon in the developing world, he says, not just because it is expensive or impractical, but because it is a new idea, not marketed commercially in the developing world, and requiring difficult design and implementation efforts at this stage. He believes the use of CBCS could do a lot more than simply improve communications among the scientists who use it:

> It is capable of allowing several teams of researchers, each subcritical in size, to develop a high degree of interaction, provide mutual support, and sustain one another. Such facilities increase the visibility of a researcher's work, and offer him membership in a close-knit community.

What is needed now, adds Ramani, is a demonstration project at the local level to prove to the research community and the policymakers that CBCS is an effective tool.

The need for action is urgent, according to Gordon Thompson, manager of communications studies for Canada's Bell Northern Research. He warns, however, that careful preliminary study is necessary, because "not every mindless installation of the latest technology will produce the desired results."

Tele-Education

As telecommunications expands, however, it will lead to a freer, cheaper, and more widespread exchange of information between rich and poor nations. Knowledge, like problems, knows no frontier. There will be stirrings in the Third World when the spread of global television brings the sights and sounds of affluence to their eyes and ears.

Both radio and television have played significant roles, not only in shrinking the world with their instantaneous news but also as a vehicle for cultural dissemination and education.

The masses of illiterate people are deprived even of basic information necessary for survival and development. TV educational programs can provide a "classroom" in remote areas of the developing countries. A community TV set can serve as a means of education to as many as 100 people. The hardware cost is scarcely one dollar a person.

In India, a successful satellite TV education program was launched in 1967, and it proved the value of such education in improving the quality of life of the villagers in the exposed areas. It would be a mammoth task to bring the latest education to 560,000 villages in India alone, but the space education industry can expedite the process at a minimum cost.

The input of modern knowledge into a developing country's education programs would enrich the quality of the curriculum and the teaching technology. A recent example of the convergence of telecommunications and computer technologies is videotex. Developed in only 10 years, systems such as Canada's Telidon are uniquely flexible in adapting to foreseeable changes in transmission and display technologies, particularly television.

Ignorance is still the greatest barrier between the wealthy and the poor. Ignorance results in despair, indifference, waste, and needless overpopulation. With virtually free computer power about to be unleashed, the potential for mass education exists. The next generation born in the underdeveloped world will be the first to benefit from the impact of computerized teaching. With it, the defeat of ignorance is in sight.

Communication and education, then, are soft infrastructures that can be extended all around the planet. It will not happen automatically; the prerequisites are open minds and willingness to learn.

Tele-Medicine

One of the world's most serious problems is lack of adequate health care in developing countries.

Tele-medicine may provide an answer to this crisis. Tele-medicine uses telecommunications technology to assist health-care delivery. Simply stated, it is healing from a distance.

It is particularly relevant to remote areas or population centers with inadequate health-care facilities or medical personnel. The system can be used to assist in diagnosis and treatment by providing consultation. It can make a major contribution to the education of professional and non-professional health-care workers, and can also reduce the social isolation that occurs in remote areas. All of this can be achieved at a relatively small increase in cost.

Such a system is in operation in the quasi-wilderness area of Sioux Lookout in Northeastern Ontario, Canada, where about 10,000 native Canadians live. There are four family physicians in the area and a few nursing stations staffed by two to five nurses.

The system converts telephone-transmitted audio signals into black-and-white television pictures. Slow-scan video units are also incorporated. Pictures of X rays, EKGs, skin lesions, pages of text, and charts can be sent and stored on tape in only 79 seconds. The cost is the same as for a long-distance phone call.

With the addition of satellite and microwave transmission, communications have improved considerably. Twenty-four-hour emergency service and comprehensive community health-care programs are now in place. Tele-medicine provides ready access to doctors and specialists, many of them 700 kilometers away in Toronto.

This system, the first of its kind in the world, goes a step beyond Australia's flying-doctor concept. Its potential for use in the Third World countries is enormous for eradicating disease and providing routine health care where none seemed possible.

Bio-astronautics is another new science of life in space that may have a great deal to contribute to our understanding and control of human illness. Already, a great number of medical applications of space industrialization are finding their way into medicine. Examples are the "laser cane" and automated body-monitoring/scanning devices.

For the developing countries, the major problems of health and medicine fall into two categories:

1. Applying available medical knowledge to the control of diseases, particularly in the remote areas through locally-trained doctors, as has been done in China.

2. Inventing new ways to control tropical diseases, particularly those that defy the terrestrial research methods, by conducting research in space.

Tele-medicine and space experiments have the potential to address both these aspects of medicine in the Third World.

Satellites for Boundless Communications

Disaster watch. Satellite pictures are helping with fire and flood management in Southern California. State officials have used false-color images from NASA's Landsat 2 spacecraft to make detailed surveys of vegetation types, age, and density, and to gather information on soils, slopes, and geology. Armed with this data, officials were able to design a program using helicopters and new techniques for controlled burning of dense chaparral areas.

As described by the report of the U.N. Regional Seminar on the Use of Satellite Technology for Disaster Applications (November 1978), satellite information on disaster warning also can be advantageously applied by developing countries. The satellite remote sensing imagery is helpful not only for storm and flood warning but also for the assessment of flood damage and other hydrological and climatological changes, including desertification as well as air and water pollution.

The photographs from Itos I showed a cyclone forming in the Indian Ocean two days before it struck on November 12, 1970, killing 500,000 people and causing over $1 billion in damage. On the average, LDGs suffer approximately $1.5 billion a year in damage from disasters of various kinds. Any successful application of modern telecommunications technology to avert or minimize such disasters would impact greatly on the rich-poor gap.

Agriculture. When combined with meteorological data, remote-sensing satellite data can be used in crop production and crop-health forecasting. Thus, one bureau predicts full-year crop figures for the U.S. on corn, soybeans, and wheat with over 90% accuracy.

By participating in the meteorological satellite programs, at a cost of only $10,000 for a ground station, the LDGs also can plan and manage their agriculture more efficiently and beneficially. Indeed, it is essential that they do so. After all, 90% of the people in China and Africa, 78% of the people in

India, and 65% of the people in South America depend on agriculture for livelihood and survival.

Fifty percent of India's national income comes from the agricultural sector, which depends on the vagaries of the monsoon rains. Space satellites offer forecasts of weather, water tables, and pests. It has been calculated that better rainfall predictions could save India $1 to $1.5 billion a year in agricultural planning costs.

Similarly, the encroaching desertification in the Sahel could have been controlled by examining the data available through remote-sensing. Information technology also helps to make formerly barren areas fertile. For example, in the deserts, in Israel's Negev as well as in the Arabian Gulf, it is now possible to farm in sandy and rocky soil. Under huge plastic covers that prevent evaporation, crops are irrigated drop by drop by networks of specially designed pipes. Water, often salt water, is rationed to each plant, to each blade of grass, to each tomato plant. A computer governs the entire system, calculates pressure, regulates salt content, monitors temperature, and measures growth under the most economical conditions of water consumption imaginable.

Landsat data has also been useful in recent years for managing forests in Thailand, aiding agricultural development in Upper Volta, and conducting crop surveys in Brazil.

Simple calculations show that with an agricultural investment of only 5 cents per farmer, the long-term benefit will be in the order of 40 cents in food production, not counting better health, nutrition, and other rewards.

The technology of information is based on people. It enables them to work in their own areas, their own villages, and thus helps stem the rural exodus. It makes soil preparation and choice of crops more intelligent and helps gauge the interplay of supply and demand in a more rational way.

Population Management

It is urgent that the rural exodus be stopped—the hideous development of the huge shantytowns of Caracas, Lagos, Calcutta, and hundreds of other megalopolises.

Decision-making needs to be decentralized toward rural villages. The village should be transformed into a development enterprise, a decision-and-management center.

Microcomputers are now the tools of this vision and provide the means that have eluded us for 30 years. By their very nature, they can work the miracle of true Third World decentralization. A village committee, for example, can help its people if it is connected to data banks and telecommunications networks that provide information, knowledge, education, and medicine.

In attempting to industrialize Third World Countries without delay, we have, with rare exceptions, aggravated their problems. We have uprooted people from their land, and they have then crowded into sprawling cities. We have followed a most unnatural path: abandon the land, which can provide nourishment, and congest the cities, which no longer provide work. Even today, rural areas continue to be abandoned, and, with 10, 15, 20 million inhabitants, the great cities of the Third World countries are becoming the ghettos of the planet. But the means for true decentralization now exist and must be put into place. What we should do is to decentralize jobs and build up the villages with the aid of computerization.

The North-South Dialogue

A most important form of communications for development, of course, is the so-called North-South dialogue. The meetings of national leaders are the first step of what will hopefully become an ongoing "global" dialogue at the U.N. level.

At the grass-roots level, hundreds of non-governmental organizations are working locally to address global problems. Thus, the Society for International Development and the World Future Society have a network of local chapters around the globe. The Global Futures Network is establishing a series of Global Cottage Meeting Places in major cities where citizens can "think globally, act locally" and "live and meet the future together"—again, across cultural and disciplinary boundaries.

Publishing

Another major facet of "communications for development" is the growing number of newsletters, magazines, and journals focusing on futures research and development.

The information rich-poor gap is nowhere better illustrated than in the newspaper industry. A total of 1,800 newspapers—23% of the world total—are published in the U.S. Even more staggering are the statistics on daily newspaper circulation per 1,000 population. These range from a high of 572 copies per thousand in Sweden all the way down to less than 1 copy per thousand in countries like Burundi and Chad where illiteracy exceeds 90%.

This deprivation is unbelievable for Westerners, who take newspapers for granted. Of the 65 poorest countries, 28 have no daily newspaper of any kind, not even a mimeographed sheet, and 43 have no news agencies. Admittedly, a number of these countries are microstates. However, they include countries like Cambodia, Laos, Mali, and Niger. Niger has one daily mimeographed bulletin with a circulation of only 3,000 copies.

Within the "information-rich" developed world, it is estimated that the information growth rate in the fields of science and technology alone will double every 10 years or less. More than 50,000 technical journals containing more than 2 million articles are published every year. Engineers and scientists produce more than 10,000 technical reports annually, containing over 60 million pages. Top executives may spend more than four hours a day just reading.

Information Flows

Many of the problems of the developing countries, and the solutions to these problems, are rooted in the generation and transmission of information through the international communication system.

Certain applications of microtechnology offer the means to advance technologies of destruction and control. Therefore, the question of who controls specific elements in the new technology becomes critical. The best strategy for minimizing the possibility of exploitation and control is to diffuse microelectronics through as many channels as possible. This is an important reason for Third World countries to get in on the microelectronic act. Failure to do so will cast them in an even more dependent relationship with the developed Western countries, and the latter will use the advantages of microtechnology to maintain their dominant position in the international economic and political system. They will sell the products made possible by microelectronics abroad at inflated prices, unless Third World countries develop the basic competence to use this technology themselves.

Developing countries also are fighting to control 20 broadcasting frequencies. The U.S. and the USSR alone use up 25 % of the shortwave spectrum. Just like the air we breathe, however, the air waves belong to everyone on the planet. Thus, the developing countries call for a New World Information and Communications Order (NWICO) through which they will be allocated a fair share of available radio-band space.

Concerns

The present structure of the international data market and the uneven distribution of the capabilities for applying transborder data flows raise a number of concerns. For the developing countries, in particular, these include the implications of transborder data flows for the international division of labor; the capacity of the developing countries to establish their own telematics and transborder-data-flow facilities; the competitiveness of domestic corporations of host countries; the bargaining position of host countries *vis-à-vis* transnational corporations and, more generally, the developed countries; and even issues relating to national sovereignty.

To the extent that information is a basis of power, the ability to collect, store, access, process, and work with it can give countries (as well as groups and institutions within them) political, economic, and social advantages. Transborder data flows may thus accentuate existing imbalances—and, in fact, create new imbalances—between the developed and the developing countries. On the other hand, if transborder data flows are made more accessible to the developing countries, they may become an instrument for these countries' advancement. An equitable management of transborder data flows also could contribute to greater economic cooperation among developing countries.

Developing countries already participate in the application of transborder data flows. They supply data—remote-sensing data, the wide variety of data that find their way into data bases, data exported (and re-imported) for processing purposes, and data sent by foreign affiliates to their parent corporations for storage or processing. They also buy the finished product—information—as it is contained in earth-resources images and processed data (not to mention such traditional media as books, journals, and technical papers), as made available by consultants, or through training, or as returned by parent corporations for the purpose of managing their foreign affiliates. And, finally, they acquire the technology and equipment, the capital goods, that they need for their own mostly rudimentary telematics sectors.

At the present time, it is clear that most developing countries participate in transborder data flows mainly as passive suppliers and, to a lesser extent, consumers of data. Only very few have the industrial capabilities to produce the technology and equipment needed to process data and participate actively in the international data market and the application of transborder data flows.

Implications for Host Countries

Information is a resource. It makes alternatives known, reduces uncertainty about their implications, and facilitates their implementation. When appropriately applied in the pursuit of well-defined objectives, information is central to decision-making. And, increasingly, decision-making depends on access to a great variety of data, which has to be stored and processed on computers to make it manageable.

In what ways does transborder data flow impact the development process and especially the capacity of developing countries to pursue a self-reliant development strategy? Two factors may be particularly important:

• The ability to fully utilize the relevant technology, equipment, and data (including those of domestic origin) and to apply them in the interest of national development and international competition.

• The ability to obtain access to the international data market.

Transborder data flows could give a growing number of users instant access to a rapidly expanding and diversifying pool of up-to-date knowledge. Such access may give developing countries more alternatives to choose from, greater possibilities for critical comparisons of alternatives, and better access to the necessary information for implementing the alternatives selected. For instance, the imperfections of the international technology market have long been considered as a major handicap for the development effort.

Access to the existing network of machine-readable data bases could therefore be of value to at least some developing countries. An increasing amount of business and economic data is becoming available on an on-line basis, and the ability to use it whenever the need arises could strengthen the bargaining power of developing countries.

For many developing countries, however, most of the value-added benefits from the production process occur at the processing and distribution stages and do not normally accrue to the developing countries. Certain spin-off effects (such as the production of software) may also be associated with processing and distribution rather than with the production of the raw material—be it mineral resources or data. Thus, Charles Dalfen of the CRTC observed that "data export for processing abroad comes to be regarded in an information age in the way the export of raw materials for manufacturing abroad is regarded in an industrial age—as the best way to fall behind, as a mark of underdevelopment."

Thus, some countries are confronted with a difficult choice of balancing the immediate benefits of importing data and data-processing services against the sacrifices associated with the long-term benefits that could result from a national developmental policy. If a country lacks data about itself and its international environment—because of a very limited capacity to collect, access, or process that data—it can be said to lack pertinent decision-making capacity about its own future. Its economic development is therefore seriously impaired.

For no group of countries is the promise of extraordinary gains in pro-

209

ductivity and of efficient use of raw materials through microelectronic technology more important than for the Third World. Unless they can increase productivity dramatically and use their resources more efficiently, they have no way out of poverty. The microelectronic revolution offers a more autonomous, less dependent role in the global political economy. The critical problems are economic and political—who controls, who benefits, and who pays. It would be naive to think that the distribution of productivity gains from this technological revolution will be easy while development and use of microtechnology is concentrated in a handful of powerful corporate and other dominant political and economic institutions.

On the other hand, we believe that these new technologies will not be used in perpetuating exploitation and inequality provided access to them is made available to developing countries. If this is achieved, microelectronic technology can bring about a transition to a more just, peaceful, equitable, ecologically sustainable world.

The New Global Economy

Servan-Schreiber has observed that the microprocessor is a wonderful device from which the three basic elements of all wealth converge: information, matter, and energy. This is the basis of the call from Southern leaders for the New International Economic Order (NIEO). If the North-South dialogue is to be successful, the North will realize that the reason for the Third World's wishing to adopt microelectronic technology is *not* to gain or enlarge their access to markets of industrialized countries, but to provide productive jobs at home and create domestic markets.

The computer explosion can be the key to solving the world economic crisis. The North cannot recover from its economic crisis unless it equips and develops the Third World with the most advanced technology. The North must realize that Third World development is in its own urgent interests. What the Third World asks is that the computerized infrastructures it seeks be used efficiently, so that it can enrich itself and become the vast market for the rest of the world. Revitalization of international economic growth depends on this transformation.

Telecommunications and the Future

by

Shirley Fetherolf

We are on the edge of a new wave that will be as important as the industrial revolution—"an electronic revolution that will change our entire economy, our city structure, our values, and even our politics." Alvin Toffler made these comments in a chapter called "The Electronic Cottage" in his new book, *The Third Wave*. A majority of industrial employees already handle information instead of things, and this trend is expected to grow as communications technology improves.

Telecommunication is the transmission and reception of messages over long distances. Indian smoke signals, telephones, television, and radio are older, more familiar examples of telecommunication. This paper will discuss recent developments in the area of telecommunications and how their impact will affect our lives.

Fiber Optics vs. Copper Wires

Hair-thin strands of glass are replacing the bulky copper wires that now carry the majority of our telephone calls. These fibers can transmit data and visual communication more efficiently and at a much lower cost. Fiber optics technology permits images and messages to be sent through light pulses beamed down glass fibers so clear "they make window glass look like a chalkboard."[1] Compared with copper wires, which carry voices converted into bursts of electricity, fiber optic wiring carries voices converted into light pulses by lasers the size of a pinhead. Copper coaxial cable used to distribute cable TV can be replaced with glass fiber cable since television images can be transmitted over them also.

How do fiber optics affect telecommunications? The main influence is economic—"It will bring the so-called office of the future down to the pocketbook of the average person."[1] Bell Telephone Company will lay more than 14,000 miles of glass fiber this year. A recent Southwestern Bell publication called "Telephone Talk" announced that they are planning the world's longest lightwave telecommunication system linking the Washington, Philadelphia, New York, and Boston metropolitan areas. The estimated cost is $79 million, but the system is projected to save nearly $50 million by 1990 because of lower construction and operating costs.

Shirley Fetherolf is a librarian at Atchison Junior High School, Atchison, Kansas.

Cable Television, Direct Broadcast Satellites, and Other Options

For those who want more than commercial network broadcasting offers, there are several alternatives: cable television (if your community is wired for it), pay television (a scrambled signal is broadcast and descrambled at home), and direct broadcast satellites (television transmissions from all over the world).

Cable television is growing in popularity. A recent survey revealed that 22% of the households in Kansas City are cable subscribers, and demand is growing faster than neighborhoods can be wired. It is estimated that half the households in the United States will be served by cable television by 1985. In the spring of 1981, there were already 30 services—news, sports, movies, concerts, plays, children's shows, and consumer action programs—transmitted by satellite to cable franchises around the country.

RCA joined with Rockefeller Center, Inc., in May 1981 to sponsor a new service called the "Entertainment Channel." It will complement existing pay cable movie services (such as Home Box Office) with a broad range of popular entertainment programming beginning in 1982. An additional monthly fee will be charged.

The cable industry has been described as "an enormous money machine"—and also has been called the only depression-proof industry in the U.S. This is probably why all three commercial television networks are now planning special programming to sell to cable television.

Some interesting innovations in cable television are "targeting" and "narrowcasting." Targeting allows advertisers to focus on the groups most likely to buy their products. For instance, MTV from Warner Amex Satellite Entertainment Company will be a 24-hour rock music network with the first stereo video signal. Sponsors of this network could appeal directly to the under-35 age group most likely to subscribe.

"Narrowcasting" as opposed to "broadcasting" has limited audience appeal. It allows sponsors to specify the segment of a show they want—pet news could be sponsored by pet products, for instance. It could also apply to special-interest programming that would not be feasible on the commercial networks.

Educational commercials, like the "Home Shopping Show," are half-hour segments in a talk-show format that feature product demonstrations by company representatives. Companies such as Pillsbury, Maytag, Hershey's, Corning, and Mr. Coffee have participated in the Home Shopping Show since it began in September 1980.

Pay television is expected to be available in the greater Kansas City area by 1982. Scrambled signals of recent movies will be broadcast over the whole area at night. Homes that pay a monthly charge for a descrambling device could view the movies, with pornography promised one night a week. The main advantage of pay television is that no cable is needed. It could reach people in isolated areas unlikely to have access to cable television. Another boost for pay television is the fact that unauthorized decoder sales have recently been prohibited by the U.S. Circuit Court.

A threat to both cable and pay television is the direct broadcasting satellite or DBS, a subsidiary of Comsat. This service would be broadcast in scrambled signals from satellites to small (two-foot) antenna dishes leased by homeowners for perhaps $25 a month after a $100 installation charge. No cable would be needed for this subscription television system.

The ultimate option, which would pick up television transmissions from all over the world, is available from the Ken Schaffer Group. It is a twelve-foot dish antenna that sells for $12,000. Schaffer predicts that over 200 stations will be available to the big dishes by 1985. He says:

> It's all a very third-wave kind of thing. It will allow people in one country to watch local programming from another country. Just the other day I watched a Calgary-Alberta ball game transmitted via a Canadian satellite, then turned the dish around and watched the Russian news from the Kremlin.[2]

Schaffer doesn't foresee mass production or lowered price for this type of antenna.

Information Utilities

Videotext is a broad term that refers to a television system that provides words and numbers on a television screen upon demand. It covers two distinct systems—teletext and viewdata. Teletext "puts data (words, numbers, simple illustrations) in an unused and unseen part of the normal television signal, the VBI or vertical blanking interval. Viewers can use a hand-held keypad to retrieve the hidden information on their screen."[3] The television studio's editorial staff decides which type of public interest material to broadcast. Station KSL-TV in Salt Lake City was the first in the U.S. to have teletext.

Viewdata (also simply called videotext) is a more interactive medium than teletext. It consists of a television connected with a computer far away by telephone lines. Like teletext, a keypad is used to call up a "menu," then the viewer selects a "page," or one screen display of information. A page consists of 20 lines with 32 characters on each one, or approximately 120 words. There is no editorial staff to select limits to what is broadcast; the computer can hold libraries full of information. "By pressing a few buttons on a keyboard, a user can command his home terminal to go fetch the desired information."[4] Since there is a direct connection between the user and the computer, the user can be billed for each page he accesses. On the other hand, subsidies and advertising must support teletext. Publishers, telephone companies, and cable companies are very interested in viewdata. The British Post Office has two versions—"Prestel" and "Viewtron."

What kind of information and formats will videotext provide? Videotext is attractive, seven colors and white plus simple graphics. Teletext, the simpler system, can provide continuous brief items of wide interest—entertainment or shopping guides, news, sports results, weather, airline and train schedules, and financial reports. It goes one step beyond similar services that have been offered for years on cable television. First, it offers more variety, and second, it permits the user to go from general to specific data.

There are three teletext systems that have been approved as international standards by the United Nations agency responsible for setting telecommunications standards (the International Telegraph and Telephone Consultative Committee of the International Telecommunication Union). The three systems are CEEFAX/Oracle, Antiope, and Telidon.

CEEFAX. CEEFAX (short for See-Facts) was developed by BBC engineers in 1972, and it is now the most widely used broadcast teletext system in the world. Although initially developed as a means of subtitling for the deaf, it does not do this at present.

Oracle, a similar and compatible version of teletext, was developed about the same time by the Independent Broadcasting Authority (IBA). In 1974, the BBC, the IBA, and British TV-set manufacturers set a common standard for teletext, and the British government began a two-year field test. In 1977, the government gave official approval to teletext, and it is now available on three television channels in Britain.

Here is how CEEFAX works: "The viewer presses a button on a special keypad and makes an index appear on the screen. On the index are three-digit combinations corresponding to categories such as weather, news, sports, travel information and TV programming. The viewer presses the three-digit combination desired and after a short pause (up to 25 seconds) gets either a lower-level index (showing, for example, the kind of sports news categories that are available) or the information sought."[5]

CEEFAX has five increasingly complex levels, which require different types of decoders. Level one, simplest and least expensive, is now in use in Austria, Germany, Holland, Flemish Belgium, Sweden, Norway, Denmark, Finland, and Australia. Level three has picture quality competitive with Antiope, the French version of teletext. Level four uses a sophisticated alphageometric code that is the basis for the Canadian Telidon system. Level five provides full color but is impractical at this time because of the amount of computer memory required and the resulting high decoder cost. The production cost of a level-one decoder is around $40, which could be reduced by half with greater mass production.

"In Britain, the post office operates the telephone service, and back in 1970 a post-office employee named Sam Fedida dreamed up the first viewdata system as a scheme to increase the number of phone calls made daily by Britons, and hence increase the post office's revenue."[6] Prestel is the brand name for this type of videotext in which the TV set becomes a computer terminal in the home or office through telephone-connections to a large central computer. Forty-two million dollars were spent to develop Prestel in Britain, but it has only 10,000 subscribers. Prestel also offers a CEEFAX type of teletext service to 120,000 customers.

Prestel sold its U.S. videotext marketing rights to General Telephone and Electronics Corporation, but GTE has never developed them. Prestel sold their teletext rights to Field Enterprises for a Chicago field test. Field Electronic Publishing and Zenith Radio Corporation are sponsoring a one-year experiment with teletext terminals in public places. These information "kiosks" will be open 24 hours a day in locations throughout the city. A Field-owned television station will send out the teletext signal. Features will be supplied by Field's *Chicago Sun-Times* newspaper and other sources. The teletext system, called KeyFax, is based on a modified CEEFAX system.

Antiope. Antiope is an acronym for *L'Acquisition numérique et télévisualisation d'images organisees en pages d'écriture* [Numerical Acquisition and Televisualization of Images Organized As Pages of Writing]. This system requires a special television with a built-in terminal. The price is 10-20% more than for a normal color TV. Like other videotext systems, Antiope has a hand-held keypad that can call up the latest news, sports, weather, traffic reports, TV schedules, and more. In spring 1981, plans were for adding airline and rail schedules, theatre and movie listings, and educational course listings.

The French telephone company is planning to give every phone subscriber an Antiope terminal instead of a telephone directory. They expect this to be cheaper than printing paper directories, and there is one more advantage. Electronic "yellow pages" can be easily updated, giving newspapers competition for classified advertising, and thereby increasing telephone company revenues.

Antiope is the only one of the three basic videotext systems to be endorsed by a major television network, CBS. It delivers the most at a reasonable cost (according to company officials), while also having capabilities to quickly correct errors in the stream of data being broadcast.

Telidon. Telidon, the most sophisticated of the three videotext systems, is a two-way TV system that can be hooked up to a regular television to give computerized information retrieval right in the home. It can operate in two modes, teletext or viewdata. Teletext piggybacks in on the unused space of a TV signal called the vertical blanking interval. One of the more exciting aspects of Telidon is the viewdata mode, which permits viewer interaction with computer data bases. By using a keyboard pad the size of a hand-held calculator, one can get many services similar to those offered by CEEFAX and Antiope.

Telidon decoders cost more than the other two types, but because it uses alphageometric display, the graphics have smoother lines and thereby are more realistic-looking. Telidon officials claim that their system is superior to the other two systems. It was developed by the Canadian Department of Communications, and $27.5 million is being set aside for worldwide promotion and marketing. Telidon Videotex Systems, Inc., a U.S. subsidiary of Canadian Infomart, has been given permission by Telidon developers to market Telidon in this country. Time, Inc., and the Times Mirror Company plan to test the viability of teletext as a cable television-delivered service. Project Ida, an experiment sponsored by the Manitoba Telephone Company in a suburb of Winnipeg, is using Telidon and Omnitext, a videotext service developed especially for the project by Interdiscom Systems Limited of Winnipeg. Here is a description of how to use Telidon from a Project Ida brochure:

> Retrieving information from Telidon is as easy as deciding what you want to know, pushing the appropriate buttons, and watching the information appear on the screen. After consulting the general index and choosing the subject— "entertainment" for example—you push the button on the Telidon keypad. From there, using the same procedure, you narrow your selection until you reach the specific information you want—for example: The Royal Winnipeg Ballet.

The Source

Viewdata is already here for many Americans via The Source, an information utility that markets data bases, or information collections, to home computer owners. Beginning operations in June 1979, The Source was the first computer network service aimed at small-computer users. They are now adding data bases and other services oriented towards businessmen, whose tax-deductible business use of the utility could generally increase its popularity.

The Source is like an electronic magazine or library that subscribers use and pay for like a phone call. The computer data banks and an electronic mail service are available 24 hours a day, but most of the 19,300 subscribers go for the non-prime-time rates that are in effect between 6:00 p.m. and 7:00 a.m. weekdays and all day on weekends and holidays. The initial hook-up subscription cost is $100. Here is a partial list of Source data bases:

U.S. and international airline schedules.
Business and financial information (including stock market quotations, advice columns, commodity reports, etc.).
Classified Ads and Bulletin Board (allows users to post their own advertisements and announcements of general interest).
Dining Out Guides to restaurants in the Washington, D.C., and New York City areas.
Discount Shopping Service (an electronic "mail-order catalog").
Education programs (including practice drills in French, Spanish, German, math, and spelling).
Energy Saving News and Tips.
Games (including simulations of economic and social planning, space flight, military tactics, bridge, poker, and others.
New York Times News Summary (contains national, world, local, and business headlines).
Political campaign reports on national and state races.
Announcements of traveling exhibits and special events at Washington area museums.
Sports (scores and news reports).
Travel Club (information, package tours, tickets, etc.).
United Press International News (unedited news stories just as they come over UPI wires to newspaper offices and broadcasting stations throughout the world; can be searched by name, subject, date, or combinations of these).
Weather bulletins or forecasts.

Who collects the information for these data bases? In the case of the "Dining Out Guides," two New York housewives—one a former restaurant critic for *Cue* magazine—originated the idea of storing restaurant data in their home computer. They called their restaurant guide to the Big Apple—New York City—"Apple Bites." Their information is transmitted to the Source, which in turn then transmits it to interested customers. Diane Hirsh, one of the partners in "Apple Bites," says, "There are so many corporations with computer access that send people here on business, and so many tourists who want to know where to eat, we decided to categorize for price, location, and ethnicity to make choosing even easier." With the bulk of their work done at home, these women have an electronic cottage industry such as Alvin Toffler writes of in *The Third Wave*.

Electronic Mail

Electronic mail is a way to send a message from a computer terminal in

New York, for example, to a terminal in San Francisco in less than a minute for about one dollar. General Telephone and Electronics Corporation started the electronic mail system in mid-1980 after acquiring the Telenet Communications Corporation in June 1979 for $55 million. Frustration with the U.S. Postal Service has made the rapid electronic mail system very attractive to corporations in large and small cities. Here is how it works:

> A company composes a message on a computer terminal and, typically, sends it on local telephone lines to one of the 11 major Telenet traffic hubs or to one of the 200 secondary switching centers. At the Telenet centers, each message is "packetized" or broken down into sections of 128 characters or less, including spaces and punctuation, each of which is then addressed with a computer code. The packets are mixed randomly with others from various sources into a single stream of electronic data. That stream is transmitted via the nationwide telephone network by means of cable and microwave. At the switching center near the destination area, the packets are put back into the proper sequence and reassembled as originally sent to Telenet. They are then sent to addressees via local telephone lines.[8]

All this takes less than a minute.

The already existing services of mailgram and telegrams will continue to serve the home market until prices for terminals come down. Electronic mail is one of the key features of the automated office of the future, and the time savings and increased productivity of white-collar workers can justify the higher-than-postal-rates cost.

Videodiscs

A videodisc looks similar to a phonograph record, but when played it produces both audio and video. There are two types of videodisc players—optical, or laser-produced, and mechanical, or stylus in groove. Although present players do not record, videodisc player-recorders are just around the corner.

Like the early days of video player-recorders, there are many noncompatible formats available to consumers, who seem to be waiting to see which ones emerge as leaders. Videodiscs offer some advantages over videocassettes. First, they offer enormous information storage density—54,000 still frames or screens of data or 30 minutes of regular video. Second, the cost of raw materials to manufacture discs is very low compared to videotape or celluloid film stocks. Third, players may be hooked up to a computer for faster access to those 54,000 frames.

The simpler version of videodisc technology is the stylus-in-groove or capacitance technology. "Selectavision" by RCA is an example of this cheaper, simpler to operate and maintain system.

"Magnavision," marketed by Magnavox and produced by MCA Philips, uses the laser system. Philips's optical disc has the best outlook for computer and eventual consumer informational/instructional/entertainment purposes. They have developed a disc that allows the operator to record in an ordinary room, not the usual ultra-clean laboratory environment formerly required. However, protection from fingerprints, scratches, and dust is still necessary. Philips has patented a "self-developing" digital disc that is based on laser-formed pits in a thin metallic film such as tellurium and bismuth. The primary disc base is plexiglas, and normal shelf life is estimated at 10 years at average room temperature.

The erasable disc will expand videodisc usage to the point that videotape machines become obsolete. Snapshots, slides, motion-picture film, and X rays now stored in bulk form could be recorded and preserved by the thousands on one disc without deterioration of color or other qualities. Implications for the fields of ordinary consumer photography, medical photography, and publications make videodisc technology worth keeping an eye on.

Sears, Roebuck and Company is testing videodiscs in 1,000 homes as a replacement for their traditional printed catalog. Shoppers will be able to push a few keyboard buttons and call up information on the television screen. The same picture of the products found in the catalog (plus, in some cases, additional information such as material found in television advertisements) will appear. This information can then be used to telephone in orders. Videodiscs could save Sears millions of dollars in printing costs.

CompuServe and EIES

There are two more networks of interest to small computer owners: CompuServe, a computer time-sharing subsidiary of H & R Block, and EIES (Electronic Information Exchange System) Network. With CompuServe, users can compare different newspapers' treatment of the same story without subscribing to or searching through a great number of out-of-town newspapers. Eleven major newspapers, including the *New York Times,* the *Los Angeles Times,* and the *Washington Post,* are available to home and office computers for a $5-an-hour time-sharing fee. Newspapers receive 20% of this fee. The company also offers information on more than 32,000 stocks, bonds, and options—as well as backgammon, Space War, Star Trek, CB, and other games. They hope to add other diversions, amusements, and time-sharing informational services for the home.

EIES is more of an idea exchange and teleconferencing system. According to an EIES brochure, it is a computer-based communications system that links together 700 people all over North America and in Europe. It is an organized communication space that provides various structures for the exchange of information. Users may send and receive messages, engage in electronic conferences or "meetings," jointly draft articles and reports, contribute to and read computer-based journals, and design computer aids tailored to their own work. The cost for nationwide use of the system is $7 an hour, which is economical compared to long-distance calls or traveling to meetings, and is less expensive than postage for user groups of nine or more who wish to exchange communications as a group on a regular basis.

Open University

"Telecourses" aimed at non-traditional students may help higher education's declining enrollments. Some schools such as the University of Mid America, the University of Maryland, and Penn State University are developing telecourses or degree programs based on them.

The University College of the University of Maryland at College Park has long offered extension courses, but it has now moved into televised instruction. For the past 10 years, it has been cooperating with the Maryland Center for Public Broadcasting to offer telecourses similar to the ones developed by the British Open University. These courses—which are heavy in content, theoretical, broadly-based, and humanistic—are more European in approach than American. (American undergraduate courses are typically practical, specialized, and pragmatic.) These telecourses appeal to students over 35, modestly affluent, and with some college background; this is also the profile of the average public television viewer.

The success of these partly-televised college courses has led to the development of the National University Consortium for Telecommunications in Teaching. Only 4½ hours of air time is used to supplement nine credit hours of instruction. (Traditional telecourses require 15 hours of air time to deliver three credits of instruction.) Here is how it works:

> The students watch a half-hour program every other week, follow a prescribed regimen of reading, and submit essays and self-administered tests to assigned tutors at University College. If they choose, students may come to a weekly discussion session. They also have telephone contact with their tutors, though assignments are often submitted by mail.[9]

The National University Consortium project plans to transmit two hours a week of these courses by satellite to all public TV stations at no charge. Public TV stations would then receive a per-student fee for airing the programs. Students could enroll in cooperating local institutions that would pay a fee to the National University Consortium. Three programs of study—Humanities, Social and Behavioral Sciences, and Management and Technology—are available, which lead to Bachelor of Science degrees.

TELENET is an educational communication system linking 34 locations in Kansas by amplified telephone. The main advantage of TELENET is that it allows people to take credit and noncredit courses from the six state universities without traveling long distances. Over 6000 participants used the network during fiscal year 1980-81, and it has been in existence for 11 years. It is owned and operated by the Regents Continuing Education Network, with faculty from the six state universities conducting the classes.

Libraries

Could librarians become obsolete if videotext becomes widely available to private homes? Videotext could provide reference service, newspapers, magazines, and even books. Of course, it would cost more for this service, but it might be faster and easier to use.

In March of 1981, a group of librarians and information disseminators concerned with this issue formed the Electronic Library Association. The organization urges participation in information industry committees working on technical standards for teletext and videotext. Because of the danger that computer-supported telecommunications systems can perpetuate information control by a few, they urge librarians to develop their own data bases and to plan on providing videotext services to library patrons in the future.

One library has developed a data base of urban information called ACCOMPLIS. The Greater London Council Research Library started this data base, which provides a wide range of information for local government. Bibliographic data is provided on-line in areas such as finance, employment, industrial development, planning, engineering, recreation and leisure, flood-protection, civil defense, housing strategy, transportation, waste disposal, and air pollution. A fee is charged for this service.

Many librarians offer similar bibliographic computer services for $3 to $30. Data bases include the *Magazine Index* (370+ popular magazines), *National Newspaper Index,* and *NEWSEARCH* (daily updated index of the two above indexes). Access to these data bases can be gained through major search services called data-base vendors. Lockheed (DIALOG) Information Retrieval Service is the largest of these vendors and offers the most unique data bases. Other data-base vendors include SDC (Systems Development Corporation—Orbit), BRS (Bibliographic Retrieval Services—STRAIRS), National Library of Medicine (MEDLINE), and New York Times *INFOBANK.*

"On-line" involves a dialogue between the user and a computer. An on-line catalog will replace the traditional card catalog, and on-line circulation, acquisitions, management statistics, and serials check-in can be developed from an on-line data base. New technology will certainly change libraries and library science as a profession, but there is an exciting possibility available. Gaining "bibliographic control," a goal librarians have long aspired to, will be more attainable. "To an increasing degree, we will be able to find out almost everything we want to know about anything whenever we want it," says Edward Cornish, president of the World Future Society.

Problems Arising from the New Technology

Will only the rich be able to afford the new home information technology? Information is so valued as a commodity that its centralization has always aroused hostility. Because the body of knowledge is doubling every five years, and the systems that provide access to this information are growing more complicated and more powerful, centralization is a very real possibility.

People are used to paying for entertainment, but are they willing to pay for information they could get from a library? Some home videotext decoders cost almost as much as a color TV set, and there is not yet enough demand to justify the mass production that could reduce the price. However, there is a willingness of business and some individuals to pay high costs for information, as long as it is tailored to their needs and can be delivered nearly instantaneously.

Consumers do not want and cannot pay for every new gadget that hooks up to their TV set. Video games, videocassette recorder/players, videodisc players, cable and pay TV services, home computers, viewdata, and videotext all compete for use of the TV screen. Marketing will play an important role in determining which of these "gadgets" succeed.

The new information technology will cause perhaps one-half of all occupations to cease to exist, and will radically affect most others. It will put some companies out of business, and make a few others incredibly wealthy. It could be concentrated in "the hands of too small a segment of the population, which could control us more comprehensively and efficiently than any totalitarian regime of the past."[10] The government could electronically monitor certain individuals on a systematic basis. Everyone in the world could be listed in a universal computer data bank.

There is the possibility of lack of copyright control in videotext systems—

"stealing" information without giving the author credit. The new technology opens up all sorts of new opportunities for crime.

What values will the new information technology communicate? The biggest selling item in the videocassette market is pornography, and Kansas City Pay TV hopes to gain subscribers through a pornography night once a week. There is such an appetite for sex and violence that one industry official predicts the development of "Viewsak" (as in Musak) tapes or discs that are totally devoid of plot and devoted to violence and/or sex. Off-track betting through viewdata is a possibility British and Canadian systems are working toward.

Reading for any sustained time off the television screen is uncomfortable. "People using VDTs and CRTs often complain of headaches, backaches, neckaches, eye strain, and more. Loss of color vision has been reported by some VDT operators.[11] Newspapers and magazines don't cause these problems, are low in cost, and are more portable than a TV set.

Positive Implications and Forecasts

One of the most positive aspects of the new information technology is the amount of energy it could save us. With more "electronic cottages" and teleconferencing, commuting could be greatly reduced. Families would be working at home together as "prosumers," both producers and consumers. Perhaps both personal and business decisions could be made more easily with instant background information. Education could become the entertainment of the future through videodiscs and viewdata. Television would no longer be a passive activity, with narrowcasting, interactive videotext systems, and satellite television being options to the bland programming on the three commercial networks. Using computers without knowing computer language will be possible, and home computers may be replaced by televisions with computers built in. Small-town libraries with videotext equipment could offer services only large libraries have had in the past.

It is true that some jobs will probably be eliminated, but many new jobs will also be created to manufacture new equipment, install fiberoptics technology, maintain data bases, and write educational materials in new formats. A prosperous and information-rich global society is on the way.

References

1. Scott Armstrong, "Fiber Optics: Wiring the Future with Whiskers of Light," *Christian Science Monitor,* April 23, 1981, pp. B8-B9.

2. "Bargain Dishes at $12,000 Apiece?" *Christian Science Monitor,* May 1, 1981, p. 23.

3. L. Theresa Silverman, "A Viewer's Guide to Radio, TV, and New Technology," *Sunrise Semester,* 1981.

4. "The Home Information Revolution," *Business Week,* June 29, 1981, p. 76.

5. Michael Nyhan with Robert Johansen and Robert Plummer, "Home Information Systems: Some Thoughts on the Role of Public Broadcasting," *Public Telecommunications Review,* 7:3, p. 21.

6. "Read Any Good Television Lately?" *TV Guide,* February 16, 1980, p. 33.

7. "Computer Cuisine," *Family Circle Magazine,* April 7, 1981, p. 2.

8. "GTE: The Promise of Electronic Mail," *New York Times,* November 2, 1980, section 3, page 1.

9. Richard Smith, "College-Level Telecourses Take a New Turn," *Public Tele-communications Review,* 7:6, p. 35.

10. "Computer Literacy a Must in the Future," *Information Hotline,* 11:11, p. 2.

11. Barbara Garson, "The Electronic Sweatshop," *Mother Jones,* 6:6, p. 36.

The Telecommunications Role of Local Government

by

Mark A. Greenwald

In recent years, urban and cultural historians have begun to write with increasing frequency of the evolutionary parallels between our socio-economic patterns and the history of scientific and technological developments. At the same time, it grows a little harder each day to separate the rush of daily events from the cumulative impacts of our own institutions upon them. Such impressions, often negatively received, have already begun to affect our conscious thinking about those values and institutions we currently embrace, and how they may be affecting the general health of the world we inhabit and claim to care for.

As early as 1968, Fred Friendly, the chairman of CBS who was also heading New York City Mayor John Lindsay's task force on CATV and telecommunications, described the power of the emerging cable television industry: "Those who own these electronic conduits will one day be the ones who will bring to the public much of its entertainment and news and information, and will supply the communications links for much of the City's banking, merchandising, and other commercial activities. With a proper master plan these conduits can at the same time be made to serve the City's social, cultural, and educational needs. . . . Cable television and cable telecommunications offer the City of New York an opportunity in good planning and good habits."

America today is almost one-third wired for cable television. Increases in productivity in the communications industry during the 1970s far outpaced those in other sectors of the economy. Technological advances in this area have likewise been nothing less than phenomenal over the last five years in particular. In 1956, by way of comparison, the coaxial transatlantic telephone cable carried 50 voice circuits. By the mid 1980s, a new underwater cable, now in the planning stages, will carry twelve *thousand* channels, and double that amount of circuits, by a fiber-optic system based on holographic and laser principles.

Two-way interactive systems, once a mere prop in sci-fi flicks, are currently being developed for commercial use in several Western nations, and within a few years operational systems may suddenly begin to proliferate. By

---

Mark A. Greenwald is a consultant on communications, networking, environmental planning, and design based in New York City.

1983, fifteen hundred subscribers in the French resort city of Biarritz should be able to enjoy picture phone, color video, data services, and telephony. By 1992, the French government postal and communications authority (PPT) plans to equip each of its 30 million telephone subscribers with a free (video) data terminal. Viewdata, the British Postal system's version, is currently being put into place in the New Town of Milton Keynes (UK), while in Canada the Telidon system, reputed to be the most technically advanced of the current videotext technologies, is being tested in a number of locations. It is being simultaneously and successfully marketed to institutional users in the United States, including the Library of Congress. Also in the U.S., Warner-Amex, after several years of testing its QUBE system in Columbus, Ohio, has begun to market it in dozens of large metropolitan areas that are first being wired for cable.

Notwithstanding this legitimate and evergrowing list of wonders, Fred Friendly's advice to Mayor Lindsay about foresight has been largely ignored, at least in the public sector. The nation's telecommunications landscape, as author and planner William Rushton puts it, is still "a foreign territory to most of the nation's planners." The city of New York, which in the early 1970s was one of only five municipalities in the U.S. to have negotiated with cable television companies for free municipal access channels, had to be compelled by a court order in 1978 to initiate comprehensive public review and planning processes for new cable franchises. Besieged by a plethora of other problems and by more limited resources than it could call upon a decade earlier, its leaders had simply lapsed into a position of noninterest concerning the possibilities of electronic communications.

Local government institutions have historically abandoned control of the telecommunications environment to the Federal Communications Commission and to Congress. They have never truly recognized the evolving role of this electronic "public utility" as a critical urban infrastructure. The FCC, on the other hand, has recently initiated a classic policy reversal by beginning to deregulate the telecommunications media, both radio and television as well as data services. While its stated reason for pursuing this policy may have been the enhancement of consumer benefits and choice, our state and local governments have been left to ponder the likelihood of this rationale reasonably fulfilling itself, and if not, what regulatory roles they may have to assume in the 1980s in order to properly look after the public interest.

Several states have responded by picking up the regulatory slack through their own Cable or Public Utility Commission. Others, having caught the deregulatory fever, are pursuing it even further through state legislatures. The Governor's Office in New York State, for instance, is currently proposing legislation that would weaken considerably the powers of its own statewide cable commission, once considered a pioneer in establishing model regulatory practices and technical assistance services to municipalities.

Communications, or information, in the current analysis, now has all the significance necessary to become a functional planning concern of municipal governments, just like housing or transportation did in previous decades. Given this possibility, and the proper state enabling legislation, what exactly might be the parameters for such a role? What concerns would it need to address, and what would be some of the problems likely to be encountered

224

from the vantage point of local and regional socio-economic impacts? On the following pages, an attempt has been made at an exegesis of the telecommunications role of local governments, simplified into three major topical areas: (direct) Policy Concerns; Economic Concerns; and Sociological Concerns.

Policy Concerns

What should the government priorities be in a decade characterized by increased diversity of communications? Four basic areas will need attention:

1. Competition or Cooperation? How should competition in information handling between government and private industry be managed, and how also can duplication of services be avoided? The U.S. Department of Commerce, in one telling example, spent almost $25 million to collect information in order to create and maintain WITS, an information service designed to expand American exports, when such a service had already been commercially available for several years. From federal to municipal levels, public agencies are too often unaware or uninterested in what is going on in the private sector. Better programs for monitoring information needs and resources must be developed within government agencies, and relevant contacts maintained with outside organizations.

2. Access to Information and Technology. How will governments respond to the "openness" that accompanies the new telecommunications technologies? How will it alter public outreach policies and programs? It took several decades before TV was allowed into Congress—now most floor sessions may easily be accessed by the public on the C-SPAN cable service, which is usually carried daily by a local cable channel. On the local level, it will not be long before town meetings, city council sessions, etc., are regularly cablecast. Examples to date include Reading, Pennsylvania, and Columbus, Ohio (QUBE). In Manhattan, local legislators and community board members have been seen for several years on municipal access Channel L.

To what degree will governments on all levels utilize "teleconferencing" capabilities between cities, and between disparate parts of their own city or region. Will this technique promote a better exchange of ideas both among policy-makers and at a more technical level of operations. Both satellite and line time are already cheaper in many instances than the physical travel alternatives.

3. The Franchise Process. Municipal or county governments, through their franchising powers, usually have the first responsibility to oversee the development of a public telecommunications infrastructure.

The areas for substantive consideration on the part of the government franchising agent are numerous. Several of the most significant are listed here:

• *Nature of the Franchise*—How large should the franchise area be? How rigid need those areas be, both over time and with regard to multiple franchises competing in the same area? Many cities and towns have lately constructed "coterminous" service districts for fire, police, water, etc., so it may make sense that telecommunications services should respond to those same demarcations. Provisions in franchise contracts might also include trading clauses, allowing franchisees to later shift territories amongst themselves for a variety of acceptable economic or logistical reasons.

- *Construction Schedules*—These need to be carefully engineered so as not to discriminate against any particular section of the community or social group. In some cases, it takes up to six or eight years to wire a city of significant size.

- *Nature of the Franchisee*—The government franchising agent must set some standards for the general qualifications of all potential franchisees. This is best done beforehand in a municipal or county cable ordinance, and not as a response to someone's petition. A second question concerns ownership of the systems. Policies must be non-discriminatory and at the same time they must respond to the desire for some home control, particularly in minority communities.

- *Access and Access Services*—What will be the nature and number of access and leased channels? The provision of access equipment and facilities is an extremely important consideration, as several cities or states already require them to be provided by the franchisee per minimum standards set by the franchising agent. Part of the annual franchise fee might be allocated for this purpose.

The administration, financing, and control of program content for Access Channels is quite a delicate matter, and might include the constitution of community oversight groups. Additional responsibilities here may include: (1) informing potential users of access opportunities; (2) providing technical training to access users; (3) securing, maintaining, and making available any necessary production equipment not provided by the cable operator; and (4) developing uses for these channels that are responsive to the community's needs. An equally basic concern, which each government must address as a generic democratic principle, is that of universal consumer access to the system at a minimum affordable base cost.

- *Public Participation in the Franchise Process*—This is important in two regards: (1) to foster comprehensive public education and feedback on the proposed system's design and capabilities, as well as its long-term adaptability to other needs; and (2) to assess the communications needs of the various communities, both current and projected.

4. Functional Planning Impacts. What impacts of the new telecommunications infrastructures will local governments need to consider in the normal comprehensive planning process? Six significant areas of concern may be identified: land use; transportation; community development and population distribution; public participation in government; technology transfers/information access; and creation of new economies.

Who in government will be responsible for the long-term monitoring and analysis of change in these functional areas due to the new information technologies?

Economic Concerns

The following trends are visible on the horizon of the information-based society:

- Movement of considerable commercial resources away from over-the-air broadcasting to cable and other technologies.
- Increasing deployment of videotext and other two-way video and data

226

services.

• Replacement of heavily energy consumptive forms of transportation and work environments by more energy-efficient forms based on electronic and fiber-optic techniques.

All three incorporate opportunities for businesses to interconnect geographically dispersed facilities, thereby fostering ad hoc conferencing and the exchange of needed information between suppliers, customers, and other businesses and institutions. Also, new types of linkages may be created between employees and their workplace(s), which may result in the partial decentralization of the office environment.

The telecommunications revolution may fuel an increasing tendency toward staggered work hours, leveling peak-usage loads for office buildings while also creating other benefits in terms of spacial arrangements within buildings, to say nothing of the travel alternatives between the workplace and home. This in turn could further affect the reusable potential of land within central cities, for residential or other purposes. The creation of Mixed Use Districts is a trend already discernable on a modest scale in places like New York City. As it becomes more widespread, it will likely foment necessary changes in the tax, evaluation, and land-use structures of cities, simultaneously impacting upon select municipal services and infrastructures (e.g., sanitation and transportation).

The effects on local comprehensive planning operations can be viewed more clearly through such potential economic dislocations. Municipal governments will be pressured to adjust, perhaps to totally reevaluate, the balance of their revenue structures in a different manner than currently dictated by "cutback-shrinkage" strategies. This will occur concurrently with tactical shifts in the allocation and intensity of services as mixed-use districts begin to supplant the traditional single-use districts that have dominated city planning for half a century. In such critical areas, the speed with which a city is able to respond to shifting service delivery needs in many different areas at once is usually a direct measure of the speed with which correct and usable information flows through the system.

This is perhaps the biggest economic challenge of the upcoming decade. Unless our big public bureaucracies find ways to reduce their bulk, synchronize their resources with those of various private enterprises, and still maintain the expected output and quality of essential services (this includes planning at all levels), it is likely that system overloads and breakdowns will begin to occur in the societal structures that are dependent upon those services and planning.

Sociological Concerns

From the government's point of view, it is absolutely essential to prethink some of the cumulative social impacts of the new technologies. While the positive impacts pass largely unreported, the negative ones will inevitably call out to one level or another of government for "solutions." It would be wise for government institutions at the local/regional level to embark now upon a course of preventive "social" planning in such areas as the following:

1. **Services.** Preventive health information and post-hospital care through video terminals may foster more awareness and self-reliance on the part of

individuals. But will it also cause tensions of reduced physical distances and human contacts without similarly reduced psychic, political, economic, and social distances? Such imbalances may generate a kind of cultural circuit overload in individuals, whereby their alienation and frustration levels would abruptly rise.

2. Crime. Electronic alarm, security, and video monitoring systems are proliferating. Many transit systems are in the process of installing closed-circuit television cameras inside trains and station facilities. It is felt that this equipment can partially offset our reliance on manned police patrols while enhancing the level of psychological deterrence. Along with the benefits of the new communications technologies, though, comes an increasing concern for the privacy of the individual. One cannot but wonder whether Public Man will be able to bridge the psychological gap that is growing between his perceived social freedom and the new electronic watchdogs.

3. Public Participation and Access. It has been generally assumed that people will react favorably to two-way television that links them with municipal government or local community forums, as well as other interest groupings. Two specific concerns, however, have recently arisen that must be neither overlooked nor forgotten: (1) fractionalization of viewing and interacting groups so that few groups will be large enough to afford to utilize electronic communication as a reasonable alternative to physical travel; and (2) increased passive viewing of television and less contact among people as a result of the enormous array of services, entertainment, and other interests available through electronic means.

Fortunately, both concerns may be somewhat overstated. The problem of fractionalization will likely be offset by electronic economies of scale that, together with the localization of new interests and of production/consumption economies, ought to foster somewhat more self-sufficient, hence balanced, communities.

The impending diversification of the media and information channels may indeed produce opportunities to create and maintain new communities of common interests along the dimensions of shared tasks and concerns. But what will these communities actually look like? How will they be structured, both physically and functionally? It is time that local government began to seriously explore the implications of new communications technologies for society, in order to find the appropriate framework for answering these questions.

Telecommunications Alternatives to Transportation

by

R. C. Harkness and J.T. Standal

Telecommunications, used as a partial alternative to transportation, can reduce the energy, materials, and capital required to support social and economic interaction, and thereby contribute to the achievement of an equitable and sustainable level of resource utilization in both developed and developing countries.

The physical infrastructure and behavioral patterns of developed countries were designed and built during a brief historic period characterized by cheap energy, abundant resources, and environmental abuse. For example, the developed countries, which contain only 26% of the free world's population, consume 85% of its energy. As developing countries demand their "fair share" of the earth's resources and seek to obtain our level of economic and social activity, a new communications infrastructure must be found to support increasingly complex patterns of social and economic interaction. This infrastructure must place less reliance on vast fleets of automobiles, expensive freeways and mass transit systems, energy intensive aircraft, and incessant mobility.

We suggest an increased utilization of telecommunications to reduce the need for travel by moving information rather than people. The following sections amplify some of the salient considerations.

The Technology and Opportunities for Substitution

In this particular paper we are concerned with person-to-person and person-to-machine communication by electronic means. Although there are many applications of telecommunications that could reduce the need for different types of trips (remote shopping, educational television, pay TV, telemedicine, etc.) and applications that might increase the energy efficiency of existing transport systems (computer control of traffic signals, truck and auto route advisory, transit passenger information systems, etc.), we will describe only telecommunications systems that can reduce the need for business travel and the journey to work. These two applications have been

Richard Harkness is senior business planner, Satellite Business Systems, McLean, Virginia, J.T. Standal is affiliated with Boeing-RCC and Seattle University, Seattle, Washington.

the focus of much recent research and are important examples from a far wider set of possibilities.

The relevant technologies fall into two main categories: teleconferencing systems and office information systems. Teleconferencing systems are designed to substitute for face-to-face meetings and business travel by conveying the voices and sometimes the images of the participants. In addition, there are often provisions for transmitting such charts, documents, and photographs as may be needed during a meeting. Even remote blackboards have been demonstrated.

There are now about 40 audio or audio-video teleconference systems in operation in the free world. Although teleconferencing systems have been used for initial meetings and even job interviews, researchers are agreed that their major application has been as a substitute for routine, periodic meetings. The U.S. Department of Energy, the Stanford Linear Accelerator Laboratory, the Bank of America, Dow Chemical, the Union Trust Company, NASA, and others have found such usage very beneficial. Much travel has been eliminated. The proliferation of such systems in recent years indicates that teleconferencing is an idea whose time has come, although much remains to be done in refining the technology and learning how to use it most effectively. The potential is large, because extensive research has shown that teleconferencing can substitute for roughly 55% of all business meetings with no loss in meeting effectiveness.

With teleconferencing systems in widespread use, it should be possible to reduce the energy and facilities needed for intraurban, intercity, and international business travel. Therefore, this is one specific application of telecommunications that can contribute toward resource conservation and thus long-term sustainable growth.

The second major technology is computer-based office information systems that are intended to replace paper-based information flows. In one such system developed over the last 10 years at Stanford Research Institute, typed text appears on a TV screen, where it can be stored in a computer data file or transmitted instantly to anyone having a similar terminal. Hard (paper) copies can be made on high-speed printers, if necessary. Although these systems are still being developed, they have been used by widely scattered researchers to jointly compose reports, send messages (electronic mail), and even converse in real time via brief typed statements.

With both teleconferencing and office information systems, one can envision another major opportunity for resource conservation, namely, the ability for white-collar or information-processing workers to work at home (or near home) rather than commuting to a common office building. These commutes often exceed one hour each way in major cities and are expensive in terms of time, energy, materials, and capital. The concept of information workers being able to work remotely from each other via telecommunications rather than congregate in large office buildings clustered in dense downtowns has been labeled *telework*. Although perhaps of most immediate benefit to handicapped people, working mothers, and others unable to commute, telework may ultimately be applicable to a major fraction of those engaged in processing information.

230

Growing Importance of the Information Sector

The major principle underlying modern economic organization is the achievement of efficiency through the specialization of labor and production. This ultimately results in a complex economy highly dependent on coordination and information exchange. Thus, as economies develop, the percentage of the work force engaged in information generation and processing, as opposed to operating machinery or handling goods, rises dramatically.

As developing countries modernize, their work force should undergo a similar dramatic growth in the information sector, thereby creating even greater demands for business travel and commuting to office buildings. The amount of energy thus consumed and the necessary capital investments in transportation systems will be a large burden for developing countries unless an alternate technology can be found to achieve the necessary level of interaction with less travel.

Bus transit is of course more economical than automobiles and can serve many short trips. However, the grade-separated subway systems needed to serve downtown office growth adequately are enormously expensive. The Washington, D.C., Metro is costing $45 million per mile and the initial segment of the Atlanta subway is expected to cost about $80 million per mile. It is questionable whether developing countries can afford to dedicate such large sums to moving commuters. Their growing external debt is now about $170 billion, due partly to higher prices for imported oil. In a major article, *Business Week* states: "Short of default, the developing countries have no alternative but to squeeze their economies and thus cut import demand. But since their level of consumption is already low, the only viable choice is to suppress capital outlays." By moving information rather than people and by moving toward the scenarios outlined above, we believe the developing countries can reduce both oil imports and capital investments for transportation.

Potential Energy and Capital Savings

The energy required for a teleconference is normally far less than that required for a trip. Table 1 illustrates some comparisons.

Recent research has shown that substituting 20% of U.S. domestic business travel by air and auto would save 190,000 barrels of oil per day in 1985. If half of all U.S. office workers were able to work in "neighborhood office centers" (a version of telework where employees work in offices near home but not at home), the savings would be 238,000 barrels per day in 1985. These savings compare favorably in magnitude with other major energy conservation measures identified by the Federal Energy Administration. The neighborhood center measure is in fact the third largest, exceeded only by higher auto efficiency standards and the industrial conservation program.

There is preliminary evidence that it may be far less expensive for society to encourage decentralized patterns of office employment, with the aid of telecommunications, than to concentrate employment in central business districts (CBD). Simply encouraging office employment to locate in suburban sites is a fairly conservative scenario and appears to drastically reduce transport costs because suburban freeways or bus systems are far less expensive than freeways or rapid rail systems that slice through high-density neighbor-

231

Table 1

**Energy Required for Two People to Make the 400-Mile Trip
From London to Glasgow for a 3-Hour Meeting
Versus the Energy Required to Hold a Teleconference**

	Primary Energy Input (Kwh)
Teleconferencing using:	
Telephone	Less than 1
Studio-based audio system	2
Viewphone	40
Confravision	250
Transport (using average occupancy rates) by:	
Rail	450
Air	2500
Car	1600

hoods, or go underground, on their way into city centers.

The more radical neighborhood office center concept creates little or no demand for new transport facilities and, according to a recent SRI study, could save between $30 and $47 billion in U.S. transport investment between now and the year 2000. The cost of telecommunications will, of course, offset these savings to some unknown degree.

Although these scenarios appear to have the potential to yield very large savings, available estimates are still very crude. Clearly, further investigation is merited since both developed and developing countries are having increased difficulty in raising capital for large public works.

Conclusions

The movement of information rather than people provides one way in which developed and developing countries alike can reduce the need for energy, materials, and capital-intensive transportation systems, and move toward a sustainable rate of resource utilization.

The huge and growing external debt in developing countries makes the search for transportation alternatives seem imperative if their economic and social progress is to continue. While the substitution of telecommunications for transportation may apply to a relatively small percentage of the work force in these countries now, that percentage will grow and the applicability of substitution concepts increase accordingly. Conversely, without substitution, resource constraints may keep the information sectors from growing and their economies from maturing.

We do not suggest that the above concepts are fully proven and merit immediate implementation. There are still far too many unknowns and, except for substituting teleconferences for business travel, the scenarios would take many years to implement. However, to the extent they prove feasible, they are permanent long-term solutions.

What we do suggest is that planners begin to question the wisdom and necessity of planning cities and transport systems as though the volume and pattern of travel now observed in developed countries must continue. The possibilities for teleconferencing, telework, and many related concepts should be fully explored. Research and demonstrations should be sponsored. New city shapes based on telework, remote shopping, and other concepts should be evaluated. Urban planners should think in terms of an emerging three-way modal split between auto, transit, and telecommunications. We should, in short, search for new, more sustainable means to achieve the traditional ends of economic and social interaction.

A Scenario of the Telematics Future

by

Henry H. Hitchcock and Joseph F. Coates

The following is one of four scenarios of America in 1995-2010, assuming continued development of telematics. The scenarios are the result of a mini-assessment done by JF Coates, Inc., of the possible environmental consequences of developing telecommunications technologies. All four scenarios are intended to stimulate creative thinking about the interaction of telematic systems in practice, about the mutual influence of other trends with telematics, and about the impacts of such developments on people, human culture, and the natural environment.

The scenarios reflect a systematic manipulation of several factors. First, we attempted to include as many variables as practical—including demographics, the natural environment, social, political, and economic factors, and technology. The focus is on the United States, but not in isolation from the rest of the world. We guided ourselves by extrapolating trends as well as salting in key events. All of this was organized around the inherent possibilities for good, bad, and other developments of telematics.

Three of the four scenarios are unequivocally optimistic and positive in their attempt to get at the profound implications for the organization of human affairs—implicit and increasingly explicit in telecommunications. The fourth scenario, taking its cue from the work of Bertram Gross, emphasizes "friendly fascism" and describes the situation in which telecommunications is both a cause and an agent for control over an increasingly disrupted society.

The four scenarios are intended to bridge the gap between the present understanding of the elements of the telematics tool kit and the profoundly complex ways in which those tools may come together to affect our world. These scenarios attempt a holistic view of the infinitely complex. They are to be provocative and stimulate the exploration of consequences. From these scenarios may come a sense of where important changes are likely to occur and where research, monitoring, evaluation, experimentation, field trials, public policy options, and alternatives may merit attention.

Henry H. Hitchcock is associate, J.F. Coates, Inc. Joseph F. Coates is president of J.F. Coates, Inc., a futures research and policy analysis group located in Washington, D.C.

234

Scenario 1: The Storm

A loud buzzer woke Libby Collins early Thursday morning. An emergency message was coming onto the home terminal. Putting on a robe, she went downstairs and read the message:

Hailstorm rapidly approaching. Will hit Collins farm between noon and 4 p.m.

"Damn," Libby thought, "Just when we were about to have the best sorghum harvest in years. I'd better wake John."

John (her husband) slept through the alarm. He'd spent the night going over the financial arrangements for the proposed Mid-Nebraska Co-op Automated Elevator project. The elevator would be operated completely by robots and computers. It would reduce operating costs and improve efficiency for the co-op. With Clem Walker, the county extension agent, John had ironed out all the details for getting federal funding for the project through fiscal year 1995. They clearly qualified for funding under the Agricultural Robotics program—the project was a significant change from past practice; it was technologically feasible and economically sound; it would pay back in less than five years; and the area needed the boost for family farms. There had been a growing amount of large corporate acquisitions of family farms in the area. They could count on George Jackson, their congressman, for the necessary political support. As finance chairman of the co-op, John had had to get all of these details straightened out before the Co-op Executive Committee meeting that night.

John reacted to the news the same way as Libby had. "Just yesterday, the Weather Service assured me it wouldn't come this far south. I even tracked the damn thing myself using the data from the co-op's receiving station. All my models told me the probability was miniscule—less than 5%. When this all blows over, I'm getting some better modeling programs from the university."

"Wake up Tad [their son] and tell him to get on the videolink with the county locator and line up a crew for this morning. I heard there was a migrant harvesting group near here; tell them we'll pay double the going rate if they can get here in two hours. The transient locator service run by the county may be a good bet for picking up some extra people. I'll contact some members of the Co-op who aren't likely to be hit by the storm and see if we can borrow their harvesters. First, I'm going to run a few problems through the computer."

John was most interested in setting his priorities for harvesting. Which crops were most ready for harvest? The data from the automated irrigation sensors would give him some indication. Which crops would get the best price on the market? The local commodities trends and projections would give him that data. How much demand was there for biomass feedstocks and at what price? If the demand and price were right, the hail might not matter. Damaged sorghum was just as good as healthy sorghum as far as energy production was concerned.

Just as the priorities were coming off the console, Tad told him that the migrant crew was bound by a previous commitment to help the Jarrel farm.

The locator service provided the names of 20 possible people and their current whereabouts. Tad had contacted 15 of them on the videolink; 10 of them were willing to help out. Using the routing program on the home console, he worked out the fastest and most energy-efficient way to get these people to the farm. Three of them could hitch a ride with the Caravan; two others would come via the Medibus. The rest would form a temporary carpool and on the way would pick up the harvesters from the other members of the co-op.

It was clear that John was not going to get the whole crop in. The computer listed the priorities for harvesting:

1. Low pesticide residue crops . . . highest yield and price . . . maximum harvest time ½ hour with 3 harvesters.

2. Sorghum crop in section E-5 . . . most ready for harvesting . . . harvest time 1 hour with 3 harvesters.

3. Sorghum crops in N-1, 2, and 3 . . . high yield areas . . . relatively ripe for harvesting . . . harvest time 2 hours with 3 harvesters.

4. If time is available . . . S-2 and 3 . . . harvest time 2 hours with 3 harvesters.

5. Remaining crops can be sold to co-op for energy feedstocks; see if you can get commitment before the storm . . . estimate drop in price following the storm of $.50 per kilo of feedstock.

John's first response was to check the current prices for biomass feedstocks around the area. Hastings Co-op was paying top rate. However, Tom Broker down at the co-op was not willing to pay that price today—"in less than 12 hours we'll have more feedstock than we can handle." John brought Jack Holmes, president of the co-op, into the negotiations. They quickly reached a compromise—John would get half the difference between the price before the storm and after the storm. After terminating the negotiations, John ran through the various possible prices that could result after the storm. Even with the most severe storm, his profit from selling the sorghum as feedstock would be acceptable. With that knowledge, John could concentrate on the high yield, high quality areas instead of trying to get the most possible sorghum harvested. At 6 a.m., John, Tad, and the 15 men from the locator service left for the fields with three harvesters.

* * *

Libby decided her time would be better spent: (a) monitoring the farm, and (b) doing some of her backlog of editing, typing, and programming work. They were going to need all the extra income they could get if the storm was very severe. Libby had worked in town for a lawyer's office. When they got the home terminal, she decided it would be more economical to take in work than to make the 18-mile drive into town every day. The law office found piece work convenient, less costly, and satisfying to all parties. They did not have to pay for office furniture, other overhead, and fringe benefits, and the work was done in pretty much the same amount of time.

In addition to her work for the law office, Libby also took in editing jobs from a local university—there was always some professor in need of help in turning his tortured language into prose. She was also beginning to be known as a competent programmer. She had helped several of her friends with pro-

236

gramming their home terminals, and now some of the local businesses were hiring her. When the Collinses got their terminal they had taken advantage of the salesman's offer of half-price tuition for programming courses. Within a year, Libby was bringing in money from programming.

Before turning to her editing and programming, Libby ran a quick check on the farm's operations and determined the following:

- The pigs were coming along nicely. The sensors embedded in their backs had worked beautifully in monitoring their heartrates, metabolism, and growth. The experiment with the Hans Seyle method of stress reduction and growth enhancement was working quite well. This year's slaughter would bring at least a 50% increase to this profit center of the farm.
- The cows had moved into the north pasture last night. The grass in the north pasture was not quite ready for grazing. Libby used the microwave prodder to move the cattle out of that pasture into the east pasture.
- The fence on the west pasture had a break. Libby's first suspicion was attempted rustling; reviewing the videotapes from last night's surveillance, she was unable to detect any unusual activity; a count of the cattle moving from the north to the east pasture showed that they were all there.
- The wind generator and storage batteries were still low. The calm days of the past week had left much of the area with little energy stored in the batteries. Libby checked the load-management network and saw a number of her neighbors in need of immediate energy. Reviewing her probable needs for the next two days and estimating the amount of energy they would get from the hail storm, she decided they could spare some of their storage. She entered her offer and within 10 minutes was contacted by Len Jarrel, their neighbor. He thanked her for her offer and said he'd send over any of the migrant working crew he could spare to help John and Tad get the crop in.

Her final check was the experimental section where their crop breeding experiments were planted. Things did not look right—the colors were off and the resolution of the zoom lens was fuzzy. Libby made a note to get a replacement monitor from town while she sent this one in to be fixed. Before turning away from the experimental section, she activated the protective covering to prevent the hail from destroying their experiments.

* * *

As Libby was checking on the farm, their youngest daughter Ellen came downstairs ready for school. Ellen's school, Hastings High School, was on an experimental program in which the students went to the central school only three days a week; the other two days were spent at home using interactive teaching programs on home computers. For those students whose homes did not have consoles, the school provided them for a nominal fee.

Yesterday, Ellen had worked on her calculus, French, and history at home using the terminal. She also had begun her advanced course in computer repair—a required part of the consumer education class. After finishing her studies, Ellen had worked on several stories for the school newspaper (she was an editor on the paper):

Microwave Effects: Fatal to Farmers?

With the rapid proliferation of microwave dishes throughout our region, some people have begun to wonder if we could be exposing our-

237

selves to dangerous radiation. Most experts agree that a single device is not likely to be harmful. However, with the numerous devices cropping up in farms around the areas, we wonder if the interactive effects have been fully explored. This and related issues will be the main topic of discussion at this week's meeting of the Science Club in Room 404.

Energy-Telecommunications Conflict

There is a proposal to put a receiving antenna for the new solar power satellite in nearby Red Cloud, Nebraska. Some argue that the microwaves from this giant energy satellite could adversely affect the communications networks in this area. In addition, if the satellite malfunctions, according to some it could harm people and animals in the surrounding area. The benefits of the satellite are a continuous supply of energy at relatively low operating costs. For the Red Cloud area it could mean more jobs and greater tax revenues.

Next month, the Debating Club will focus on this conflict between energy, environment, and communications.

She put the stories on the school's computer network with messages to several of her fellow editors.

For entertainment, Ellen participated in an episode of *Space Battle*. Several of the kids at the local high school had formed a *Space Battle* club; they played every Monday and Wednesday. After last night's episode, Ellen's starship fleet was minus two battle cruisers and in danger of being completely destroyed by her best friend's forces. Before retiring, Ellen tuned in the cable TV to see the last half of the semifinals of the women's pro basketball championship. Her favorite team, the Iowa Marauders, had won and was well on its way to another championship.

Ellen had to fight with her older brother Tad to watch the game; he had wanted to use the viewer to participate in a junior grange meeting. They were preparing an agenda for the meeting of the Young Grange party. Tad was hoping to be elected to represent Hastings. This would give him extensive exposure, as Grange party members from all over the nation would be participating. When Ellen had succeeded in capturing the viewer, Tad decided to use some of his remaining monthly gas allotment to take the car into town to be at the meeting. Before he left, he put in another plea for buying another viewer.

* * *

Today, Ellen was going to Washington, D.C. Not really—her travel club was trying to decide whether to go to Washington, D.C., or New York City over Christmas break. To help them decide, the school video library provided them with travel tapes. With these tapes, the club would experience the sights, sounds, and smells of the places they could visit. She remembered the thrill of her first experience with the travel tapes: as a thriller-diller extra, the tape on San Francisco had ended with a jump off the Golden Gate Bridge.

After the travel club meetings, Ellen and her friends in the Computing Club were meeting to discuss the alternative plans they had devised for improving the efficiency of the Caravan and the routine Medibus trips. Over the past two years, both the Caravan and the Medibus had exceeded their fuel allocation; the co-op had offered the students a prize of 10 new game programs if they could come up with a more efficient routing system.

* * *

When the price of gasoline went through the roof in 1985, the Hastings community decided to move to a less energy intensive/more communications intensive existence. Along with the local co-op, the community government invested in a transmitting station and receiving disk. With these facilities, they could offer the excess capacity as inducement to communications-intensive firms that might want to locate in Hastings. Currently two companies—an insurance company and a major mail order business—were interested. Much of the program had been funded with low-interest loans backed up by the Rural Electrification Administration's "Wired Farm" program.

The most widely used element of the program was the twice-a-week Caravan—a consolidated delivery and pickup service. The Caravan combined trash pickup, package delivery, and grocery/shopping deliveries into one service. Most of the community participated, significantly reducing the number of trips they made into town.

The community groups in Hastings also took advantage of the burgeoning communications capabilities. Using the facilities of the high school on its two vacant days, they prepared and broadcast programs of interest to the community. To complement the broadcasts, the community built a unique teleconferencing center. Using the home-to-center video relays and innovative video programming, community groups could hold face-to-face meetings without extensive travel. John Collins's presentation to the executive committee of the co-op was going to use these facilities later that evening. But actual get-togethers were still common in Hastings—especially on Sundays when people would come into town for church. For church services, the interdenominational bus service brought people in from the surrounding countryside.

One of the most popular elements in the community's communications program was the Medibus. Libby's mother had been ill recently with the flu; the Medibus with its physician's assistant/driver had visited her mobile home several times during her illness to bring her drugs, check on her condition, and give her some company. While at the house, the assistant called in the current symptoms and put Libby's mother on the remote medical sensor. The doctor in town scanned the readout and ordered new prescriptions or instructions. At one point, Libby's mother had become so ill that they left a continuous monitoring device with her.

* * *

During her lunch break, Libby called up the day's mail from computer storage. Sorting through the advertisements, Libby noted a sale on self-teaching programming cassettes. Getting on the videolink, Libby contacted Ivan Greenwald at the computer store in town; he had just one self-teaching cassette left. After debiting her account at Hastings National Bank, he agreed to send the program out on the next Caravan. Next, Libby contacted the John Deere outlet to get a new monitor for the experimental crop section. After paying a few bills, Libby turned to her personal correspondence.

After two months, she had gotten a message from her computing comrade in Greece. Helena looked well; she'd gained a little weight, but it looked good on her. The weather in Athens looked beautiful. Helena had just gotten back from a trip to the islands and had the tan to prove it. She apologized for not having been in contact sooner, but life had been just one great whirlwind. After reviewing the comings and goings, births, deaths, marriages, divorces, and assorted peccadilloes of her family, she thanked Libby for her last communication. The English learning tape she had transmitted would help her son Nikos brush up on his English before his visit to the United States next summer. Helena asked if it was still all right for Nikos to spend a few days with the Collinses when he got to the U.S.

* * *

While Libby was watching Helena's message, John activated the tractor's computercator to signal her. One of the harvesters had broken down and he needed some help from the local John Deere service center.

Fortunately, John's harvester was equipped with the latest trouble sensors and a transmitter. Plugging in the code for the harvester, the technician saw immediately what was wrong with the harvester. He radioed John with step-by-step instructions for fixing the harvester. Within an hour of reaching Libby, John had the harvester working once again.

Around 1 p.m. the hail began. By 2 p.m. the ground was carpeted with hail. John, Tad, and the others had harvested more than they had expected. What was left of the crop would go for biomass feedstock. All in all, they had responded much better than they could have a mere 10 years earlier.

Communicating with One's Self: A Wave of the Future

by

Thomas E. Jones

"Know thyself." This dictum, addressed by Socrates to his compatriots 25 centuries ago, poses no less of a challenge to each member of the human species today. Unless we know ourselves, we cannot communicate well with ourselves; and unless we communicate well with ourselves, we find it difficult to communicate with others. The prospect of using emerging communication technologies to promote understanding and cooperation in our diverse, yet increasingly interpenetrating, world depends significantly on the extent to which people learn to communicate better with themselves as unique individuals who nonetheless resemble each other.

Despite the enormous gains in knowledge of human behavior achieved since Socrates' time, many of us still feel as if we are strangers to ourselves. However, recent breakthroughs in such areas as cognitive psychology, neurophysiology, holography, kinesiology, brain lateralization research, psychic research, biofeedback, laser- and electro-acupuncture, brainwave entrainment, and holistic medicine—breakthroughs fostered in part by increasingly sophisticated instrumentation—have begun to yield reliable knowledge about conscious and unconscious processes and especially about human energy fields. Although this creative fringe makes its share of excessive, uncorroborated claims, it appears to constitute the vanguard of a convergent movement devoted to loosening the shackles that unduly restrict holistic self-communication. The flowering of this seedling might even encourage intelligent international cooperation to cope with interrelated global problems. In spite of the highly problematic future of such an emergent tendency, forecasters cannot afford to ignore its potential consequences.

Clearly, breakthroughs toward enhanced communication with one's self are occurring in many areas. Yet in the limited space available here, I will focus only on human electromagnetic fields and on several promising technologies—most of them little-known or emerging—that measure these fields and modify them to promote physical and mental well-being.

Thomas E. Jones is an adjunct associate professor at the Graduate School of Management, Polytechnic Institute of New York, Brooklyn, New York. A frequent writer on futurist topics, including the book Options for the Future: A Comparative Analysis of Policy-Oriented Forecasts *(Praeger, 1980), he holds doctorates in both philosophy and social science.*

241

Technologies for Communicating with One's Electromagnetic Field

Every object, whether inanimate or alive, possesses a unique electromagnetic field that exhibits antagonistic, complementary (resonant), or neutral reactions when it interacts with other fields. Recent investigations provide evidence that:

• Each human being, as well as each other living system, appears to have a distinctive electromagnetic life-field interpenetrating and surrounding its body.

• This field and its subdivisions can be measured accurately and repeatedly.

• Certain precisely specified frequencies, amplitudes, and waveforms are regularly associated with—and seem to be causally related to—healthy, electrically balanced (homeostatic) functioning of various parts of the body and of the body as a whole.

• Certain other frequencies, amplitudes, and waveforms generally accompany, or serve as early warning signals of, various types and degrees of disease and degeneration that disrupt this balance.

• Specific kinds of instrument-mediated, non-invasive stimulation by frequencies, amplitudes, or waveforms (or corresponding ingested remedies) that are incompatible with those of the pathogens and resonant with those of optimal organic functioning can frequently alleviate an incipient or established pathological condition and help to rebalance the entire organism.

Evidence that favors the diagnosis and treatment of diseases via electromagnetic life-fields derives largely from the use of new instrumentation to stimulate organisms, record their responses, and note correlations. The resulting communication with the complex, tendency-prone psycho-bio-physical organism encourages a shift toward holistic preventive medicine.

Furthermore, several established technologies call attention to the importance of electronic currents in the body. By using sensitive electronic instruments—for instance, the EMG (the electromyograph, which measures muscular tension in terms of electrical activity), the GSR or EDR (galvanic skin response or electrodermal response, which measures skin resistance to an electric current), and the EEG (the electroencephalograph, which records the electrical activity of the brain)—to record, measure, and feed back information about certain physiological functions in the form of auditory or visual displays, an individual may learn how to consciously regulate functions that had been regarded as involuntary.

Life-fields, Electronography, and Acupuncture Devices

From the 1930s until his death in 1973, Harold Saxton Burr of Yale University collected evidence to support his claim that an electromagnetic life-field or "L field" performs a directive, organizing function on the physical structure of an organism. Leonard Ravitz found that a person's mental state measurably affects the L field that is detected by electrodes placed a short distance away from the skin. According to one interpretation, Kirlian photographs of electroluminescent discharges from a person depict part of the L field. The intensity and character of the energy emissions seem to be closely correlated with the physical and mental health of the person photographed. Ioan Dumitrescu of Bucharest, Romania, has modified the Kirlian technique, thereby devising "electronography." It produces images of the configurations of human elecromagnetic fields in ways that facilitate detection of pathogens such as cancer long before they are disclosed by such established procedures as X rays and blood tests.

Further evidence that human electromagnetic fields can be detected and modified therapeutically comes from electro-acupuncture technology that measures and corrects pathogenic imbalances in bodily energy flow. The computerized Accupath 1000, a new diagnostic instrument designed for the Nevada Clinic of Preventive Medicine in Las Vegas, measures in terms of skin resistance the responses of meridians, organs, and organ systems to electrical current that enters at corresponding points on the skin. Readouts disclose whether the meridian, organ, and organ system associated with each "acupoint" is in an electrically balanced, inflammatory, or degenerative condition. After completing a review of bodily electrical paths, the Accupath 1000 surveys a table of approximately 1,700 preparations to determine which remedies and remedy strengths will rectify observed electrical imbalances.

The Biotech Multi-Modality Laser/TNS/Electronic Acupuncture Apparatus, designed by G. Dean Peterson and scheduled for production by Dynatronics at Salt Lake City, is the epitome of hybrid acupuncture technology. This versatile, portable computerized instrument combines electro-acupuncture, laser acupuncture (irradiation of acupoints with appropriate wavelengths of coherent light, thereby repairing damaged DNA and rejuvenating weakened bodily systems), transcutaneous nerve stimulation or TNA (therapeutic electrical stimulation of the central nervous system by means of electrodes placed on the skin), and galvanic skin response measurement (which here refers to the resistance of underlying tissue, as well as skin, to electronic current flow).

Quite popular in West Germany is still another electrical stimulation technology: the "biopulse" or "magnetotron," which creates a low-intensity, low-frequency (about 10 Hz) electromagnetic field that improves cellular oxygen-utilization.

Becker's Electrical Stimulation Therapy

Yet the most dramatic of these technologies is that pioneered by Robert O. Becker of the Veterans' Administration Hospital in Syracuse, New York (described lucidly by Kathleen McAuliffe in her *Omni* article, "I Sing the Body Electric"). From his measurements of increased voltage generated at injury sites, Becker discovered clues to the mystery of why a salamander can regenerate as much as a third of its body mass. Red blood cells at the location of a salamander's wound lose their specialized function and become a "blastema," a cluster of temporarily undifferentiated cells that proceed to regroup themselves into the complex tissues of the body part they replace. Becker's research led him to conclude that in mammals the blastema appears to be derived from nucleated cells in bone marrow, and that only the controlling factor—electricity—is missing. His measurements of stable voltages on the skin of different kinds of organisms suggest that nerves provide the electrical signal for blastema formation. Furthermore, measurement of voltages on the outside of nerve fibers indicates that the cells coating the outside of peripheral nerves carry a constantly flowing current, in contrast to the short bursts of electrical activity that the nerves conduct. Becker infers that his continuous current radiates throughout the body's network of peripheral nerves and produces electromagnetic field patterns, which are disturbed by injury. When cells detect an injury, they begin repair that eventuates in scar tissue unless the nerve mass is large enough to generate the voltages required for regeneration.

By means of electric current from an implanted electrode, Becker stimulated a rat to regrow its amputated foreleg to the elbow joint. When Stephen Smith of the University of Kentucky Medical School made an electrode migrate down a limb as new tissue grew back, he was able to regenerate an amputated frog's leg in complete anatomical precision. Andrew Bassett of Columbia-Presbyterian Medical Center in New York City conducted animal studies in which electric current consistently doubled or tripled the growth rate of peripheral nerves, thus furnishing hope that electricity will prove successful in repairing damage done to the human central nervous system. In a healing procedure approved by the U.S Food and Drug Administration, Bassett places electric coils around a bone fracture to create a pulsating electromagnetic field that induces tiny currents in the bone.

Results of the experiments conducted by Becker, Smith, and Bassett indicate that cells can respond as well to induced electric current as to the body's own. Yet the artificial electromagnetic pulses must be fine-tuned, in terms of amplitude and frequency, to the biological waveband required to exert cellular control. Electrochemist Art Pilla, a colleague of Bassett, uses a computer to devise pulsed waveforms that move ions across the selective membrane of cells and thereby start the needed chain of chemical reactions within the cells.

By intercepting electrical messages that bodily communication networks transmit, researchers have discovered how to code electrical signals that cells understand. Thus the researchers, without fully understanding the information encoded in the signals, have brought about healing by mimicking the internal signals by which organisms regulate growth, development, and repair.

Electrical stimulation therapy for humans in the near future will probably center on bones, skin, and peripheral nerves, all of which manifest some regenerative capability. Increasing numbers of scientists think that regeneration of parts of the human body will be achieved, probably within the lifetime of many people alive today. Another possibility is cancer control.

A further prospect is the use of electric current to augment cognitive processes. Ross Adey has increased the rate of learning in primates and cats by focusing electromagnetic fields on their heads during training. He believes that electrical signals carried over a radio frequency, modulated in amplitude, and adjusted to the frequency range of alpha and theta brainwaves result in neurological changes that enhance learning and memory.

Brainwave Entrainment

ELF generators. Despite rapid progress in recent brain research, little is known about the complex operation of the human brain. Nevertheless, available knowledge and new technologies are facilitating our rudimentary, yet highly significant, communication with our own brains. Several devices that are designed to influence brain performance emit frequencies or waveforms that entrain brainwaves. One example is Adey's instrumentation. It resembles another: the frequency generators used by investigators of the marked psychophysiological impact of extreme low frequency (ELF) electric and magnetic fields on an estimated 25% to 75% of all humans and animals. As an electronic pacemaker can induce correct heart rhythms, so a personally-worn pocket-size ELF generator can entrain brainwaves at selected frequencies.

The naturally occurring oscillations of the earth's magnetic field span a resonant ELF range identical with that of human brainwaves. These predominantly beneficial oscillations display slight variations corresponding, for instance, to the phases of the moon and sunspot activity; and correlations suggest that these variations can encourage frequency-related moods.

Frequencies emitted by certain modern technologies inadvertently interfere with the "cosmic drummer," to whose life-enhancing beats humans have been attuned for ages. A further danger is the apparent feasibility of mood-manipulating "psychotronic warfare," in which harmful frequencies might be targeted for distant, geographically large areas via pulse-modulated radio frequency carriers.

Numerous EEG experiments have demonstrated brainwave entrainment and neuronal synchronization or desynchronization when the subjects are in the vicinity of intentionally generated, as well as naturally occurring, ELF oscillations of appropriate intensities. Symptoms exhibited at different, precisely specified frequencies can display dramatic contrasts. For instance, ELF magnetic fields of 6.67 Hz and 6.25 Hz produce symptoms of anxiety, confusion, fear, tension, depression, insomnia, mild nausea, headaches, and so on. Conversely, fields of 7.8, 8, and 9 Hz engender anxiety-relieving, stress-reducing states.

Other instruments. The electronic circuitry of G. Patrick Flanagan's Neurophone presents audio information to the skin in such a way that it can be received and decoded by the central nervous system and the brain without passing through the eight cranial nerve systems, thus enabling individuals to hear without using their ears or bones.

Instead of supplying pulses to entrain brainwaves, Jean Millet's "light sculpture" EEG instrument provides biofeedback information from which users may learn to synchronize the discharging or "firing" of neurons in their left and right cerebral hemispheres. Synchronization in the alpha frequency range, for instance, turns on a corresonding row of distinctively colored lights and produces a tone. This helps the user to become acquainted with, and duplicate, the bilateral synchronization state that promotes the focus of attention associated with creative insight.

A number of devices employ flashing lights (e.g., the Psychelitic Strobe Light Stimulator), pulsating sounds (e.g., one type of Silva Mind Control training device), or a combination of light and sound stimulation (e.g., Denis Gorgas's Brainwave Synchro-Energizer) in partially successful efforts to entrain brainwaves. As the pulsed stimuli are repeated, the evoked cortical electrical responses may assume the rate set by the pulses. When higher percentages of brain cells fire together, brainwaves become more orderly, stronger, and more coherent. An increase in brainwave amplitude indicates that many more neurons are brought into phase to communicate with each other. The supposition is that this renders more of the brain's potential intelligence available for use.

The Synchronous Field Generator

A particularly promising emerging technology is G. Dean Peterson's Synchronous Field Generator. Peterson is producing a battery-operated instrument that will generate the highly specific frequencies and waveforms that ELF research has shown to be associated with various mental and physical states and processes. Since the timing of neuron firing is so important to brain performance, Peterson has designed his equipment to produce precisely-timed stimulation of neurons. Such precise operation seemed to require computerized controls, but a dramatic breakthrough in computer chip engineering now allows the same goal to be achieved with the less expensive chips. Pulsed stimulation will be auditory and photic as well as magnetic. Although ELF research has disclosed that magnetic field induction is the most powerful entrainment mode, the sound and light display via goggles and earphones will contribute to the overall effect.

The unit may be used with such accessories as a tape recorder. A number of researchers maintain that listening to special tapes while experiencing brain entrainment at specific frequencies can facilitate relaxation training, hypnotherapy, and speed-learning, and can also help to induce particular altered states of consciousness. Monitoring devices that measure galvanic skin response and brainwave patterns can be employed to check the efficacy of the Synchronous Field Generator in producing desired mental and physical effects. Special safeguards to prevent the selection of harmful settings will be built into the unit.

Possible Socio-Cultural Consequences

Will a brainwave entrainment device, such as the Synchronous Field Generator, promote measurable increases in IQ, creativity, and other indicators of intelligence? Will it expedite the learning process? Will it enable psychotherapy to become appreciably more effective? Will it make possible the enjoyment of quasi-psychedelic trips while permanently enhancing brain efficiency? Will it bestow the flexibility to function at frequencies and amplitudes appropriate to achieving a variety of goals? Will it encourage bodily healing and health maintenance?

Assessment becomes even more problematic when we seek to project possible second-, third-, and n-order consequences that might be touched off by the success of the instrument. It could, for instance, be distributed in ways that exacerbate conflict-engendering inequalities among people, or in equitable ways that encourage individuals to attain the increasingly available self-knowledge and self-control needed for rewarding self-actualization.

A technology assessment confined to the major technologies just surveyed is beset by a high degree of uncertainty concerning both their future performances and the wide-ranging consequences that might stem from their implementation. Uncertainties are compounded when we view these technologies as stepping-stones to more powerful ones, and take into account the many related technologies not mentioned here. Yet the spectrum of desirable and undesirable possible consequences dramatizes the urgent need for perspicacious technology assessment. Moreover, the problematic character of these consequences, coupled with the significant extent to which they depend on human choices, suggests that normative planning could be applied judiciously to channel change away from disasters and toward beneficial outcomes.

One concluding speculation. If conclusions resembling those drawn by neurophysiologist Karl Pribram concerning the holographic character of human information processing, and by physicist David Boem concerning the holographic character of the universe, prove to be well-founded, our increasing technologically based knowledge of ourselves may help us better understand the behavior of other people and even of the universe itself. Recognition of this underlying interrelatedness and unity might provide the psychological underpinnings for a paradigm shift that would open up a range of beneficial futures to the human species.

Politics and the New Media

by

Richard M. Neustadt

The first thing Congressman Jim Coyne does when he gets to his Capitol Hill office each morning is read his computer. Coyne is the first congressman to set up an "electronic mailbox" to receive messages from constituents and others who have their own computers. Coyne says he likes his system because it gets him fresh ideas faster than they get to his colleagues.

Coyne's flickering screen is a sign that the notorious "communications revolution" is about to hit politics. A wave of new technology will transform campaigning, political organizing, news coverage, lobbying, and voting. Some of these changes may make campaigning less costly and bring decision-making closer to the people. But the greatest impact may be to fragment our politics, narrowing people's perspectives, shifting more power to special interest groups, and weakening the glue that holds our system together.

The turbulence ahead will be reminiscent of what television did to politics two decades ago. TV turned campaign schedules into a string of "visuals" to draw the cameras—candidates started wading into polluted rivers to deliver position papers on the environment. It started frantic hunts for money to buy precious seconds of air time. Presidents and candidates learned to use TV to talk directly to the people, over the heads of the political parties and the press. Television even changed the kinds of faces, voices, and personalities that win elections.

During the 1980s, television and other media will be reshaped by cable TV, satellite-to-home broadcasting, videotape recorders, personal computers, and electronic publishing. Politicians will have to learn the political implications of these devices, just as they had to learn about television. And all of us ought to start thinking now about how we want politics to work in the new era.

Campaigning with "Narrowcasting"

The combination of new technology and deregulation is creating a flood of new television channels. A quarter of U.S. households now subscribes to cable TV; by 1990, the number should be over 50%. All the new cable systems have at least 32 channels, and the frantic bidding war for franchises is push-

Richard M. Neustadt, a former TV news writer and a policy adviser in the Carter White House, now practices communications law in Washington.

ing cable companies to promise as many as 200 channels in some cities. The number of regular radio and TV stations on the air has doubled since 1960. The FCC is about to award hundreds of "low power television" licenses, creating new outlets in the coverage gaps between existing stations, and it will soon have hundreds of new radio licenses to give away. Direct-broadcast satellites may be operating by 1986, sending as many as 20 channels of television directly from space to low-cost roof-top receivers.

This wave of new channels is creating the economic base for "narrowcasting." The big three networks will survive and will continue to aim at mass audiences, but dozens of new services will spring up to serve smaller audiences with particular interests. Already, the new economics of television has spawned networks dedicated to news, sports, weather, movies, culture, Hispanics, Jews, Blacks, seniors, children, and even health.

Up to now, politicians used television to send short, universally appealing messages to large audiences. The new television will mean longer messages tailored to smaller audiences. When we watch the narrowcasting networks, we will see campaign ads and news programs showing candidates advocating bilingual education on Spanish channels, defending Social Security on channels aimed at the elderly, and playing football on sports channels. Politicians will find the all-news channels particularly fertile ground—viewers with enough appetite for news to watch it continuously will be good prospects to contribute, volunteer, and vote.

The new media's greatest impact may be on congressional and local campaigns that could not afford to advertise on old-style television. For example, a candidate running in Lansing, Michigan, has to pay at least $500 for a 60-second ad on a regular TV station, and most of that money is wasted because the station covers half the state. The same commercial on the local cable system costs $30 and reaches just Lansing residents. Advertising is new to cable—only 10% of the systems take local ads today—but it will be universal in a few years.

Cable even offers free time at the local level. Most cable systems have "public access channels," which are available to anyone who wants to use them, first-come, first-served. In many cities, the cable system even supplies the studio and cameras. Few access channels have regular audiences, but they are ideal for a campaign manager to brief volunteers or a political party to run a weekly talk show for its activists.

The New News

Most Americans get their news from television. Up to now, TV news has meant mostly 90-second stories, Sunday morning interview shows, and a few "specials" on presidential speeches, election nights, and the like. The new media will turn "specials" into daily fare and change politics in the process.

The cable system in Reading, Pennsylvania, was one of the first to provide live coverage of city council meetings. Viewers got to know who the council members were and what they did, and that changed Reading's politics. Those TV shows helped the current mayor, Karen Miller, attract a following, beat a political machine, and win her seat. "People definitely are watching us," says Mayor Miller.

The Madison, Wisconsin, cable system is another pioneer in local coverage. City councilmen accustomed to anonymity find themselves treated like TV personalities—strangers stop them in the streets to praise or revile their performances.

Most of the cable systems now being built will dedicate a channel to this kind of programming. There is talk in several states about letting cameras into the legislatures. A cable network has carried the U.S. House of Representatives live for the past three years, and the Senate will vote this year on whether to do likewise. Early reports from the House indicate that television has produced some grandstanding but also some improvements. Congressmen have a strong incentive not to look foolish when they speak on the House floor—their opponents can use TV clips in campaign ads.

These channels are creating a novel kind of television news. They bring events directly to people, "gavel-to-gavel," without editing or interpretation. The audiences are small compared to "Laverne and Shirley," but they are huge compared to the numbers who actually show up at city council meetings or House debates.

These channels operate without reporters, but electronic journalism also is growing. Two 24-hour cable news networks are on the air, and two more will start this year. Reporters for these networks will be able to do stories four or five minutes long, increasing substance and subtlety. In Washington and many other cities, newspapers are teaming up with cable systems to produce local news channels. All these services will give us more in-depth reporting and more of what television does best—live coverage of breaking stories.

News coverage on the old media also is improving. CBS is considering expanding its evening news program to an hour. Many local TV stations are increasing their own operations and bringing in more national and international coverage. (The new technology is helping canny political organizations take advantage of the local stations' interest. For example, the Republicans bought half an hour of satellite time to transmit clips of senators praising President Reagan's State of the Union Address to their home-state TV stations.)

Taken together, these trends will provide more information for those who want it. Politics will be more accessible and understandable, and that may get more people involved.

Unfortunately, many people may end up knowing less. Most Americans get their news from television, and the old broadcasters' news programs, superficial though they are, provide a homogenous information base for the most diverse society in the West. In narrowcasting, by contrast, some channels will provide only news about their particular themes, and many—such as the movie and sports networks—will offer no news at all. Narrowcasting may fragment Americans' perception of events, and the vast menu of entertainment channels may draw some people away from the news altogether. An electorate awash in video information may end up less informed.

One result is that when the president goes on television in 1990, he may be carried on six networks, but he will not be on two dozen others. For the first time since FDR's fireside chats, the mass audience that presidents have automatically commanded will begin to erode.

250

Campaigning with Computers

Politics requires mountains of paperwork. Candidates and causes need people to make lists, stuff envelopes, and so on. These tasks have helped make housewives and high-school students the indispensable footsoldiers of campaigns. In the last two years, however, computers have become cheap enough to let most campaigns automate their paperwork. In the 1982 election, the most prized volunteers will be those who bring their personal computers to campaign headquarters.

The newly-liberated volunteers will be turned loose to contact voters, but computers will play a role there, too. A few campaigns have started using automatic dialing machines that call hundreds of people an hour and play a message when they answer—e.g., a tape of the candidate urging them to vote. The next step will be "voice recognition" machines that "understand" what the person at the other end of the line is saying. Several companies already have built prototypes that can handle callers' airline reservations with startling accuracy. By the end of the decade, we may see electronic canvassing—once people get used to talking to computers.

Computers also will help "target" messages and money to particular groups of voters. A Republican National Committee study last year recommended giving local parties access to the national party's sophisticated data banks, to provide instant information and analysis in the heat of campaigns.

The advent of computers will help well-heeled candidates who can afford the fanciest equipment, but falling prices will let even impoverished candidates use automation. The only certain gainers will be those who move quickly to take advantage of these machines.

Organizing by Video

The new technologies will help candidates, but they will do even more for interest groups. The U.S. Chamber of Commerce has taken the lead by launching its own television network. "BizNet" will use a satellite to broadcast six hours per day of business news, interviews, and—of course—lobbying messages, directly to receivers placed at corporate headquarters around the country. The Chamber has spent $5 million on studios and will spend several millions more each year to run the operation.

BizNet is pioneering a migration that will sweep through political organizations—the shift from paper to electronics. Up to now, most interest groups have relied on mail to raise money and communicate with members, but the cost of mail is going through the roof. Today it costs about $250,000 to print and mail a fundraising pitch or a newsletter to a million people, and that price may double in five years.

In electronics, by contrast, most costs are stable or falling. For the price of a fundraising mailing, a group can now reach over a million people with 100 two-minute ads on a cable network. For the price of a newsletter, an organization can produce up to 10 one-hour television shows, and some of the new networks are so hungry for programming that they will give away air time. Such opportunities are unavailable on the old networks, which sell only 30- and 60-second spots—too short to be substantive—and charge tens of thousands of dollars each. With the new channels, an environmental group, for example, can spend a relatively small amount of money to produce a weekly "nature hour" that gets its message to its members and to anyone else who may tune in.

Apart from cost savings, this approach takes advantage of the emotional impact of pictures—in an America reared on TV, video is the way to get people excited. That is why Richard Viguerie, the leading fundraising expert for conservative causes, says that "cable television will be to the politics of the 1980s what direct mail was to the 1970s."

Only one group has really exploited the new media so far—the churches. In the past few years, several denominations acquired their own UHF TV stations and created satellite-fed networks that reach millions. Most political organizations are hanging back because of ignorance or penury, but a few savvy groups are moving now, while channels are still available and narrowcasting network time is still cheap. The United Auto Workers, for example, has applied for 24 low-power stations to create the base for its own TV network.

By the end of the decade, trade associations, corporations, unions, and political parties will be turning out oceans of videotape. This "electronic direct mail" will be a key tool of political organizing.

Electronic Lobbying

The new technology is giving political organizations another potent tool: the "video teleconference." Last December, for example, Vice President Bush had promised to speak to a group of GOP contributors in California, but he could not spare the time for a full day of traveling. Instead, Bush went to a studio a mile from the White House and talked by satellite. The audience watched him on a screen while he gave his speech and answered their questions. The contributors were happy, Bush saved a day, and the Republican Party saved the cost of an airplane charter.

The National Education Association tried a much bigger teleconference last year. The Association wanted to mobilize 1,000 of its organizers across the country for a letter-writing campaign on a budget issue. Instead of flying everyone to Washington, the Association brought them to 49 sites around the country and plotted strategy over a satellite. The conference worked, and it saved a quarter of a million dollars in air fares and hotel bills.

By 1990, similar electronic meetings between congressmen and constituents will be a routine part of lobbying. These sessions will be cheaper and faster to arrange than the traditional flight to Washington, and lobbyists will find it much easier to recruit busy constituents for a one-hour teleconference than a two-day trip. Electronic meetings will not have quite the impact of face-to-face contact, but they will get the message across.

One company already is building a studio within walking distance of the Capitol to exploit this market. Eventually, Congress is likely to wire its own buildings so that members can hold teleconferences from their offices and committees can hear testimony from out-of-town witnesses.

Electronic Polling

The most dramatic changes of all may be in polling. The 1980 Reagan-Carter debate gave us a primitive picture of what lies in store. After the debate, the ABC network asked viewers to call a special telephone number and record their preference. Within hours, an AT&T computer tallied millions of votes and pronounced Reagan the winner.

A two-way cable TV system in Columbus, Ohio, called "QUBE" illustrates the next generation of the technology. Subscribers are given a small black box with several buttons, which is connected to the TV set. The announcer on a television program asks a question and gives the audience four choices, and viewers at home then push the button for the answer they like. Within seconds, the results flash on the screen.

This year, cable companies will install two-way gear in Dallas, Omaha, Pittsburgh, and several other cities. Other companies are developing two-way systems that use the telephone network. By 1990, as much as a quarter of the population may be using these so-called "videotex" systems to get information, bank, and shop from home. All those people will be able to participate in electronic polls.

The new technology may even be used for actual elections. San Diego showed what can happen when it ran a bond referendum by mail last year: the turnout was twice the normal level. Registrar of Voters Rudy Ortiz commented, "In the future, elections may be done by telephonics. We may just be showing the way." If Americans are willing to trust their banking to electronics, voting should be an easy step. This may be a good way to help the disabled and ill vote, and it might do something for all the healthy people who do not bother to go to the polls.

QUBE is popular—subscribers apparently like talking back to their TV sets. Larry Wangberg, the cable executive who oversees the project, says it is "boosting the citizen interest-level" in politics. Alvin Toffler's new book about the information age, *The Third Wave*, predicts that in time this technology will "combine direct citizen participation with 'representation' into a new system of semi-direct democracy." Toffler promises less alienation and better government from this automated politics.

However, electronic polling can be dangerous. First, the results are skewed. The ABC and QUBE polls count only those who bother to respond —hardly a cross-section. Most poor people will not have videotex terminals for a very long time, so the new technology will deny them even the chance to participate. Moreover, the existing two-way systems have no way to tell who is actually pushing the buttons. Many of the "voters" could be four-year-olds.

Second, these polls measure people's instant, emotional reactions to issues. Electronic polling is powerful because it involves many more people than the old-fashioned Gallup and Harris surveys, and it gets answers a week faster. In the process, these polls deny people the chance to think about the issue and omit the old surveys' follow-up questions that measure how deeply people feel. One shudders at the idea of instant referenda on the Panama Canal treaty or what to do about the hostage seizure in Teheran.

Finally, electronic voting offers a perilously convenient way for politicians to bias results or escape hard decisions. "Any fool knows you can control the outcome by how you ask the questions," warns Mayor Miller. "You could have some pretty atrocious acts justified by this." The greatest pitfalls are at the local level, where survey polling has been rare and where it would be all too easy to "go along with the people" on tough zoning or budget decisions.

The press, seduced by novelty, has given heavy coverage to QUBE results. Journalists should be more wary. In a few years, however, millions of people will be pushing buttons, and electronic polls are bound to have an effect.

Fortunately, people have too much common sense—and politicians too much instinct to protect their own power—to turn decisions over to fully automatic "teledemocracy." The subtler but more profound impact of electronic polling and the other new technologies will be on the distribution of power.

The shift of power from the political parties to narrow interest groups has been underway for decades. Radio and TV contributed to this trend by giving candidates a way to talk directly to voters, without having to go through party organizations, and by making candidates more dependent on money.

The new technologies may further dilute the fragile glue of the parties and of public identification with broad ideas. If television shapes the public's image of the world, narrowcasting can splinter that image. As former CBS News President Richard Salant put it recently, "Instead of a common data base, we'll have smaller and smaller groups knowing more and more about less and less." Meanwhile, politicians and causes will use the new media to bind people more tightly into narrowly focused groups. The art of saying different things to different people is hardly news, but the advent of narrowcasting and electronic direct mail will make it easier to do and harder to catch.

In addition, the new technology will touch off a new scramble for money to buy teleconferencing studios, satellite transmitters, and fancy computers, and only the well-heeled interest groups will have the money to use all the new machines. Few liberal groups can match BizNet's millions.

On the other hand, some of the portents are good. The new technology may increase public participation in politics, through viewing and voting. Live television coverage may make politicians more responsive to the general public, rather than powerful lobbies. It certainly will help politicians speak directly to large numbers of people, with whatever length and depth the audience will tolerate. Low-cost ads on cable, free-access channels, and cheap computers will give impoverished candidates and causes their first chance to buy time on television and use time-saving automation. The parties themselves can use the technology to raise money and organize supporters.

Some of the effects on the balance of power will depend on how the new media are regulated. The Communications Act requires regular TV and radio broadcasters to sell time to candidates at minimum rates, to treat all candidates equally, and to provide balanced coverage of controversial issues. The application of these rules to cable and satellite-to-home broadcasting is thoroughly confused at present, and Congress and the FCC have barely begun to think about the matter.

In 1952, few politicians paid much attention when the first TV cameras were trundled into the national party conventions. Eight years later, television helped elect Kennedy and defeat Nixon. The political impact of the new media will be at least as traumatic. This time around, politicians and the rest of us had better take note and help shape this new world.

Communication Systems, Technology, and Culture

by

Brent D. Ruben, Josephine R. Holz, and Jarice K. Hanson

Communication is the process by which humans and other organisms create, send, receive and interpret information in order to adapt to and affect their environment.[1] Among human beings, the ability to communicate has been extended through the development and use of symbols and a variety of means for their production, dissemination, reception, and storage across time and space. It is through the process of communication that societies are developed, maintained, and changed. Communication and culture are, therefore, closely interrelated. In order to better understand the potential significance and impact that new communication technologies are likely to have for existing cultures, the intricate relationship between communication and culture must first be understood.

Communication and culture. In any ongoing relationship among two or more people, certain common symbols, understandings, rules, and characteristic verbal and nonverbal patterns develop as a natural consequence of reciprocal message processing. This standardization and patterning occurs in a very natural way, as the individuals involved adapt, over time, to one another. These dynamics are perhaps easiest to visualize in two- or three-person relationships. As casual friendships between individuals evolve toward greater intimacy, each person adapts to the communication patterns, rules, and maps of the other. In a process of compromise and negotiation of which the individuals involved are only partially aware, the body of joint rules, habits, greeting forms, symbols, knowledge, and standardized meanings is forged in a developing relationship. Collectively, these shared patterns are the *culture* of the relationship. The same process occurs in groups and organizations involving larger numbers of people. As networks are formed and evolve, shared patterns are created in families, clubs, prison communities, social groups, educational institutions, and business organizations. In each, particular words, phrases, gestures, conventions of dress, and greetings

Brent D. Ruben is professor and chairperson, Department of Communications, Rutgers University, New Brunswick, New Jersey. Josephine R. Holz and Jarice K. Hanson are assistant professors in the Department of Communications at Rutgers University.

evolve over time, as a result of communication and mutual adaptation of the members of the unit.

Though societies are larger, far more complex social units, the same communication dynamics are at work. The *symbols* of a society are perhaps the most obvious signs of the process. Of these, *language* is the most pervasive symbol system. The currency and coinage—and the monetary system to which they are necessary—are perhaps the second most universally significant symbols within most societies. There are also many other significant symbols—heroes and heroines, monuments, buildings, flags, songs, and places that have important symbolic value for the citizens. For us Americans, George Washington, Martin Luther King, the Capitol Building, "Old Glory," "The Star Spangled Banner," the Statue of Liberty, and Gettysburg have important symbolic value. Through shared communication, orientations toward religion, politics, sex roles, race, and other facets of social life also develop and become a part of the culture of any society. Patterns of courtship and marriage, eating, and child-rearing also evolve.

Thus, in terms of the general dynamics underlying the creation of culture, relationships, groups, organizations, and societies have much in common. In the same way that individuals in a small social unit come to share common symbols, knowledge, and rules—a *subculture*—members of a society are linked together and given a collective identity through the *culture* they create and perpetuate through their activities.

While interpersonal communication serves to establish and maintain a common "culture" between and among individuals, large groups and societies are also united by common symbols, values, rules, and knowledge through various forms of mass communication. Since social consensus and a common culture depend on communication, the boundaries of social subsystems or subcultures arise through communication channels.[2] In this context, the mass media have become increasingly important, spanning group boundaries and thereby providing the elements of a common culture to disparate segments of society.

Communication technology also contributes to the "portability" of culture. It is largely due to this technology that knowledge, symbols, and rules developed within one subculture or culture are available to individuals who were not involved in their creation. With the increased capability for transmitting, duplicating, and storing data, the knowledge of one generation need not die with its creators. Rather, it becomes a permanent part of the symbolic environment. And these data can be transported through space. They are available not only to persons in the society where they were created, but to any individual or group with technologies that permit their transportation and/or acquisition.

By extending our creating, copying, and storing capabilities, such communication technologies as writing, printing, and telecommunications have broadened the pool of data available in common to individuals within a society. This "data base" consists of the news, information, and entertainment programming provided by traditional mass media, along with other mass communication institutions like libraries and museums. Collectively, these institutions provide members of a society with a common menu and an agenda of concerns, issues, values, personalities, and themes that occupy a central role in the symbolic environment to which individuals must adapt. The data are a kind of societal mirror, providing potential information as to how society works and how the individual fits within it. As many popular and scholarly authors have noted, the mass media do provide society with a view of political, economic, social, aesthetic, and religious reality, and in this way play a fundamental role in the socialization process of the individual and contribute, at the same time, to stability and social order within a society.[3]

Communication technology. In addition to our ability to create and use symbolic languages, our capacity for tool-making also distinguishes us from other animals. Although monkeys have been observed using sticks and coconuts as weapons, no other animal is able to create tools to assist in adapting to and altering the environment at anywhere near the level of sophistication of humans. This capacity has given us better ways of growing food, creating shelter, and fashioning bodily coverings. It has also led to the creation of an impressive array of devices through which we extend our communication ability.

From Smoke Signals to Telecommunication

It was about 20,000 B.C. when early humans first carved symbols on the walls of caves and used drums and smoke to signal one another. With these very primitive communication devices, the foundations of our modern message-processing technologies were put firmly into place. While smoke signals and cave drawings served their purpose well, the development of the first systems of writing dramatically increased the possibilities for making messages both permanent and portable. By about 1,000 B.C., early pictographic writing had given way to systems of writing that made use of an alphabet. Paper was invented around 100 A.D., and by 1500 Johannes Gutenberg had completed the printing of a Bible using the movable type and printing process he had developed. In many ways, the printing press revolutionized the communication process, because it greatly increased the rate at which written and other visual documents could be produced.

The impact of printing began to be felt in the 1500s and 1600s, and it was during this period that newspapers appeared in their present-day form. In the 1600s, regular mail service was also established to link major cities in Europe, and by the 1700s postal services were operating in many countries. The 1800s brought the advent of telegraph and the Morse Code, and with them the introduction of electronic technologies that greatly increased both *range* and *immediacy*.[4]

There were a number of other notable advances in the 1800s. In 1866, the Atlantic was crossed by cable, further extending the capability for rapid data transmission, and it was during this same period that the typewriter and the telephone were patented.

Prior to Marconi's development in 1895 of the wireless telegraph—or radio, as it is commonly termed today—the source and the destination had to be connected physically by wire. With the means for sending coded data and later voice through the air, many new options were available. These advances paved the way for the development of television in the 1930s.

The mid-1950s saw the widespread use of television, and the 1960s the development of communication satellites that served much the same relay function as did the early and far less sophisticated "fire towers" of ancient Greece. In the years that followed, a number of new devices became widely available, including miniaturized transistor radios, stereophonic audio equipment, home movie systems, photocopying devices, and 8-track and cassette audio recorders.

More recent developments in the 1970s and early 1980s have included video games, cable television, videodisc players, home computers, videotext, popular use of computerized data bases, word processing, advanced telephone systems, and telecommunication technology.

Functions of Communication Technology

In the most obvious respects, it is difficult to see much similarity between such diverse technologies as smoke signals, telephones, typewriters, television, and computers. If we think of these in terms of basic concepts of communication and behavior, however, the relationship between tools such as these becomes more apparent. Each of these items, along with many others, qualifies as communication technology if it *expands* our *visual, auditory, olfactory, gustatory, or tactile capacities for creating, distributing, or receiving messages.* We can define *communication technology,* then, as any *tools, special devices, or media that assist in the production, distribution, storage, reception, or display of data.*[5]

Production, transmission, and display. Perhaps the most obvious contribution of communication technology has been the extension of our ability to create, transmit, and display auditory and visual data at great distances in time and space from their point of origin. Beginning with spoken language, early humans progressed in their utilization of auditory communication, to make use of drums, musical instruments, telegraph, telephone, and later commercial AM, FM, and citizen's band radio.

Our use of visual devices to extend our capacity for the production and dissemination of data began with cave drawings and early forms of the alphabet. Later, the use of hand and arm signals, signs, billboards, flags, lanterns, and printing, photographic, and copying equipment of all sorts further broadened our visual abilities. Television, film, projection systems, videodisc, and videocassette extend both the visual and auditory modalities simultaneously.

A number of other tools serve many of these same basic functions, though less obviously. For instance, pencils, pens, typewriters, and the materials of the artist further our human capability for creating, transmitting, and displaying visual messages. And computers, video games, and even many of the hand-held electronic games and calculators have equivalent uses. Without too much stretch of the imagination, even such devices as heating pads, saunas, and hot tubs would qualify as communication technologies, in that they extend our tactile, data-producing capacities.

Multiplication, duplication, and amplification. Some of the data produced, transmitted, and displayed by means of communication technologies are sent by one individual to another whose identity is known. In situations such as this, technology essentially extends our capacity for *one-to-one,* or *face-to-face,* conversation. There are a number of times when we use communication technologies in this way, as when we call a friend on the phone, write a letter to a relative, or use an inter-office intercom. Communication technologies that assist in exchanges among two or several people in this way are called *interpersonal* (or *personal*) *media,* because they are being used in *interpersonal communication.*

In a great many other situations, messages are created and transmitted to a large number of individuals who are unknown to the message originator. This sort of *one-to-many* situation is generally termed *mass communication,* and technologies used in this fashion are termed *mass media.* Whether one thinks of cave drawings, printing presses, videotext, photocopying machines, or public address systems, the essential role of each in communication is quite similar. Tools such as these make it possible for what begins as a single message to be *multiplied, duplicated, amplified,* or *enlarged,* thereby making *mass* communication possible.

Reception, recording, storage, and retrieval. In one sense, any technology that aids in the production, multiplication, display, or amplification of data plays a vital role in message reception. Other more specialized devices, however, play an even more basic role in message reception. Eyeglasses, contact lenses, microscopes, magnifying glasses, binoculars, radar, periscopes, and telescopes, for instance, are invaluable to us as devices for extending our capability for receiving visual messages. And tools such as hearing aids, earphones, stethoscopes, and sonar systems give us capabilities for the reception of auditory messages unavailable to any other species.

The way we store and later remember and use the messages we receive has an important impact on our behavior and that of other persons. Here, too, our human tool-making capacity helps us in extending our native abilities. Though we are not accustomed to thinking of diaries, wills, files, and appointment calendars as communication technologies, they fit our definition in that they further our capacity for message storage and retrieval. Among the more familiar technologies that assist us in these ways are tape recorders, dictating and copying machines, phonograph records, microfiche and microfilm, videocassette and videodisc. Certainly, the most noteworthy information-recording tool to be developed is the computer, through which data of all sorts can be stored, classified, reclassified, and retrieved at any point in time.

The Evolution of Form

Over the course of human history, the form of our communication technology has changed in dramatic, almost incomprehensible ways. Our first messages using communication tools were fashioned with sticks, rocks, smoke, and fire. We have progressed, today, to the point where we are surrounded by machines and electronic devices of all shapes and sizes, which extend our message processing modalities incredibly. Where, not too many years ago, the advent of television made it possible for us to view as well as listen to local and national programming for the first time, we now have cable television, projection television, and even television sets that double as telephones. Where we once made our program selections from among a handful of stations, we are now able to choose between any number of offerings in most locales in the country. And with cassette, videodisc, and home video game and computer systems, we are not limited in our selections to programs being broadcast to us. In effect, we are able to create our own programming with such luxuries as rewind, slow motion, stop-action, fast-forward, and stereo sound.

Further advances in computers, cable, and telecommunication technologies provide still other options. Using relatively inexpensive microcomputers and especially created software programs, one can send and receive acoustically coded alpha-numeric data bases that contain current newspapers, magazines, stock market quotes, international weather reports, airline schedules, and a variety of games. With this same equipment, it is possible to bank, shop, and make restaurant reservations from home, order "handprinted" copies of desired materials, and "converse" with other computers.

In a growing number of cities, "two-way" television is also becoming a reality. With cable systems like QUBE, subscribers not only select between standard and local programs, but are also able to interact with the broadcast center. Using a small keypad device similar to a hand-held calculator, users may participate in programmed instruction or an opinion poll without leaving the home. A centrally-located computer scans all sets connected to the cable system every few seconds, and in the case of opinion polls, tabulates viewer responses instantaneously. The results of the polling can then be displayed on viewers' sets.

As impressive as these home technologies are, there is little doubt that they will seem elementary in comparison to the communication centers to which we will become accustomed in the years ahead. In all likelihood, these centers will combine the data storage and retrieval capacity of the computer and disc with video display, stereophonic audio reproduction, and print capability.

With these systems, we will have a variety of pre-programmed fare from which to choose—films, network shows, video concerts, news and information documentaries, games, national and international news services, stock market quotation services, airline schedules, international weather and travel services, a range of newspapers and magazines, and even off-track betting. Through these home centers, we will be able to electronically access and display back issues of newspapers, magazines, and other publications, or single out articles on particular topics of our choosing. With a press of a key we will receive a printed, permanent copy of any of these documents.

Through the system, we will scan the pages of store catalogs and the list of sale items at the supermarket. With a touch of the keyboard the order will be placed, the bank notified to forward payment, and our balance updated and displayed on the screen in front of us. If we need to know the phone number of a friend, or whether a particular book is available in the local library, that information, too, will be available at the touch of a keyboard. A few additional keystrokes may well place the necessary call or display the pages of the selected book on the screen.

Interconnected burglar and fire alarm systems will be linked to the center, and in the event that sensors detect a fire or break-in, information will be automatically conveyed to the fire or police department for immediate action. Our health records, favorite books, set of encyclopedias, even family pictures can all be stored on disc for immediate access and display, with "hard" copies available whenever desired. Writing a book, composing a song, creating visual art forms, and "personal publishing" of all sorts will be options for anyone who has access to the technology.

The new communication technologies have already begun to have a dramatic impact on our organizations and society, as well as upon us as individuals. Mechanical cash registers, typewriters, and checkwriting machines are rapidly becoming antiques, being replaced by electronic data processing systems. An entry in the electronic cash register not only records a sale but also updates inventory records in the same transaction. Word processors tied to a central computer and printer are used in place of the single-function typewriter. The same technology that creates reports and memos also prepares mailing labels, keeps personnel records, computes employee salaries, and writes out payroll checks. Increased capacities for data storage, production, transmission, and display make linking various divisions, offices, locations, or branches of any organization a trivial matter. At the same time, these devices provide instant access to a broad range of information that may be useful in management decision-making throughout an enterprise.

In hospitals, paper-and-pencil systems are being replaced by complex information-processing packages. Using these new tools, even the results of lab tests, X rays, and other diagnostic procedures are relayed to the appropriate destination electronically. And in the profession of law, the drafting of wills and many other documents requires no more than entering the names, addresses, and special clauses and stipulations into a computer-printer facility capable of turning out such documents in a matter of seconds.

The Information Revolution

Throughout the history of human invention, our tools for communication have given our species capabilities wholly unmatched by other animals. Rapid advances in our technologies in the recent past and those projected for the immediate future promise even more dramatic impact upon our lives.

We are moving rapidly to the edge of an "information revolution" that may well parallel the industrial revolution in its impact and far-reaching consequences. Given our current tools, it is not difficult to imagine ourselves an "information society" in which communication technology will play a central role in virtually every facet of our personal, occupational, and social affairs.

There is little doubt that our rapidly changing technologies will have a number of implications for the way we live in the years ahead. Among the more obvious will be an ever-increasing volume of available data in our environment, merging of transportation and communication technologies, blurring of the distinction between home and office, blending of media uses, and a sharpening distinction between information "haves" and "have nots" based on economics. In the next section we will discuss very briefly each of these in relation to human behavior.

Increase in the volume of data. With each new technological advance, particularly those with the capability of multiplication, amplification, or duplication, comes an increase in the number of messages available to us. Many of the new technologies also expand our abilities to record, store, and access information.

Today, collecting recordings of favorite singing groups, old television programs, classic movies, daily newspapers, magazines, books, articles, and monographs is a time-, space-, and money-consuming activity. In the near

261

future, however, it will be possible for those who can afford certain basic technologies to have copies of nearly any visual or auditory material they desire available for instant access and use.

As this becomes possible, the very real challenge facing humans shifts from "how to get it" to "what to do with it." The storage capacity of emerging technology literally boggles the mind. One videodisc can store 108,000 separate color television images together with stereo sound. At present, the clarity is not adequate for reproducing a printed page. If and when the quality is improved, the text of about 3,200 books could be stored on one two-sided disc, making "video publishing" a formidable new technology.[6]

As we move progressively toward a time when we will have ready access to virtually all current news and entertainment, as well as documents of all sorts, the problem of "information overload" may very well become even more critical than it is today. There seems little doubt that the increased volume of data will demand new communication competencies in identifying those messages that are relevant, organizing and categorizing them in an appropriate manner, and using them efficiently.

Merging of transportation and communication technology. There has always been an interesting relationship between the functions of transportation technology and those of the tools of communication. Even with the earliest automated message transmission devices this relationship was apparent. Instead of delivering information in person, one sent it on horseback or ship. One need not *go* and look at something if information about it can be transported. One need not take a message to someone personally if the message can be sent there on its own.

Moving data can be an efficient, economical, and speedy alternative to moving things or people. More than ever before, our emerging communication technologies provide new options. Today, business conferences are held between individuals across the continent using telephones and video hookups. Using telephone lines, doctors at a hospital are now able to monitor the heart rate and other vital signs of a patient miles away. With similar systems, medical personnel also have access to current research in their efforts to diagnose and treat illness. When connected to a nationwide network and computerized data base, lawyers can instantly search through the equivalent of whole libraries to find key cases or legal opinions. Newspapers, magazines, research reports, goods, services, health care, banking, conferencing, and interfacing with other computers are now accessible without any travel whatsoever.

Evolving concepts of office and home. When one considers these possibilities along with others discussed earlier, it seems likely that the time will come when the concepts of "home" and "office" are much less distinct than they are for most of us today. In the very near future, there will be little in the way of data sending and receiving that one cannot do from home. For most of us, "work" has been somewhere you went—a place away from home. In the years ahead, it seems likely that work will be less a place and more an activity. The idea of an office as a place filled with individuals conversing face-to-face about social and business matters may gradually be replaced by the concept of office that implies an individual alone, at home in front of a computer terminal, able to access people and information by a touch of the keys.

262

Today one can do little more than speculate about the nature of these changes, and wonder about the kinds of life-styles and occupational existence that future communication technologies will inspire.

Changing uses of media. Traditionally, there has been a reasonably clear distinction between various communication technologies. Newspapers, for example, have historically provided their audience a summary of current happenings of the day. Though they have increasingly broadened their scope to include features and other items, the primary focus has remained news.

Film has been essentially an entertainment medium. Radio and television, in terms of the majority of their content, have been primarily entertainment media also. Telephones have been used socially and in business contexts, generally as a substitute for short, face-to-face conversations. Institutions like libraries and museums have served their users by providing documents that serve reference, archival, and, to a somewhat lesser extent, entertainment functions.

Many of these traditional distinctions are rapidly becoming obsolete. Those who have cable television now may select channels that play recordings of rock groups much like those aired on radio, but these are accompanied by visual effects. Cable users also have a channel that functions as a local bulletin board, much as one is accustomed to finding in the newspaper or on the wall of a local supermarket. Other cable channels are available on a subscription fee basis, bringing films to television via satellite. Another cable channel displays stock market quotations, wire service copy, and the local weather.

With some fairly inexpensive equipment and a flip of the switch, television becomes a video arcade game. Connected to a microcomputer, television becomes a book—a self-instructional guide to French, finance, the stock market, or computer programming. With some additional hardware and software programming, the telephone also changes function to become a device for the transmission of acoustical data.

Together, the computer, telephone, and television can become a newspaper, magazine, game, reference tool, catalog, index, and a variety of other things. When a printer is added, the telephone, television, and computer become a typewriter and paper, a card catalog, and the stacks of books at a reference library in medicine or law. When connected to a videodisc player or videocassette recorder, television is a movie screen. When the tapes are played or recorded on a portable video tape unit, television is a home movie—a family album.

As a result of these many technological changes, media that were primarily associated with mass communication are now being used in interpersonal communication, and vice versa, perhaps indicative of more fundamental shifts in the nature of each in the years ahead.

Communication technology and cultural change. In surveying the major changes in and additions to the communication technologies available to us in the past and likely to occur in the not too distant future, it seems that these technological devices have brought about significant cultural and social transformations. And it is certainly true that such previous additions to our techniques for transmitting and storing information as the development of writing and printing promoted significant alterations in education, government, business, religion, and other aspects of culture. From this perspective, it is tempting to see these communication technologies as autonomous phenomena that "caused" a series of ensuing social and cultural "effects." Yet the development of writing and printing—and such later devices as photography, telegraphy, television, and computers—occurred only after a complex set of cultural elements had appeared and accumulated within the existing culture, creating the social and cultural preconditions within which such devices could emerge and flourish.[7] These technological developments were consistent with and responsive to the needs and possibilities opened up by changes in other cultural institutions and practices at the time.[8]

This is not to say that changes in communication technology do not have significant and often unanticipated effects on the cultures in which they are developed and diffused. It is only to suggest that, as much as culture is defined, shaped, and transmitted through communication techniques and devices, the reverse is equally accurate. The evolution of our communication symbols, codes, and media, the circumstances surrounding their production and use, and the effects they have on individuals, society, and culture have been and will continue to be shaped, directed, and constrained by other cultural needs and forces.

Given the interactive relationship between communication and culture and the sociocultural functions that communication serves within any culture, what impact can we expect new communication technologies to have on the cultures that use them?

Culture consists of the shared body of knowledge, meanings, symbols, values, rules, and rituals among the members of a social system, and communication both depends upon, and makes possible, this sharing. While interpersonal communication creates common "cultures" and subcultures among interacting individuals, mass communication is one of the means by which the same function is carried out among and across different subcultural groups. By distributing common messages, images, and symbols to large, diversified audiences, broadcasting and other forms of mass communication contribute to the maintenance of a common culture that, to some extent, cuts across religious, ethnic, racial, political, socio-economic, and regional lines. At the same time, the mass production and distribution of common images and messages also results in a degree of standardization, lack of diversity, stereotyping, and audience passivity for which the mass media, particularly television, have long been assailed.

New technologies like cable TV, videocassette recorders, videotext, home computers, and a growing host of other communication technologies, channels, and services promise to create somewhat more diversity in the data pool and allow the communication receiver to exercise more control in selecting his or her own specialized information and programming. Yet, just as broadcasting and other forms of mass communication served to maintain cultural consensus at the cost of cultural standardization and uniformity, narrowcasting and other forms of selective communication may bring more cultural diversity at the cost of cultural fragmentation. Rather than strengthening the cultural linkages among us, the new communication technologies may just as easily strengthen and exacerbate the cultural divisions among us.

New communication technologies usually increase the amount of information available in a society. But, as numerous studies of communication effects have demonstrated, increasing the flow of information into a social system does not necessarily result in equivalent information gains among all groups within the system.[9] In the distribution of information, as with any resource, those groups whose status, values, and behavior patterns are already conducive to using the resource will acquire and use it at a faster rate than others. Furthermore, information, like other social resources, tends to be distributed and controlled in ways that direct it to those groups that can most easily utilize it. In the case of much of the communication technology mentioned above, differences in purchasing power may further accentuate such tendencies. While the unit cost to play a video game, attend a movie, or even purchase a radio or television set is well within the range of most consumers, the newer technologies are much more expensive. The cost of home computers with the capability for transmitting and receiving data through phone lines ranges from $400 to $6,000 with a printer. And while the price of videocassette recorders has dropped markedly, the base price is still nearly $500. Satellite antennas, large-screen TV, and projection TV are much more expensive.

The relatively large expenditures now required to purchase some of the more advanced communication technologies may well have the potential to broaden the gap between the "haves" and "have nots" within our society, if not within the world. It seems quite likely that those who have financial resources will have much greater access to tools for creating and receiving information than those who do not. To the extent that these technologies afford an individual or a society power over their own or others' lives, the economics of communication technology may well have important implications for human behavior in the decades ahead.

On the other hand, if public policies are enacted to overcome some of the differences in access to these new technologies due to differential purchasing ability, the new technologies' potential for reducing or eliminating the need for travel and transportation may help to bring previously excluded social groups into the cultural mainstream. For the physically disabled, the elderly, mothers with young children, and other homebound groups, electronic banking, shopping, and home employment opportunities could help these persons to remain in or re-enter the cultural mainstream.

Communication Technology and the Quality of Life

For all the obvious changes in the *forms* of our communication technologies over the years, it is important to question the extent to which their *functions* have also changed. There can be little doubt that data processing today is much quicker, more flexible, and better arranged and displayed than ever before in our history. To what extent, however, have these changes been matched by improvements in the quality of life? In any given day, do we know more as a result of all the technology we have available? Are we better entertained by all the new media? Are we better organized and better prepared by all the storage-and-retrieval technology? Are we happier? Have the quality of communication and the nature of human life improved for all the advances?

In our excitement and enthusiasm for the new technologies, it is probably important to give at least passing consideration to these sorts of issues. Questions such as these remind us that communication technologies are, after all, no more than extensions of our own human message-processing abilities and liabilities. They can do little more than display, transport, store, duplicate, or amplify the data we create. The nature of those data and the uses to which they are put depend upon us and not our technologies. To expect communication technology to do more may well be to misunderstand the nature of technology and its relationship to human behavior and culture.

NOTES

1. The discussion of communication, communication technology, and their relationship to one another as presented in this chapter is based upon Chapters 6, 7, and 14 of *Communication and Human Behavior* by Brent D. Ruben (New York: Macmillan, 1983).
2. Tamotsu Shibutani. "Reference Groups As Perspectives," in J. Manis and B. Meltzer (eds.), *Symbolic Interaction: A Reader in Social Psychology* (Boston: Allyn and Bacon, 1967).
3. Cf. Hugh D. Duncan, *Communication and Social Order* (London: Oxford University Press, 1962) and Hugh D. Duncan, *Symbols in Society* (New York: Oxford University Press, 1968), especially Parts I and II.
4. Cf. Don L. Cannon and Gerald Luecke, *Understanding Communications Systems* (Dallas: Texas Instruments Learning Center, 1980), pp. 1-8 through 1-19.
5. Brent D. Ruben, Op. Cit., Ch. 7. "Communication Technology."
6. Lewis M. Branscomb, "The Electronic Library," *Journal of Communication,* 31, 1, 1981, pp. 148-149.
7. Melvin L. DeFleur. *Theories of Mass Communication.* Second ed. (New York: David McKay, 1970).
8. Raymond Williams. *Television: Technology and Cultural Form* (New York: Schocken Books, 1975).
9. Phillip J. Tichenor, George A. Donohue, and Clarice N. Olien, *Community Conflict and the Press* (Beverly Hills: Sage, 1980).

Microcomputers—Order Through Fluctuation: Implications for Education

by

Michele Geslin Small

Just as the plow, "the instrument of surplus" (Burke, 1978, p. 9), served to trigger change in the human communities in which it appeared, allowing those who were not food producers to contribute in many different ways (crafts, commerce, administration, entertainment, etc.) to the life of the local population; just as the triangular sail, the rudder, and the compass allowed increased commerce and trade among the Mediterranean countries and initiated the great trans-oceanic voyages that led to the discovery of new worlds; just as the stirrup, the longbow, and gunpowder led to the collapse of the medieval feudal system, many innovations or seemingly singular discoveries in the centuries before ours have launched irrevocable waves of change, altered our environment forever, and led to our present, taken-for-granted, social amenities such as electricity, the automobile, telephone, television, or to more terrifying and potentially destructive forces such as nuclear bombs and intercontinental ballistic missiles.

In his brilliant analysis of the patterns of the forces of change, called felicitously, *Connections,* James Burke affirms:

> The reason why each event took place where and when it did is a fascinating mixture of accident, climatic change, genius, craftsmanship, careful observation, ambition, greed, war, religious belief, deceit, and a hundred other factors. (Burke, 1978, p. 13)

What is certain is that, not unlike a pebble that when thrown into a still pond causes an ever-expanding pattern of concentric circles that will reach the farthest shore, those innovations, whether they were the fruit of chance or necessity, can be considered as what Maruyama has so aptly called "deviation-amplifying mutual casual processes"; small kicks that send waves of change, increase differentiation, develop structure, and increase complexity. (Maruyama, 1976, p. 200) Today, such an example of positive feedback is the chip. This tiny, man-made artifact, a small piece of silicon as big as a

---

Michele Geslin Small is associate professor of English and French at Northland College, Ashland, Wisconsin.

thumbnail, has initiated a revolution whose known implications boggle the mind and whose unsuspected ones remain hidden in the recesses of the future and are at this point beyond comprehension.

The first law of thermodynamics tells us that the energy of the universe is constant; and the second, that the entropy of the universe (a measure of the unavailability of energy for work, of disorder, of a high degree of probability and a loss of information) is constantly increasing. The universe is thus continuously, irreversibly becoming less ordered than it was, and it is this behavior that accounts for the one-way direction of events and the irretrievable passage of time. (Prigogine, 1979, p. 136) While these principles of thermodynamics apply to closed, stable structures, they are incompatible with the concept of evolution in biology and sociology, which is characterized by the formation of structures that are more and more organized, ordered, and complex. Prigogine's research in the new field of non-equilibrium thermodynamics postulates the principle of "order through fluctuation," whereby open, complex biological systems (e.g., man) or social systems, characterized by a high degree of matter and energy/information exchange with their environments, can develop instabilities that, as they amplify, instead of leading to random behavior, drive the system into a new dynamic regime that may correspond to a new state of complexity. Prigogine states:

> If we examine a cell or a town, we find that not only are these systems open, but they survive because of it. They feed on the flow of matter and energy which comes to them from the outside world. It is impossible for a town or a living cell to evolve toward a mutual compensation, an equilibrium between the inflows and outflows. If we want, we can isolate a crystal, but the town and the cell severed from their environment will die rapidly. They are an integral part of the world which feeds them; they constitute a kind of singular and local incarnation of the flows which they do not cease to transform. (Prigogine, 1979, p. 142, my translation)

This theory of "dissipative structures" in non-linear, non-equilibrium systems accounts for the rise of more complex and more stable civilizations across the centuries through constant change. As we have observed, and as Taylor points out, technological innovations have consistently served as positive feedback processes in the development and transformation of socio-cultural systems, while social institutions and mores, designed to maintain continuity and persistence, act as negative feedback processes to ensure overall stability and social invariance in the face of technological and environmental transformations. (Taylor, 1976, p. 173)

We find ourselves today at the dawn of the chip era, which is destined to produce a new, unprecedented major fluctuation on our planet. It would be beyond the scope of this paper even to consider the variety of social impacts that will be generated by the microcomputer revolution as it affects the family, government, international relations, urban and rural communities, transportation, crime, etc. What we choose to focus on will be some probable happenings in the realm of education.

Implications for Education

The educators. A major problem perceived by futurists, as they review contemporary education in America, is the tremendous discrepancy between

268

the information explosion outside the walls of our schools and the resistance to it inside. While information technology has progressed by leaps and bounds in the last five years, the reaction it has caused in educational circles is cause for concern.

Instead of perceiving the liberating and exciting promises of the new technologies, most educators seem to view them either as instruments of the devil, bent on depriving them of their jobs and livelihood, or simply as irrelevant to their own professional concerns. In every technology, there is always potential for abuse, but there is also potential for good. The defensive reactions of educators are simply a matter of perception, a symptom of what Clarke calls "failure of nerve and failure of imagination." (Clarke, 1973) They are expressions of fear, the fear of the unknown, often exacerbated by feelings of personal insecurity and inadequacy in the frightening context of a flagging economy, rampant inflation, and demographic forecasts that project declining enrollments and potential massive retrenchment in the labor-intensive institution of education.

Certain trends are clear, however: within a decade we will have fewer fiscal resources at our disposal for salaries, facilities, equipment, maintenance, etc., and the taxpayers' revolts indicate that people are not willing to increase their contributions to education. The new information technologies (home TV programs, calculators, videodiscs, home computers) can and must provide a support system as we search for new solutions. As Dede points out:

> *For what machines can do well,* people are not competitive economically. So our labor-intensive position in education has caused us steadily to use up more and more of the consumer dollar, just as have all the other labor-intensive industries; and we have finally reached the limit. We need the resources. We're losing teachers now due to our relatively poor salaries compared to the rest of the economy, but the money is *not* going to be there . . . just as funding is being cut back for medical care. To get past this fiscal problem of being labor-intensive, we must find a way legitimately to use more technology in education. (Dede, 1980, p. 85)

Unless educators alter radically their viewpoints in the face of the inevitable, and decide to seek the opportunities embedded in what they consider a crisis, their fears of losing their jobs might be well-founded and turn into a self-fulfilling prophecy. The microcomputer, like any other technology, will eliminate jobs, but then any teacher who can be replaced by a machine deserves to be. There will always be work available to those who look upon a "job" as a creative, problem-solving opportunity to benefit society.

Once educators recognize fully the potential, as well as the limitations, of these new machines, they might well forget their earlier prejudices and start thinking about how to take advantage of their new options. Some will see the machines as a means to be relieved of the most mechanical chores of pedagogy (drills, information delivery, grading, tutoring, etc.) and will dedicate their time and energy to the higher and more exciting task of education: to foster critical thinking, creativity, open-mindedness and the joy of learning. Others, more farsighted perhaps, will not fail to perceive the new opportunities that reside in the making and packaging of educational software in a new but burgeoning market, or in the need to exercise the rigorous quality control that must accompany any standardized, widely distributed instructional material, since one critical mistake in a program could mean that millions would learn the same error.

The students. But what about the students? They too will be affected profoundly and in markedly different ways by the chip revolution. Like the Chinese ideogram for crisis—which consists of two characters, one for danger and one for opportunity—the new technology holds both promises and perils. Let us examine briefly two aspects of the effects on students: access to the technology and impact on the individual.

On one hand, the new technology can provide infinite storage and easy retrieval of information across the arbitrary boundaries established by nation-states all over the world, making everything there is to know universally accessible and by-passing the time-consuming, elitist, and affluent concepts of education based on the ability to read, write, and do arithmetic. Wagschal reminds us that "only a minority of the globe's population can afford the time and resources required to learn the three R's." (Wagschal, 1980, p. 39) And we might add that elements of what has been called "the fifth world" are present in the most powerful and wealthiest nations. Any attempt on our part to preserve the status quo would simply mean that, like the medieval scholars who feared the newly printed books, we want to preserve locally our professional advantages and globally the supremacy of our Western culture. Yet one cannot resist forever the tide of change. In the long run, any society or subculture maintained in ignorance by force and repression might become a time bomb in a world that is growing more and more interdependent by the day.

Yet, on the other hand, the darker side of the coin is still very conceivable. Since information is power in the sense that the more information we possess, the wider the variety of options and choices we have, then this fact alone raises the specter of the ultimate discrimination beyond those of race, sex, age, and religion—that of access. Unless we proceed with extreme caution and think of the long-range consequences of our actions, we might well have to face a new generation of "haves" and "have nots," locally as well as globally: those who have access to and control over information and those who do not. As computers become increasingly indispensable in the sciences, government, business, education, and everyday life, those educated in their use will have a tremendous advantage over the rest of the population. Computer illiteracy may well become the major handicap of those who will live in the twenty-first century.

Fortunately, current trends seem to go in the direction of wide dissemination and lower prices, if one can judge by the proliferation of pocket calculators, digital watches, video games, home computers, etc., and the mushrooming of private electronic cottage industries and do-it-yourself kits. Together they allay the nightmarish vision of a 1984-like, highly centralized, computerized, elitist, totalitarian global regime.

If they become cheaper, the new electronic technologies have the potential to become the private tutors of a new Renaissance, transcending the constraints imposed by socio-economic factors that, as recent research has indicated (Coleman, 1966; Jencks, 1975), seem to play such an important and detrimental part in the education of our children. All students will be able to learn at their own pace with the mode that is most appropriate for them.

The "slow" student could find in a robotlike machine a private tutor—kind, considerate, and patient, programmed to know his background, his level of achievement, his strengths and weaknesses, his personal temperament, and even his tastes and hobbies. Such "robots" already exist and are in use in some classrooms. They can wait for an answer, give immediate positive reinforcement, or go back a few steps and reiterate information that has not been properly assimilated. They can also establish a change of pace, tell a joke, and are not altogether devoid of a sense of humor. This process can do much to teach the child what he needs to know without the negative pressures imposed by a competitive classroom atmosphere and help him feel more at ease, more confident, and more successful, qualities that in themselves are self-reinforcing and self-generating. (Freeman, 1980)

For the "bright" student, the limits will be set by his own talent and imagination. He could listen to a lecture delivered at Harvard, plug into countless data bases, use computer-conferencing facilities to discuss and share ideas, converse with another student in another part of the globe, etc. In short, the chip revolution can contribute to making education a truly democratic process where each student can "become all that he is capable of being." This highly individualized instruction, in conjunction with a truly synergistic "regular classroom" where students can discuss, debate, and share ideas, hone and refine their own perceptions by exposure to others' views, and enjoy much needed human and social contacts, will foster tremendous diversity, heterogeneity, and true learning. Let us not forget, as Clarke remarks, that "electronics can never completely convey all the nuances of personal interaction with a capable teacher." (Clarke, 1980, p. 76)

Yet, serious doubts have been raised about the fate of the democratic ideal of "equality," as well as about the burden of the "solipsistic predicament." We must remember first that equality of opportunity has never guaranteed—nor should it ever—equality of results and that, too often, as pointed out by neo-Marxist educators, this very ideal has been used as a cover for homogenization, conformity, indoctrination, and mediocrity. Secondly, we must not forget the lessons of biology. All of us can, do, and *must* contribute in many different ways if we want to ensure the survival of our species. A society bent on enforcing commonality of thought, attitude, and behavior is doomed to failure.

Breaking down generational barriers. Finally, the chip revolution in education will lead the way in breaking down the factitious barriers that have been erected between the school and society. When all—adults as well as children, workers as well as students—can learn through home TV programs delivered on multiple cable TV channels, play simulation games together, and increase their knowledge in whatever area they may choose, learning will become truly a lifelong experience for all, reducing the fundamental age segregation that has plagued all educational systems in contemporary highly industrialized nations.

Once again, grave concerns are being raised about the political implications of such a major transformation, and Prigogine himself gives thought to the question:

We could pose this question, made very concrete today because of the progress of information technology: What would happen to the "democratic system" in a society in which the means of communication would allow permanent consultation of each individual by a central representative organization and allow the speed of communication to exceed that of local, non-linear interactions between individuals? Would it not in fact be the realization of a new order, stable and conservative? (Prigogine, 1979, p. 179, my translation.)

Perhaps, but could we not also argue that this new, stable, and conservative order would itself be subjected to new fluctuations? With such a variety of electronic tools in their hands, would men, women, and children of the twenty-first century tolerate any particular nationalistic values and commitments, or would they not also transcend the man-made geographical and political boundaries and come to the realization that we are all citizens of one planet, a world that we much share and whose survival we must preserve, ensure, and cherish?

What Do We Do Now?

This brief look at some of the possible direct impacts of the silicon-chip revolution on education shows us that this innovation, albeit tiny in size, will be powerful in its effect. If we invoke one of the cardinal principles of biology, that "one can never do merely one thing," or, put in systems terms, "everything is connected to everything else," this event, by virtue of its complexity, poses formidable challenges. Our educational system fits the description of what Ackoff has called "a mess," a term that he defines as a "system of problems." As he points out:

> ... No problem ever exists in complete isolation. Every problem interacts with other problems and, is therefore part of a set of interrelated problems. ... Furthermore, solutions to most problems produce other problems. ...
> (Ackoff, 1974, p. 21)

We can then expect many different impacts on other sectors of society, directly or indirectly connected with the school. Will the book survive? Could we not save tons of paper, when all there is to know can be contained in a few information centers and made available to the public? What effect would this have on loggers, paper manufacturers, publishing companies, and others whose livelihood depends on books and paper? When it is possible to learn anywhere, would we need to congregate daily in the buildings that we call schools? Precious energy wasted on heating and cooling those buildings year round could be saved, but what of the fate of those hired to maintain those buildings? What about the issue of transportation and busing? The savings in terms of gasoline and community satisfaction would be great, but what about the bus drivers, maintenance crews, bus manufacturers, and so forth? Obviously, the ripples caused by the wide use of microcomputers will be numerous and far-reaching, leaving no corner of the school or of society untouched.

If we look at the problem in light of the principles of cybernetics (the science of communication and control within organized systems), we realize that the curve of unimpeded positive feedback approaches infinity with the passage of time. As Hardin has pointed out: "Ours is a finite world. Positive feedback is not tolerable as a permanent state of affairs. It can be tolerated only for short periods of time." (Hardin, 1978, p. 152) Since an effective cybernetic system produces stability, i.e., fluctuations within limits, we must find a way to introduce in our transitional period negative feedback processes that are conducive to the reestablishment of homeostasis. Yet, at the same time, too much control too soon may deprive us of the "benefits of serendipity" which, as Burke has shown us, "are at the heart of the process of change." As he aptly puts it:

> Without Apollo, would we have had minicomputers? Without Moissan's search for artificial diamonds, would cyanamide fertilizer have been discovered? Without the atomic bomb, would fusion be feasible? (Burke, 1978, p. 293)

And we may add: if we limit too strictly the use of microcomputers in order to minimize the social ills they might cause, might we not ultimately prevent a new evolution of the mind of man, another fluctuation triggered by constant immersion in an environment awash with information?

The lessons are clear. We have passed the point of no return as to the existence of microcomputers. They are here and here to stay. What we must do now is establish some control over the development of the new technologies: how much and how soon? Aware of the dangers of a positive feedback process running wild with catastrophic consequences for society, and aware that major fluctuations do lead to new order in complex social and biological systems, we must chart a transitional course guided by three key principles: anticipation, design, and planning.

Anticipation: Studies of technological assessment and social impact assessment should be conducted with global coordination and the results disseminated worldwide. Since we are rushing headlong toward what McLuhan has called the "global village," we cannot afford selfish isolation in our efforts, which could lead to disastrous political, economic, social, and cultural side-effects.

Design: We must introduce self-correcting feedback loops for control. Interestingly enough, to manage the information and electronic age, one must be educated about information and electronics.

Participative planning: In such a rapid and pervasive transformation, planning cannot be left exclusively in the hands of the "experts." Since ". . . the role of the professional planner is not to plan for others but to facilitate their planning for themselves" (Ackoff, 1974, p. 28), we must inform and involve all, so that each individual can understand better the new technologies and organize his life to maximize its benefits and minimize its dangers.

In the educational sphere, this will mean preparing the younger generations for the massive changes that are going to occur within their lifetime. We would advocate three curricular directions: future studies, systems thinking and global learning at all levels, and the study and use of computers from kindergarten on, so that children, raised with the new technology, can be in a better position to understand its limits, appraise its potential, and control its development. In addition, more efforts should be put toward strengthening the science curriculum. It should come as no surprise that the Soviets and Eastern European nations have already taken a decisive lead in this area. Ephthalia and John Walsh, in a special report "Crisis in the Science Classroom," state:

> Comparing educational systems in different countries is notoriously tricky. Evidence is accumulating, however, that the Soviets and countries of Eastern Europe are making an extraordinary effort to raise the level of scientific understanding among the masses, which in this case really does mean everybody. Of course, this is what the Russians have been saying they meant to do all along. Marxist-Leninist theory provides an ideological basis for a scientific world view that puts a high value on scientific knowledge, theoretical and applied. But the Soviets are not so naive as to assume that identifying ideology with science will be sufficient to motivate students. Education is the chief mobility mechanism in Soviet society. Success in school, above all in science and math, opens the way to careers with high prestige and pay. This is well understood, and it is a powerful incentive to parents and children. (Walsh and Walsh, 1980)

This heavy emphasis on the sciences, we might add, also includes the science of cybernetics.

As for teachers and future teachers, as stated before, if they want to remain competitive and save their jobs, they will have to retrain themselves in the use and understanding of the new technologies through courses, seminars, and workshops, possibly with the help of private enterprise, which is already quite competent at training its own recruits and is decades ahead of academia in accepting and using micro-technology.

But schooling is only a tiny fraction of what education really is. Broadly conceived, education is life, in the sense that we are doomed to learn by the very fact that we are alive (a very refreshing thought). Education occurs in the world of work, the family, the community, the church, and those major spheres of influence cannot be discounted. Moreover, the school is already suffering from the burden of everyone's expectations for solving society's problems (not only does it have to teach conceptual skills but it is also supposed to form character, teach values, foster equality, babysit, etc.), and, as we have stated before, it will itself be subjected to major transformations in the years ahead. We must therefore take another tack and, on a parallel course, make massive efforts to "educate" the population at large through the media, radio, print, and—why not?—the electronic gadgetry already on the market.

Too often, due to the image created by advertising, people have perceived the advent of the microcomputer as an interesting and clever improvement for entertainment purposes (Superstar Football, electronic chess) with, occasionally, some added educational benefits (simulation games). But the microcomputer means more than "neat toys." It is of grave concern that the majority of the population seems unaware of the momentous repercussions of the chip industries on their lives and in their societies. Unless they are warned and made aware, they will be unprepared for the rapid developments ahead that, like a brick, will fall on their heads and leave them stunned, frustrated, and in despair.

In recent years, many magazines (*Science News, Science 82, Omni, Next*) and TV programs (*Nova, Connections, Cosmos*) have attempted to convey to the masses some of the awesome and sometimes frightening frontiers of science and technology. These efforts are most commendable, since popularization does not necessarily have to mean vulgarization, but they are not enough and are still restricted to an educated and interested minority. Since familiarity breeds confidence and information is power, we must find ways (and find them fast) to inform, educate, and prepare our societies for the major fluctuation that has already begun. Then, and only then, can we look forward to the exciting promises of what has been called "the Second Industrial Revolution."

References

Ackoff, Russell L. (1974). *Redesigning the Future, a Systems Approach to Societal Problems*. New York: John Wiley and Sons, Inc.

Burke, James. (1978). *Connections*. Boston: Little, Brown and Company.

Clarke, Arthur C. (1973). *Profiles of the Future*. New York: Harper and Row.

Clarke, Arthur C. (1980). "Electronic Tutors." *Omni*, Vol. 2, No. 9, June issue, 76.

Coleman, James S. et. al. (1966). *Equality of Educational Opportunity*. Washington, D.C.: U.S. Government Printing Office.

Dede, Christopher J. (1980). "Educational Technology: The Next Ten Years" in *Education and the Future*. Edited by Lane Jennings and Sally Cornish. Washington, D.C.: The World Future Society, 84-90.

Freeman, Michael and Gary P. Mulkowski. (1980). "Advanced Interactive Technology—Robots in the Home and Classroom" in *Education and the Future*. Edited by Lane Jennings and Sally Cornish. Washington, D.C.: The World Future Society, 41-45.

Hardin, Garrett J. (1978). "The Cybernetics of Competition" in *Stalking the Wild Taboo*. Los Altos: William Kaufmann, Inc., 148-176.

Jencks, Christopher. (1975). *Inequality*. Hardmonworth, England: Penguin Books.

Maruyama, Magoroh. (1976). "Toward Cultural Symbiosis" in *Evolution and Consciousness: Human Systems in Transition*. Edited by Erich Jantsch and Conrad H. Waddington. Reading, Massachusetts: Addison-Wesley Publishing Co., 198-211.

Prigogine, Ilya. (1971). "La Thermodynamique de la Vie." *La Recherche*. Vo. 3, No. 24, 547-562.

Prigogine, Ilya and Isabelle Stengers. (1979). *La Nouvelle Alliance: Métamorphose de la Science*. Paris: Editions Gallimard.

Prigogine, Ilya. (1976). "Order Through Fluctuation: Self Organization and Social Systems" in *Evolution and Consciousness: Human Systems in Transition*. Edited by Erich Jantsch and Conrad H. Waddington. Reading, Massachusetts: Addison-Wesley Publishing Co., 93-126.

Taylor, Alastair M. (1976). "Process and Structure in Sociocultural Systems" in Evolution and Consciousness: *Human Systems in Transition*. Edited by Erich Jantsch and Conrad H. Waddington. Reading, Massachusetts: Addison-Wesley Publishing Co., 169-182.

Wagschal, Peter H. (1980). "Illiterates with Doctorates: the Future of Education in an Electronic Age: in *Education and the Future*. Edited by Lane Jennings and Sally Cornish. Washington, D.C.: The World Future Society, 39-49.

Walsh, Ephthalia and John. (1980). "Crisis in the Science Classroom." *Science 80*. Vol. 1, No. 6. September/October issue, 17-22.

Problem/Possibility Focusers: A New Knowledge System for the Communications Era

by

Robert Theobald

It is generally agreed that no one today can gain an overall picture of the nature of the problems and possibilities in any field of human concern, e.g., energy, food, climate, health, education, economics, etc. This situation is a direct result of the patterns of knowledge creation and distribution derived from the norms of the industrial era. In their place, I have proposed a new means of creating and distributing knowledge designed to clarify on a continuing basis *why* people reach their conclusions, and to give citizens a chance to determine whether they agree or disagree. I call the products of this new approach to knowledge "problem/possibility focusers."

There are three key assumptions in industrial-era decision-making. First, it is believed that there is a right answer to any question and that this is known by the most expert individual or the most expert group. This approach results from the concept that it is possible to look at any situation objectively, to perceive all the realities within it, and for the person who is most skilled to give the right answer. It is this assumption that leads to the ever-growing conflict between "expert" testimony. Second, it is assumed that it is possible to consider the results of policies and actions in one field without thinking seriously about their interconnections with other areas of the socioeconomic system.

The committee structure that exists, for example, in the U.S. Congress and state legislatures, makes it possible to consider energy policy without a systemic look at the consequences on ecology and the economy. It is seldom recognized that there are secondary and tertiary results of policies besides the desired primary effects. As people and systems become more sophisticated, they learn to respond in ways that limit or palliate the negative effects of any set of legislation. This is the reason why most types of control mea-

Robert Theobald is president of Participation Publishers, Wickenberg, Arizona, and founder of Linkage, a networking organization. A lecturer and writer in the fields of communications and future studies, Theobald lives in Wickenberg, Arizona, and Dingwall, Scotland.

276

sures (price control, for example) are necessarily ineffective.

It is fascinating that both those who see the *certainty* of improvement *and* those who see global catastrophe ahead are willing to trust the same information-structuring techniques. While their conclusions about the future are diametrically opposed, the ways they structure their thinking are very similar.

The Challenge of the Communications Era

Given these serious difficulties with our present decision-making system, why are people still so confident of our survival and success? The reason stems from the third hidden assumption of the industrial era: that we can think about our socioeconomic system as a machine that may break down but that can always be mended. Thus it is assumed that, although there will be sticky moments, we shall always eventually "muddle through."

But people who have learned system theory know that this is not an appropriate model. We must recognize that systems behave in three ways: they have oscillations that decrease in magnitude, oscillations that increase in magnitude, or they are stable. Systems that have increasing oscillations are unstable and will break down: the only question is when. Most system analysts would agree that the industrial era is suffering through cycles of increasing magnitude and thus that it will not be possible for us to continue to "muddle through" indefinitely.

It is urgent that we recognize the instability of present systems and start to find ways to minimize the dangers that result from this instability. We also need to create new information systems that defuse current instabilities by helping people to gain different perceptions of their self-interest in the light of the new conditions that are emerging. An effective community needs to be recognized as one that can deal with its problems before they become acute and can recognize possibilities while they are available. The problem/possibility focuser is one technique designed to move us in this direction.

General Description of the Problem/Possibility Focuser

A problem/possibility focuser (PPF) aims to provide a picture of the status of debate on any subject under consideration on a continuing basis. Those engaged in producing a PPF recognize that they will necessarily disagree; they try to find what can be understood and agreed upon to clarify the nature of the real issues involved. Instead of looking for a technological fix, the PPF approach accepts the need for continued "messiness" in the culture.

The problem/possibility focuser approacher can be applied at various geographical scales and for any subject of real concern. For example, one can think about problem/possibility focusers on the water problem in Tucson, the educational issues in the central areas of Detroit, the nuclear power issues in the United States, and the global food problem. Problem/possibility focusers, however, are also suitable for use within any institution: a business could use the technique to determine whether it should enter a new activity, a church could use it to decide what its attitude should be toward poverty, an educational institution could use it to determine how to deal with the possibility of declining enrollments.

The existing conception of the problem/possibility focuser (which is, of course, still evolving) has four parts:

277

The first section of a PPF describes the agreements that exist around a particular issue, especially the factors that cause people to accept that issue as one deserving continuing attention. Taking as an example the issue of food, one might list, among other problems: the maldistribution of worldwide food reserves; the growing evidence of climatic shift; the existence of chronic malnutrition and starvation; and the loss of arable land to bad farming practices and to building.

The second section of a PPF describes the disagreements that exist around a particular issue and identifies the reasons for such disagreements as best they can be determined along with the type of knowledge that would need to be developed if agreements were to be reached. Again on the issue of food one might list, among other points the following: the degree to which the climate is actually shifting—a technical issue; the true impacts of land reform—a values issue and a disagreement about human behavior patterns; the potential for controlled agriculture within large greenhouse structures— a technical issue; the viability of triage and lifeboat-ethic strategies—a value and human behavior question; the impacts of the energy question—affected by facts, technological questions, and human behavior questions; and the ecological impacts of fertilizer- and pesticide-intensive farming—a technical and value issue. (Obviously the distinctions between facts, human behavior, technical issues, and values issues are to some extent arbitrary: for example, if any issue is pushed far enough it becomes a values issue, for any accepted behavior is always based on cultural norms.)

The third section sets forth the scenario implications of the various models being proposed and suggests policy measures that would be needed depending on the various views. The different scenarios can then be challenged by those who disagree with them. Thus, to continue with the global food problem, there are some people who would argue that we need to take immediate large-scale measures to avoid worldwide famine and others who would argue that existing patterns of agriculture are adequate to improve worldwide nutrition without "heroic" measures. There are some people who argue that our only hope is to abandon large parts of the world population to starvation and others who claim that such a stance is both immoral and ineffective.

The fourth section of a PPF would state what resources are available for further understanding. The most important of these resources would be the people and groups who are working on various parts of the food issue (and related subjects). In addition, print, video, audio, and computer-based information would be included.

"Translation" of Problem/Possibility Focusers

An important benefit of the problem/possibility focuser technique is that a PPF is ideally suited to take advantage of the potentials of the new electronic technologies to be updated rapidly as new information becomes available. However, the PPF would have only a limited effect if we did not deal with the enormously different ways in which people learn. We need to begin, as a society, to make provision for the "translation" of information from one media format to another. We must take steps to ensure that the knowledge we gain is made available to all levels of understanding from kindergarten upwards and also learn to use the various media in ways that are most effective.

During the industrial era, we believed that people received the message that was sent to them: that there was a tidy correlation between the teachings we aim to make available and the information that people receive. We now know that people's receipt of messages is mediated by an immensely complex screening process of the sense organs and the brain. We still understand far too little of the implications of this reality.

Some pioneering work has already been done. For example, Piaget has shown that there are some ages at which children can learn certain skills and knowledge more easily than at others. Some work has been done on sensory inputs. But in general we still pay very little attention to knowledge regarding the process of translation from the sent message to the received message.

Uses of Problem/Possibility Focusers

The frustration with existing methods of structuring knowledge, the extraordinary difficulty in conducting research, the grotesque overload of published material all point to the necessity for fundamental changes in knowledge patterns. Today's public decision-makers are often so overwhelmed by the noise of special pleading that it is almost impossible for them to gain any grasp of the really key possibilities and problems in any area. Assumptions and values are hidden by a frantic lobbying effort to achieve the goals that have been set by each group.

Private decision-makers are equally in need of good information to determine the directions in which they should turn their attention. The manufacturer who continued to turn out buggy-whips long after they were a declining market is an example of a failure to reconceptualize the market in which one is active: if the buggy-whip manufacturer had thought in terms of being in the transportation industry, he might well have survived.

One of the greatest gains would, of course, occur in education. At the present time, most of the material that is available—whether in print, audio, or video form—is at best obsolescent and is quite often obsolete. This is inevitable given present patterns of publication. But a computer-based problem/possibility focuser can be kept up to date on a continuing basis. In addition, instead of it being necessary for an individual to read or see several different presentations in order to get a perception of the extent and significance of the existing range of views, the necessary information is all contained within a single document. Indeed, it seems reasonable to see the problem/possibility focuser as the base for the communications-era encyclopedia.

Finally, this whole approach to knowledge would necessarily have an extraordinary impact on the media and methods of reporting. The media are presently trapped into the need to report major stories in a fragmentary way. Each day they interview somebody who has a different slant on the story and they dutifully report what they have learned to their public. Unfortunately, the overall impact of this style of reporting is to leave the reader or viewer increasingly baffled. Holistic, large-scale stories are outside the capacity of most media. Even when "in-depth" reporting is attempted, it is within an objective frame. Viewers are told that they are only seeing "factual material." However, there is nearly always an implied or expressed conclusion—a slant—with which the public is expected to agree.

The problem/possibility focuser could alter this situation. It could provide people with an overall perception of the real differences that exist, the reasons *why* people disagree, and could also suggest the tools people could use to be involved in thinking about their own futures.

Obviously, these patterns of use would change the socioeconomic and political system of the country. Problem/possibility focusers would enable people to have a better perception of the real issues that face us. We pay lip-service to a well-informed democracy. Whether we are able and willing to take steps to create such a well-informed democracy is the issue that lies behind the problem/possibility focuser model and will determine its success.

Necessary Personal Skills

There are, of course, many possible objections to the problem/possibility focuser model. The first question that nearly always emerges is "Where are you going to find the people who are willing and able to work with knowledge systems in the way you describe? Obviously, everybody will try to distort the picture to ensure that they gain the maximum advantage."

I find this reaction fascinating. Any response to it must have several parts. First, I deny that I expect to set up a perfect system in which we will know all that we need to know about any subject. I am not arguing that the result of a problem/possibility focuser system will be a pattern of knowledge that will answer every question we need to ask; rather, I am stating it should be within our competence to define the relevant questions that we need to consider at this time when humanity is controlling the evolution of the earth.

Second, within this context, I state that all those involved will choose the best people we can find for the initial work on any problem/possibility focuser. Obviously, the initial group will not be the final group: people will move in and out. There is no need to worry excessively about people staying when they cannot contribute because one will be working with competent people who always have more to do than they can manage and who are delighted to give up any activity when their help is not needed.

Third, one will be working with people who have already changed their perception of self-interest. This group will consist of people who have recognized that their own development, the long-run success of themselves as individuals, of the institutions with which they are associated, and indeed the survival of the human race depend on fundamental changes in values and patterns toward more responsible behavior. Given this reality, the people involved in the creation of problem/possibility focusers will be prepared to try to understand the real issues rather than to set forth their narrowest self-interest.

Computer Implications

We are still treating the computer as if it permitted us merely to do the things we have done in the industrial era better and faster. We are not recognizing that computers are forcing us to adopt new authority patterns. Computer-based knowledge systems are making it impossible for decisions to be imposed on the basis of power rather than knowledge. It is therefore somewhat amazing that many people concerned about social reform and change see the computer as a block to achieving a more democratic society rather than as the prime route toward it.

This does not mean that the required transition will be easy, but it does mean that if we come to accept the logic of the communications era—rather than the industrial era—we shall find that our society will be forced into a democratic mode. The problem/possibility focuser will be both chicken and egg in this process: helping people to see the possibilities first and then providing the structure for an alternative form of society.

Methods of Drafting

The suggestions that follow offer an idealized statement of the way in which early problem/possibility focusers can be drafted. Later, patterns and norms will necessarily change substantially as networks are established and as efforts are more fully computer-based. It is assumed that a significant amount of face-to-face contact will be necessary for early problem/possibility focusers.

Step 1. Find a number of people who represent the various views about the issue under consideration and who are willing to work within the PPF format. It is suggested that this number should fall between eight and twelve in order to meet what we know about small-group interactions. As already stated, the group will not be "ideal" and we may well expect to see movement in and out of it. "Expertise" is not a condition for membership in the group, but passionate interest is.

Step 2. Two promising groups of talent for assembling the first PPF teams would be competent retired people who would like to continue using their skills and graduate students with competence in the subject who could gain credit toward a degree from working with the group and who would choose this experience because there is no way they could learn more.

Step 3. Bring together problem/possibility focuser creators and staff for a three-day session. While work would certainly be done at this time to try to begin to understand the patterns of agreement and disagreement, it would be recognized that a great deal of the time would be taken up getting to know each other and establishing rapport within the group. Thus, play and games would be part of the first meeting. One possible approach for the work portion of this first meeting might be to ask each person to draft a statement that he or she thought would be acceptable for the whole group. This could lead to one of two results: either there would be people present who would disagree, thus beginning to define the area of controversy, or there would be genuine agreement and this statement would then form part of the agreement section of the document. Another critical goal for the first meeting would be to define some areas in which the staff could start to do research and think.

Step 4. After a period of time for reflection—say two to three months—the group would meet again. The purpose of this second meeting would be to create the first draft of a problem/possibility focuser that people would comment upon and criticize.

Step 5. If at all possible, staff and participants would be linked at all times through a computer-based telecommunications system. The contact that would thus be possible would increase both the work and the relationship potential of the group. However, the success of early problem/possibility focuser creation does not depend on the availability of teleconferencing.

Step 6. Comments, ideas, and responses to the PPF draft would be solicited from those most competent in the field: but circulation would be kept relatively limited during this period to avoid overloading those involved. It is probable that many people will have difficulty understanding the difference between the problem/possibility focuser and existing methods of knowledge structuring. Therefore, efforts would have to be made to ensure that this understanding was achieved, for otherwise many of the comments would be useless. During this period, efforts would also be made to contact media, publishers, and "translators."

Step 7. Feedback would continue. Plans would be laid for initial publication and translation.

Step 8. A revised problem/possibility focuser draft would be approved for widespread publication. The feedback and revision process would continue as long as the issue was important.

Other approaches to initiate problem/possibility focuser studies may also prove fruitful. We must remember however, that any movement toward a PPF format will not only involve a shift in ways of structuring knowledge but also require fundamental changes in patterns of behavior. The shift from the industrial era to the communications era will demand alterations in perceptions and patterns of action that will be at least as far-reaching as those that took place during the shift from the agricultural era to the industrial era. Thus we are necessarily considering a different pattern of social skills than those that were taught by industrial-era societies. The difficulties to be faced are greater than we can imagine; but the benefits that can be achieved are greater still.

The Future of the Rural Public Library

by

Bernard Vavrek

This is a particularly fortuitous time to be considering the future of the rural public library among society's multifaceted levels of communications. As a matter of perspective, it is important to understand that 82% of all of the public libraries in the United States can be found in communities of 25,000 or fewer individuals. Further, within the last few years more attention has been focused on this sleeping giant, i.e., rural libraries, than since the beginnings of the public library movement in the mid-nineteenth century. This fresh look at libraries in rural communities has occurred because of the growth rate of small towns (an unprecedented demographic phenomenon has emerged in that for the first time in the history of the United States more people are moving to nonmetropolitan areas than to metropolitan areas) and the fact that transportation and technology permit access to both cultural and economic centers while one lives in the country.

It is generally assumed because of national reporting trends and the hype generated by large models of public libraries found in cities such as New York, Philadelphia, Boston, Baltimore, etc., that these libraries are, in fact, typical of public libraries in the United States. While these institutions are cultural achievements of worldwide importance, they distract the viewer who seeks an image of the mainstream of public librarianship. The mainstream public library is in rural America—whether located in Knox, Pennsylvania; Stone Mountain, Georgia; or Lebanon, Illinois.

The word "rural" can be defined with the aid of a dictionary, but it is better interpreted in a context. The U.S. Bureau of the Census definition considers it as a population base of 2,500 or fewer individuals, although other agencies of the federal government define "rural" conveniently as "nonmetropolitan." The Center for the Study of Rural Librarianship (CSRL) uses as a definition a community of 25,000 or fewer people and the criterion that a library must be an independent agency as opposed to a part of a larger system.

More subjectively, however, there are some additional glimpses of rurality that this author would like to add to provide a proper interpretation. First, although not everyone in a small town is friendly to the same degree, usually

Bernard Vavrek is professor and coordinator, Center for the Study of Rural Librarianship, School of Library Science, Clarion State College, Clarion, Pennsylvania.

it's simpler to get to know one's neighbors (and personal greetings, such as "Good Morning," take on an individual significance and satisfaction). Second, it's easier (after a break-in waiting period reserved for outsiders) to become known in a community because of one's participation in social and/or civic activities; this, of course, can work to one's disadvantage because rumors and impressions spread faster than the proverbial wildfire. Third, it does seem that rural areas have a higher proportion (than the city) of individuals who are willing to volunteer their time for the good of the community; this may be witnessed in activities from the Little League to the volunteer fire company. Fourth, cable television is a condition of rural living, at least for hopeful TV watchers; otherwise, stations are usually too far away to receive viewing signals. Fifth, although I haven't made a scientific study, on a per capita basis, I am convinced that there are more pick-up trucks and recreational vehicles in rural towns than in cities; further, prominently visible in these vehicles are racks holding rifles or shotguns (or fishing rods) with National Rifle Association decals on the windows or bumpers. Sixth, in rural areas, the daily *New York Times* can't be purchased and the absence of a bookstore is taken for granted. Seventh, rural towns rely heavily on mail-order stores around the United States; otherwise, it is frequently very difficult to obtain even basic necessities. Eighth, emerging symptomatically as an aspect of the rural environment is the shopping mall—a characteristic of suburban living that is now creeping into small towns.

Quite realistically, there are many rurals, all of which are altered by geography and socio-economic conditions. The problems that affect the midwestern states (such as the MX missile system and large-scale agro-economics) are not the same issues that are confronting the Sunbelt states, which are experiencing unprecedented population growth in rural towns. While it is convenient to consider only two types of rural, i.e., the town or area that is booming because of population growth and the rural town that is dying because of a lack of people and a nonexistent economic base, clearly one must consider the rural phenomenon on a linear scale, with these two examples at either end of the measure. Symptomatic of "boom town" rural, as mentioned earlier, is the fact that for the first time in the history of the United States people are leaving metropolitan areas to live in nonmetropolitan regions. Demographers indicate that unless some totally disruptive event occurs (e.g., the total absence of fuel for the family automobile), this outmigration from American cities is going to continue. It is beyond this author's interest to speculate on all of the reasons why this population shift is occurring, but presumably it has something to do with seeking a better life. Personally, it's my belief that living in a small town has become the chic thing to do. Irrespective of whether it is fashionable or not to live in rural areas, increasing numbers of people are doing it, not necessarily to the delight of the current inhabitants of towns that are doubling in size because of this current demographic trend. And curiously, some of the new settlers in rural areas are more interested in preserving the environment than those long-time inhabitants who take the country for granted.

Serious challenges are developing for librarians, who now must face the demands of citizens who have previously lived in metropolitan areas and have come to naturally expect a greater variety of alternative informational packages from which to choose. It has been convenient to think of the rural library as being insulated from such things as on-line data bases, videotext systems, etc. But the new wave of rural people includes those who have already experienced some of the latest technological achievements in controlling and disseminating information and will expect the same services to be available in their new community. First, of course, some decided effort must be made to be certain that all libraries have telephones before grand systems of electronic connections are contemplated. In a national survey just completed by CSRL dealing with public libraries in areas with 25,000 or fewer people, it was discovered that 6.0% of the responding libraries were without telephones. Of the libraries serving populations of 2,500 or fewer individuals, about 14.0% were without telephones. While 6.0% or 14.0% of public libraries without telephones may seem to be an inconsequential matter, this must be considered as only one of a variety of unique problems complicating the future of communications in rural areas.

Additional problems are more generally applicable to a majority of rural public libraries than the absence of a telephone, however. The most obvious of these is geographical remoteness, which means that the librarian has few other cultural and/or informational centers from which to draw support. This situation is considerably different in a metropolitan area, where one has relatively easy access to a multitude of resources, frequently within a few block radius. In many rural communities, except for the public library, there are no additional sources of information to augment the library's role. The only other type of library frequently available is the public school library. Unfortunately, however, this communications resource has fewer publications than the community's public library and is normally open only during school hours.

Geographical remoteness also manifests itself in that it precludes the rural librarian from having regular professional contacts with other librarians or information specialists. The exchange of ideas and the facilitation of discussion are largely eliminated because of the absence of resource people. It should be noted, however, that in some instances the librarian may be faulted for not identifying and/or contacting these individuals.

The discussion above about professional isolation is very much a nuance of what I believe to be the single most pressing matter facing rural library service: the lack of trained staff. Emerging from research done by CSRL both in Pennsylvania and nationwide is a rather clear picture of staffing patterns. While situations do vary, of course, academically trained librarians are simply not available in sufficient number to insure their availability in every library. In most states, if it were not for volunteers who help staff public libraries, many could not remain open. Pennsylvania's ratio of academically trained librarians when compared with volunteers is approximately .8 to 6. I can think of no other institution in society where volunteers play such a major role.

It is possible to continue discussing the limitations inherent in providing informational service in rural communities, but one additional example is sufficient. It deals with the size of the resource collection available in the rural library. In research conducted by CSRL, it was discovered that the size of the average book collection in the public libraries surveyed was approximately 19,500 items. Compare this with the simple fact that over 40,000 new books are published in English each year. As a consequence of collection inadequacy, and not only as it relates to books, decided emphasis and strain is placed on the interlibrary loan of resources in rural America. To meet citizen demands it is not surprising, for example, for a rural librarian to borrow a thousand books from other libraries during a one-year period. While the interlibrary loan process is both simple and effective, the inability to satisfy user demands immediately, as opposed to waiting several weeks or months, reinforces the image of the public library as only a modestly helpful place. A seventh-grader told me recently that she liked to buy her own books rather than using the library's because of the dead insects, crayon marks, and yellow tape found on the pages of library books.

Since this paper is a statement dealing with communications in rural areas, it is of some importance to consider what channels of communication are available to public librarians, while recalling those comments made earlier about the absence of daily national newspapers and bookstores. In an article written about two years ago, I compared attempting to have one's name placed on a preferred list of individuals who had access to the Sunday quota of the *New York Times* as tantamount to obtaining tickets to the Metropolitan Opera in New York City. This situation has now changed in my own community because there is no longer any list. It has been eliminated since the Sunday *Times* is no longer available at the newsstand.

On the positive side of utilizing existing communication facilities, the rural librarian does have access to sources such as the town newspaper or radio station—if in fact such channels exist. One librarian related an amusing but, in reality, sad story of attending a workshop conducted by someone from a metropolitan area dealing with the techniques of developing television announcements. The irony rested with the fact that no television stations existed within 100 miles of the librarian's community. So television (excepting cable television) can hardly be considered a viable source of communication in most rural areas. Personal contacts continue to be a basic and crucial method of contact for rural people, but it is a decidedly slow process when one wants to reach "large" numbers of individuals at one time.

Given the geographical and intellectual isolation of the rural public library, coupled with its sometimes low community profile, it is an easy matter to develop a critical indictment against this institution and to ask, "Has technology eliminated the need for the public library?" Rather than answering this last question directly, I shall attempt to respond to the public library's apparent weaknesses with the following discussion. First, regardless of its shortcomings, no other agency in society is charged with the responsibilities of collecting, organizing, preserving, and disseminating the total products of our communication. While so many other institutions (e.g., newspapers, book publishers, archival data centers, etc.) concern themselves with selected varieties of information, none of these is oriented toward or committed to drawing the products of communication from all other sources and creating a "balanced collection" of information, in which supposedly all views are represented. And to make these resources available without "direct cost to the consumer." Even if this, in reality, is an impossible task, the public library's societal role is unique. In spite of the fact that the rural library lacks funding (which in Pennsylvania means that the rural library is supported with a per-capita subsidy approximately one-half that of a metropolitan area), it is refreshing to be reminded of the contribution it makes. Irwin Shaw, the novelist, was recently quoted:

> As in the case of almost all American writers, my real education and the first hope that I might be a writer myself came to me in a public library. It was a small and modest one, in Sheepshead Bay, run by a prim lady who always kept a bowl of narcissus on her neat desk. . . .

Considering the fact that the average price of a trade book is approximately $20.00, it is not unrealistic to assume that the public library's historical role as society's collector will continue. Book publishers will price themselves out of the general consumer market—except in cases of well-known authors—if book prices keep pace with inflation. And although comments about the library's resources in this paper so far have been made in relation to books, this has really been meant to be symbolic of all library materials. In reality, libraries are collections of both print and nonprint materials. What other public agency, for example, will provide the free loan of film materials, including a projector as well?

The uniqueness of the public library, wherever it is located, also extends to include a national network of other public libraries from which resources may be borrowed. Although the over-use of interlibrary sharing was cited earlier in this paper as an example of the inadequacy of individual library collections, this loan network (a cooperative arrangement without direct charge back to the customer) constitutes an unparalleled information service available to Americans, regardless of where they live. In rural America, this ability to draw resources from other library repositories is the only "lifeline" against geographical and intellectual remoteness.

Today, because of the existing and emerging technology, one finds considerable emphasis placed upon individualized access to information. In the public library, however, a member of the staff is available to assist with one's information searching. Unfortunately, as mentioned earlier, academically trained librarians are in short supply; but even if we allow for the possible uneven service that may result from this shortage, the very fact that a resource person is available to assist one in information gathering must simply be viewed as a unique societal function. No other community institution provides for this in such a sweeping fashion.

In addition to the unequaled services already described, and in conclusion, it should be stressed that the public library also functions as a community information center enabling a wide cross section of information to be available in one locus; provides "free" programs intended for citizens of all ages and backgrounds; and, particularly in rural areas, offers a town meeting place for all types of functions—a gathering spot that otherwise is non-existent. Given the excitement inherent in both the concept and reality of the public library, society's main fault is having taken this institution for granted. Arthur Miller commented, "The public library is the foundation of our freedom, and cannot be diminished without diminishing the essence of what we are and have to become."

It is extremely difficult to clearly picture the future of communication and the rural public library. There are too many contrasts that are beginning to confuse my already meager concept of what is occurring. To suggest an immediate contrast, I recently spoke before a group of librarians in a rural school district, not far from Clarion, about microcomputer application in school libraries. The distressing thing I discovered was that 11 microcomputers had already been purchased by the school district but the individuals involved had little notion of what to do with the new equipment. The issue was not one of programming the computers, but rather simply determining what library routines or programs might be used. In my view, this incident is too characteristic of how technology is being badly managed today.

The patient reader will undoubtedly be relieved to know that a discussion about the future of communications and the rural library will finally be attempted. It is hoped that the preceding discussion, rather than seeming extraneous, will be viewed as a necessary introduction to attempt a discernment of the future. The reader should also realize that it is not with total confidence that one attempts to predict the future, even if it is an exciting challenge, because change, whether it is the symptom or cause of technology, defies one's logical descriptive ability. There can be little doubt, however, that rural libraries will be affected both by change and by technology, and it is my belief that the following developments will occur:

The Library's Public. First, from the viewpoint of the library patron, it will become less necessary for personal visits to the institutional library, unless one chooses to do so. For those individuals who can afford a home microcomputer, information requests will be made by utilizing this device with an acoustic coupler and telephone line. Transactions, whether in the form of the loan of books or other resources, will be conducted from the home microcomputer to the library's microcomputer. Requests will also be made via the home computer to enable one to have one's name placed on a waiting list for a bestseller (physical books will still be available for a while longer) or to enable the reader to suggest an item that he or she would like to access in the future.

Second, what would be described currently as the library's reference services (basically, assisting in answering questions of all types) will be supported also through microcomputer linkage and/or cable television. Depending on the nature of the inquiry and the answer required, reference information from the library will be sent to the consumer from CRT to CRT— or, if more detailed graphic rendition is necessary, through a high-resolution television screen and "community" cable linkages. Searching through electronic data bases along with conventional sources of information will be considered a standard service in the rural library (as it now is in most larger libraries).

Third, at present only 10% of public libraries utilize, either directly or indirectly, on-line bibliographic data bases such as Dialog. Within the next decade, the same libraries will become brokers for a wider variety of data bases. Extensive bibliographic searches will be done in the library on a fee basis for business people, farmers, educators, politicians, and the general public, and the results will be provided by the library's computer to the consumer's computer. One may wonder why indeed would the library be a necessary and viable part of this electronic network when already a wide variety of videotext and other data bases are available for individual and home use? The proliferation of data bases is precisely the reason that ultimately the library will be looked to, to sort out from the variety of electronic communication that which is the most important. An interesting historical parallel may be referred to here because public libraries, as well as other libraries, did not really have a significant cultural role to play until the individual management of information became untenable. One will remember the earlier discussion in this paper characterizing the uniqueness of the public library as the only institution which consciously attempts to collect, organize, preserve, and disseminate society's communication. Why should electronic forms of information be excluded?

Fourth, because of the increased proliferation of information and the technology available even in the smallest library, it is my view that librarians will assume an additional level of service within the next decade. This will take the form of more individualized assistance given to readers in the preparation of reports (descriptive as well as statistical), reviews of literature, bibliographies, and perhaps even speeches. Some libraries provide these services now, but not at the interactive level suggested above. Regardless of the "Library of Congress Reduced to a Shoebox" mentality, the proliferation of resources and the current lack of compatability among computers and software programs will strengthen the mediating role of the public library in the future. Some reprogramming will have to be done as well, within the curricula of library schools, since present educational approaches do not accommodate what is being suggested for the future.

The Librarian. First, national systems that enable librarians to catalog library resources, e.g., OCLC (Online Computer Library Center), currently being used in 43% of the country's small libraries, will become less important in the next decade. As microcomputers become more sophisticated and memory capacities enhanced, which is now occurring, the regional control of bibliographic information will become more important. Radio Shack's newly announced ARCNET system is just one example of emerging technology that will allow microcomputers to interact with other microcomputers rather than with mainframes.

Before long, librarians, if they choose to, will be able to print out on-line their own catalog records from Daisy Wheel or Epson printers. The questioning reader may scoff at the notion of conventional card catalogs continuing in any libraries, but it should be realized that many rural libraries will not be able to afford enough CRTs to satisfy reader needs. And not all homes will become electronic cottages. It must also be remembered that, on a developmental scale, rural libraries have the greatest distance to travel.

Second, collections development and management will also be promoted because of the microcomputer. Libraries will be able to place orders and make transactions with local print and nonprint jobbers for library materials. This is currently being done around the country, but not necessarily by rural librarians. Simple software programs will allow the librarian to do the financial tracking needed in any enterprise; management reports also will be facilitated because information about the collection will be available in a machine-readable format.

Third, as a matter of convenience it seems a reasonable thing to summarize together those additional instances in which the rural librarian will be affected in the future, since technology will have a relatively even impact on all record-keeping aspects of library services. These include keeping account of materials circulated from or within the library; tracking books and other resources sent outside of the library for repair or binding; and booking films for group showing—although in the future, Saturday afternoon film programs will not only be shown in the library but will simultaneously be broadcast by cable television to those individuals who for any reason choose to or are forced to stay at home. In fact, the whole sphere of library services to the blind, the physically handicapped, and the elderly will be improved because the library will really make itself available outside of its own physical space. Perhaps the money allocated or needed to improve existing physical structures to allow access by the blind or physically handicapped can be channeled to improve home microtechnological applications. Those who have traditionally been unserved by the rural public library will benefit the most in the future.

Undoubtedly, to some the preceding discussion about change and the rural public library will seem pale in comparison to more highly advanced and/or intriguingly conceived future systems. What futurists must understand, however, is that for the vast majority of libraries in small communities the scenario being suggested here will be considered light years away. As decidedly nonfuturist as it may appear, one must remind the reader again that not all libraries even have telephones. While the absence of a phone would seem a simple matter to overcome, it is symptomatic both of the problem and the solution.

Where Are the Peasants?

by

Charlotte Waterlow

When Soviet Premier Nikita Khrushchev visited the United States in 1959 as the guest of President Dwight D. Eisenhower, he exclaimed in wonder: "Where are the peasants?" North America is almost the only region in the world that has never known this phenomenon. Elsewhere, for millennia 90% of the population has consisted of peasants, who lived in traditional and essentially static societies in which their beliefs, habits, and life-styles were dictated by immemorial customs derived from religious revelations.

There is growing realization in the West of the fundamental dangers inherent in the confrontation between "North" and "South"—between societies that have acquired the knowledge and wealth to visit the moon, put satellites into orbit, computerize banking systems, talk and fly across the world, and those in which the majority are still peasants. Many people are now aware of the material dimensions of this confrontation: the population explosion in the developing countries from over 3 billion in 1981 to a projected nearly 5 billion in 2000; the daily hunger of a billion people; the need to create a billion jobs in the next 20 years to provide work for all; the lack of decent housing, clean water, and disease control; and so on. These are facts that can be quantified. Not so many people are aware of the psychological dimensions, which are largely the fruit of the communications revolution.

Before the modern age, the average peasant's range of conscious experience was limited to the life of his village and perhaps the neighboring market town. In 1970 I met a Swiss shepherd in the mountains above Lausanne who had only been to Geneva—an hour's journey by train—once in his life. In 1982 a British journalist asked an Indian peasant how much, including interest, he owed the local farmer to whom he was a debt slave. "Such complicated sums were beyond him. 'Ram Singh keeps the accounts,' he said." The average peasant was illiterate, and he often communicated with others in a language that was unique to his village. The consciousness of women was usually even more limited. They were often restricted to the four walls of the family courtyard and shrouded in veils when allowed to go out into the lanes with other women. In 1972 a British journalist in Algiers reported, "Most

Charlotte Waterlow teaches on global problems at Buckingham, Browne and Nichols School in Cambridge, Massachusetts, and is the author of four books in the field.

women are still shrouded from head to foot, or locked away altogether from public view, domestic drudges condemned to breed until exhaustion."

This profound ignorance of his or her global, national, and even regional environment kept the average peasant, for thousands of years, in a childlike and passive state of mind.

And now modern communications have suddenly impacted on his consciousness. First, there are the media. Transistor radios are everywhere. A Palestinian engineer in Boston, brought up in a refugee camp, told my students that the unemployed refugees, living on United Nations charity, were among the best-informed young people in the world, because they spent their time listening to world news on their transistors. In the mud-hut villages of the Third World, the village loudspeaker will blare government propaganda into the ears of the men sitting in the coffee shops. In the shanty towns that ring the cities, someone will buy an old TV set and charge his friends a small fee for coming to watch. Movies also penetrate the towns and villages. In India, which has the second biggest film industry in the world, traveling movies go from village to village; in each case, the sentimental love story is preceded by a government documentary on hygiene or some didactic subject. Of Latin America, Salvador de Madariaga has written:

> Hollywood bids fair to be . . . the most potent source of revolutionary ferment in the world. The film is the book of the illiterate. Millions of simple beings lost in their villages had never imagined how a rich man lived. Hollywood brought to their astounded eyes the lavish lives of the rich. "Why should I go on lying on my mat of lice?" asks the illiterate Indian. And so he goes to swell the mass of those whose sons will avidly devour cheap pamphlets from Moscow. That the film comes from the United States only adds mustard to the salt.

Although most developing countries are governed by some form of dictatorship, it is now "with it" to have a constitution and elections. The dictatorship often tries to base its support upon a mass party, or in Communist countries, on mass support for an elitist party. For the first time in history, the peasants are a political force to be wooed, and modern media are an essential tool in this courtship. It is true that Gandhi awakened the Indian masses by spending 30 years walking the length and breadth of the huge country, talking to them in a language they could not understand and often could not hear. But now the politicians have microphones at their command. And recently cassettes have become a potent political tool. The Ayatollah Khomeini, for instance, prepared the way for his revolution by sending cassettes of his talks from his French retreat to the Iranian bazaars, and the revolutionary flame was thus ignited among the urban masses with whom the Western embassies had no direct contact.

The media are complemented by the advent of modern systems of mass travel. Millions of peasants are moving from village to town, and even from country to country, by bus or train, or even—in the Soviet Union, for example—by air.

In addition to the media and mass travel, there is the massive development of education. The very idea that every child, male and female, *ought* to be educated is entirely new in these societies. And the content of the education now provided by governments is revolutionary. In olden days the limited education, offered to boys only, consisted largely in memorizing the scriptures. Today, boys and girls are being taught modern science, Western languages, and secular social studies. Adult literacy is also spreading rapidly. Eighty per cent of China's billion people can now read and write simplified characters, and Cuba's peasants were taught to read by high-school kids in a crash literacy campaign in the early sixties. In non-Communist countries, the progress is somewhat slower, but 50% of the world's people are now literate, despite the population explosion and the problems of the diversity of languages and scripts.

The question of language is crucial. In many areas, particularly those where written scripts did not develop in the traditional societies, neighboring villages speak mutually incomprehensible languages. In Africa, for instance, there are at least 800 languages; among the Mexican Indians, about 90. All-India Radio broadcasts in 51 languages and 82 tribal dialects. A peasant who wishes to communicate in the modern world may have to learn the national language, which may in effect be a foreign language—Spanish in Latin America or Swahili in Africa or Hindi in India—and also the language of a completely alien culture, such as English or French. This creates an identity problem.

The communications revolution is therefore jolting the peasants of the developing countries out of the immemorial ruts of tradition and making them aware that their poverty and oppression *need not be.* This has been called by the Brazilian educator Paulo Freire *concientizacia*—consciousness-raising—the awakening of the political and social awareness of the masses. The consciousness-raising of three—soon five—billion people is one of the most fateful developments in history.

What are the thrusts of this mass awakening? First, there is the often noted "tide of rising expectations"—the desire of the billions to enjoy "modern" living standards—proclaimed as their "right" in Article 25 of the United Nations' Universal Declaration of Human Rights. They are becoming aware of the unequal distribution of the world's wealth (three-quarters of the world's population have access to only 20% of its wealth). Unless the modernized countries take major steps to redistribute this wealth—minor steps have been taken—the developing countries are likely to turn into infernos of the mass, mindless violence of millions of semi-moronic, semi-literate unemployed young people (malnutrition in the first year of life does permanent damage to the brain), who *see no hope* that their future will ever provide the conditions for a life of "dignity and the free development of his (and her) personality" (Article 22 of the Universal Declaration).

Second, a less well understood cultural transformation is taking place. The impact of modernity, whether in a Western humanistic or Marxist mode, is forcing the billions to replace religious revelation by secular science as the source of "knowledge"; to replace revealed customs and laws by man-made secular systems of law and government. This transformation represents a leap forward from societies based on a group consciousness, in which the individual did not count *as such*, but only in terms of his or her function in the group. The experience of modernity, however, has shown that in order to achieve this transformation it is necessary to secularize society. In the West,

293

religion has been made a private matter; in the more primitive Marxist societies, it has been brutally replaced by "scientific atheism." But in reality religion has been undermined in modern societies not by laws but by science. The sprites have fled from the sacred groves; the aura of the numinous no longer blesses every daily activity; the sense that human society is a *cosmopolis*, a city of gods and men, of animals and plants, has vanished; the "communion of saints" has become an empty phrase. And so just when "persons" matter as never before, modernized societies are developing as impersonal machines, treating persons as "things."

A Third World peasant who tries to escape from the stagnant misery of his village by emigrating to a big town, as millions are doing, finds himself at best working long hours in unhealthy conditions for a minimal wage at some assembly-line job in a factory—which is quite likely owned by a Western multinational corporation. At worst, he is unemployed, living by scavenging and crime in the slums that ring these cities. Like his counterpart in the modernized countries, he is "alienated"—with the added trauma of material misery.

The communications revolution has, in a profound sense, cheated the peasant. In eagerly jumping into the modern world that calls on him to be a person, enjoying undreamed of material affluence, he finds that in fact he has exchanged the traditional human group, which enclosed its members in its warm embrace from the cradle to the grave, for the impersonal "organization" in which he is but a cog in a machine. His economic insecurity is therefore compounded by psychological rage.

Leaving aside Marxism, two ways of dealing with this psychological trauma are emerging. The first is to turn back to traditionalism, to retreat into the nest, to cling to or revive past customs and laws and to try to limit the influx of Western science, secularity, and humanism, while adopting Western technology in order to raise living standards. This is surely the explanation for the wave of Islamic fundamentalism that is sweeping through the Muslim world, for the Hindu fundamentalism that Nehru said that he feared more than Marxism, for the violent protests against secularism of the gentle Buddhists of Burma and Sri Lanka, for the obdurate conservatism of a large section of the Roman Catholic Church in Latin America, and perhaps for the continuing tribal tensions in Black Africa. But the clock cannot be put back. Dogmatic religions that assert the infallibility and superiority of their own particular ancient revelation cannot survive in their traditional form, because both human potential and scientific discovery, the foundation stones of modernity, are in their very nature open-ended. "The spirit bloweth where it listeth." Western Islamic scholars such as Professor H.A.R. Gibb and Wilfred Cantwell Smith have explored sympathetically the failure of Islamic "modernists' to relate orthodox Islam creatively to modernity. The experience of the Iranian revolution, the great laboratory for this experiment, is already indicating that the circle cannot be squared.

But there is another way forward, which offers a solution to the psychological problems of the rich countries as well as of the poor. This lies in distilling from the traditional religions their essential *spiritual* content and applying this at the ground level as the motive force for social transformation. Thus dogmatism, authoritarianism, sanctified laws and customs, and credulous su-

294

perstition would all be shed, and the *mystical* element in all traditional religions—the aspiration of the soul to *experience* the love, wisdom, and power that stem from union with the Divine—would be cultivated. From this state of mind springs the spontaneous desire to promote social justice and human rights for all. And when the mind sees the world through the eyes of the soul, it finds that science and religion are two sides of the same coin.

Two great movements have arisen in the developing countries that aim at spiritualizing the consciousness-raising process. The first was launched by Gandhi in India in the inter-war years. His genius lay in distilling from traditional Hinduism the concepts of *ahimsa*—universal benevolence—and *satyagraha*—"firmness in truth"—and applying them in the form of non-violent civil disobedience to secure social and political change. But he also affirmed the need for simultaneous self-transformation, for he knew that a good end cannot be achieved by bad means or by bad people. Gandhi's ideas and actions and example have profoundly influenced many Third World leaders, particularly in Africa, as well as Martin Luther King and his followers in the United States.

The second movement is the growing radicalization of a fairly large sector of the Latin American clergy, from archbishops to parish priests. Like Gandhiism, it has two dimensions; first, a reformulation of Christian theology in "the theology of liberation," which points to a vision of the spiritual evolution of consciousness for all humankind, looking to Christ as the great Model; and second, *action* by the clergy to promote consciousness-raising and social reform, leading towards a "communitarian" society free from the "institutionalized violence" practiced by the established regimes. These phrases are taken from the statement issued by the Second General Conference of Latin American Bishops held at Medellin in Colombia in 1968—a truly revolutionary document. The bishops abjured the use of violence to achieve the radical changes that they advocated.

"Communitarian" is probably a key word for the communications revolution of the future, for humankind stands on the verge of the transformation of consciousness. The individual, liberated from the traditional group to achieve personal self-development, must now learn to communicate, not only at the technological level but at the soul level, the level where person blends with person. Then alienation will be ended, and the brother-and-sisterhood of persons will emerge. And this transformation is likely to be pioneered not by the developed but by the developing countries.

Telepropinquity: Implications for Business Trading Systems

by

Barry J. Witcher

The combination of information and shopping together in the same place and time, in consumers' homes, through television and computer based telecommunications systems, is called *telepropinquity*. This new development is likely to be a valuable aid to complex and special shopping decisions, and will have substantial consequences for business as well as consumers.

Malcolm McNair and Eleanor May, writing in the *Harvard Business Review* in 1978, traced the basic idea for in-home television computer systems, together with automated shopping and programmed household needs, to Edward Bellamy. He was writing in 1888 of a utopia (of sorts) in the year 2000. In the same tradition but more recently, in 1967, Alton Doody and William Davidson predicted teleshopping as commonplace sometime in the 1970s.

Doody and Davidson were a bit early; the armchair shopper had not taken his seat by the end of the seventies. However, he should be there in time for 2000. If so, the implications for marketing and retailing seem considerable and they may be unexpected.

McNair's Wheel About to Turn

McNair advanced a hypothesis called the *wheel of retailing*. This has it that new types of retail outlets begin as low-status, low-margin, low-price operations. They prove to be successful competitors of traditional outlets that have become mature over the years. In time, they too become mature as facilities are upgraded and operating costs become higher. Eventually they are vulnerable to new competitors, and find other new retail forms taking over. The wheel has made another turn.

McNair and May argue that developments over the next few decades will be closely connected with these past trends. The evolvement of retail institutions, shortening retail life cycles, and the influence of consumers and lifestyles on retailing will combine with developments in technology to turn the

Barry J. Witcher teaches in the Department of Marketing at the University of Strathclyde, Glasgow, United Kingdom. This essay is based on a paper produced as part of the Prestel Innovation and Marketing Strategy Research Project, funded by the Joint Committee of the Social Science and Engineering Research Councils, United Kingdom.

wheel afresh. Specialty stores will thrive, but retailing of routinely ordered staples will be transformed.

Consumer goods can be categorized according to the reasons for purchase. Following the terminology proposed originally by Melvin Copeland, the categories are *convenience goods*, *shopping goods*, and *specialty goods*. Each is associated with a different kind of retail outlet. They are outlined in Exhibit 1.

Exhibit 1

Consumer Goods and Associated Retail Outlets

CONVENIENCE	Frequent, often routine purchase; bought immediately with a minimum of effort. Outlets in local, convenient sites; small general independent stores, small-unit discount stores and supermarkets.
SHOPPING	Factors such as suitability, quality, and style important. Often complex products with high unit value, and non-routine purchase; such as consumer durables. Outlets are department stores, often in town centers, and large-unit, often out-of-town, discount stores and supermarkets.
SPECIALTY	Special purchasing effort made; may be the subject of "shopping expeditions." Include ego-intensive products such as fashion items or hobby and recreational items. Outlets are often small units catering to differentiated life-styles.

Teleshopping, argue McNair and May, is likely to displace convenience shopping. This kind of activity is a chore and can be readily programmed. But it will not be frequency of acquisition but preselectivity that will determine which goods are teleshopped: those where appearance, feel, smell, and personal service are unimportant. Thus, the food trade may be less affected than household products, such as paper and hardware. The view that teleshopping will most affect convenience trade is based almost entirely on two ideas: that adequate information for consumer buying decisions with regard to shopping and specialty goods will be unavailable, and second, there is a social function behind this kind of shopping. But these assumptions seem unsound.

Mail Order

If there is inadequate information, the consumer will need to see the goods he is to buy and will depend to a large degree upon personal communications for high-risk purchasing; hence, the importance of sales assistance in shops. These arguments have been used before in the context of mail order and self-service. Yet both categories of trade have grown to include both shopping and speciality goods.

The popularity of mail order is often cited as evidence to help prove the coming of teleshopping. Yet most of this trade is not for convenience goods. Hard-to-obtain products are some of the most popular, and these include specialty items for hobbies, house, and garden. Just as in the United States in the nineteenth century the general mail order business increased with the growth of the railroads and the U.S. Post Office, so now will growth of electronic communications widen the choice still further.

Convenience shopping seems likely to develop slowly through tele-shopping. The main reason is that delivery systems linked to programmed ordering seem unlikely to develop quickly, since consumers must be tied to a single or a small number of outlets. Slow growth is likely to be most true for the grocery trade. Telephone delivery systems have not developed for this reason.

Shopping and specialty goods trade will develop faster since postal services are designed for this kind of trade. It seems likely that the mail order houses will keep pace with changes in business, and could develop improved delivery, including break-bulk facilities and consumer pickup points, as teleshopping grows. Delivery costs are likely to remain low and mail order prices continue to compare favorably with traditional selling.

Information plays a vital part in mail order, through catalogs. In the future companies will be able to reach their customers in much better ways. Teleinformation will be up to date, and linked to video catalogs and question-and-answer sessions.

Shopping's Social Function

Convenience shopping is said to be a chore whereas other shopping is fun (particularly when expeditions to suburban shopping malls might be with the family). But is this so? And is the social role of shopping—getting out and about with the family—really linked to shopping and specialty buying? Perhaps not. Most family shopping outings seem to be associated with routine purchasing of the week's groceries.

Social conditions, particularly as they affect women (such as two-career, two-children families), are working to make consumers more time-conscious. They are also bringing about changes in other time-saving technology, and some of this has become part of the shopping scene, such as automatic cash dispensers. These developments will create a society that is used to handling electronic buying aids.

Despite these doubts about the joy of shopping and the requirements to see goods prior to purchase, there are other reasons for thinking new media effects may not be greatest for convenience trade. The most important is the novelty of having information side by side with shopping in completely new forms.

Telepropinquity

Television could bring shopping into the place where the need for new goods is felt most keenly, and move the shopping context close to where buying decision processes start, namely, the home. To understand the implications, it is necessary to look at the different aspects of the information-shopping relation, brought close by *telepropinquity*. This is best done by considering separately the following: the nature of new communication media, the buying decision, changed marketing communications, and consumer knowledge.

Changed Media. The medium is the message: if so, messages are in for a change. Computer-based communication systems offer new media. The most important change is their interactive and real-time character, which allows users great selectivity. Information is called up by users when they require it, and usually in the latest, most up-to-date form. The user may act on this immediately through the medium, either to send a message to a service provider, request further information (perhaps from conventional media), or reserve or buy something. The user may also use the medium to contact other users.

This cannot be done with mass media, and is difficult even with a combination of, say, newspaper and telephone. Mass media information tends to be too general for use by individuals for specific purposes. There may also be problems of obsolete information and difficulties in taking follow-up action. In the sense that an interactive communication medium could become available for use in everyone's home, it is the first approximation of a kind of individualized mass media.

The Buying Decision. The context of buying has also changed. It will be as if many shop sites have collapsed into one and that one is conveniently inside the home. Time is saved. Product information and availability can be checked easily and purchases made from a variety of locations are possible in a matter of minutes.

Above all, consumer buying ability and confidence will be enhanced. Quality of advice will cease to be tied to purchase and less confused with loyalty. For example, if the quality of teleinformation is objective and detailed, there is no longer a need to seek a shop assistant's advice in a department store, then go skulking off to a discount store to make a purchase at a cheaper price. The captive market of local monopolies where "loyal" consumers buy a variety of products in one place will begin to leak. Point-of-sale advice and service will become less important. There will be less identification of products with the sales agent. Product advice and messages through the new media will be subject less to problems of perception, attitude, distortion, and lack of retention. Many failures in communication are simply failures of memory. Information presented at the moment of shopping will minimize this. In addition, aids such as computer data storage and printers will help jolt memories.

Changed Marketing Information. Interactive media will be a useful aid to promoting sales directly, improving links with company distributors and customers. Both can be kept informed about the latest stock and delivery information, and reviews. The marketer could monitor advertising promotion effects by observing and linking media use with information. As part of mixed media campaigns, new media should be seen as an extension of old forms, perhaps to provide more information on products and services advertised in traditional media. All that a conventional advertisement need do is include a teleinformation reference number to refer the interested party to further details. Books and directories could be updated in a similar way.

Another kind of multi-application for old and new media might be used for newspapers. Electronic newspaper readers could be provided with a facility enabling them to request follow-up analysis of interesting reviews or features about products, or a collection of previous items of interest. This may be supplied as conventionally printed material, by radio, or by cable television.

These and other changes are likely to mean that marketing information will become more factual. There will be less concern with prompting interest and awareness, or trying to influence the factors that bear on "attitude."

Point-of-sale presentation and packaging will be of less importance. Instead, more emphasis will be placed on product information, on "knowledge" and "action" in the determining processes. The consumer will find it easier to get the advice in the form he wants, so that buying complex shopping items should become much easier.

Suppliers will be able to target their information more effectively. Though traditional media permit some degree of market segmentation, the marketer is nearly always dependent upon his customer discovering the message, usually among a motley collection of advertisements. With the power to monitor information use, such as the new media provide, and a more active role taken by the consumer who can comment easily on his purchase experience with complaints, ideas, and requests, it will be easier to reach particular groups of consumers. Potentially, this should prove helpful for launching new products, because marketers would have a clearer idea about who is first to show interest and buy new products. This knowledge can be used to test products through teleshopping before expensively distributing them in other ways.

Media Displacement Effects. The greatest change may lie in the possibility that some publications could cease altogether as competition for advertising revenue shifts in favor of transactional media. It may be argued that the swing away from printed-media advertising to electronic forms has already been in progress for the past 20 years or more. Television and radio have taken a greater share of the constant media revenue cake.

But the new media will also do things much better than the traditional forms. Specifically, they will satisfy the need for quick, convenient, and up-to-date information of the sort provided by directories and yellow pages or by classified advertisements and mail order catalogs. Interactive media are nearly perfect for direct marketing and selling.

Additionally, the greater effectiveness of the new media is likely to be felt in another way. A curse of our times is information overload, or the piling up of reports, magazines, papers, and so on. This may be most true of technical and managerial fields, but it is also true, to an extent, for consumers, particularly of durables. Product and service advertising abound, and libraries and consumer advisory groups can only counter with more reports and leaflets. Only a small proportion of the paper received will actually contain wanted information, the rest being too general and irrelevant.

This is essentially a problem of information push. Interactive media offer the potential of the user pull, where users can individually select the material they need from a primary source. In the long run, this is likely to have a major contracting effect on traditional media.

Consumer Knowledge. There are also likely to be completely new roles for media. The most likely will emerge from opportunities in evaluative and consumer advisory services. These are likely to include new ways of marketing products and services, and more testing procedures. There are likely to be new roles for publishing groups as information system organizers and information brokers, as final consumers move closer to primary data sources. Using the new media, these roles could be performed not by vendors and marketers, but by specialized business and consumer agencies, able to target advice and run viable services.

There is already an existing consumer advisory industry: consumer associations, citizen advisory groups, libraries, government and public agencies. Some of these act as consumer vigilantes; others have members who are recognized as representatives of consumers as a whole. Often, because members tend to use formal information sources more than ordinary consumers, they serve as opinion leaders and message amplifiers.

But these sources of information are often difficult to use for the ordinary consumer. They have to be found, and in the case of consumer associations, membership fees must be paid in advance. Advice often takes the form of generalized leaflets or bulky reports. Interactive media are likely to make this information more accessible and in a form suitable for easy references, so that it can be used quickly at the same time as teleshopping.

In time, the consumer information business could become very big business indeed. Product testing may grow, and some groups may eventually become home consultants. Such developments could include independent groups acting with vendors in "official" trials, or service approval schemes (particularly in instances where design, health, and environmental regulations apply). Later on, integrated computer control systems in the home may provide access, through the new communication media, to home consultants. These systems would also allow monitoring, testing, and servicing of domestic equipment. Data thus gathered could be used as "experience," stored and used later when replacements are considered.

Some Skepticism

Innovation rarely ends up in the form originally envisaged. Many things can happen along the way, and the road to commercial success is littered with the disappointments of inventors and product champions.

The new media may not be welcomed without compromise and change. They may bring about a way of life that is artificial and complex. Information pull mechanisms, widening choice, could lead to an information overload; too much choice might lead to inconsistent trading patterns. Some companies might not wish to be associated with teleshopping because of a danger of superficial trading, where teleinformation is likely to concentrate too much on price and encourage the fly-by-night trader, at the expense of established consumer trade founded on personnel and quality of service. Brand-switching, it is argued, can only upset trade and, in the long run, increase costs.

It is by no means certain that teleshopping will be widespread by the year 2000. Prestel, the world's first public-service application of these services, has failed to quickly capture the imagination of residential consumers. As a result, the system's marketers have changed tack and begun to emphasize business applications.

The approach also seems to be having only slow results, and there is no sign yet of "take-off." Radical service innovation probably requires a lot more time than was originally thought necessary for commercial success. New developments in technology seem likely to improve the product greatly, but there is a danger that the original idea of a social information and trading network will be forgotten in a more profitable world of electronic captive markets. Several countries continue to run trials, and the international outlook for teleshopping remains optimistic.

Conclusion

The nature of teleshopping and its consequences have yet to be properly understood, particularly the importance of telepropinquity.

Information is important to the freedom of trade. If teleservices develop slowly, it is likely that the scope of information and variety of services will be limited, if the electronic market turns out to be just a collection of captive markets and trapped consumers. The message for all those concerned with business policy is to keep watch; it may be necessary to change the rules to get the desired outcomes.

Problems

The Future of High Technology in America

by

James Botkin, Dan Dimancescu, and Ray Stata

Below the glittering hills of Monaco, in a Riviera hotel hugging the Mediterranean harborside, a little-noticed but highly significant meeting took place in early 1982. Founders and chief executive officers of America's booming electronics industry presented one success story after another to more than 275 of Western Europe's barons of the financial investment community. The message: not only are America's high-technology industries thriving but they are emerging as a global economic force. Their success is leading toward a new world economy based on knowledge and advanced technology.

Within weeks, a quite different meeting of equal size and importance convened—this one in a crowded suburban hotel conference room on the East Coast of the United States. Many of the same chief executives listened to presidents of American universities and other institutions of higher education confirm a shared concern: that the shortage of scientists and engineers, the lifeblood of high-tech companies, would get worse before it gets better. Many universities were operating well over capacity in engineering classrooms and laboratories, faculty salaries could not keep pace with competitive industry rates, and equipment in most engineering departments was sadly outdated. And in high schools and primary schools, a dismal picture of declining standards of education was producing children who for the first time

James W. Botkin is a coauthor of the Club of Rome report No Limits to Learning *and a principal in the Technology and Strategy Group, a book writing and research/consulting team based in Cambridge, Massachusetts. Dan Dimancescu is a consultant and writer on high-technology strategy and policy issues and is a principal in the Technology and Strategy Group. Ray Stata is founder and president of Analog Devices, Inc., a high-technology company in the Boston, Massachusetts, area. The authors wish to acknowledge the participation of John McClellan, who is completing his doctorate in future studies at the University of Massachusetts. This article is from the author's forthcoming book* Global Stakes: The Future of High Technology in America, *to be published this fall by Ballinger Press.*

were less well-educated than their parents. Not only were reading scores down, but math and science training was diminishing as teachers left their profession for better-paying jobs in industry.

America's high-technology industry is a rising star in an otherwise declining economy, but whether its future will be one of success or stagnation will depend on yet another challenge—international competition. While a number of once predominant industries like shipbuilding, steel, textiles, and now automobiles have succumbed to foreign competition, the United States still leads the world in computers, electronics, telecommunications, and other high-technology fields. But continued leadership is far from assured.

International competition and Reaganomics have caught the high-tech industry—and with it, the American economy—in a squeeze play. While Japan challenges our technological leadership, burgeoning defense programs soak up the engineering skills critical to continued American innovation. National economic policy is increasingly at odds with the needs of America's high-technology future. In the short run, misplaced investment priorities and the high cost of capital are discouraging high-risk investments in new technological development. In the longer run, a growing shortage of scientists and engineers and a neglect of our systems to educate them threaten to stunt the growth of high-technology companies. We seem to be spending more to sustain traditional, stagnating industries than to encourage new emerging industries that are key to future economic power and social well-being.

An old-fashioned, home-spun national economic policy could not have come at a worse time. Sophisticated global competition is intensifying in the high-tech sector as Japanese and European companies scramble to close the technology gap. Foreign governments, especially in Japan and France, are becoming active partners in subsidizing their export industries. Their well-crafted national policies leave no room for doubt. Our competitors see that the stakes of the game are global and that the future of high technology hangs in the balance.

Much of the U.S. competitive strength in high technology happened almost inadvertently. It did not emerge from a consciously formulated national plan, as it has in Japan and France. Following World War II, America undertook a vast program to build a technically sophisticated national defense system. At the same time, the G.I. Bill provided generous subsidies for servicemen returning from the war to pursue higher education. Later, in reaction to Sputnik, America launched a buildup of technical education and resources to lead the world in the exploration of space. All these programs, along with the massive infusion of technical talent from Europe before and during the war, combined to propel America on an unforeseen and revolutionary course of technological development. From this era of government-sponsored research and development emerged the computer, semiconductor, communication, and instrumentation products that today provide the most promising foundation for new economic growth for the rest of this century. By the year 2000, for example, the high-tech industry is expected to be second only to energy in its impact on the economy of America and indeed the world.

The United States, having achieved technological leadership and commercial success as an offshoot of these other objectives, has no game plan to sustain its momentum in high technology. We take our success for granted

306

without really appreciating the underpinnings that have supported our achievements and that will be required to maintain our leadership.

National economic policy in recent years has focused on capital formation as the key to increasing productivity, reducing inflation, balancing trade deficits, and ultimately improving our standard of living. This policy, embedded in the new tax laws, provides accelerated depreciation of capital investments, liberalized investment tax credits, and a new twist—"safe harbor leasing"— whereby losing companies can sell their investment tax benefits to profitable ones. On the face of it, incentives for capital investment seem like a good economic idea, and in some respects they are. But a close examination of the trade-offs as to where new investment is likely to be made leads to the conclusion that this policy reinforces capital-intensive "sunset" industries at the expense of knowledge-intensive "sunrise" industries. Even worse, this policy prolongs the life of dying companies and ignores the needs of growing firms. Scarce capital resources are dissipated, providing marginal returns to the national economy. Also, this policy reduces a source of government funds that could be used more wisely to repair a faltering but strategic resource critical to a knowledge-intensive era—a system of higher education on which our economic and national security will increasingly depend. In the context of tomorrow's economy, it makes economic sense to invest more in education than in steel.

The needs of fast-growing, knowledge-intensive, high-technology companies are significantly different from those of slower-growing, capital-intensive industries. Slower-growing companies generate most of their capital from internally generated profits. Thus, accelerated depreciation and investment tax credits are important for them. By contrast, fast-growing high-technology firms that are not so capital intensive look to the equity market for start-up and expansion capital. Moreover, their future growth is dependent on high-risk investments in research and development (R&D). Thus, a lower capital gains tax and R&D tax credits are more attractive than accelerated depreciation to high-technology companies.

While the present high cost of capital disproportionately discourages investments in high-tech development, the growth and vitality of America's new industry will be impaired more by a lack of human capital than financial capital. It is significant that the cost of capital is three times greater in the United States than in Japan; what is more significant is that the Japanese graduate three times more engineers than America on a per-capita basis and also more in absolute numbers despite a population half our size. Technical talent is the raw material that feeds the growth of the high-technology industry, and we have reason to be concerned about the adequacy of our supply. There is a serious shortage of engineers in America, which limits the breadth and depth of product and technology development we can undertake. Underlying this shortage is an underfunded and overstretched system of education.

Neither the strategic importance of education nor its close link to high technology is widely recognized and understood in America. Characterized by rising costs and falling test scores, our educational establishment has reached a low ebb in public opinion and governmental support, which is being drastically cut back. This is a "San Andreas fault" in government policy that creates a potential for disaster in Washington. A shifting economy and an unsupported system of education will create pressures throughout society. This fault in national policy is most visible in the recent phase-down of National Science Foundation support for engineering education at a time when demand for engineers outstrips supply by two to one. Somehow the nation has lost a strategic recognition of education that two decades ago was a national commitment.

Even more incongruous is the massive buildup of defense spending in the face of serious manpower shortages without a commitment to expand the pool of engineering resources as an integral part of the defense budget. Will the government's demand for scarce human resources crowd out private-sector needs in much the same way that government demand for financial capital has driven the cost of capital to crippling levels? In a sense, the United States is fighting for leadership on two fronts—militarily with the Russians and economically with the Japanese—but with the same troops, namely, our technical work force. It is far from clear which battle is more decisive to our national security.

The incongruities in national policy, particularly with regard to the role of education, can at least in part be explained by the fact that our society has failed to grasp the full significance of the transition that is now underway. We are moving from a capital-intensive, physical resource-based economy of the first half of this century to a knowledge-intensive, human resource-based economy of the last half. The formulas, policies, economic theories, and conventional wisdom that facilitated the earlier transition from an agrarian to an industrial society are no longer applicable to the transition now in progress from an industrial society to an information society.

It should come as no surprise that we cling to old ideas and values long past the time when evidence clearly calls for change. Research on changing patterns of history has shown that societal forces tend to reinforce the status quo and even to condemn as heretical new facts and ideas about the world and how it functions. The persecution of Galileo and the demands that he recant his discoveries and theories serve as a constant reminder that our well-established, well-intentioned, and best-educated contemporaries can be dead wrong about what makes for a better world.

Thomas Kuhn in his seminal work, *The Structure of Scientific Revolutions*, carefully analyzed and documented the dynamics of change that involve significant transitions of ideas and values. His study focused on changes in the physical sciences; later authors extended these same concepts to political, religious, social, and economic patterns of change as well. In the history of science, supposedly the most factual and objective of all human endeavor, Kuhn points out that established views of how the world works prevail long after new discoveries have rendered past theories obsolete. For example, Einstein's theory of relativity and of quantum mechanics revolutionized Newton's mechanistic perspective of the world. Yet at that critical juncture from old to new, nearly all the experiments, scientific work, and research policies continued to be based on the validity of Newtonian laws long after the time when these efforts could yield useful results. Today we are at a similar crossroads of economic and social history, insisting on using old theories when we already know what works better.

From another perspective, Jay Forrester, an MIT professor who is building a national economic model based on engineering feedback theory, notes that economic vitality waxes and wanes in 50-year cycles—the so-called Kondratieff long wave. He explains this long-term business cycle by changes in the underlying technological base of the economy and by the tendency toward the end of a 50-year cycle to overaccumulate capital stock in old technologies, which are subsequently rendered obsolete by developments in new technologies.

The United States is now experiencing a basic change in technological dependencies from steel- and energy-based products such as cars to knowledge-based products such as computers. Whether or not the Kondratieff wave presages further economic malaise for the mid and late '80s, Forrester makes a significant point that there are long lags between the time when capital investments are made and when the results and payback from the investment can be measured. During periods of transition, this can lead to an "overshoot" of investment in old technology, which then produces a drag on the economy until these marginal investments are written off.

When juxtaposed with the observations of Kuhn and others that societies tend to continue their most recent behavior pattern regardless of evidence to the contrary, Forrester's theory takes on added meaning. What about the wisdom of tax policy that retains large amounts of the nation's investment resources in corporations whose technologies are obsolete and whose markets are dying? It makes one wonder why the Chrysler Corporation gets $1 billion in public financing and new high-technology firms are left to compete for overpriced capital on the open market. It raises the question of whether a billion-dollar investment in a North Sea oil platform will ever be recovered when the search for alternative energy sources is so pressing. In other words, incentives for capital investments can in fact amplify and prolong the stagflation they are intended to cure.

Robert Hayes, a professor at the Harvard Business School, also challenges today's conventional wisdom. The usual reasons given for declining productivity in the United States, he says, do not hold up under close scrutiny. Such impediments as insufficient capital formation, high energy costs, labor problems, and government red tape may contribute much to our problem but little to our thinking about its solution. He observes, for example, that France and Germany have these same problems and then some; yet their rate of productivity growth has been significantly higher than ours.

Hayes concludes that meaningful strides in productivity do not come so much from incremental investments to improve existing products and manufacturing processes as from investments that create products and markets based on substantially new and different technologies. What is wrong, Hayes argues, is the preoccupation by American management with short-term incremental investments in existing businesses to the detriment of long-term investments in new technology and market development. By this reasoning, it is technological innovation more than capital formation that will solve our productivity problems. And innovation comes from investments in people as well as investments in machinery.

From many perspectives, it can be argued that more of the same is not what is needed. The decade of the 1980s promises to be a time of fundamental change. The longer we resist and prolong the transition, the more radical and painful the adjustment will be to a new economy. To those in high-tech industry, the transition has already taken place; it is a fact of life. But among the wider public and most decision-makers, the realities of a new era have not yet been fully understood or accepted. This is why U.S. national economic policy remains only marginally relevant to the most promising segment of a new American economy and why our educational institutions are slow to respond to the needs of a knowledge-intensive society.

The fact that high-technology products embody an unprecedented amount of human knowledge and technically sophisticated labor will change the equations by which national priorities are calculated. Whereas American wealth and power have traditionally been based on natural resources and on capital investment in physical plant and machinery, the balance is now tipping toward investments in people and knowledge as key resources. This is not to deny the continued importance of natural resources and the need to conserve nonrenewable ones more wisely. Nor is it to repudiate the role of capital and the need to control inflation more vigorously. But once the concept is fully grasped that knowledge should be seen as a strategic resource with an importance equal to or exceeding natural resources and physical investments, then a chain of propositions follows that will change the way national priorities and strategies are set in America. The most important among these propositions concerns education, and the strategic long-term need to resupport and reorient the American system of education.

The Serpent in the Garden

by

Howard F. Didsbury, Jr.

The telecommunications revolution now taking place in the United States is being welcomed enthusiastically. Many see in this revolution the realization of a technological paradise—comfort, ease, and convenience for all—resulting from the wizardry of innovative telecommunications.

But look more closely and one sees a serpent lurking in this paradise! This serpent may be taken as a symbol of unanticipated effects of these much-heralded innovations. Let us note briefly some of them.

A dramatic increase in the number of TV and cable channels will undoubtedly contribute to an acceleration of the ideological fragmentation of American society. In essence, this means a rapid, increasing loss of commonly shared assumptions, values, and attitudes throughout the nation. In the past, in a real and subtle sense, mass audiences—divided as they have been among a comparatively small number of carriers, each stressing, for all practical purposes, similar, if not identical, assumptions, values, and attitudes—have been a way of sustaining a common plane of discourse and generally shared values. For example, the similarity of network news broadcasts and telecasts, the career models and aspirations of material success in TV soap operas, and the propagation of a certain life-style and cultural tone (note the virtual absence of all save Anglo-Saxon names and life-styles, etc.) are obvious instances of mass electronic indoctrination to a certain limited range of values. Viewing much of TV, one would be led to believe that there are only four careers in contemporary America: medicine, law, advertising, and journalism.

Having a limited number of media outlets—all conveying essentially the same message in varied settings—has served an important social function. They have been an effective means of public indoctrination into a similar view of life. As "general education" courses in colleges and universities were originally designed to develop an appreciation for the achievements and values of Western civilization in students and provide them with a common cultural frame of reference, so, in a sense, telecommunications media, when few in number, have served as a kind of electronic "general education" in values and attitudes for the average person. This particular media structure

Howard F. Didsbury, Jr., is professor of history and executive director, Program for the Study of the Future, Kean College of New Jersey, Union, New Jersey. He is also director of media projects for the World Future Society.

may have contributed greatly to the creation of the psychology of the consumer society.

Confronted with the current telecommunications revolution, one cannot help but wonder how common values and attitudes will be nurtured and sustained throughout the nation. Few, indeed, would argue that the educational establishment can compete with the pervasiveness and impact of the telecommunications media. Furthermore, there is little to suggest the educational establishment is capable of the necessary radical restructuring needed to meet this challenge.

Another undesirable effect of the advent of a multiplicity of carriers may be the increasing proliferation of "special interests" and their power. One consequence of this will be a diminished concern for "the public interest" understood as the general common good devoid of narrow partisanship or ideological demands. Also, there may be a marked increase in the growth of religious intolerance and/or political extremism. A mushrooming of "special hates" and fanatical causes hardly bodes well for communal harmony.

In a worst-case scenario, one could imagine parochial, racial, national, or cultural groups, each with its own "network," ultimately developing into antagonistic "separatist movements." In this scenario, such groups might end up demanding political autonomy along with linguistic and cultural autonomy. This would pose a serious challenge to the concept of "One Nation Indivisible." Indeed, it would be ironic if the communications revolution were to succeed where the Civil War failed—in the breakup of the Union! Social fragmentation and political separation are dangers not to be treated lightly.

Turning from the national to the personal level, let us examine some effects of the telecommunications revolution on the individual. These may make his life more pleasant and also easier. However, these may also in fact heighten the individual's sense of personal "isolation" from other human beings. Much of the enthusiasm surrounding the telecommunications revolution tends to ignore a marked tendency today to have "things"—gadgets and machines—replace human beings and human contact in people's lives. There is much wisdom in a perennially popular song that contains the observation that "people need people." This sentiment can be ignored, but at great peril to the human psyche. One cannot help but wonder what role TV has had in the death of conversation. Surely, there is widespread daily evidence of a growing inarticulateness among people of all classes in society from the State Department to the local shopping center. The Orwellian age of "Newspeak" has long since arrived. With these and other unfortunate developments before us, we must have some serious doubts about the roles of telecommunications as "companion" and "teacher." In sum, the new media may not only increase the individual's isolation and passivity but now ensnare him in compulsive interaction with new, more sophisticated electronic gadgets. It would be sad indeed if people became more "at home" with gadgets than with people.

Insofar as the current revolution may serve to augment the artificial technological environment in which humans live, the effects may be grave. In such an environment, the human being vicariously experiences life more and more removed from the real world. The long-range detrimental effects of such an existence may be profound. The short-range consequences may be clear before us. It is conceivable that one of the causes of growing crime and violence in a highly developed society stems from the stresses and strains of its sheer artificiality, its foreignness to living as a human being in some communion with nature. Like Antaeus of Greek mythology, who was invulnerable while his feet touched the earth, human beings may need to draw refreshment and strength from the actual experience of nature's realm. What roles will the new telecommunications media play in all of this? Will the vicarious enjoyment of living be further enhanced electronically? Will "appearance" be substituted more and more for "reality" ("for the real thing")?

The modern mania for substitution—machines for muscle, computers for minds, drugs for sensations—may ultimately find a substitute for being human.

These questions may come close to dissolving into the mists of philosophical and metaphysical speculation. Let us return to the practical.

The potentialities of the telecommunications revolution are greeted ecstatically by its egalitarian admirers. They are fascinated by its prospects for genuine democracy. There will be "instantaneous electronic plebiscites," we are informed. These will be held on political, social, and economic issues confronting American society. The electronic plebiscite, we are advised, restores genuine democracy. It provides an opportunity for all to participate actively in the political process and dispels, once and for all, feelings of alienation and political impotence. From this perspective, adjectives fail to describe adequately the many wonderful results that will follow the arrival of popular instantaneous plebiscites. And that may be. Nevertheless, there are some good reasons for having second, less sanguine, thoughts about the whole prospect. For one thing, as everyone knows, there are fads and fashions in ideas (economic, social, and political) as there are in clothes. They come and go with notable swiftness. In the realm of style, no harm results from this; in matters of statecraft and society, the results could be calamitous. Popular fickleness on issues is demonstrated repeatedly by the results of consecutive polls. What is a burning issue one instant becomes a dead issue a short time later.

Secondly, there are the dangers that arise from ignorance, hysteria, and passion—not to mention problems created by the oversimplification of difficult, complicated issues. Electronic plebiscites would create a field day for the politician with the catchy slogan and the easy, simple solution. It is chilling to think that one's freedom or survival might hang upon the electronic whim of his neighbor—a neighbor who might be a passionate ignoramus, a religious fanatic, or a well-meaning, completely uninformed person. Who would rest secure a single night in such a society?

The new telecommunications media may have equally undesirable effects on the social structure. It seems reasonable to suppose that this revolution, like all revolutions, will create its own new class structure—with all the attendant privileges and antagonisms associated with such a change. In this case, one can discern at least two classes, each of which has very unequal prospects in this new telecommunications society (or, as it is now increasingly designated, "the information society"). On the one hand, there are the "information-rich"; on the other, the "information-poor."

313

The "information-rich" are those who have access to abundant sources of information, the technical means of processing and utilizing the information, and the requisite intellectual acuity to capitalize on its possession. For them, no doubt, there will be stimulating careers and much power. The "information-poor," however, may have dull and routine work—unless it is considered wasteful and inefficient to permit them even this. Conceivably, they might have a definite, special, and important "service role" in this new society. They could constitute a new servile class whose major function would be to make life more pleasant and convenient for their "information" betters.

In this new social order, there is another important role they might play—the role of a perpetual "audience" that must be busied, distracted, and entertained. Meeting these voracious audience needs will be one of the great challenges facing the "information-rich." It will be they who have their ingenuity taxed in providing escapism. They will have to create a kaleidoscope of vicarious pleasures—some harmless, some educational, some inspirational, some violent and sexual—for this massive, potentially dangerous audience. It should be noted that nothing prevents the "information-poor" from fulfilling both of these latter roles at the same time. Here we have a faint outline of the "finely tuned" manipulated society.

These brief notes on some of the negative effects of the telecommunications revolution suggest that the Golden Age that many envision may not be as golden as we are led to believe. This being the case, prudence dictates that thoughtful, concerned citizens strive to anticipate undesirable effects of this revolution without delay. They should seek to formulate policies to prevent or, at the very least, alleviate the inhumane effects of this revolution. They should make sure that the benefits as well as the costs associated with telecommunications innovations are equitably shared throughout the society. Informed action may achieve some good; inaction assures mischief.

The MacBride Commission Report: Issues and Process in Global Communications

by

William G. Harley

At the 19th UNESCO General Conference, at Nairobi, in 1976, the U.S. concluded its participation in the Culture and Communications sector by proposing that the Director-General appoint a special commission (following the pattern of the Faure Commission on education) to study thoroughly international communications issues, including those that, as the strident debate on the Declaration on Media demonstrated, had divided the member states. This suggestion was duly noted in the Conference report and subsequently adopted by the Director-General as his own.

Late in 1977, he appointed an International Commission for the Study of Communication Problems, commonly known as the MacBride Commission, after its chairman, Sean MacBride, of Ireland.

The Commission was asked "to undertake a review of all of the problems of communication in contemporary society against a background of technological progress and recent developments in international relations with due regard to their complexity and magnitude." It held eight sessions spread over two years and five countries and in this connection organized round-table discussions on topics of particular relevance to its work. Some 100 papers on various aspects of communication were prepared by specialists from around the world. In addition, the Commission received a wide range of comments, research, and documentation contributed by organizations, institutions, and individuals.

The Commission also had the benefit of comments—including those of governments—on its 1978 Interim Report. It completed its work on November 30, 1979, although its Final Report, including a Preface by the Director General, was distributed to UNESCO member states only in August 1980.

Structure of the Report

The MacBride Report attempts to be a comprehensive set of statements about communications issues. Part I analyzes communications in its histori-

William G. Harley is communications consultant to the United States National Commission for UNESCO. This paper is drawn from a much more detailed presentation prepared as a briefing document for members of the U.S. Department of State.

cal, contemporary, and international dimensions. Part II is concerned primarily with the structure, patterns, and means of communications, together with the "disparities" among countries. Part III analyzes communication flows and the problems of imbalance and possible solutions. Part IV is devoted to communications policies and the role of professional communicators. Part V consists of Section A, with four general "Conclusions and Recommendations," and Section B, "Issues Requiring Further Study."

Section B is not properly a part of the report at all, but simply 12 suggestions added by individual Commission members, that had not been approved by the Commission; several were not, in fact, even discussed. Even so, due to this structuring, Section B is now being mistakenly treated by critics as a formal and integral part of the Commission's report.

Though an effort has clearly been made to be equitable in setting forth the range of views on the issues covered, there are some subjects, from a Western perspective, that are treated with something less than impartiality.

Indictment of Western Media

There are implications that Western domination of the international news flows causes a disequilibrium in world communication that prohibits developing nations' participation, promotes neocolonialism, disrupts national cultures, and fosters "transnationalization" of information. The free flow of ideas—branded as really a one-way flow—is seen as a veil for commercial penetration and perpetuation of the West's dominant position. Furthermore, the Western international news agencies are criticized for being insensitive to the needs and concerns of the Third World.

Western authorities do not dispute the reality of the imbalance in flows of news and information between the industrialized and developing countries. Disagreement arises on the reasons for imbalances and the remedies to be applied. These are the central issues in contention.

In some respects, the report appears to be trying to convert a doctrine of free-flow—and the diversity that implies—into one of an unspecified balance by spelling out a series of reforms in the world communications system. Western news professionals and policy-makers, while recognizing the need for remedying the more conspicuous imbalances, reject the notion that this should be done by imposing international restraints and restrictions upon the communications activities of the industrialized countries—the apparent target for these reforms. Nor can it be done by unconditional sharing of Western information resources.

From a Western viewpoint, the correct approach is to strengthen the communication capacities of the developing countries. Indeed, the report calls for national efforts at greater self-reliance, building appropriate infrastructures and national news agencies, and establishing national and regional production centers.

One particular implication requires special attention: the suggestion that reporters and news editors tend to be guilty of narrow ethnocentric thinking in reporting of foreign news and that press and broadcasters in the modernized world are not alloting sufficient space and time to foreign news, especially news from developing countries.

The underlying question here is over the definition of news. Clearly in any

316

society news values are inseparable from national values, and editorial judgments will be made on the basis of the interests of subscribers and listeners.

Western media executives agree that they are not doing as good a job of Third World press coverage as they would like—particularly on development news; on the other hand, some recent research seems to contravene the charge that the Western-controlled media report only "bad news." In fact, some of it shows that Western-controlled media carry a higher proportion of foreign news than the media in Third World countries carry about their developing neighbors.

Transnational Corporations

The tendency to view critically the role of private commercial institutions is especially evident in the report's attitude toward transnational corporations (TNCs), whose practices are seemingly regarded as having only negative consequences.

Two recommendations in the report, calling for information disclosure by transnational corporations and legal measures to circumscribe their actions, presuppose negative TNC behavior without admitting any positive benefits of their activities.

The U.S. does not disagree that monopoly situations warrant careful scrutiny; however, this examination should be made on a case-by-case basis, for in certain instances there is evidence to prove that monopolistic arrangements best maximize economies of scale and scope, and thus serve the public interest with low costs.

The need for case-by-case analysis is also relevant to the critical comments in the report regarding media concentration. The free-marketplace, pro-competition position is supported by several U.S. laws; and the FCC has long limited cross-ownership and multiple-media ownership in given localities. Thus the U.S. has traditionally opposed concentration in the media, and cannot quarrel with the report so long as it merely urges "special attention" and "critical review" of this matter, and proposes that the process of concentration and the action of transnationals be circumscribed only at the national level.

Advertising

Advertising is singled out both as a pernicious influence and as a target for taxation. Although the text of the report acknowledges that advertising undoubtedly has positive features (fostering, for instance, economic health and independence), its primary purpose is "selling goods and services so that it tends to promote attitudes and life-styles which extol acquisition and consumption at the expense of other values."

The U.S. is clearly opposed to deceptive or unfair advertising (see FTC regulations), but feels that any regulation of the industry must be done at the national level; and, while recognizing that further research by advertisers is needed on the effects of advertising in LDCs, it believes that the net impact of advertising can be beneficial (i.e., informing consumers of available products, stimulating industry responsiveness to consumer needs, enabling distant buyers and sellers to reach one another, and providing essential revenues for media).

317

An international tax on commercial advertising, suggested as a possibility, is clearly discriminatory, for there is no rational basis for taxing advertising as opposed to other goods and services.

Private Commercial Media

The most obvious of the anti-Western attitudes is contained in recommendation 31. It calls for giving preference "in expanding communication systems to noncommercial forms of mass communications." This embodies the presumption that commercial media are bad *per se*. The U.S., of course, has recognized that commercialization has some negative effects on the quality of mass media; in fact, this is why it has supported the introduction of public broadcasting as a partial balancing factor to the mass audience appeal of commercial broadcasting. But again the U.S. is at once opposed to commercial domination and in favor of diversity and competition as safeguards of the public interest. Here again this is a national issue—to be decided democratically by the people (not imposed by the government) of each country. The choice and form of national media institutions are not the proper concern of international bodies.

Stating that noncommercial forms of mass communication are preferable appears to endorse the "noncommercial" system of the socialist states without also balancing this by pointing out that this system has led to the establishment of a press whose primary aim is to support the objectives of the governmental regimes.

International Communications Center

One of the most controversial issues the Commissioners debated concerned the recommendation that UNESCO might undertake establishing an International Center for the Study and Planning of Information and Communication. But the controversy has since been overtaken by events. At the UNESCO intergovernmental conference convened last April to discuss this matter, the U.S. joined in the consensus agreeing to establish a new international mechanism, within UNESCO but working with other UN agencies, that would coordinate communication development assistance internationally. The idea for such a coordinating mechanism was originally introduced by the U.S. at the 20th General Conference. Although the original proposal has undergone several changes, it is hoped that it will increase the effectiveness and efficiency of bilateral and multilateral assistance programs in this field.

Correcting Imbalance

In addition to calling for increased regulation of transnational corporations, advertising, and commercial practices, the report introduces the dangerous notion that journalists' behavior should be judged by the *effects* of their reporting. Thus, according to that view, if they are to behave responsibly, they would have to determine whether or not their reporting would foster peace, promote international understanding, enhance national identity, etc. In the U.S. view, *pursuit of truth*—wherever it may lead—is the *duty of the journalist*.

A constant preoccupation of the report is with the relationship between power and communications. Communication is identified as a critical source of power and influence within the global system that creates relationships of domination and dependency, cultural imperialism, and political disruption.

There are implications that transnational corporations (including global wire services, though they are not singled out) exert and abuse vast influence, and therefore need to be held accountable and possibly taxed and circumscribed by "effective legal action."

Not only does the exercise of such communication "power" carry with it responsibility; but there is also the implication that the concentration of too much power is *per se* not good for the world; and consequently, there should be a sharing of this "power" among the developing countries—one way of reducing the information imbalance.

How the sharing of communication "power" is to be achieved is not clear, though there are recommendations that suggest directions it might take (e.g., "the electro-magnetic spectrum and geostationary orbit should be shared as the common property of mankind"; "reform of existing patent laws and conventions"; "mechanics [should be established] for sharing information of a nonstrategic nature . . . particularly in economic matters"; and "exchanges of technical information on the principle that all countries have equal rights to full access to available information").

The U.S. position is that the "common property of mankind" is not a concept of legal property rights shared in common, but a general term applied to depletable natural resources in areas outside national jurisdiction. The U.S. is committed to the concept that outer space, including the geostationary orbit, is not subject to national appropriation by claim of sovereignty or otherwise and that all are to share in the benefits of space communication.

As for existing patent laws and conventions, the U.S. has already acceded to several international conventions relating to protection of property and copyright, so it is not opposed in principle to international measures in this field; however, the international acquisition and distribution of technical and cultural materials that are subject to proprietary rights must take into account the valid remuneration of the authors and publishers of such materials.

The U.S. supports the principle of an international free flow of information; however, given the vital significance of economic and business, scientific, and technical data, it recognizes that the proprietary rights in information must be balanced against full free-flow principles.

Communications for Development

Another theme flowing from the basic premise that communications must be considered in a social context is the insistence that media should be used to further economic and cultural development.

The report brings out the need of developing countries to evolve national communication models of their own in which the media can be used as essential catalysts in nation-building. Contrary to the Western concept of journalism's role, the media should mobilize society behind the government program in the course of development, national unity, and cultural identity. This not only involves a search for forms of development that reflect indigenous needs and traditions, but also links national communication policies to "overall social, cultural, economic, and political goals."

319

The Commission does warn, however, of the danger of state-developed policies leading to state controls.

Conclusions

The MacBride Report did not provide the definitive statement on the New World Information Order (NWIO), though some expected such a proclamation. What the Commission did do was to state that the NWIO was an "ongoing *process* of successive changes in the nature of relations between and within nations in the field of communications."

In fact, perhaps the major benefit of the MacBride Commission's work, from the Western perspective, may be the modifying effect it had through the recognition it makes of the NWIO as a *process*. Chairman MacBride, in his preface, specifically calls the NWIO a *process* whose goals are: "more justice, more equity, more reciprocity in information exchange, less dependence in communication flows, less downward diffusion of messages, more self-reliance and cultural identity, more benefits for all mankind."

The U.S. has no quarrel with the concept of the NWIO conceived in terms of these goals. The question is how they are to be achieved. The use of the word *process*—an evolving, step-by-step patient procedure to remedy acknowledged imperfections in the existing system—provides an opportunity to move the discussion from the abstract to the concrete, so as to focus on practical ways to work cooperatively to help all nations to participate to the fullest extent possible in the production and dissemination of information.

The MacBride Commission report demonstrates that rationality and realism can be brought to bear on the highly sensitive communication issues. Given the diverse political and philosophical perspectives of the Commissioners, a remarkable degree of agreement was achieved during the two years of their discussions. Although certain positions continue to be irreconcilable, the Commissioners were able to find common ground for practical action in several areas, and to agree that there are legitimate concerns and communication deficiencies that require some far-reaching changes. To a considerable degree, the Commission succeeded in reflecting the strong differences in world opinion and the diversity of cultures and practices but still managed to produce findings that may have practical value in terms of encouraging effective international cooperation.

The report emphasizes the need for a global view of communications and the need to understand how national and international aspects are so interrelated that they must be considered together if policies are to be effective.

Actually, this voluminous report is so encyclopedic that every nation can find in its pages support for its own views. The Soviets will find some support for their positions on advertising, commercialization, and private enterprise (though they will be displeased with the recommendations on access and censorship); in general, Third World countries will find comfort in the recognition of their concerns and of the need to reduce and eventually eliminate existing communication gaps—though not all will find the report so fully responsive to their interests as they had hoped. The U.S., despite the presence of what it considers lack of balance in treating the activities of private enterprise, feels that, in view of its minority voice on the Commission, values of importance to U.S. communications professionals were well preserved.

The test of the report, of course, is not in this or other similar critiques. That test will be whether groups everywhere are stimulated to take actions that are of practical value in all forms of communications at local and national levels and in promoting effective international cooperation.

The Medium Is the Madness: Television and the Pseudo-Oral Tradition in America's Future

by

Tony M. Lentz

In the sixties, Daniel Boorstin developed in painful detail the characteristics of an American society obsessed with *The Image*. Celebrities became known, not for anything they actually did or for any skill they possessed, but because they were seen on television celebrity shows. *Reader's Digest,* a magazine ostensibly created to summarize articles from other journals, actually planted most of the articles it published in other journals so that there would be enough "appropriate" stories to digest. "News" conferences were called to create the image of a newsworthy event, when in actuality the speakers presented well-worn arguments: nothing "new" happened at all.

This trend from the recent past seems to be continuing into the eighties and beyond. Film, for example, has become an exercise in the ability of technology to present a flashy image. As film critic Vincent Canby wrote recently:

> There is no dearth of filmmaking talent, young and old, but the economic circumstances of our era are directing these talents toward an increasingly parochial kind of movie, the kind that has the effect of being about nothing more than filmmaking itself, or to put it another way, about what the filmmaker can do with his advanced technology.

The rush of films such as *Star Wars, Raiders of the Lost Ark, Superman,* and *Blow Out* indicates that flashy technological imagery is an integral and growing part of the formula for financial success in filmmaking.

Novelist John Gardner, meanwhile, has created a furor over "commercialism and immorality" in modern fiction, attacking works that present glittering but outrageously shallow images of the world. I find it difficult to argue with his position when I read works like John Irving's *The World According to Garp,* in which the "climax" of the work's dramatic structure is a scene that strains all pretense to probability or taste. The hero-husband acciden-

---

Tony M. Lentz is assistant professor, Department of Speech Communications, The Pennsylvania State University, University Park, Pennsylvania.

tally slides his car into the rear of his wife's lover's car while she is having oral sex with said lover, with the result that she bites off a particularly male portion of his anatomy with her teeth. Whatever one's evaluative reaction to the entire work, much of its success seems to rest on arresting violent or humorous imagery unrelated to the real world, a sort of visual hyperbole.

A partial explanation of this fascination is suggested by controversial studies of the influence of media in America. In one experiment, children were attached to an electroencephalogram that measured their brain waves while they watched television. The hookup was arranged so that the television would remain on as long as the child maintained an active brain pattern. The set was turned off if the child slipped into an alpha wave brain pattern associated with light sleep, meditation, or unfocused daydreaming. Out of 40 children, not one kept the set on for more than 30 seconds. The images from the television were apparently streaming into the child's brain with little or no critical thought. Indeed, as McLuhan said, the medium appears to be a message.

Lane Jennings noted the importance of the media as an influence on the English language in the June 1981 issue of *The Futurist*, and suggested that the growth of literacy was related to a decline in the status of spoken language. "Decreased emphasis on teaching children such skills as careful listening, persuasive rhetoric, entertaining conversation, and even story-telling," he wrote, "may have made reading and writing appear more necessary to education than they really are. But without some special effort to teach better speaking and listening, the average citizen of the future may be an 'oral illiterate.'"

This statement is certainly threatening to those of us in the field of speech communications, but it is particularly unnerving at a time when the young people we teach appear to be losing their writing skills as well. How is it possible that modern children could lose both their ability to speak *and* their ability to write? Can it be that we are witnessing a decline in *both* oral *and* written traditions at the same time?

A possible explanation for this contradictory situation is suggested by the gradual change in ancient Greece from an oral to a written culture. The relationship between writing and speaking in Greece can be compared to the relationship between television, writing, and speaking, offering a sobering explanation for both the current wave of fascination with the image and a vision of our future as a society of potential "oral illiterates." Plato's theory of writing and the Greek attitude toward writing in ancient society present a picture of communications technology (writing) and the nature of human knowledge that may help explain "why Johnny can't read" and "why Johnny can't speak" today. They also suggest a few of the dangers that face our Western heritage in the pseudo-oral tradition of the future.

The pre-literate oral traditions of the ancient past were far from "oral illiteracy." We tend to think of the society and its use of language as being a little simpler than that which followed the introduction of writing as composition, but scholars are discovering that oral literature is anything but simple, as Eric Havelock notes in his new book *The Literate Revolution in Greece and Its Cultural Consequences*. The great poems of Homer are highly complex, the ancient Minoan and Mycenaean civilizations were extensive and powerful, and the ancient educational system apparently made efficient memories a common goal for every student. As late as the time of Plato, for example, eight of his dialogues have a dramatic frame in which men meet in the street. One says, "I heard you were there the other day when Socrates and Protagoras were talking," and the other replies, "Yes, I was there; it was an interesting discussion." The first then asks his companion what was said, and the second man then *recites the entire dialogue,* apparently from memory. Memories that could control that kind of detail were a sure guarantee against "oral illiteracy." The stress on memory and public speaking in schools was a reflection of the ancient Greek's idea of knowledge.

Before writing and the alphabet combined to create a written tradition of composition (as opposed to lists and record-keeping), knowledge and literature were thought to exist in the mind and inspiration of a person. One story that illustrates the idea is told about the poet Philoxenus. He was walking along one day past a group of brickmakers, who were apparently mixing clay and straw to make mudbrick to be dried in the sun. The men were singing a song composed by Philoxenus, and they were doing a clumsy job of singing. Outraged, the poet marched over to the brickmakers and jumped up and down on the wet bricks, crushing them to worthless clods and mud. "As you utterly destroy things of mine," Philoxenus raged, "so I utterly destroy things of yours." The poet in this story was the source of accurate information about his song; he composed the words and the vocal pattern, and he was considered the ultimate judge of its performance.

Plato applies the principle to knowledge in general in the *Phaedrus.* Our knowledge of the world around us, he said, is found in the mind of a person who knows something about it. For knowledge of architecture, we must look to the mind of the architect who has taken his experience of building and shaped it into an understanding of his art. The same is true with all arts or crafts; the few glimpses we imperfect humans get of the way things really are must come from those of us with knowledge about the subject. The great problem this presents is that we're constantly distracted by our imperfections. Just when we're about to get an idea, we have to go to the bathroom, or we get hungry, or a pretty girl walks by and raises our blood pressure. Worse, we become over-impressed with ourselves, and when we're successful as lawyers we decide we're smart enough to tell doctors how to do their jobs as well. We decide that expertise in one field makes us the source of true knowledge about everything else in the world.

The only way to counteract this conflict between ego, bodily functions, and the truth, Plato decided, was to sit down with the expert in dialectic combat, to fight it out "through talk." Talk to the supposed expert, ask him tough questions, and see if he really understands how things work. This is the way in which Socrates got into such trouble with the Athenians: He spent his life talking to people to prove to them that they didn't know as much as they thought they did about the world. If we assume that he carried on this activity for most of his life, it isn't too difficult to understand how they got an overwhelming vote by a jury to condemn him. Telling people that they aren't as bright as they think they are is no way to win popularity contests.

True knowledge, at any rate, was something in the mind of a wise man who could answer tough questions about his ideas. The spoken word was the symbol for the thoughts in the man's mind, and through question and answer we can determine if he really knows as much as he thinks he does. Notice the importance of memory in this view of knowledge; the wise man has to remember the glimpses of truth that he has between trips to the bathroom if he's to share them with the rest of the world. As we compare present experiences with past glimpses of truth, we must rely on our memory to remind us of the things we already know, making new ideas possible.

This position makes sense in light of our modern understanding of language and communication. To put Plato's conception in a modern context, let's take the example of a modern candidate for president. John Q. Publican wants to become leader of our nation, and he tells us that he knows how to solve the energy problem, defend the national security, and make America great again. According to Plato, the way to test the man's wisdom is to sit down with him and ask him questions, face-to-face. "How are you going to reduce inflation?" you ask him, and you observe his physical behavior, the details of his intonation pattern, and follow his argument step-by-step to determine if his plan really makes sense.

Modern research shows us that this one-on-one situation gives us a lot of information. Physically we tell each other if we're tense or relaxed, interested in each other sexually, or confident in what we have to say. If our candidate doesn't look us in the eye, for example, we would suspect his honesty. The variations of meaning in physical "body language" are almost infinite. Scientists tell us that there are over 20,000 facial expressions possible. These gestures and those of the rest of the body give us a tremendous amount of information about the words being said.

The candidate's voice also gives us a great deal of information. Linguists have analyzed a very complicated system of variables in American English, including changes in pitch level, pauses, loudness, stress, and voice qualities. Our candidate for president, for example, could say "I'm a Communist" with an exaggerated intonation and a twinkle in his eye, and we'd laugh at his joke. If he used a calm intonation, nervous voice qualities, and a serious look, we'd think he truly was a Communist. If he was uncertain of the things he was saying, we'd note the anxious qualities in his voice as he explained his economic policies. If we calculated all the possible permutations of his intonation, the speaker would be able to say "I'm a Communist" over 10,000 different ways, each with a different shade of meaning. And the one-on-one situation would make it difficult for him to "fake" his responses if the questioning was tough. If he was too polished in voice, with the overstressed and overloud volume of the television announcer, and if his physical movement was graceful to the point of being artificial, we'd suspect him of being phony.

Spoken language in a face-to-face context, then, is the most accurate method of testing the truth of our knowledge of the world, according to Plato, since the spoken word is the symbol for the thought in our minds. As we have seen, the face-to-face situation also gives us a great deal of information about what is being said. The difficulty with writing, as he saw the new technology, was that it presented the polished appearance of knowledge without the reality of the author's intention behind it. In terms of our example, if we receive a newsletter from John Q. Publican's campaign, we get much less information about the man's actual intentions, and about his knowledge regarding the topics discussed in the newsletter. We wouldn't be able to see his face, and we couldn't hear his voice. We apparently make up an intonation pattern for his words as we read, taking a guess as to the precise vocal and physical behavior he intended if he were to speak to us in person. But the message is much less exact already. Worse yet, we can't ask him questions about his intentions, or check his facts to find out where he got the figures. We don't, in literal terms, have access to the knowledge in the mind of the writer. The written style may be elaborate and impressive, the words may sound nice in our "inner ear" as we imagine the author's "tone," but *we* provided much of the information from our own imaginations.

Wait a minute, one might object. How is this possible? Haven't we communicated accurate information about the world in writing for, lo, these many centuries? Surely writing can communicate something about our knowledge of the world? This is certainly true in several ways. Words that refer directly to our senses are one example. The smell of a skunk is an unforgettable experience, and if you mention "skunk smell" in writing, the reader can clearly reconstruct the impact of that sensory experience in his memory. We can also communicate precisely about blue sky, the texture of sandpaper, and other sensory experiences that we all have had. Written language also makes permanent the complexes of meaning that we build into language as we get further and further away from the actual sensory experience that the words ultimately symbolize. The word "lion" is more abstract than brown, soft fur, sharp teeth, powerful legs, long claws, roar, and so on. If I write, however, that a certain boxer is a "lion" in the ring, we select those qualities of lion from our experience that could logically be associated with a boxer in a fight. Stylistic devices also allow for communication of meaning. If I write that "this is not the beginning of the end, but the end of the beginning," I have placed information in the written letters that tells you something about the order of the events I am discussing. In Plato's terms, however, you have less information about my intentions than you would if you sat in the same room with me and asked me questions about the way in which I meant that metaphor, or the experiences I associate with the words in my mind. I might intend the "lion" statement as a compliment, while you interpret it as an insult.

There is considerable conflict among literary critics today regarding this question of "interpretation" and the written word. E. D. Hirsch and P. D. Juhl, for example, hold that texts can be interpreted accurately according to the intentions of the author. Plato would answer that we must sit down with the author and ask him questions if we would know his intentions; the reader must normally determine for himself what he believes the author meant in each passage of the work.

Plato's mistrust of the accuracy of the written word is reflected in Athenian society, the law courts being the clearest example. Written evidence and statements from witnesses became an accepted part of legal procedure, but, as Isaeus tells us, written evidence had to have a group of credible witnesses to reassure the jury that the witness did, indeed, sign the statement in question. Forgeries were common, and witnesses apparently prone to simply deny they had said the things written down on a deposition. Those involved in litigation, then, collected a group of trustworthy men to witness the signing, and they spoke from their personal knowledge at the trial, assuring the jury that Alexandros did, indeed, make that statement. The ultimate measure of truth then became the credibility and spoken testimony of the living witnesses, men who knew from experience that the deposition was accurate as signed.

Written contracts also presented a serious problem. One poor Greek was so excited by the prospect of owning a handsome boy slave that he paid little attention when the contract was read aloud by the seller before it was signed. The reader apparently skipped over part of the "fine print" in the contract, and the buyer signed it without having a friend along as a credible witness to the proceedings. Later he discovered that the written word had left him responsible for any debts the slave owed anyone else; the pretty boy, it seems, had an expensive addiction to perfumes and ointments.

Many other cases turned upon interpretations of the law, as the litigants argued over the intentions of the written law. Other controversies were generated over written letters that were easy to forge, and over written wills. In most cases letters were sent by trusted messengers who could vouch for their authenticity. So while writing grew in importance to the society, the spoken word remained the ultimate authority as to the written word's veracity.

We find similar situations in today's society, situations in which the value of the potential information trapped in the written word is validated by the spoken word of a trusted individual, or "one who knows." When I was interviewed for my job at Penn State, for example, the search committee decided to invite me to the campus on the basis of the written record on my résumé. The purpose of the interview was to determine if I knew the things (in person) that my written record implied that I should. I delivered a paper orally (an important test in a speech department), but then I was asked a lot of difficult questions. The group was testing my knowledge in a face-to-face situation, attempting to determine if I knew as much as I thought I did.

Think of the other similar situations in your own experience. When a written contract between businesses is signed, doesn't the real negotiation take place in a face-to-face bargaining session? Each side has lawyers to protect the official interpretation of the written version of the agreement, but the negotiations take place orally and, if the deal is big enough, in a face-to-face situation. Isn't this why the "businessman's lunch" remains so important in our society, because we want to size up the person with whom we're doing business? If we're hiring someone to work for our office, don't we always want to talk to the individual to see if they're impressive in person? People may call it the "old boy network" when someone picks up the phone to ask a trusted source "what kind of person" this job applicant is, but in Plato's view it's only logical that we trust the living intelligence of a person who knows the applicant more thoroughly than the written record of his accomplishments.

When the point at issue affects our lives directly, we contact a trustworthy individual to interpret the written word in light of his knowledge of the subject. Who do you trust when the plumbing in the basement leaks? The library? The written ads in the newspaper? Or do you call a friend who does construction work to get him to recommend a trustworthy plumber? The odds are that you call someone you know who has had experience with local plumbers or contracters, and trust their judgment. Unless, of course, you've had personal experience with a good plumber, one who has demonstrated knowledge of his trade.

The danger that Plato saw in writing was that it could present the appearance of knowledge where there was none in actuality. The speechwriters of his day, for example, wrote words that sounded impressive, and the words were memorized by citizens who had to defend themselves in court. The jurors heard what may have sounded like an impressive rendition of the facts of the case, but they didn't reflect the knowledge of the speaker so much as they did the knowledge of the speech*writer*. The written words were literally removed from direct knowledge about the facts of the case.

The saving grace of writing in Western civilization has been its permanence, its structure, and its relationship to an author. With writing we can refer back to our ideas, read over a passage several times, refine the expressions, and thus control ideas and problems of great complexity in a permanent way. Its value as a record of ideas has been proven over and over throughout our history. It was no accident that the Renaissance began in Italy after Western scholars were given access to more accurate written versions of Plato that had been missing in their culture for many years. The reappearance of Plato's thought in a more accurate form was one of the forces that allowed a new perspective on the world to arise, because men were reminded of ideas that had been forgotten. Writing also preserved the definitions of many words in dictionaries, providing great subtlety and specificity in our vocabularies; reading those words in written works helped to improve vocabularies.

Writing also forces us to structure our thought, usually in a linear visual fashion; I believe that has had a great influence on the Western scientific tradition. We see the letters laid out upon the page in a line, subject doing something to an object. The basis of much Western progress is the experimental method, which is essentially a careful examination of cause-and-effect in the world around us. Writing did not invent cause-and-effect reasoning, certainly, but I think it's fair to say that the linear left-to-right structure of writing in Western culture has reinforced that basic pattern of organization and that mode of thought. Ancient Greek, for example, appears to be a much more "three-dimensional" language, the more complicated verb forms in the Greek's memory allowing lengthy convoluted sentences. The words had to be held in the listener's memory through the whole sentence, in many cases, until the verb appeared at the last of the sentence to make the whole idea clear. Most modern languages in the West, however, seem to rely upon a much more linear written structure, with subject-verb-object, parallel structure, and dependent clauses that mirror many of the basic forms of reasoning that we teach in argumentation classes today. Spoken language has those structures today, but how much of that has been influenced over the last several hundred years by writing? Hasn't our modern journalistic writing style been an outgrowth of a more complex style in the past, and doesn't it parallel the growth of the publishing industry and the newspaper industry? At any rate, the permanence of writing (and its capacity for detailed consideration of complex ideas) has provided one basis for progress in Western society over past centuries.

In artistic terms, writing has led to great complexity and depth in literature, allowing the creation of such masterworks as Joyce's *Ulysses*. The best of our literary artists have been able to capture worlds of experience in great detail and richness, giving the reader an experience with a world beyond that of his own personal viewpoint. Such involvement with a work of literature reinforces our basic ability to imagine what the world looks like from another individual's perspective.

Notice that the association of writing with an individual perspective matches Plato's conception nicely, although his view of literature was another story. The written word, Plato said, must rely upon its author to defend it. Many times that has been the case, as literary critics and other scholars composed reams of articles about what was meant where and by whom. There has always been an author whose views the written word reflected, and who was often criticized if his work was inaccurate or unrealistic or simply bad. The written word reflected the world view of an individual, his knowledge and perception of the world, and that person could be trusted, mistrusted, or held accountable for his views. The written word has given us insight into the way another human being saw the world, another person's knowledge of experience. Written works in all fields have traditionally been based upon the perception of an author or authors, and the complex vocabularies and the permanent abstract structures of written language gave us considerable insight into the "knowledge" of that one person.

The combined spoken and written traditions have given us great flexibility. We still rely on the spoken word as the most authoritative reflection of the mind of an author or expert. Witness the crowds at poetry readings who want to hear the poet read his own work, the audiences at speeches by other authors, the continuing reliance upon eyewitnesses in our courts. In a sense, we have listened to Plato's criticism of writing, employing the spoken word of trusted men and new technological controls on forgery to vouch for the written words upon which we base important decisions.

As Plato predicted, our long-term memories have suffered. The permanence of writing combined with our short-term memories have replaced the study of memory and recitals that were a part of ancient education. We may have suffered inaccuracies in some cases, but in many others writing has given us an ability to discuss complex problems at length that the vagaries of memory might not allow. There are problems, of course. The complex meaning potential of written language as we climb up the ladder of abstraction gets further and further away from the realities of experience. Very often we would like to shake an author out of his abstract tower and ask him what the hell he means in a more down-to-earth arena of one-on-one conversation. On the whole, however, the combined written-oral tradition has functioned effectively in Western society.

Now, however, both the spoken word and the written word appear to have become "lost arts" to a great extent. Verbal scores have fallen on major national tests during the 1960s and 1970s. (In 1981, they didn't improve; they merely didn't get worse.) Graduate instructors at my university have complained in the student newspaper that many students write at a grade-school level. In my personal experience, many papers by college sophomores and juniors that I have graded are not written as well as my junior English theme written at a small rural high school. Vocabularies are limited, apparently

329

because students simply don't read. Only a handful of students in a given class read any newspaper except the student paper, and only one or two have recently read a book that wasn't assigned for a class. Many students are unfamiliar with well-known authors. I will never forget the chill that went down my spine when I mentioned William Faulkner in a lecture at a small college and received only blank stares in return. These Southern students had simply never heard of him.

Spoken language skills have also declined. Barnet Baskerville, a distinguished scholar in the history of oratory, recently published a book with a chapter entitled "The Decline of Eloquence" in which he notes the influence of the media upon modern public speaking. "Audiences come not to hear good speaking," he writes, "but to see celebrities in person, and whenever possible to hear an assault on the 'power structure.' The lecture is too often merely a branch of show biz—a showcase for television personalities." Baskerville blames much of this decline on the growth of television, and television's concentration on the images projected by the television "show."

If we draw a parallel between the influence of writing on the ancients and the influence of television on modern society, Plato's theory of writing offers us a sobering but rational explanation for many of the changes we perceive in our society. If writing is twice removed from knowledge, television is even more seductive because it is a pseudo-oral tradition. TV is false because it gives us the detailed illusion of reality reinforced by the full power of the old maxim that "seeing is believing." Surely some critical thought takes place in the minds of audiences watching television, but are we not constantly faced with color and sound images of the world that are divorced from reality?

Surely television gives us powerful sensations of "being there." We see the action, the color, hear the voices, and we have the powerful impression that we have experienced the reality of the situation. In truth, however, we see only those portions of an event on the evening news for which interesting camera work is available. In a football game, for example, the television coverage shows us a face or two from the crowd, a pretty girl or two from the cheerleading squad, and the "action" following the football on the field. We are not free, however, to choose what we pay attention to; we can see only what the camera lets us see. We don't often get to see the alignment of the defense, for the standard camera shot at the beginning of the play shows us only the offensive team's lineup. We don't see the defensive backs following the man in motion, and we don't see the receivers in their patterns until the ball lands miraculously in their hands. Perhaps that's why passes seem to leave such a dramatic impression on our images of football. We don't see where the quarterback is looking, and the catch is a thrill because we don't know where the pass is coming down until the moment it gets there. One wonders if this "thrill" led to the recent rule changes that have emphasized the passing game. At any rate, we turn off the set with the impression that we have "seen the game," and we talk to our sports fanatic friends as if we had been there to see it all.

On the television news, we see a group of demonstrators in a balcony, and we hear then President Nixon make a dramatic quip that draws a roar from the crowd, and we get the image of a powerful speaker in command of the situation. We don't see in the picture that the audience is overwhelmingly

330

Republican, that the president has just given a plaque to the college's football team for being number one in the Associated Press Poll that year, and we don't see the members of the Young Republicans Club who set up "cheerleading" sections in the hall an hour before the general public arrived. The impression goes straight into our consciousness, creating the image of a successful speech on a college campus, when in fact Nixon could have spoken on only two or three campuses during that time frame without generating a riot of protest. The appearance of reality is there in all its colorful glory, with movement and sound to match.

Most of the other programming on television makes no pretense of being tied to reality. Programs are conceived and written on the basis of very simple vocabularies to draw the largest possible audiences. The extremely limited time frame of each show after commercials requires a very simple plot, and many shows now handle three or four extremely superficial plot lines at the same time—*Love Boat* and *Fantasy Island*, for example. These shows reinforce over and over again the implied message that what we see is real, because we have seen it with our own eyes. We begin to believe that everyone (except perhaps us) lives in a $300,000 house in California, that everyone wears $1,000 suits and has their hair done every day. We have commercials constantly reinforcing the theme, implying that if we wear designer jeans and have our hair done by Sassoon we'll not only be successful, but happy as well. The story lines of commercials suggest that all human problems can be solved with money; the plot lines of the shows suggest that all human problems can be solved in half an hour without much effort (and certainly with only minimal discomfort to the hero). The characters are given only surface treatment, and we find out little about their innermost thoughts and feelings. Clearly the images we see on television are different from the realities we face as individuals each day; usually they don't represent the experiences of a single author, either.

Writing, it can be argued, also creates the appearance of knowledge when the individual who composed the words isn't present. Television, however, usually has no single author or authority who is responsible for its content. In the first place, Plato would argue, television does not allow us to ask questions. In some cases, we are offered the illusion of a question-and-answer session. Take the two meetings of Jimmy Carter, or better yet the panel discussions staged by Richard Nixon's campaign, in which carefully chosen "friendly" questioners were selected to ask the candidate prepared questions. The program was designed to create the image of the candidate meeting the people and answering tough questions on the spot. In reality, none of the questions were new; they had been standard in all his meetings with the local press, and most questions were stated in friendly terms that invited the candidate's prepared answer on that issue. The press wasn't invited. In Nixon's campaign for a second term, this technique went so far that the press saw his frequent speeches on closed-circuit television; they weren't allowed in the same room with the candidate. Everything was carefully designed to control the image of Nixon that the nation would see on television. In most cases the same principle applies; we don't get to see even the appearance of an information source answering questions about his statements.

Our continual need for an individual source of trustworthy information, however, leads us to unreal expectations of our politicians. We are given an image of the politician in the media that suggests to us that he is strong, powerful, in control, and we develop expectations based upon those images that no president can fulfill. This cycle has been evident in many recent political campaigns; the Jimmy Carter phenomenon, the boom and bust of the Teddy Kennedy campaign, and the growing dissatisfaction with Ronald Reagan as people begin to see beyond the candiate's image to the ways in which his policies will really affect their lives. The television image Reagan presented suggested to all of us that he was fatherly, strong, and friendly, and that he would do what was best for all of us. It isn't possible to keep all the people happy all of the time, however, as Reagan is beginning to find out. These unreal expectations based on media images can affect other parts of our lives.

The faceless entity called the "media" (ironically, only an image itself) gives us no one source whose credibility we can use as a measure of the image's relationship to reality, to truth in Plato's terms. We are given the suggestion that what we see is reality, bypassing both thought and questioning. The concentration on the image encourages us not to think, not to use our imaginations. We don't consciously think of television as a representation of reality, as we do the written word or the spoken word; television appears to *be* experience. To think or imagine something, we look beyond the written or spoken word to find a picture of someone else's human experience; television short circuits the process of imagination. The pictures for each story are presented to us in living color; we don't have to imagine them. The voices are presented for us in their clear, regular, sanitized intonation patterns; we don't have to imagine them. The emotional experience of the show is suggested to us by the musical scoring or the canned laughter; we don't even get to laugh when *we* feel like laughing. We sit in our chairs and the waves of light and sound roll over our glazed eyes and ears, the bright colors and sounds carefully crafted not to involve us too deeply or to upset us.

This conception suggests an explanation for the students who never sit down and involve their imaginations deeply in the images and sounds suggested by a work of literature, hearing and seeing the potential sensations trapped in the written word by the author. They don't search for the "knowledge" of the author's experience symbolized by the written word. It isn't that they don't have the ability; it's merely that they've rarely had to involve themselves deeply in worlds beyond their own, or beyond the world of television. On the tube, the work is all done for their imaginations; they grow to expect the world to be simple and obvious.

This is a serious cheapening of our lives, one that injures our ability to understand and feel for each other. We begin to base our behavior on illusions, not on our experience. It's no wonder that this is known as the "me" generation; we're brought up with the suggested image that everyone else is nearly perfect, lives in a clean, neat house, never has a hair out of place, and never cries unless the lighting is positioned so their eyes aren't too unattractively red for the cameras. On the one hand, we are made to feel insecure because others seem to be so cool and together, and on the other we are discouraged from imagining what the lives of others must really be like because television presents such a seductive and convincing image. This basic

332

ability to imagine things as they never were—to see new combinations, new possibilities—is vital to Plato's conception of questioning as part of the search for knowledge about the world around us. Thinking about the ideas and perceptions of another, trying to imagine their point of view and make sense of it, this is vital to our personal creativity and happiness. A medium that constantly reinforces unexamined images (or conclusions) can strongly influence the assumptions on which we base our lives.

A preliminary report on a 10-year study by the Annenberg School of Communications, for example, indicates that Americans are influenced by television in their behavior regarding health. Television reinforces the image of the "all-powerful doctor," able to cure anything, implying that one can smoke, drink, and not exercise because the medical profession can always fix it. The leading characters in prime-time series remain healthy, slim, and sober in spite of all the shooting, drinking, and eating. These images are clearly not related to the realities of life in the world outside the television cabinet. As a result of the image on television, however, Americans who watch a lot of television tend to have unhealthy attitudes toward eating, drinking, and exercise.

There is also an apparent relationship between television and study habits. A 1980 California study found that of 500,000 public school students who took tests in reading, language use, and arithmetic, the more television the student watched, the lower the score on the tests. Certainly, drawing conclusions from such data is risky, but there seems to be a strong possibility that people tend to imitate behavior they see on television.

People on television don't worry about eating, drinking, or exercise, so neither do we. Children on television don't study, make literary allusions, or deal with complex problems that don't allow for happy endings, so why should we? In our everyday lives, however, such assumptions will eventually catch up with us. One has to wonder how much of the mental stress faced by future psychiatrists will be generated by individuals attempting to bridge the gap between the assumptions generated by television images and the harsh realities of life away from the tube.

The implications for the future of society as a whole are just as serious. The *Chicago Tribune* reported that a new update of a study by the U.S. Surgeon General's office will confirm a connection between violence on television and violent behavior by both children and adults. The images presented on television, in short, may influence not just the individual who watches, but the society around the individual. If television reinforces the image that problems can be solved by violence, not by talk, the implications for society can be serious indeed. One can envision a society of people who have two modes of behavior: They either sit passively, involving themselves mindlessly in the unrealistic world of television, or they react violently. Perhaps such violence arises when the images of the media world are so unrelated to the reality of their personal life that they can no longer sustain the fantasy that they are a part of that image.

The passive receivers of the television world attempt or pretend to be as happy, attractive, and well-to-do as the people in the illusionary world of the image. They buy the flashy cars, designer jeans, and try to look "together," avoiding realistic and involved relationships with those around them that delve beneath the surface image. The violent imitators of the television world strike out, they believe, at those around them who are as happy and well-to-do as the perfect television characters they can never hope to imitate. We begin to evaluate ourselves and others not on the basis of real evidence, on the basis of experience with the person, but on the basis of the appearances we see, on the basis of images we have begun to believe because we "saw" them on television.

This inability to imagine or understand the thoughts or motives of others is one of the basic characteristics of those who are unable to communicate effectively. They believe their personal worthlessness is the cause of their lack of success in society. Those members of society who absorb the unspoken assumptions and unreal expectations of the media image could well be part of the statistics on divorce rates, alcoholism, and other social problems, because we tend to measure our personal success against that of those who populate the unreal world of television.

This fascination with the image may also have serious future consequences for the nation's politics. The last few presidents have apparently been elected on the basis of style, not substance. We can point back to the studies that showed that radio listeners believed that Richard Nixon won the 1960 debates with John F. Kennedy, while television viewers rated Kennedy as the winner. The difference was largely the image of cool, professional "presidentiality" that Kennedy presented in comparison to the poorly made-up and ill Nixon. One feels that this was an underlying motive behind the election of the smiling Jimmy Carter over the bumbling image presented by Gerald Ford. The same holds true of the election of the fatherly, friendly images projected by Ronald Reagan, although in terms of arguments and facts Carter apparently "won" those debates.

More disturbing than the influence of the image of the candidate on the election, however, is the influence of the image of the president upon the conduct of the nation's affairs. Witness the following paragraph from a recent *New York Times Magazine* article on the "Marketing of the President":

> The President's strategists are at the center of the new political age. At the end of the day, they become spectators, seeing their performance tested by the contents of the television news programs. For the Reagan White House, every night is election night on television. How an Administration action is placed and portrayed on the network news often determines what initiative the President will take the next day.

Surely politicians of the past have reacted in their decision-making to the impression they have created in the written media, and before the time of writing to the spoken advice of their counselors. The danger for the future is that we will begin to believe too completely the images created before us in the little black box.

A democratic society ultimately depends upon the ability of individuals to make decisions regarding complex issues. The results will be traumatic enough if we continue to vote for the image a politician projects through the television, and then are always disappointed because he cannot possibly live up to the implied perfection that we had let ourselves believe. One must wonder how long our government will survive, however, if the politicians themselves begin to measure their success or failure primarily based upon the image projected by television. The measure of reality regarding a given problem then becomes not what a thoughtful individual with knowledge of the subject believes, nor what any knowledgeable person makes of experience, but the image projected on television. To paraphrase Abraham Lincoln, we may become a government of the image, by the image, for the image.

The question then becomes not whether a proposed policy is good, or whether there is evidence that it will work, but how it will look on the evening news. The result is that we are faced with a hall of electronic mirrors, literally basing our decisions on illusions. Presidential advisors, for example, make decisions based not upon written reports of factual data, not upon the spoken arguments presented by their sources, but upon the image that the action would present on television.

Beyond the presentation of illusion as reality, however, television offers another threat to human knowledge. Remember that memory is a key part of Plato's theory of knowledge, for a man has to remember the perceptions of truth that he has if he is to use them to shape his actions. Television may endanger our memories in a more insidious fashion than writing. Writing tempts us to write down rather than remember, making our mental perception of the world less complex and less accurate. Television offers two apparent threats to memory. First, television stuffs our heads with thousands of images that are not related to any personal experience, but images that take up space in our memories nevertheless. Writing discourages the use of our memories, but most of us today have our heads filled with images of television programs and commercials that we will remember until we die. Captain Midnight, Superman, "double your pleasure, double your fun"—think of the zillions of memory cells occupied with worthless trivia that you can remember perfectly. Surely that takes up room that we might use for more serious matters, especially when we remember that much of it apparently sinks in without apparent thought. On an everyday basis we select that to which we will pay attention; most television we accept in mesmerized silence without selectivity. All the images pour into our circuits to be filed away.

At the same time, television is as ephemeral as speech, in that the words and pictures are gone as soon as they have been said. In most cases we cannot doublecheck the scene to make sure we have remembered the moment correctly, so the illusions that strain our brain capacity may be inaccurate. The image reinforces a kind of oral tradition, but does not require or encourage the kind of memory that made ancient oral traditions possible. The result is a pseudo-oral tradition based upon images that are divorced from reality.

One of Plato's famous lines is inscribed in Greek at the entrance to the Liberal Arts building on my campus: "The unexamined life is not worth living." We might paraphrase for today's media-dominated society that "the unexamined life is not worth dreaming." Allowing ourselves to be influenced by the subtle but powerful illusions presented by television leads to a kind of mass madness that can have rather frightening implications for the future of the nation. One could reasonably define madness as behavior that is not based on reality. If we accept Plato's perception that knowledge of the world rests in the mind of someone who has knowledge of the subject based upon personal experience, then allowing the images on television to influence our behavior is truly mad. To the extent that we accept the unspoken assumptions that looking successful is being successful, that everyone else is perfect and in control, that people won't love us if we have ring around the collar, etc., then we are mad as well. We will have begun to see things that aren't there, giving someone else the power to make up our illusions for us. The prospect is frightening, and given our cultural heritage we should know better.

One old maxim states that "he who knows not and knows not that he knows not, he is a fool. Shun him. He who knows not and knows that he knows not, he is a child. Teach him." Western civilization can survive those who behave like children, for they can be taught. For the sake of the future, however, we must continually remind ourselves that through the media we do not see what we think we see. Otherwise, we shall truly be fools, and the future will truly be "a tale told by an idiot."

The Decay of Purposive Communication

by

Gerald M. Phillips

Oral communication is customarily considered as either expression or rhetoric. Expression is personal talk designed either to release tension or to draw attention to oneself. Rhetoric is planned talk designed to convey information, direct or inform behavior, or modify ideas and attitudes. Rhetoric is always directed at someone else. It seeks to provide other people with the information they might need to make satisfactory decisions. Often, individuals are confronted with rival rhetorical messages from which they must choose the point of view they prefer.

Generally, rhetoric is found on a public platform. People with ideas present them to other people who have the power to make decisions. The clash of ideas sometimes creates political parties, but, when society provides the means, it virtually always provides decisions.

Most of us prefer to believe that we are not rhetorical with our friends and loved ones, but close relationships and family activities are, in reality, based on rhetorical exchanges. In fact, when members of a close-relationship unit begin expressing themselves, the unit is in trouble, since expression has no direct purpose other than to call attention to particular individuals and to insist that their demands be met.

Relationships in which rhetorical talk is exchanged last longer than those built on expressive speech. Families and friendships cannot sustain themselves if individuals communicate largely for their own purposes without considering the welfare of others involved. The decay of rhetorical talk has contributed to the dissolution of family units and to the growth of narcissism.

In recent years, there has been a decay of rhetorical talk in interpersonal relationships. Surveys of more than 3,000 people taken in 1972 and again in 1981 indicate a strong trend away from purposive talk in relationships in favor of narcissistic expression. Authorities seem to agree that our whole society is tending toward narcissism. In particular, Christopher Lasch's *The Culture of Narcissism* decries the trend. More recently, Daniel Yankelovich's *The New Rules* explains the narcissistic trend as a shift in values away

Gerald M. Phillips is a professor of speech communication at The Pennsylvania State University, University Park, Pennsylvania, and editor of Communication Quarterly.

from an urgency to acquire personal goods and power toward acquisition of intangibles like personal satisfaction and inner gratification. Whatever the explanation, there are three situations in our society that grow directly out of the narcissism of its citizens.

First, there is a trend away from meaningful relationships. Not only is the nuclear family a decaying unit, but people seem to be moving away from a willingness to take the responsibility for having children and rearing them to adulthood. Evidence of this trend is the untidy flood of divorce cases where neither parent seems to want custody. The trend toward increases in the number of single-person living units indicates a desire by people to be alone so that they can have their own way. Furthermore, there is evidence of a flood of neurotics in the population under age 35. All of this adds up to a society of people who are socially underdeveloped, unable to speak to people for the common good, or, for that matter, even for their own good. Isolation from other human beings encourages the development of expressive speech.

Second, the trend to single-issue politics indicates a tendency for people to oversimplify personal and social issues to the point where they are willing to jeopardize the common good in favor of achieving a goal they find personally satisfying regardless of its impact on others or on the society in general. One good example is the current battle over abortion, an issue of some moral consequence but hardly central to the existence of the society. Supporters of the anti-abortion position have been noteworthy in their uncritical support of candidates who will promise conformance on that issue, regardless of their position on other social or economic matters.

Third, the general trend to production of low-quality goods and slipshod services stems from concentration on the self. Workers who are not committed do not care how their product comes out, nor are they interested in talking about how to make it better. By the same token, they are quite urgent about getting quality goods, and so they purchase imports, further complicating matters by sending needed dollars out of the country. Noteworthy here is Theory Z, a type of management characterized by intense participation by individual employees. In Japan, employers regard employees as experts on their jobs and solicit their advice on how work should be done. This is quite different from the plaintive wails that characterize contemporary American personnel relations, where employees may avail themselves of counseling at company expense or expensive grievance procedures guaranteed by their union contract, neither of which has anything to do with quality production. Thus, narcissism impedes the flow of accurate information needed for improvement of quality of merchandise. Furthermore, so long as workers are guaranteed an outlet for their narcissism, they tend to avoid involvement in the more difficult tasks of purposive communication.

The consequence of these three trends is a lack of participation in community affairs and politics. The decline in the number of voters in recent years signals this trend, as does the movement toward government funding of political parties. The proliferation of small political parties indicates that appeals to narcissistic interests can have some political effect, although it is questionable whether it is a healthy one. Furthermore, the decline of purpose in maintaining basic family and social units has even more serious consequences.

338

Purposive talk in social relationships is imperative to the maintenance of social units. Without it, people separate from each other despite their common need for close relationships. Once people isolate themselves from one another, they lose the ability to work together to solve their problems; rather than "work things out," they separate. Continued avoidance of problem-solving activity in political and social life results in atrophy of the ability to engage in rhetorical discourse. Rather than attempt to cooperate to solve problems, individuals seek attention to their personal needs through expressive talk. They air their troubles, refuse to honor the problems of others, and, in general, look out for "number one." They no longer recognize the purposive aspects of communication, and since participation in problem-solving is difficult and sometimes frustrating, their inherent narcissism leads them to avoid it. Thus, as they fail to solve problems, they make themselves more likely to fail at solving future problems. The result can be total alienation, endogenous depression, or affiliation with causes and movements that enable them to submerge their identities into the ideology of a "guru."

Purposive talk is important on the job. Production is a social effort during the course of which little compromise can be made with personal comfort, convenience, and necessity. Without the directed contribution of experts, management cannot make the kind of decisions it needs to compete properly. Furthermore, when people in social communities concentrate on their personal interests as opposed to the common good, decisions tend to be responsive, long-term needs cannot be anticipated, and segments of the community are polarized into adversarial positions. This, in essence, is the source of the litigiousness that characterizes contemporary society. In general, skill at purposive talk is fundamental for citizens of a democracy to provide maximum participation.

The trend to narcissism is a precursor of a trend to totalitarianism. Narcissists cannot participate in democratic action because they cannot identify with the position of the other. Skilled rhetorical speech is directed at the needs of an audience, following Aristotle's dictum, "the fool tells me his reasons, the wise man persuades me with my own." Democratic societies are considerate and protective of the rights of minorities. Narcissistic societies are characterized by expressions of need and want from individuals and their factions, but since there is no recognition of the needs of others there can be no means of reconciliation. Thus, the powerful party wins regardless of the consequences. The bastion against this totalitarian trend is the integrity of the courts, but the advent of single-issue politics seems to bode ill for the independence of the courts, and the "loyalty test" attempted by the 1980 Republican Platform may signal a trend away from the separation of the courts from the volatility of the community at large.

Social Forces Encourage Narcissistic Expression

The main pressure toward narcissism comes from the premise that individuals can transcend their mundane existence and achieve some sort of personal euphoria and nirvana through the process called self-actualization. The actualization myth was introduced by Abraham Maslow, who adapted it from the German radical sociologists who believed that the supply of wealth and goods was sufficient to sustain all of the people of the earth with a reasonable standard of living. In the last few years, however, there has been a real threat to maintenance of high standards of living even in industrialized Western societies, and realists have had to revise their programs from the quest for actualization to maintenance of some reasonable living standard. The narcissistic myth has been exploded by depletion of natural resources. This seems to have little effect on narcissistic reactions, however, for the decline in availability of goods seems only to have exacerbated the search for inner tranquility and personal satisfaction.

The actualization myth promised that people could free themselves from dependence on others and fulfill themselves through art or intellectual endeavors, as well as through intensive relationships (mostly sexual). To serve the myth, a training enterprise evolved from the T-Groups initiated by the followers of Kurt Lewin. Such movements as encounter and sensitivity training, pedagogical methods such as assertiveness training, personalized therapies like Gestalt and primal screaming, and commercialized enterprises like est and Lifespring catered to narcissistic urgencies and promised that number one could look out for himself, say "no" whenever necessary, and find satisfactory orgasm, success on the job, and personal identity with minimal effort. In essence, what was offered was a medical model that suggested that people who were not actualized were, in some way, sick, and through the application of the proper therapy, could be healed and made whole. Unlicensed trainers and therapists offered "therapy for normal people" designed to provide them with skills with which they could actualize.

The record was spotty. Most people showed no change at all. Some estimates, however, put the number of casualties at two to one over gains, with gains estimated at 5% (at best) of those in training regardless of the orientation of the trainer. Some types of programs seemed to be particularly productive of psychiatric emergencies. Moreover, all seemed to emphasize narcissistic goals, and most made the point that any attempt to control one's communication was manipulative. Thus, the whole narcissistic movement tended to subvert the development of purposive rhetoric. The consequences are obvious. Today's students are particularly bewildered when asked to present persuasive speeches or write rhetorical messages. They seem to regard one idea as equal to another—except their own ideas, which, of course, take precedence over everything else. The watchword is "do your own thing" and/or "anything goes between consenting adults."

The media supported the narcissistic quest by showing characters fulfilling themselves in short episodes. People were led to believe that life's problems were also episodic, and when solutions were not forthcoming in a short time, frustration and anger set in. The tendency of the narcissistic is to blame others, thus generating conflict that cannot be resolved. While there was no problem that the media did not tackle, the solutions were quite unimaginative and generally unrealistic, since the "live happily ever after" theme seemed to prevail. Thus, a male could live with two females, a female could live with a creature from another galaxy, and soap opera characters could commit egregious acts of betrayal and adultery and things would still come out all right. Virtually all lived in decent housing with quality furniture and appliances and were well dressed and groomed even when poverty-stricken. Thus, it was made clear to at least two generations that the worries their parents had about the source of the next meal were not their worries and they could get about the business of actualizing themselves through hot tubs, sexual therapies, physical manipulations, religious experiences, oriental philosophies, and traditional "let it all hang out" pseudo-therapies, not to speak of engaging in arts and crafts. One of the most interesting developments in recent years, for example, has been the "arts fair," in which whole communities cooperate on giant displays of personal crafts by setting up sales. It is intriguing that people can cooperate on ways and means to express themselves narcissistically, but cannot cooperate on such issues as zoning or water conservation.

The prime message of narcissism was that people did not have to be dishonest with one another. People were advised to be open with one another, to "tell it like it is," to announce what bothers them, and to get in touch with their feelings and not be reticent about sharing them. Everyone was to receive unconditional positive regard, that is, everyone's ideas were to be tolerated, but one's own were to be acted on. Once again, the message that purposive discourse could provide results beneficial to the community was subverted by the message that personal growth and development were most important. There was a latent notion that once everyone was fully actualized, the community would be perfect, but this was never really expressed as a political ideal. As a matter of fact, there did not appear to be any political ideals expressed by the narcissistic movements. The main premise was that at the core of every person was a "real self" waiting to be discovered. It was a distorted sort of Freudianism that promised instant discovery of hidden qualities followed by complete growth and total fulfillment. The result could be development of real loving relationships, without strings, in which adult couples could seek sensual gratification that lasted up into the geriatric period of their life. To cater to this form of narcissism, sex clinics were provided. Counseling, of course, was very important, as was continued participation in various movements designed to reinforce narcissistic capabilities.

Actualized people would, of course, be effective on their jobs, since their full powers would be released. Androgyny was also in order. Men could learn to embrace one another, women could learn to compete. Men could be tender, women could make aggressive sexual advances. There would be plenty of leisure time during which one could be fulfilled through art, crafts, relationships, or whatever.

Through actualization, our society would experience a "Golden Age" like that of the Greeks. But hardly anyone took note of the fact that Greek society was made up of people whose actualization was built on slavery. Maslow had provided surrogate slaves in the corpus of copers—sad folks whose destiny it was to serve the needs of actualizers because they could not accomplish actualization themselves.

The Bubble Bursts

The first oil boycott started the nightmare. While California held firm, the rest of the country began to feel queasy. Philosophers and editorialists began to rail about narcissism. Some of the sensitizers faded from the headlines and others began campaigns to save the world. The schools started to go back to basics, though it was not clear whether the movement was pedagogically or economically based. Economists discovered how the Japanese and Germans were beating us, and enlightened business executives began to inquire into the meaning of Theory Z and the Quality Circle. The advent of single-issue politicians activated other segments of the community to organize themselves as political units. The presidential campaign of 1980 was a strange blend of narcissistic demands and old-style political combat. The result was a drawing of political lines as they had not been drawn in years, and real issues like welfare, interest rates, national defense, ecology, and natural resources drew greater emphasis. The gulf between the narcissists and the mainstream was growing wider. Many retreated into religious cults or took refuge in the remaining therapies. While private lessons in narcissism were made available in the form of self-help and personal-therapy books, the society began to take on an issue-oriented caste. Once again, politicians made promises about the problems they were going to solve rather than try to convince people how much individuals would benefit if they only devoted themselves to dedication to the nation. Political crusades became a thing of the past. Politicians concentrated on problems to be solved. Working hard and holding a job became virtuous once again, and there was increased attention to preserving the family and producing children. The conservative trend in society was a trend away from expressive narcissism and toward rhetorical discourse.

The Present Consequences

Voter apathy was, perhaps, the major consequence of the decline of purposive communication. People who had been taught to concentrate their talk on their own internal needs were not interested in participation in the give-and-take of purposive problem-solving. It remains to be seen, however, whether we will return to training people in the civic skills of parliamentary participation and group problem-solving. Clearly, the focus is on problem-solving, but there is still the outside chance that society will not be able to shake its narcissism and will opt for the man on horseback rather than the more difficult method of citizen participation.

A second consequence of the decline of purposive communication was the inability of people to resolve personal issues. The society became intolerably litigious. Courts were required to solve the relatively uncomplicated problems of neighborhood conflicts, family disputes, and community issues like zoning and licensing.

A third consequence was the increase of sociopathology. Crime rises when people can find no other occupation. The diminished concern with the economic problems of ethnic minorities, single parents, the aging and infirm, and the uneducated and undereducated pushed large numbers of people into sociopathic endeavors like crime and addiction, and produced a large number of ambulatory mentally ill. It was never clear, for example, whether turning inmates loose from mental hospitals was motivated by civil liberties urgencies or by economics, but the present result is that a great many people who need treatment are unable to get it. Furthermore, the failure of society to develop the prison system to accommodate increasing numbers of convicts and to renovate the courts to handle the increased number of criminal cases means that society has been burdened with a component that is both sociopathic and threatening to itself. Furthermore, society does not appear to know what to do about it. Only recently was the discovery made that the American crime rate would be the lowest in the world, were it not for racial and ethnic minorities who were not getting their fair economic share and thus turning to crime as a primary occupation. Whether society will face this issue politically or not may be the acid test of how deeply narcissism has permeated the nation. Presently, we have two societies that are confronting each other, one without superego and the other without id.

In business, the idea of distinguishing the doable from the desirable has not yet fully taken hold, although it appears that the business and industrial communities are more sensitive than society at large to the need to alter methods and procedures. Recent events—in which workers gave back hard-won advantages in order to keep their jobs while businesses began to integrate worker opinion and expertise into the planning and problem-solving circuit—indicate that the business community may well be the bellwether of a changeover from expressiveness to rhetorical activity.

The Future

The next two decades do not appear hopeful. There is presently no effort being made to train Americans in orderly discourse. Schools still seem primarily interested in training students to "express themselves" or to "unlock their creativity." The late Robert Maynard Hutchins, just before his death, issued an impassioned statement advocating that schools concentrate on the communication modalities: reading, writing, speaking, listening, and figuring. These, he believed, would enable the citizens of the future to utilize the immense technology of information that has grown up in the past 25 years. Nothing else matters, he believed, if people could not communicate purposively. More recently, in the June 1982 issue of *The Futurist,* Lane Jennings announced that rhetorical capabilities were about to become "endangered skills."

The problems our society faces in the decades to come clearly require full citizen participation. If we develop an elite class of technologists, governmental specialists, and mediologists, the rights and privileges of the citizens will be sacrificed to the urgencies of those who control the technology, administration, and communications of the nation. Narcissistic fulfillment will be impossible, but once the citizens give up their right to participate by being unable to exercise it, they will be unable to take their power back by any means short of revolution.

The more likely event will be apathy. The economic dream can never be realized in a world of resource shortages and increasing demands from the Third World. The actualization dream cannot be fulfilled without fulfillment of the economic dream. With all dreams turned to nightmares, it would be reasonable to expect the citizen to eschew citizenship by avoiding the tasks it requires. People cannot participate if they are not trained to participate. Without concentration on training citizens in rhetorical techniques, the trend to a controlled society will continue unchecked.

At the time of the Three Mile Island incident, one expert predicted that the nuclear reaction would continue for 10,000 years and the reactor would have to be tended to prevent meltdown. A science-fiction-oriented individual then drew a word picture of a society of "natives" tending the "Fire God in the River," not knowing why, but knowing that if they failed in their task, the God would consume them. That is the apocalyptic vision of a society in which people cannot engage in problem-solving rhetoric. They will do what they are directed to do, not knowing why, and in general, not knowing enough to improve the society. The informed and enlightened communicator is imperative to successful confrontation of the economic, social, and political problems that will be posed to us up to the turn of the century.

Future Communications: Problems and Possibilities

by

S. C. Seth

Communications has more than one meaning. Likewise, the future for any society consists of numerous happenings and events. Education, technology, and management are means to make certain events possible over time or to avert certain undesirable events and crisis situations.

Communications is an instrument of change and transformation. Communications is also an instrument of control. Ideal communications has to be that system which acts as a two-way process, giving as well as receiving information and direction from those it is attempting to change. We must give equal emphasis to carrying other people's messages to "us" as to carrying "our" messages to other people.

The first criterion by which to judge a good communication system is to see whether we are building channels of information downwards as well as upwards and laterally. The objectives of socio-economic development imply a to-and-fro dialogue; and this can be enhanced through mass communications that can help teach people skills, create opportunities to share national and cultural excellence from people in different countries, and internally promote a knowledge-based society.

No communications system should smother regional and folk media and beauty. Decentralized communications systems are a desirable goal, but a decentralized society should not be denied the advantages of "excellence" that science and technology have given to modern man. The degree of decentralization of a society is directly proportional to the technological and managerial competence it can command.

Assessing Future Needs

Communications needs should be sectorally assessed. We need to project current and future demands, in terms of communications response in the fields of agriculture, industry, health, literacy, and formal and non-formal education.

S.C. Seth is a leading futurologist in India. Presently, he is working with the Department of Science and Technology (GOI), New Delhi. The views expressed here are exclusively those of the author and do not represent those of any official agency.

Let us look at the educational needs integral to the communications task in the Indian context. We are 630 million odd people and it is our rough estimate that, if we continue to add people as we are adding them (on an average of one child every 1.5 to 3 seconds), we would have approximately 960 million people by 2000 A.D. Our first concern must therefore be to provide satisfactory living conditions for 960 million people. How does one manage such a large human system?

Many will feel tempted—and perhaps rightly—to suggest that if "numbers" be our problem, let us control our exploding population. Yes, we should do that. But there are one or two facts to keep in mind. Firstly, in 1973 we had 104 million couples in the fertility zone. This number has since increased. Secondly, 44.2% of India's population is today below 15 years of age. Thirdly, when one launches a birth control program, it takes 25 to 30 years to achieve fertility equilibrium, and 30 to 35 more years to attain zero population growth. Thus the impact of the birth control program India launched in the 1970s will be felt only towards the third decade of the next century. But by then we will have almost doubled our population.

This fact has then some serious implications. Take the educational needs of our youngsters. What is the nature of the demand profile here? When the Indian Constitution was first drawn up in the 1950s, the Constitution makers offered their vision of a preferred future for the children of this country. They said, in Chapter III of the Constitution, that we should provide free, universal compulsory education to all children between the ages of 6 and 14. They did not realize that the children in this age group then numbered almost 50 million. Today we have more than 85 million children in this age group. By the turn of the century, there will be 145 million children in this age group. How does one go about educating 145 million children?

This task cannot be accomplished using conventional methods. In this context, we have made a rough estimate that if we follow conventional teaching methods of text books, teachers, and class rooms, then we should open a new 250-pupil school every tenth minute for the next 20 years and employ some 6 million people (1% of India's present population) as primary school teachers. Do we have adequate resources to do this? If not, what alternatives are available to us?

Choosing Technology

It is in this way that we must assess the resource and demand picture of the country in various sectors and choose appropriate communication technology options. It is only thus that we can seriously consider numerous alternatives for new systems whereby we can begin to manage the various needs of a large human system such as India. And our actions must commence right now. In this sense, the future is essentially with us today.

Key factors governing technology choices include the following:

1. Current need must always be the first factor to consider in choosing a technology, a management system, or a social organization. Nevertheless, by anticipating future needs now, we can improve the current decision-making process and invest in options whereby we may reap dividends and meet future needs with ease.

2. The methodologies suitable for smaller populations may not fully meet

the needs of a large human system such as India. [The entire population of Sweden, for instance (9 million), equals the population of just one city of India, i.e., Calcutta.] Therefore we should create an indigenous R & D base in India for future communications technologies.

3. We must examine the economic health of people. The Indian poverty condition is such that 300 million people have to meet their needs for food, housing, education, health, transportation, and communications—all on only one rupee per day!

4. We must examine the diversity and uneven growth of societies. (In India, we have co-existence of agrarian, industrial, and post-industrial societies.)

5. We must consider language diversity. In India, we have 1,652 dialects. Communication has to be in the local language, but this alone is not enough. Research indicates that many TV and radio broadcasts failed to establish good communication because their content did not respond to local experiences, etc.

6. We must take notice of technological plurality. In India, no technology fades out. All technologies co-exist. From bullock-cart to jet, from nineteenth century telephone exchange to electronics, we have everything.

Today there is no lack of knowledge concerning the range of technological developments available to mankind. Each technology, however, has a cost. Each technology also has a consequence.

How does one choose between various technologies anticipating future needs? There is a need to undertake technology assessment studies, and to judge each technology in terms of its long-range consequences.

Do people have a voice in the choice of a technology? Is this a possible proposition? How to accommodate people's views remains an unresolved dilemma.

The principle, however, is clear that we need to consider a technology-choice-and-control mechanism that will permit us to assess a technology in terms of its long-range impact applications, and first-order consequences. This should be supplemented by legislative measures and an organizational and institutional framework. We should also develop a national system wherein public opinion plays a dominant role.

Essentially, the State should have a right to satisfy itself that a given technology (whether indigenous or imported), industry, or product has no harmful consequences for man, nature, and society.

International norms need to be established for technology assessment; from these norms will flow guidelines for technology transfer.

New communications technology, like any other technology (for example, nuclear energy), has two aspects; what can help people can also be used to destroy basic human values. The possible social consequences of the "wired city" concept, for instance, need to be studied in depth.

A new world information order has to lay down a code of communications ethics. Science and technological developments in the field of communications can lead to such negative consequences as information warfare and microwave pollution.

Internationally, do we have any system whereby the people of the world can be told about a technology's long-range implications? What, for example, are the implications of the communications science and technology developments for national and international legal systems? A great deal of thought needs to be given to this area. We have made a mere beginning in the field on sea laws and space laws.

As we near the twenty-first century, we must categorically reject toying with the romantic idea of a return to the happiness of pastoral living. Times have changed. Developing societies that have missed the industrial revolution cannot afford to miss the technological revolution. What we need today is to learn and institutionalize a system to decide how best to choose and manage our affairs for the greatest good of the greatest number of people, ensuring basic needs today and ushering in a better future.

Technology needs to be socially adapted. To give just one small illustration, during the SITE experiment when TV programs were beamed via satellite to 2,400 villages in six different clusters, 300 to 500 people watched programs on a single 23-inch screen. Instead community viewing screens were needed.

UNESCO can play a leading role in the training and education of those who develop software. In paper and printing, policies regarding transfer of technology and avoiding waste need to be evolved. Of course, this is primarily the responsibility of each UN member state but UNESCO should draw up some particular guidelines, for one can safely predict a paper crisis in the future. International communications and energy relationships also need to be ascertained. Not enough studies are available in this area.

In terms of international cooperation, technology costs are prohibitive for many developing societies today (although over the years usually technology costs go down). This is an indication that regional-level cooperation for hardware and software is necessary. Are international funds available to establish these regional communications cooperation subsystems (e.g., two or three or more countries sharing one satellite)?

If the future of our children is to be ensured, and if they are to grow in a knowledge-based society, then it is necessary that the challenges posed by science and technology developments are met consciously, anticipating first-order consequences, second-order consequences, and so on. International cooperation in the field of communications will, by influencing the "minds of humanity," serve the cause of global peace and socio-economic developments.

The Radio Frequency Spectrum and the New World Information Order: Implications for the Future of Information

by

Thomas T. Surprenant

It is axiomatic that major societal or cultural transformations are accompanied by a transition period as the shift to a new society occurs. Whatever the label—post-industrial society, information age, or Third Wave—it is becoming increasingly obvious that we are in what Kenneth Boulding calls a break point in the dynamic process of world culture beyond which there is no return. When Daniel Bell spoke of the transition into the post-industrial (or information) society, he predicted that the way would not be smooth: " . . . the post-industrial society will involve more politics than ever before, for the very reason that choice becomes conscious and the decision-centers more visible." Nowhere can this be seen more clearly than in the emergence of the concept of the "info-sphere," a catchword that has been coined by Alvin Toffler to describe the production and distribution of information. And since it forms the basis of progress in the techno- and socio-sphere, it can serve as a barometer for the transition now occurring.

A confrontation is now taking place over access, control, and use of information as the nations of the world attempt to cope with change. This confrontation is likely to develop into a crisis over two major components of the "info-sphere": radio frequency (RF) spectrum allocations and the concept of free flow of information. The former deals directly with the technological or access components of information and the latter with control and use of it.

Part of the transition into the information environment is the realization that we live in a "global village" where the actions of one nation affect others in ways never considered. The United States and the other developed countries bear the burden of assisting the rest of the world community. In fact, most of the burden is on the United States to develop public policies and initiatives that will help the rest of the world make the transition.

Thomas T. Surprenant is assistant professor, University of Rhode Island Graduate Library School, Kingston, Rhode Island.

Allocation of the Radio Frequency Spectrum

The radio frequency (RF) spectrum covers "the entire range of electro-magnetic communications frequencies, including those used for radio, radar, and television." It is a worldwide environmental resource that cannot be expanded or extended, although the use of the spectrum can be enhanced through increasingly sophisticated telecommunications technologies. Any misuse of the spectrum results in radio frequency interference (RFI) preventing or inhibiting signals from reaching their destination. The RF spectrum is an extremely fragile environment that has to be managed efficiently as well as effectively. Thus, some form of regulation is necessary, taking the form of voluntary and cooperative treaties between all who use it. Formal concern over telecommunications extends back to 1865, with responsibility for cooperation and coordination now held by the International Telecom-munications Union (ITU), which is part of the United Nations. The ITU is responsible for the international uses of radio, telephone, and telegraph. Membership in the ITU has changed dramatically from 65 nations and seven groups of colonies attending the 1947 conference to 142 nations with no colonies attending the 1979 World Administrative Radio Conference (WARC-79). Of the 155 member nations in the ITU, two-thirds can be identified as developing or Third World countries.[1] Not only does this reflect growing use of the RF spectrum but it also illustrates a definite shift from technological to political concerns related to allocation.

ITU conferences are convened every 20 years to consider the allocation of the entire spectrum, with a number of specialized conferences held during the interim. A series of international agreements result from these conferences. Specifically, the full conferences produce a table of frequency allocations and operational agreements necessary for efficient and interference-free use of the radio spectrum. These agreements are reached through the work of committees and subcommittees culminating in a vote of the assembled members. Any nation that disagrees with the allocations can add what are called footnotes or reservations. In essence, they are declarations of intent, objections, or practices concerning a particular portion of the spectrum. Thus, even though a majority votes to accept the table of allocations, exceptions can be made that exempt certain countries from adhering to specific portions of the agreements. The more reservations, the greater the danger of RF interference and disputes with other nations. It must also be pointed out that the reservations and footnotes allow everyone to win regardless of the outcome of the vote.

The World Administrative Radio Conference (WARC) convened in 1979 to produce a 984-page document that set forth the regulations, resolutions, and recommendations for worldwide radio communications. The major issues of the conference were spectrum reallocation, Third World or developing country demands for equitable access, and technology transfer. The United States was well prepared technically but not as well prepared politically. As a result, "the phrase 'America against the world' was sometimes heard epitomizing the notion of WARC as a zero-sum game of 'us against them,' " reported David E. Hornig (*Journal of Communication*, Spring 1980).

Prior to this conference, the United States, as well as many of the developed countries, could count on both leadership and control of the allocation process through the use of consensus. There is no doubt that technical sophistication combined with relatively few uses of the spectrum permitted such activities. But increased use of the spectrum and the realization of the importance of information have altered the rules of the game. The Third World countries, while recognizing the technical superiority of the developed nations, view the spectrum in a completely different manner. They take the political view of conflict between the haves and have-nots, between the information-rich and the information-poor. The spectrum is viewed as an environmental resource of limited capacity, and there is a need to reserve a place in the spectrum for future uses by every country. Otherwise, they fear that all of the places in a particular portion of the spectrum will be taken before they have the capability to utilize it. Associated with the issue of access is specific pressure for a reserved place in the geostationary satellite or fixed satellite service (FSS). While relatively few satellites are now in orbit, larger numbers could eventually create interference problems and thus limit the number of satellites that could be accommodated. The Third World countries want to insure that they have access to a portion of the geostationary orbit for their own uses. From the purely political standpoint, telecommunications could be used as a "tool for development" and are a key resource to increase information capacity and power. The Third World countries are pressing for a transfer of technology that will allow them to control the flow of information. Technology transfer includes both the hardware and associated technology to maintain a sophisticated telecommunications network, as well as the knowledge and skills necessary to produce the software. In other words, the Third World countries are seeking to control both the means and the messages.

As a result of the deliberations of WARC-79 the following trends can be identified.

1. Developing or Third World countries now form a majority in the ITU.

2. Basic differences exist over the principles that should govern allocation and use of the spectrum, especially where satellites are concerned.

3. Third World countries are increasingly able to influence and shape communications policies in international forums—voting has replaced consensus.

4. A shift towards nontechnical factors (political and cultural interests and values) is occurring.

5. There is a growing disparity between nations in their ability to use the spectrum, which is leading to disagreements over specific portions of the spectrum.

6. Regional and domestic policies are beginning to predominate.

Policy Options for the United States

The next WARC is scheduled for 1999. However, a number of interim conferences will be held to deal with specific issues that need to be addressed before the next reallocation conference. Prime among them is the 1982 Plenipotentiary Conference, where the ITU convention will be renewed and modified. Since this conference sets the rules for how the ITU works, it is a

351

critical meeting. For Region 2, which includes North America, a High Frequency (HF) Broadcasting (1984) and a Space Planning Conference (1985 and 1987) for all nations are scheduled. In addition, 10 administrative radio conferences are on the docket over the next seven years.

The U.S. Congress's Office of Technology Assessment (OTA) has examined six policy options for the United States in dealing with the international spectrum issues and the ITU. The first option is to withdraw from the ITU. This does not seem to be a viable way to deal with the political issues confronting the ITU. In all probability, it would mean the end of attempts to regulate the RF spectrum and lead to its fragmentation. Fewer international channels of communication would likely result, along with difficulties with the interoperability of common systems as well as a general increase in RFI.

The second policy option is to attempt to revise the ITU voting formula of one country, one vote. Weight would be given to such things as land area and population, present use of the spectrum, total investment in telecommunications, and the relative proportion of overall contributions to the United Nations and its agencies. Implementation of this option is unlikely because it would be strongly opposed by the Third World.

A third option is increasing the regionalization of the ITU. By reassigning countries to smaller regions and focusing on specific concerns, it would be easier to keep negotiations on track. Not only could unnecessary contention be held to a minimum but regionalization would also eliminate nations voting on issues that did not directly concern them. Certainly, decentralization through regionalism is not applicable to all problems. However, it would go a long way toward the establishment of closer cooperative ties between nations who live as neighbors both physically and in the electromagnetic environment. Regionalization would also make it easier to assist Third World countries with telecommunications projects that would be of direct benefit to them as well as their region. The OTA suggests further study of this option because of potential RFI problems with other regional groupings. There is also a need to examine ways to coordinate decentralized decisions.

Better coordination and planning is the fourth policy option. It is suggested that the United States make a major effort to develop long-term plans. The planning process would take into consideration the requirements of developing nations and assist them in the exploration of short- and long-term policies. The provision of necessary technological and economic assistance would also be needed. Concurrence by all of those involved in the planning process would be sought through fair, objective, and realistic proposals. Some form of cooperative planning would help clarify the national interests of all countries and smoothen negotiations. The OTA also feels that this option, or the alternative of having the ITU undertake the effort, is the most viable and effective path for the United States.

Option five proposes a common-user system for satellite communications. Joint ventures in satellite communications would be undertaken between the developed countries and the Third World. INTELSAT provides a model that could easily be emulated. The effect of implementing this option would be to provide service without designating specific slots for each and every nation.

The sixth OTA option is "a priori allotment." This option would eliminate

352

one of the major problems that surfaced at WARC-79—assigning orbital slots to all nations. OTA points out that this option, while totally different from unalterable opposition, might not be as bad as originally envisioned. Advanced technologies in the United States, especially the Space Shuttle, would permit placement of one wide-band satellite in orbit that would handle the telecommunications of many satellites.

The options listed above serve to illustrate the flexibility of response that is open to the United States in its relations with members of the ITU. WARC-79 demonstrated that new initiatives and strategies are necessary if the United States is going to retain a stance of progressive leadership in RF spectrum matters. Exercising some of the options offered by the OTA would go a long way toward achieving this goal. To regain the initiative, it is necessary for the problems of spectrum management to be considered at the highest levels of government.

Option four—better coordination and planning—is the best place to start. Initially, the focus should be on producing a plan for telecommunications within the United States. Presently, a number of agencies have some say in the writing and enforcement of laws, rules, regulations, etc., concerning all types of communications. A permanent planning and coordination committee, with the power to make and enforce decisions, should be appointed solely for communications management. This committee would streamline and coordinate the bureaucratic process as well as planning for future development of the spectrum.

Decisions made in the United States over the next few years will set the stage for world response for the remainder of the century. The better the planning by the United States, the easier it will be on the rest of the world. Internationally, a coherent foreign policy needs to be articulated that outlines the American position within the ITU. While there might be some short-term advantage in withdrawal from the ITU, the long-term disadvantages outweigh it. The United States relies more on telecommunications than other nations, and a well-managed RF spectrum is in the best interest of the country. Refusing to negotiate through the ITU would hardly seem to serve this interest.

Attempting to revise the voting policies of the ITU is also a futile exercise that would result in increased tensions. It should be recognized that the Third World is not a monolithic voting bloc. Thus, a more constructive approach would be to concentrate on individual countries. This could be best accomplished by extending coordination and planning through regionalization. The United States should work for a plan to reorganize the ITU regional structure into smaller, more workable groupings. Once these new regions are established, a complete telecommunications system should be put into place to form a spectrum-management network. This system—which would link up all countries within a region, all regions, and a centralized planning group within the ITU—would have a number of benefits. First, it would allow nations to communicate with each other on a continuous basis to coordinate, plan, and implement telecommunications policies and systems. This system would also provide firsthand experience as well as training in advanced telecommunications systems. Thus, it would aid technology transfer. Third, as participating nations became better informed, they would be

353

able to identify more clearly their self-interests and negotiate them within their region prior to international conferences. Thus, the specific needs of individual countries would be identified at a stage where they could be understood and steps made to meet them. The better informed each nation becomes, the easier it will be to conclude worldwide agreement for RF spectrum management. The clearinghouse, centered in the ITU, would monitor the various regional networks, act as a resource for needed documentation, and provide technical assistance. Finally, such a system should be based upon satellite communications as part of the network. Once countries within a region get used to cooperating with each other, the expansion into a common-user system for other communications needs would be an easy step to take. The United States initiative in establishing a regional, satellite-based, telecommunications system for use in coordination and planning RF spectrum matters would be a bold step that would meet most of the political objectives of the Third World countries. By one action, the United States could defuse the tensions that are building over radio frequency use and management.

Controlling Information Worldwide

Two acronyms identify the attempt by many nations of the world to control and regulate the flow of information. They are NIIO (new international information order) and NWIO (new world information order). Both of these terms mean the same thing, an " . . . international exchange of information in which nations, which develop their cultural system in an autonomous way and with complete sovereign control of resources, fully and effectively participate as independent members of the international community."[2]

UNESCO has been interested in information flow almost since its establishment. The earliest documentation of the United Nations incorporates the goal of global "free flow of information." During the 1960s, it took on new meaning as the Third World began to pay attention to what was called "media imperialism"—and in 1972 the debate began in earnest. The 17th General Conference of UNESCO considered what became, in 1978, the Mass Media Declaration. Though it was never formally adopted, its basic tenets involved the responsibilities of nations to regulate information moving in and out of their own countries. This conference also passed a second resolution calling for a declaration of guiding principles on the use of satellite broadcasting, including provisions for prior consent; it was subsequently passed in the General Assembly in 1973. The 19th conference resulted in the implicit agreement by the United States that an imbalance in information did, in fact, exist—coupled with a pledge of assistance to Third World countries in the development of communication capabilities. This conference also laid the groundwork for the MacBride Report that was issued at the 21st General Conference.

The overall motto of the NWIO is the "free and balanced flow of information," as reflected in the MacBride Report. This report attempts to take a comprehensive look at the problems of information worldwide and makes recommendations for change. It is clearly admitted that the report is the result of negotiation and is not a scholarly analysis; in other words, the Mac-Bride Report is a political document prepared by a panel of experts for a large international audience. Yet, despite its political nature, the report does address the totality of communication problems in modern society. There is no doubt that it deals with issues that have been ignored or glossed over in the past. A full discussion of all of the issues would take a book, but what one gets from reading it is a sense of the many problems that have to be overcome if we are to progress fully into the age of information. A few of the key issues in the report are: censorship, information or communication imperialism, ownership of the means of communication, transborder data flow, gatekeeping of information, advertising, effects of communication on weak or developing countries, international code of ethics for journalists, and increasing information and communication access to those currently deprived of the right. The thread running through the entire report—and, indeed, through the NWIO—is that of " . . . elimination of 'cultural imperialism' and 'information dependency' and the fostering of communications technology transfer and the balanced flow of information between 'have' and 'have-not' nations."[3]

Response by the developed countries, especially the United States, has been less than positive and has tended to focus solely on the issues related to control of the mass media. While the concept of freedom of the press is an important American cultural value, as well as an important element in the transition to the information society, it should not be allowed to obfuscate other important elements in the report. The attempt by the media to label the MacBride Report as a document written by Third World communist puppets does little to address the problems associated with the NWIO and the post-industrial society.

An example of a major concern other than mass media is transborder data flow (TDF) in the NWIO. Cees J. Hamelink has argued that the international news is only a small part (10%) of total worldwide information flow. The word "informatics" is used to describe the other 90%. Informatics consists of the infrastructure and management techniques employed to transmit, use, apply, and integrate information. Included is data transmitted by computer to computer as well as all data transmitted via the traditional telecommunications networks that are essentially computer-based information sources. He also goes on to point out that informatics is the third-largest industry in the world and is controlled by a few Western transnational corporations.[4]

Not only is TDF a problem for the Third World, it is also a growing problem for the developed countries. A number of nations—including Germany, France, Luxembourg, Denmark, Norway, Sweden, Austria, Canada, Australia, Japan, and Brazil—have enacted data protection and privacy legislation that restricts and controls the flow of data out of their countries. Similar legislation is under consideration in at least a dozen others. For the most part, the reason given for such legislation is to protect the privacy of citizens. However, the debate over TDF reveals that there are at least four additional reasons for concern. The first is American dominance of the computer and service industries. This dominance has retarded the development of competing industries in other countries and has made them dependent on the United States for equipment as well as the software and related services necessary to operate it. The second reason is the use of TDF by transnational corporations and the implications for national sovereignty. In essence, the fear is that decisions about how to run a particular industry can easily be made outside of the country wherein the industry resides. The net effect could be actions that work directly against the best interests of that country and threaten its sovereignty. The third reason is the coming of what has been termed the "vulnerable society." This is a concept of national vulnerability to the hostile actions of other nations or terrorist groups in the selective destruction or withholding of vital computer-based information in order to create chaos. The fourth concern is the impact of increased TDF use on international, national, and local affairs. The sophistication of the electronic technology and the volume and quality of information create fear that established decision-making structures will be disrupted. Thus, the underlying reasons for control of TDF are primarily economic and political and seem aimed specifically at the United States.

The NWIO presents a substantial number of challenges to the developed countries, particularly, the United States. The transition into the post-industrial society must include a series of interfaces designed to handle the problems of countries that are still pre-industrial or in other stages of industrialization. The United States, as the country most advanced into the information age, bears the responsibility to take initiatives that will smoothen the transition for others. The issue of "free and balanced flow of information" must be addressed in a serious manner. As stated previously, the "free flow" of information can be split into two parts. The first concerns the communications media and its freedom to report the news without censorship or control. The United States must take an unequivocal stand in favor of freedom of the press. However, this does not mean that there is an unwillingness to discuss the concept with the Third World. All must cooperate to attempt to resolve real differences to the satisfaction of everyone. The second, and largest, portion of the "free flow" of information is TDF. Here also, there is need for specific actions by the United States. Michael Blumenthal, in a 1981 speech to the National Computer Conference, makes four recommendations that can serve as a framework for fostering a free exchange of information worldwide. The first step is to recognize that protectionist barriers will not fall until the "information gap" between the United States and the rest of the world is closed. This is a problem that must be met head-on with direct American assistance. In order to achieve this, corporate dealings abroad should be cooperative through partnerships with companies in the developed nations and technology transfer in the Third World. Third is the establishment of an intraindustry clearinghouse. It would monitor, compile, and disseminate information about TDF legislative activities throughout the world. The clearinghouse would work to identify legal issues, increase awareness of problems, and generally work towards nonrestrictive solutions to data-flow problems. Finally, a comprehensive national communications and information policy has to be worked out that would enable the United States to have constructive interactions with the other nations of the world.[5]

The proposed common-user system utilizing satellite telecommunications for the ITU is also a major step in meeting the concerns of the Third World about information. In fact, the implementation of some of the OTA options for the RF spectrum management would meet the needs expressed in the

NWIO. The ITU regional satellite conference system could easily be expanded to cover many of the telecommunications/information needs of participating nations. It is in the best interest of all nations for the United States to develop mechanisms for the placement of common-user satellites in orbit, to install the necessary hardware to access them, and to train the technical personnel in the use of the system. The United States should also expand training programs aimed at producing Third World personnel who have the information skills necessary to utilize such a system effectively. Once control of both the ways and means of communications is decentralized, the "information gap" will begin to close and the balance of information sought by the Third World will become possible.

Conclusion

This paper has examined the issues of control of the RF spectrum and the free flow of information as they will affect the transition into the post-industrial society. The United States is in a position to go a long way towards solving a wide variety of political problems worldwide by building a common-user satellite-based telecommunications sytem for use by all who seek access. Through this initiative, the United States can continue its leadership in the management of the RF spectrum and work towards the NWIO concept of a "free and balanced flow of information." Information and telecommunications are inexorably intertwined and they must be handled politically as well as technically. The United States must continue to exert leadership in these areas if it is to continue to move into the age of information.

References

1. Office of Technology Assessment, Congress of the United States. *Radiofrequency Use and Management: Impacts from the World Administrative Radio Conference of 1979—Summary*. Washington: GPO, 1982, p. 8.

2. Beebe, George. *The Media Crisis . . .* Miami: World Press Freedom Committee, 1980, pp. 4-7.

3. Clippinger, John H. "Hidden Agenda." *Journal of Communication*. 29(1), Winter 1980, p. 198.

4. Hamelink, Cees J. "Informatics: Third World Call For New Order." *Journal of Communication*. 29(3), Summer 1979, pp. 146-148.

5. Blumenthal, Michael. "Transborder Data Flow and the New Protectionism—A Comprehensive National Communication and Information Policy." *Vital Speeches of the Day*, p. 553.

World Future Society

An Association for the Study of Alternative Futures

The World Future Society is an association of people who are interested in how social and technological developments will shape the future. It is chartered as a nonprofit scientific and educational organization in Washington, D.C., U.S.A.

The Society was founded in 1966 by a group of private citizens who felt that people need to anticipate coming developments to make wise personal and professional decisions. In our turbulent era of change, the Society strives to be an unbiased and reliable clearinghouse for a broad range of scholarly forecasts, analyses, and ideas.

As outlined in its charter, the Society's objectives are:

1. To contribute to a reasoned awareness of the future and of the importance of its study.

2. To advance responsible and serious investigation of the future.

3. To promote the development and improvement of methodologies for the study of the future.

4. To increase public understanding of future-oriented activities and studies.

5. To facilitate communication and cooperation among organizations and individuals interested in studying or planning for the future.

Since its inception, the Society has grown to include more than 40,000 members in over 80 countries. Society members come from all professions and have a wide range of interests, and the Society counts many distinguished scientists, businessmen, and government leaders among its ranks.

The Society publishes a number of future-oriented periodicals, including:

• THE FUTURIST: A Journal of Forecasts, Trends, and Ideas About the Future. This exciting bimonthly magazine, which is sent to all members, explores all aspects of the future—technology, life-styles, government, economics, values, environmental issues, religion, etc. Written in clear, informative prose by experts, THE FUTURIST gives every member an advance look at what may happen in the years ahead.

• The World Future Society Bulletin. This bimonthly journal is intended for professional futurists, forecasters, planners, and others with an intense interest in the field. The Bulletin carries articles on forecasting methods, news of special interest in the field, book reviews, etc.

• Future Survey is a monthly abstract journal reporting on recent books and articles about the future. Each 16- to 24-page issue contains more than 100 summaries of the most significant futures-relevant literature.

Books published by the Society include The Future: A Guide to Information Sources, The Study of the Future, Education and the Future, and The Information Society of Tomorrow.

The Society's "bookstore of the future" stocks hundreds of books, and also a number of audiotapes, games, and films.

At the local level, the Society has active chapters in a growing number of cities scattered throughout the United States and around the world. These chapters offer speakers, educational courses, seminars, discussion groups, and other opportunities for members to get to know each other in their local communities.

Membership in the World Future Society is open to anyone seriously interested in the future. For further information, write to:

World Future Society
4916 St. Elmo Avenue
Bethesda, MD 20814, U.S.A.
Telephone: (301) 656-8274